Democracy

What is democracy? Under what conditions does it thrive? And what are the consequences of democracy?

This book – written by the eminent team of Jan-Erik Lane and Svante Ersson – answers these, and more, highly topical questions of exploring different varieties of democracies around the world. A democratic regime exists, more or less, in almost 50 per cent of the countries of the world, and is possible in many more countries. But how likely is it?

Beginning with definitions of democracy, the book divides the concept into three dimensions, which provide the framework for the study of democracy in all its forms. These dimensions form the three main sections of the book:

- constitutional democracy, which explores political rights
- participatory democracy, which focuses on participation of citizens
- egalitarian democracy, which examines outcomes of democracy in terms of equality.

This book uses data from countries around the world to estimate the probability of a stable democracy or the probability of democratic consolidation, and asks whether democracy is more determined from outside the political system or from inside it. It suggests an entirely new approach to democracy, focussing on endogenous democracy and not exogenous democracy as in the literature. It also deals with the principal–agent approach to politics and democratic participation. As well as looking at factors conducive to democracy, this book also considers the consequences of democracy, by focussing upon the link between democracy and outcomes such as equality, social protection and the environment.

With its methodological positivist approach and comparative perspective, this book will be an invaluable reference tool for students and researchers studying democracy, democratic theory and democratization, comparative politics, political science or public policy and administration.

Jan-Erik Lane is Professor of Political Science and head of RESOP (Laboratoire de Recherches Sociales et Politiques Appliquées) at the University of Geneva, and is also Visiting Professor at the National University of Singapore. His publications include *Constitutions and Political Theory, The Public Sector* and *New Public Management.* **Svante Ersson** is a lecturer in Political Science at Umea University. He and Jan-Erik Lane are joint authors of *Culture and Politics, The New Institutional Politics, Politics and Society in Western Europe, European Politics* and *Comparative Politics: An Introduction.*

Democracy

A comparative approach

Jan-Erik Lane and Svante Ersson

Routledge
Taylor & Francis Group

LONDON AND NEW YORK

First published 2003 by Routledge
11 New Fetter Lane, London EC4P 4EE

Simultaneously published in the USA and Canada
by Routledge
29 West 35th Street, New York, NY 10001

Routledge is an imprint of the Taylor & Francis Group

© 2003 Jan-Erik Lane and Svante Ersson

Typeset in Baskerville by Wearset Ltd, Boldon, Tyne and Wear
Printed and bound in Great Britain by Biddles Ltd, Guildford and King's
Lynn

British Library Cataloguing in Publication Data
A catalogue record for this book is available from the British Library

Library of Congress Cataloging in Publication Data
Lane, Jan-Erik.
 Democracy : a comparative approach / Jan-Erik Lane and
Svante Ersson.
  p. cm.
 Includes bibliographical references and index.
 1. Democracy. I. Ersson, Svante O. II. Title.
JC423 .L336 2003
321.8–dc21

                                                    2002035838

ISBN 0-415-26587-8 (hbk)
ISBN 0-415-26588-6 (pbk)

Contents

Illustrations

Preface

The question of regime variation is as classical in political science as Aristotle's analysis of it in his *Politeia*. Aristotle employed what we will refer to as a 'positivistic approach' to the problem(s) of the causes and consequences of altern ative political regimes. What we mean by 'positivism' is that the enquiry's conclusions are based on empirical evidence, which confirm or disprove the models which guide the empirical enquiry. Aristotle carried out a large-scale investigation (*The Constitution of Athens*) into most of the known real regimes existing at that time, arriving at inductive conclusions concerning his parsimonious classification of regimes, which was in fact the first theory of comparative politics.

Methodological positivism (MP) is an effort to combine theory and data, as – following Kant – theory without data is empty, and data without theory is blind. MP has proved to be so successful in various fields of the sciences and economics that its canons of research should also be employed in political science. Much has been written about the impossibility of using MP in the study of politics. However, the difficulties pointed out by several scholars should not be seen as fatal to the endeavour of using the same methodology that has so benefited the field of economics (Friedman, 1953; Blaug, 1992). MP (when used with care, as several pitfalls exist) is relevant to the questions raised by the system transformation initiated in 1989–90, resulting in a rapid increase in the number of countries with a democratic regime. These questions include:

- what conditions encourage the spread of democracy as well as its consolidation?
- which are the outcomes of democracy?

In political science, sociology and economics, one finds a large literature concerning the conditions for and the consequences of democracy, including the field of development studies. One may distil a number of central hypotheses in the form of models, which may be tested for truthfulness by examining how well they are supported by observation. Looking at the world around 2000, how does the available evidence confirm or disconfirm the central models in the literature on democracy as a political regime?

The focus in theories concerning democracy is on its causes and effects.

The relevance of this perspective – democracy and causality – cannot be doubted when one is confronted today with a situation where roughly half of the countries of the world have democratic or semi-democratic regimes, whereas the other half are non-democratic. Why this pattern of variation in democracy? And which are the consequences of different degrees of democracy in a country?

We believe that MP is the best available method for an enquiry into these problems, as it offers a method for confirming or corroborating generalizations or models which formulate key hypotheses. The causes and effects of democracy can be best understood when models are explicitly formulated and tested against a large body of data relating to the countries of the world, using the canons of inductive enquiry such as the analysis of correlations (reduced form evidence) and regression technique (structural model evidence). We cover a maximum of 150 countries in our data set, that is, almost all states with a population of more than 1 million people.

Our ambition is not merely to test the well-known theories of democracy that have been launched in the post World War Two era, but we also endeavour to suggest a new model of democracy. Thus, we examine not only the *genus proximum* of democracy but also its *differentia specifica*, meaning the causes and consequences of alternative democratic regimes such as parliamentary democracy and presidential democracy. The literature has focussed on exogenous democracy but we suggest that the time has come for an analysis of this macro political regime with models of endogenous democracy.

All the chapters in this volume have been written in order to give coherence to our analysis, with the exception of Chapter 8, which is based on an article, 'The probability of democratic success in South Africa' in *Democratization* (1997) 4, 4: 1–15. However, the ideas contained in a few chapters were presented at conferences, where we benefited from criticism and debate: Santiago de Compostella (2000) and Kottayam (2001). The concluding chapter includes a mathematical appendix on endogenous democracy written by Florence Dieterlen in collaboration with one of the authors. Svante Ersson's work has partly been sponsored by a grant from the Bank of Sweden Tercentenary Foundation. We are grateful to Sylvia Dumms in the secretariat of the political science department at the University of Geneva for much assistance.

Jan-Erik Lane (Geneva)
Svante Ersson (Umea)

Introduction

Tocqueville's question

On voit que toute science consiste non seulement dans la connaissance des faits en eux-memes, mais dans la connaissance que l'on a de l'ordre de la regle, des lois que suivent les faits don't on s'occupe.

(Say, 1996: 88)

Alexis de Tocqueville carried out the first empirical study of how a democracy operates in real life. His two-volume book, *La Democratie en Amerique*, (1835–40) was a remarkable achievement not only due to its originality but also due to the relevance of its perspective – democratic stability – and its findings. Tocqueville derived the vitality of American democracy from three sources:

1 its geographical environment;
2 its civil society;
3 its political institutions.

This is exactly our approach in starting with so-called exogenous democracy and then investigating so-called endogenous democracy.

Democracy may be measured by various indices which tap into the implementation of civil and political rights. A number of indices have been elaborated over the years, resulting in national scores which express how constitutional democracy is put in place in different ways around the globe.

Thus, much work has been devoted to measuring the occurrence of democracy around the world. A number of scales have been developed by various scholars and they all show that democracy as a macro political regime varies considerably from one country to another. Thus, one may speak of degrees of democracy measured along a scale from 0 to 10, for instance, and not only about the dichotomy between democracy and dictatorship. Using the macro democracy scales, one may make empirical enquiries into the causes and consequences of democracy. This is the chief focus of this volume, where we will employ a rigorous methodology for studying macro democracy and its conditions and effects, namely methodological positivism.

There is today a large literature concerning macro democracy. We survey this literature systematically and test a core set of key hypotheses derived from the main approaches to democracy within this literature. Our contribution is both theoretical and empirical. First, we classify the main approaches in a novel fashion, using the distinction between exogenous and endogenous democracy. Second, we base the empirical analysis on a data set concerning the countries of the world which is large both in scope and range. Thus, we arrive at several new findings which are systematized in a theory of endogenous constitutional democracy.

A preliminary definition of 'democracy'

Democracy is both a real regime and a political ideal. Our enquiry into the conditions for the real occurrence of democracy in the countries of the world does not say much about the normative debate about democratic ideals such as participatory democracy (Pateman, 1970; Barber, 1984), associative democracy (Hirst, 1994) or deliberative democracy (Elster, 1998). The new normative models of democracy may change real democracy. However, we focus on democracy as a political regime – human rights and party competition – as it occurs around the world.

Let us suggest a definition of the word 'democracy', although we are well aware of the fact that there are already a great many such definitions in philosophy, normative political theory and in empirical political science. It contains a few key concepts which will be elaborated on later in this chapter. Thus, we propose the following definition (DF1):

> A democracy is the political regime where the will of the people *ex ante* becomes the law of the country (legal order) *ex post*.

DF1 is true to the historical semantics of the Greek words 'demos' and 'cratein' while bypassing entirely the characteristic separation between citizens and slaves in ancient Greece. At the same time, DF1 makes a connection with modern social theory, which approaches democracy as the aggregation of individual preferences into a group decision. The key terms in DF1 are 'political regime', 'will of the people' and the 'legal order'. We emphasize these terms because they help us answer the question about the possibility or impossibility of a democratic regime. Let us develop these concepts somewhat and also contrast DF1 with a few other well-known models of democracy.

A group may legislate about its affairs when the individuals within it find that they have something in common. People participating in such choice processes will have preferences over the alternatives of choice. One of the key problems of democracy is to deliver a rule of aggregation concerning how these preferences are to be added so that there emerges a group winner constituting the social choice in question. The problem is to introduce certain restrictions on this aggregation of individual preferences into a group decision, called 'democratic requirements'.

Preferences about choice options – bills, candidates, initiatives, etc. – constitute the building blocks of democratic decision-making processes. They may be called 'wants', 'interests', 'ideologies', depending on how elaborated they tend to be in terms of a system of belief. What is important to emphasize here is the social choice perspective on democracy, which, although highly abstract, may be employed for the purpose of analysing real-life democracy. Each person is assumed to have rational preferences concerning outcomes, that is, preferences which are transitive and connected. And the problem is to find a rule of aggregation which takes the preferences as given, and scores one among them as the winner.

The social choice literature is rich in alternative requirements that a proper aggregation rule should satisfy. This is not the place to review the extensive debate on so-called social choice functions, but we will emphasize three requirements that figure prominently in this literature. In order for the will of the people to become the law of the land, a democratic decision-process must harbour an aggregation rule which satisfies:

a   neutrality: no choice alternative is given a favoured position *ex ante*;
b   anonymity: no person is given a special position *ex ante*;
c   simple majority: an alternative is the winner *ex post* if it receives 51 per cent of the votes.

The Apartheid regime in South Africa did not satisfy anonymity, whereas the veto power of a president against the legislature does not agree with neutrality. Thus, we favour parliamentary democracy based on the principle of one man or woman = one vote. Finally, we adhere to majoritarian democracy, that is, we favour the decision rule of 51 per cent versus 49 per cent, meaning the employment of simple majority as the main decision rule of a group.

DF1 constitutes only a minimalist definition, which requires elaboration in order to include the requirements of constitutional democracy. A democracy is a constitutional state when its legal order contains rights and immunities which restrain the power of government, achieving the Rule of Law. This is institutional democracy where the will of the people is expressed through a variety of rules. From Tocqueville we take the emphasis of simple majority as the typical decision rule of democracy, which may be combined with other political and economic institutions.

The positive argument for majoritarian democracy can be spelled out by means of a quick review of other models of democracy. Thus, what follows is a negative argument for a majoritarian conception of democracy based on the rejection of the key alternative models of democracy.

Alternative models of democracy

Majoritarian democracy, or democratic decision-making based on the use of the simple majority rule, may be contrasted with other models of democracy. These alternative models of democracy require more inclusive decision-making rules or they extend the application of democracy to areas other than politics. Let us state our criticism of these models in a short and succinct manner.

Against democracy as unanimity (Buchanan)

In the public choice school, the dominant approach to democracy is to underline the virtues of unanimity as the decision-making procedure. This is the
classical so-called Wicksellian position, named after the seminal article by
Swedish economist Knut Wicksell from 1896 translated as 'On a just principle
of taxation'. Democracy as unanimity is most ardently propagated by J.M.
Buchanan in an effort to reduce politics to economics. The link between politics as democracy and economics as efficiency is the Pareto principle, which
may be interpreted as either the maximization of output or utility on the one
hand, or as the guarantee of an individual veto, which is what the rule of
unanimity accomplishes.

One fundamental objection against the unanimity rule is that it has proved
very impractical to employ due to so-called transaction cost reasons. It is so
unwieldy that only the Security Council of the United Nations use it in an
approximate fashion. The drawback here is practical, unanimity being conducive to a so-called Polish parliament where historically no decision could be
taken because of the *liberum veto* of each nobleman.

Another basic objection to unanimity is that it violates neutrality, since all
choice options do not have the same probability of being adopted. Unanimity
favours the status quo (SQ), giving everyone a veto against proposed changes.
Thus, unanimity is biased towards enhancing the capacity to block and reducing the capacity to change. If some of the choice participants have a vested
interest in protecting the SQ, then unanimity will also violate anonymity.

The argument for unanimity is that some issues are so sensitive that everyone must have a capacity to say 'No' when their most basic interests are at
stake. However, there is another method for protecting vital concerns, namely
the protection of rights, for instance in the form of immunities. Also, a majoritarian democracy may find it advantageous to introduce and implement a list
of rights, or basic political and civil liberties. It would stabilize democracy and
diminish the probability of cycling, which is one Achilles heel in majoritarian
democracy.

Unanimity in the polity would enhance Pareto-optimal solutions in political
decision-making. But this merely begs the question: why endorse Pareto-
optimality in politics? Majoritarian democracy may produce so-called Condorcet winners (an attractive winner or a proposal/alternative which defeats
all other proposals/alternatives) in pairwise comparison, which is sufficient.

Against consociational democracy (Lijphart)

Another kind of difficulty is much talked about in consociational democracy,
where it is argued that majoritarian democracy cannot handle decision-
making in so-called divided societies, i.e. countries with strong ethnic and/or
religious cleavages. To Lijphart (1999), the Achilles heel of majoritarian
democracy is neglect of minorities which cannot realistically hope to become
majorities. When societies are locked into a historically inherited conflict
between primary groups, then simple majority rule is a recipe for civil war,

according to Lijphart. Thus, he calls for the employment of other kinds of decision-making institutions, such as concurrent majorities and the right of nullification, concepts already suggested in 1851 by John Calhoun from Carolina (Calhoun, 1992).

The original idea with consociational democracy was to emphasize the capacity of grand coalitions to enhance political stability in a country. When all key players are brought on board by means of oversized coalitions or through the making of pacts between social groups, then the risk of conflict and civil war is reduced. Consociational democracy focussed on the behaviour of elites, calling for a politics of accommodation. However, in recent developments of consociationalism, the emphasis is on rights and institutions to such an extent that Lijphart is almost talking about constitutional democracy instead of consociationalism.

Consensus democracy would be the institutionalization of democracy by means of all kinds of rules which lead to power sharing. Thus, Lijphart suggests federalism, *trias politica*, constitutional review, multipartism and bicameralism. The opposite of consensus democracy is, according to Lijphart, majoritarian democracy, which would endorse unitarism, plurality election techniques and the supremacy of parliament. One difficulty with the Lijphart taxonomy is that there is no clear-cut example of either consensus or majoritarian democracy. All existing democracies are mixtures of consensus and majoritarian institutions.

Another difficulty with consociational democracy is that it would violate both neutrality and anonymity, favouring the SQ as well as providing certain groups with more say than others. It also runs into heavy transaction costs, as the making and unmaking of oversized coalitions is a costly business in terms of time and effort. Almost all European democracies hesitate to support grand coalitions, which remove politics from popular influence. In fact, consociational democracy is close to the model of democracy as a game played among elites.

Against elitist democracy (Schumpeter)

Consociationalism has a strong elitist tone, almost reminiscent of Schumpeterian democracy. Yet, Schumpeter defined democracy in an almost majoritarian fashion, focussing on the modern political elites, i.e. the big political parties (DF2):

> the democratic method is that institutional arrangement for arriving at political decisions in which individuals acquire the power to decide by means of a competitive struggle for the people's vote
>
> (Schumpeter, 1976: 269)

Modern democracy is very much focussed on political parties, pointed out in a systematic fashion by Max Weber in his writings about Germany and the possibility of a democratic regime there after World War One. Actually, Weber anticipated the theory of presidentialism by Linz by arguing that parliamentarism was more prone to enhance stable democracy than presidentialism (Weber, 1978, 1994).

The role of political parties in mobilizing people for democratic decision-making was underlined by several scholars writing in the early twentieth century, when modern democracy was introduced in Europe and Latin America (somewhat later than in the USA). Here one may mention the theory of political elitism with the so-called Machiavellians: Pareto, Mosca and Michels. Yet, the elitist features of modern democracy may be tempered by the use of institutions as well as the legal order. Thus, the referendum is a basic majoritarian instrument in democracy, entirely bypassed in the theory of consociational or consensus democracy, which limits elitism. Similarly, a set of immunities in the constitution could guarantee that democratic elitism does not develop into fascism.

Schumpeter, like Weber, stayed away from the totalitarian temptations inherent in an elitist approach to democracy. Competition among elites would ensure that democracy prevailed over fascism. In an economic approach to democracy it would seem natural to focus on competition, as it would have beneficial results in the polity as well as in the economy. Downs showed in his path breaking analysis, *An Economic Theory of Democracy* (1957), that policy-making according to the left–right dimension in a polity produces unique solutions, or Cordorcet winners. Such core solutions would increase the attractiveness of elitist democracy, which, however, always appears unattractive due to its emphasis on the role of political elites. One may further increase the institutional fabric around the political elites, as within Madisonian democracy.

Against Madisonian democracy (Tsebelis)

A recent interpretation of democracy as Madison conceived it, together with the other authors of *Publius*, is to be found with Tsebelis, arguing in favour of so-called veto players. We have here a broader conception of institutions which complicates the aggregation of citizen preferences into democratic decisions than that found in public choice or consociational theories. A veto player could be any individual or group with the capacity to say 'No', either for the time being or definitively. Thus, a president with a suspense veto or a supreme court with an absolute veto would constitute a veto player.

Madison derived his conception of democracy from a Machiavellian theory about human beings and their capacity to succeed in life through tricks and cheating. Tsebelis offers a more sophisticated approach, employing the Arrow finding – the Condorcet paradox or cycling – in social choice theory in order to state a case for rules which stop or reduce instability (Tsebelis, 2002).

There are actually two kinds of political instability that may afflict a democracy. First, there is Lijphart instability, where strong minority groups remain forever outside of government, being incapable of becoming a majority as ethnic and religious cleavages are so deeply rooted that they threaten the polity. Here one may cite as examples Northern Ireland, Sri Lanka and Lebanon. Second, there is Arrow instability with massive cycling among all conceivable proposals for decision-making – the case of the Fourth French Republic, for example. Tsebelis does not recognize that, by using a veto player to solve for Arrow instability, he may actually promote Lijphart instability.

The basic difficulty with the notion of democracy as a nested game between veto players is that it does not satisfy neutrality and anonymity. A president with substantial blocking powers against the legislature may bring a political system to the brink of disaster (Zimbabwe) or such power resources may invite the president to bypass popular will entirely (Latinamericanization). When the Supreme Court or the constitutional court engages in extensive legal review against the legislature, then the SQ is favoured over all other options.

The basic reason though for introducing *thick* constitutionalism or rules about veto players is to marry democracy with constitutionalism. However, constitutionalism does not require all the paraphernalia of Madisonian democracy, as majoritarian democracy may also satisfy the elementary requirements of constitutional democracy as the rule of law and the protection of human rights. We will emphasize this point several times in the empirical enquiries that follow in later chapters, focussing on *thin* constitutionalism.

Madisonian democracy is rich on institutions, but can it really identify and implement the popular will? One may wish to claim that there is no such thing as the popular will, as all interests among the social groups are minority ones, expressing narrow-minded egoistic concerns. What democracy is all about, then, is to prevent one minority from suppressing the other minorities. But is there really no popular will?

Against populist democracy (Rousseau)

Madisonian democracy could be appropriate if one admits that the conception of the popular will or the public interest is hardly a very precise concept and that it may be combined with metaphysical notions, as with Rousseau and his idea of *The General Will*. Yet, majoritarian democracy would still be an acceptable political regime if there are situations where the population harbours a majority will which could be identified and implemented without a threat to the rights of the minority.

Popular sovereignty or the supremacy of the general assembly representing the people are typical notions in majoritarian democracy, which are not to be found in alternative theories of democracy such as unanimity, consociationalism and elitism. It has been pointed out several times that majoritarian democracy may degenerate into populist democracy, as happened for the first time during the French Revolution, when democratic authoritarianism was first manifested. Robespierre, for instance, was inspired by Rousseau's ideas about unlimited democracy as the implementation of The General Will. However, according to Sieyes, the notion of the sovereignty of the nation could also result in totalitarian conceptions (Talmon, 1960a, b, 1981). The conception of *La Volonte Generale* with Rousseau became a source of confusion, as he never clarified whether it was merely a procedure or whether it was, in addition, a true objective.

Populist democracy harbours a preference for the people and underlines that political elites must serve the broad interests in the population. However, it must be married with constitutionalism, as within majoritarian democracy. We suggest that Tocqueville was the first scholar who fulfilled this marriage. Before we examine him, we will reject the framework which moves democracy from the polity to the economy.

Against economic democracy (Lindblom)

The theory about democracy as an economic regime is altogether different from the previous arguments. The theory of economic democracy argues that political democracy is not enough, in the sense that a society must introduce democratic principles not only in the polity but also in the economy, that is, in the enterprises. Two versions of the theory of economic democracy can be distilled.

First, we have the argument that political democracy is threatened by capitalism in the sense that private enterprises, especially multi-national corporations, restrict the expression of the popular will through various mechanisms. Thus, economic power is often used for political purposes in order to influence public policy or policy implementation in such a way that private actors gain at the expense of the public. The techniques of the market for influencing the state range from simple corruption to advanced forms of pressure, which may take a subtle form as merely rational expectations undoing government policies through the financial markets of the world. To make political democracy work, the power of markets must be restrained – this is the conclusion of this argument suggested by Lindblom (1977, 2002).

Second, there is the slightly different argument that democracy is not merely a political regime, it is as relevant for the private sector as it is for the public sector. Thus, the enterprises of the market economy may be directed according to democratic principles, where the workers would constitute the main stakeholders of the economic corporations, especially the huge ones. Whereas the argument about the power of the market may lead to state control over the economy, this argument results in the conception of industrial democracy, as suggested by Dahl (1985).

It does not matter essentially whether economic democracy is conceived of as the control of a democratic polity over the market or as the participation of workers or employees in the running of the private enterprise. Perhaps a combination of these two arguments captures the core in the claim for economic democracy? What needs to be emphasized here, however, is that both of these arguments contradict the theory about the market and democracy, presented below (pp. 89–100).

We wish to argue that the theory of economic democracy is flawed. On the one hand, political democracy stands on its own feet. It need not be combined with economic democracy, as it is not incomplete when it operates only in the polity. On the other hand, economic democracy could counteract political democracy, if indeed it is the case that economic democracy fails to deliver the affluence that is crucial for democratic stability (Lipset, 1959; Cutright, 1963).

We will examine the impact of the economy on political democracy in

Chapter 3, where we will argue, against Dahl and Lindblom, that the market is important for political democracy, being one of the critical conditions for a stable democracy. The positive impact of the market on democratic longevity works both ways, on the one hand through its generation of affluence, as well as through its endorsement of economic freedom on the other. However, we will not go as far as Hayek (1944) and Friedman (1962), who claimed that a big public sector in the form of a full welfare state is also a threat to political democracy.

In favour of Tocquevillian democracy

DF1 states that democracy is a political regime. This is a deliberate emphasis. The problem of democracy is to devise the institutions which make it stable over time. This was the starting point of Alexis de Tocqueville's painstaking reflections on modern democracy, which – he predicted as early as 1835 – would become *the* political system in the future.

However, according to Tocqueville, political democracy suffered from a profound difficulty of instability, as democracy could be replaced by dictatorship, which – Tocqueville suggested – would be far worse than traditional monarchies. Tocqueville searched for the conditions that stabilize democracy and found them in a vibrant civil society as well as in political institutions that decentralize power. In addition, he suggested that peace, or the lack of hostile neighbours in the environment of a country, promotes democratic longevity. This sets up the *Tocqueville question*: what stabilizes democracy the most – civil society or political institutions?

It should be pointed out that constitutional democracy is not the same thing as consensus democracy. Also, majoritarian democracy may satisfy the requirements of constitutionalism. In fact, all existing democracies are more or less constitutional democracies, that is, democracies where the political regime is based on a legal order which includes both constitutional law – written or unwritten – and institutions that guarantee the rule of law.

DF1 takes into account the requirements of a constitutional state and Rule of Law. The will of the people can only become the law of the land if there is a legal order which recognizes the 'Rechtsstaat'. The central question in relation to constitutional democracy is not whether modern democracy can do without it, but instead how much constitutional inertia there ought to be. Consociationalism argues in favour of many constitutional breaks on the will of the people. In Madisonian democracy, the will of the people is replaced entirely with the conception of democracy as checks and balances – countervailing powers. Majoritarian democracy can operate with a minimum of institutions which safeguard the rule of law. We will underline the crucial role of the Ombudsman, that is, the special Scandinavian contribution to constitutional democracy. Thin constitutionalism is necessary for democracy but it is also sufficient.

The possibility and impossibility of democracy

Political democracy has been introduced in many countries during the 1990s. It is an open question as to whether some of the countries will achieve a consolidated form of democratic regime. Yet, what we wish to speak about now is not the conditions for successful democratic consolidation, but the prospects for democracy in the countries which are still non-democratic today. Our definition DF1 presents a few clues to this question relating to the possibility or impossibility of a democratic regime.

One may suggest four kinds of impossibilities which make democracy very difficult to introduce in several countries. First, if there is a higher law than the will of the people, then a democratic regime is unlikely. One clear example would be Islamic societies where religious law appears to be unchangeable. When Sharia is declared as the supreme law of the country, then democracy is very much restricted in its operations. Second, in societies where some form of elitism is institutionalized, there democracy cannot breathe easily. One example would be traditional monarchies of various kinds where political power is confined to the circles of a royal family. Another example could be a Communist democracy, as it was practised in the so-called people's democracies, where political power was restricted to the *nomenclature*. Perhaps the most extreme forms of elitism have been practised in fascist countries where power is the monopoly of either a single party or the military.

Entirely different difficulties are to be found when the people lack a will, i.e. common set of interests, or a denominator which founds a general will. When a people is highly divided and cannot identify a common core of interests, then democracy is not viable, not even in the form of federalism. Perhaps this is what Rousseau meant by his concept of '*volonte generale*'? The question is whether religious or ethnic fragmentation constitutes such a form of democratic impossibility. We will argue that democracy can thrive from multiculturalism, but it may be that some countries have such a divided population that separation is the only solution to political instability and civil war. The former Yugoslavia and Czechoslovakia are examples of such a situation.

Finally, we arrive at the fourth kind of impossibility, namely that a country lacks a legal order. We are referring to a predicament that many Third World countries have fallen into, namely the breakdown of state operations. Stateless societies are now more numerous than fifty years ago, especially if one broadens the concept to cover not only countries suffering with civil war or complete anarchy but also countries where there is political authority but it is challenged by warlords. One may point at Somalia, Liberia, Sierra Leone, and perhaps also Afghanistan and Colombia, at least to some extent.

Tocqueville's problem, or the tendency of a democratic regime towards political instability, may be researched in relation to the present states of the world: why are roughly half of all states democratic and the other half non-democratic? Tocqueville suggested that the probability of a democracy depended on:

a   civil society,
b   political decentralization, and
c   peace with neighbours.

We will pose the same question and focus on *exogeneity versus endogeneity*, i.e. the extent to which democratic probability depends on outside factors, the so-called exogenous variables, compared with inside factors, i.e. endogenous variables.

Democracy is a system of human institutions for governing a country. Its probability depends on, we argue, exogenous conditions. The great problem in democracy research is to clarify whether democracy is determined from inside the political system or from outside factors, i.e. which set of factors weigh most heavily, the unchangeable exogenous or the endogenous conditions? Democratic probability depends on three major factors: the economy, the culture and the institutions. The first two constitute the exogenous conditions, whereas the third forms the changeable exogenous conditions.

Civil society theory underlines the contribution of the market economy to stabilizing democracy. The link between the market economy and political democracy is affluence, as underlined by Lipset (1959) and Diamond (1992). The theory which links democratic stability with economic affluence seems to be well confirmed in numerous empirical studies, linking the degree of democracy with various measures of country affluence such as the GDP or the HDI. The hypothesis that affluence promotes democracy was proposed in the 1960s, but it is also to be found in a recent theory about the contribution of the market to democracy, linking democratic stability with the degree of economic freedom.

The cultural approach underlines the role that ethnicity, religion and values plays in either restricting or facilitating democracy. If the economy or the culture of a country is decisive for democratic probability, then there is little space left for constitutional engineering. However, if institutionalism is correct in stating that institutions matter, then the framing of political institutions opens up a great promise for enhancing democracy. This is exactly what this book sets out to determine: what is the impact of political institutions on democracy in relation to the exogenous factors?

We remain sceptical towards the socio-biological theory that democracy could be explained in terms of an evolutionary argument, at least if one relies mainly on a biological approach (Wilson, 1998). The probability of a democracy is clearly affected by the adaptability of democracy to societal changes and economic fluctuations. But it has not been shown that democracy is the regime with the highest survival score of all possible polities. And the choice of democracy cannot be seen as genetically conditioned, as it is an open question as to which regime is the most adaptive. However, if one employs evolutionary game theory, then one could perhaps present an argument about democracy as an evolutionary stable state (ESS).

The question of the conditions for democratic probability is a classical one in political science. One may speak of democracy as the dependent variable, and social structure, culture, legacies and institutions as the independent variables in an explanatory framework for understanding why the occurrence of democracy varies around the globe. Yet, we will use the classification of variables used in economics, i.e. the separation between exogenous and endogenous factors. Let us explain why.

Exogenous and endogenous democracy

Although much controversy still characterizes discussion on the ends and means of democracy, the stunning result in the research on democracy, as it occurs in various countries, is that all these indices on constitutional democracy give almost the same country rankings. Table I.1 shows how a number of democracy indicators go together when a large number of countries of the world are covered. The table reports the findings from a factor analysis undertaken for four democracy indices covering two periods of time (1990 and 1998). This analysis suggests that these democracy indices seem to measure a similar phenomenon, which we interpret as being democracy.

Thus, the problem to be resolved is: why do countries score differently on all these indices and almost in the same way? One may elaborate two different kinds of models.

Exogenous democracy: The variation in democracy is determined by affluence, ethnicity, religion, state age or the global economy. These factors are decided outside of the political system of the country in question.

Endogenous democracy: Countries differ in democracy due to the operation of different institutions, which may be changed by the country in question, i.e. they are determined inside the polity. In models of exogenous democracy the emphasis is on the impact of GDP (Lipset), or ethnic and religious fragmentation (Lijphart), state age (Huntington) or the core–periphery position (Frank, Wallerstein). We suggest that one endogenizes democracy by looking at the role of factors which are determined within the system, i.e. the polity of the country.

A common terminology used in econometrics for sorting variables is *endogenous* and *exogenous* variables (Geweke, 1987; Darnell, 1994; Maddala, 2001). Although this is not the place to enter into the discussion of how to distin-

Table I.1 Democracy indices: factor analysis

Democracy index	Factor loading
PRZEWORSKI, 1990	0.883
POLITY, 1990	0.953
FREEDOM HOUSE, 1990	0.908
VANHANEN, 1990	0.952
POLITY, 1998	0.928
FREEDOM HOUSE, 1998	0.917
VANHANEN, 1998	0.886
Explained variance	84.4
KMO	0.857
N	111

Sources: see Appendix 1.

Note
KMO measures the degree of sampling adequacy of the factor solution.

guish between exogenous variables (causes) and endogenous variables (effects), which depends on the model specified, we focus here on the notion that exogeneity refers to outside factors and endogeneity to inside factors.

In economics, endogenous variables are those determined within the economic system, and exogenous variables are those given from outside the system. Most variables are endogenous as the only truly exogenous variables one can think of are factors beyond human control such as weather conditions, such as cyclones, etc. Yet, 'in any problem this is a matter of approximation,' states Maddala (1977: 5). In the study of the demand for an item by households, we can treat the quantity demanded as endogenous and income and price as exogenous, because a household does not have control over these factors. Here, one can also treat government expenditures and taxes as exogenous. However, Maddala states: 'as we lengthen the time period of our observations, these variables will also become endogenous. In general, the greater the level of aggregation – whether it be over time periods or over individual cross-section units – the more exogenous variables will have to be treated as endogenous' (Maddala, 1977: 5).

This is the meaning of 'exogenous' and 'endogenous' democracy that we will refer to later in our study in our analysis of the causes of democratic probability. The question is whether democracy is determined by factors outside of politics or by factors within the political system. Thus, we will enquire into which conditions are the most important for democracy: exogenous ones (predetermined variables) or endogenous ones (political factors). If democracy is exogenous, then it is predetermined by conditions that cannot be changed. Exogenous democracy is fixed from outside of the political system, for example, by macroscopic economic conditions, entire social forces or historical legacies. If, on the other hand, democracy is endogenous, then it is generated through the political system, that is, chiefly through its rules or norms.

To us, the degree of endogeneity of democracy hinges mainly on institutions. This entails that we will try hard to estimate the role of political institutions in enhancing democracy as well as their impact in the transition to democracy. Democracy may also be strengthened or weakened by constitutional policy-making. However, we argue that, at the end of the day, policies impact on the rules of the political game, that is, on institutions.

Theories of democracy focus either on exogeneity, as when democracy is explained with affluence (Lipset, 1959) or social fragmentation (Almond, 1956); or endogeneity is underlined, as in the pact approach to democracy (O'Donnell and Schmitter, 1986). When democracy is regressed on economic conditions (Cutright, 1963) or cultural factors such as religion (Huntington, 1984, 1991), then strong exogeneity applies. Governments cannot change these outside factors, at least not in the short term. On the contrary, when the role of institutions is emphasized, then endogeneity is underlined (Linz, 1994; Lijphart, 1999). What needs to be researched is how democracy is to be understood as both conditioned by exogenous and endogenous factors. Our aim is to show that institutions play a major role in shaping democratic outcomes, but there are also powerful exogenous factors at work conditioning democratic probability. Later (pp. 140–80) we will consider how exogenous and endogenous conditions interact to shape democratic longevity (long-term perspective) and democratic consolidation (short-term perspective).

Constitutional democracy

Constitutional democracy combines two political dimensions, namely the rule of law with the active participation of people in politics. Thus, in a constitutional democracy, there will be both human rights and political contestation between political parties or politicians.

A country can have one dimension – human rights – without having the other – political contestation. Rule of law may be found in several semi-democracies where one party maintains a hegemonic position, as for example, in South East Asia. This is why many democracy scholars have underlined the occurrence of actual competition among parties or politicians as the crucial aspect of democracy. Rule of law or human rights is not enough. The key argument is that a state may endorse the rule of law and guarantee many citizen rights without operating a fully competitive polity. Thus, R.A. Dahl always emphasized the level of contestation as the essence of modern democracy.

Political contestation entails that no party or politician exercises hegemony. When political parties are the key players in a democracy, then party governance implies that no party becomes dominant, either legally or behaviourally. Thus, when one party is a state dominating one, then democracy is at risk. One-party states achieve this position by legal means, for example, through prohibition on other parties. State dominating parties accomplish the same position through other means, for instance by monopolizing a national legacy or staging elections, inviting minor parties to also participate, although they have no chance to win.

Endogenous democracy will be determined by forces inside a country. The basic model that we propose here is a model which endogenizes democracy. Therefore we suggest that:

$$\text{Democracy} = d(\text{Election system, Corruption, Size of Largest Party})$$

The more a country suffers from corruption, as well as the more one political party, dominates the election outcomes, the less the probability of democracy. Thus, we expect democracy to be stable in countries with old states where corruption is controlled and there is party contestation between two or more political parties. On the other hand, democracy will be non-existent or fragile in countries with young states where corruption is massive and one party has a dominant position, formally or factually.

Rights and duties figure prominently when democracy is discussed. It is impossible to define 'democracy' without talking about citizenship and citizen rights. The rights and duties of people in relation to government and public officials are considered to be of such importance that they are enshrined in the most basic form of law: constitutional law. Most countries have constitutional provisions about rights and duties, but only some of these countries actually implement them. Why?

We will enquire into two problems that democracy (when conceived of as a constitutional order) poses:

1 Why is the constitutional order stable in some countries and unstable or non-existent in others (the stability problem)?
2 Does thick constitutionalism make a difference compared with thin constitutionalism?

We will enquire into these two questions by means of a macro analysis covering all the countries of the world for which there is information available. In Chapters 3, 4, 5 and 6 we consider the stability question from a long-term perspective, whereas in Chapter 7 we look at the short-term perspective. In Chapter 8 the difference that thick constitutionalism makes for democratic stability will be compared with thin constitutionalism.

When a country is classified as democratic or non-democratic, then the evidence used involves estimations by experts of how human rights are implemented. What is at stake is whether the basic political institutions are identified in a transparent manner and whether they are enforced without too much hesitance and ambiguity. Often the focus is on the written constitution as one wishes to know whether it exists and whether it is a liberal one. However, merely having a written constitution is not enough, as in reality the key question is whether the real constitution – the actually enforced political rules – is a liberal one, meaning that basic human rights are respected. A country may lack written constitutions but still respect human rights. Or its formal constitution contains little information about the human rights that are enforced in the country, as these rights may have been identified in case law through judical interpretation.

For a long time, the research on the sources of democracy focussed on a simple dichotomy: democracy versus dictatorship, reflecting the realities in the 1950s, 1960s and 1970s. However, with the many system transitions initiated in 1989–90, this dichotomy is no longer appropriate. One needs to add the consolidation of a democratic regime to the simple democracy versus dictatorship distinction. When the consolidation concept is added to the separation between democracy and dictatorship, then one may take into account the possibility that a country has neither a democratic nor an authoritarian regime. It hangs somewhere in between as the democratic institutions may not be fully implemented or the authoritarian regime may have collapsed into anarchy.

Up until the regime transitions began in 1989 and 1990s, it was the case that many more countries were non-democratic than democratic. With the move towards democracy that both former Communist and fascist countries displayed in the 1990s, the situation is now that half of the countries of the world are democratic and the other half non-democratic, roughly speaking. Yet, it is not a question of completely democratic and fully authoritarian countries, as many countries find themselves somewhere in between, and they may have to stay so for a long period of time. In reality, the consolidation process may be more difficult than the transition process.

One may look on democratic consolidation as the same as democratic longevity, that is, the capacity of a democratic regime to maintain itself over a long period of time. Democratic longevity or democratic vitality refers to the capacity of a country to enforce democratic institutions, especially human rights and contestations. One may look on this capacity as a probability phenomenon, meaning that certain forces in a society increase or decrease the probability that democratic institutions can be maintained. The virtue of such an approach is that it allows one to grade the probability of democracy in a country between 0 and 1, which recognizes the many countries which are neither strictly democratic nor non-democratic.

What, then, increases or decreases democratic probability? Later in this study (pp. 89–139) we will consider the impact of macro factors on the likelihood of a democratic regime. One may also inquire into the micro level support for human rights, asking why people demand civil and political rights. However, the problem of the sources of constitutional democracy has been posed in such a manner that it asks a macro-level question. In any case, there is not enough data available for aggregating the attitudes of individuals in various countries into macro-level scores, except for a few well researched factors such as social trust. Later (pp. 89–184) we will test macro models relating to the sources of constitutional democracy or democratic longevity, with the unit of analysis being the country or state. In the literature the emphasis has been on exogenous democracy. Let us briefly explain the traditional way of analysing democracy.

The traditional requisites of democratic longevity

It is generally believed that constitutional democracy, once introduced into a country, will last while certain social, economic and cultural conditions are at hand. If this general statement is true, then we must make it a specific one by stating which social, economic and cultural prerequisites these are. This is a question for research into probabilities, as one may not expect that one condition is a both necessary and sufficient condition for constitutional democracy. The social sciences know few such strong generalizations. Which conditions could have a positive impact on constitutional democracy, although far from determining democratic longevity? One may suggest a long list of social, economic and cultural requisites, but one must ask for the connection between a requisite and the democratic regime, that is, a mechanism which takes us from one to the other.

Modernization

The structure of society – modernization – has been singled out as a major requisite of constitutional democracy. Constitutional democracy requires a modern society – this is the argument firmly entrenched in the so-called modernization school. Countries which have a pre-modern structure or a pre-modern society cannot sustain a democracy. A modern society is urban and industrial, where communications across status and tribal ties occur on a daily basis through mass media and the operations of political parties. On the contrary, an agricultural society cannot support a constitutional democracy, as it is based on traditional distinctions of prestige which run counter to the egalitarian spirit of democratic politics.

Modernization is a social process which has been going on since the industrial revolution started in the United Kingdom in the eighteenth century. It does not stop when an industrial society has been achieved, as modernization today continues in the transformations leading to the post-industrial society. If the modernization argument is correct, can we then conclude that the Internet society will be an even stronger source of democracy?

It is true that agricultural societies have been governed by non-democratic regimes, feudal ones in Western Europe and Japan and despotic ones elsewhere. Can one conclude that societies where a majority of the population works in agriculture cannot be run by democracy? Perhaps the modernization theory is no longer as applicable as it used to be, because in most Third World countries the majority of the population now lives in urban areas. Cannot an urban and industrial society be ruled by dictatorship? Certainly, one would be inclined to answer, as it has happened many times.

The modernization factor can only be a rough condition which, to some extent, increases the probability of constitutional democracy. Of course, an advanced society could be run by means of an authoritarian regime, and an agricultural society could be run by radical democrats in search of agrarian socialism. A modern society would have an advanced economy. Perhaps this is the key factor: affluence?

We will test the modernization theory by using two measures:

1   the relative size of agricultural employment;
2   the length in time since the industrial revolution was initiated in a country.

We predict that modernization is a weak positive factor for constitutional democracy, but that is all. It is true that agricultural societies used to have a system of stratification based on or conducive to such large inequalities that they are not in agreement with a democratic regime. When democracy is introduced into agricultural societies, then political unrest is the outcome, as traditional and new leaders clash in the fight for power.

Affluence

The economy – affluence, openness and economic institutions – has often been mentioned as the foundation of constitutional democracy. An affluent economy pays for a civil society with all its free associations which adhere to democracy in principle. Poverty is the source of dictatorship or political instability, as dissatisfied people support strong leaders who promise quick solutions and deliver repression. Constitutional democracy requires a state with a certain amount of resources, which in turn presupposes a society that can be taxed. Massive poverty denies this possibility and is conducive to a weak or authoritarian state.

Affluence is connected with modernization, as high levels of affluence are only feasible in advanced economies. However, not all modernized countries have a highly advanced economy. Affluence may also occur in societies which are non-democratic. It can only be a rough positive condition for democracy, which raises to some extent the probability of democratic longevity. One may conceive of a stable poor society like India, which is safe for democracy. And one may refer to the rich Gulf states, where affluence has not pushed the countries to accept democracy.

Like modernization, affluence is neither a necessary nor a sufficient condition for constitutional democracy. But both contribute to the probability of democratic longevity. Thus, they are not negatives, but in themselves they are not enough to assure a constitutional democracy.

Culture

Beliefs and values – culture – may be linked with democracy by examining the logical coherence between the culture in question and the principles of a democratic government. Whether such a logical relationship between a culture and democratic ideology matters in real life can only be tested through an examination of probabilities. Two major forms of culture come to mind: ethnicity and religion.

Ethnic diversity has always been regarded as a challenge to democracy, especially democratic stability. Sooner or later, high levels of ethnic diversity generate social conflict to such an extent that civil war or anarchy may result. Societies that have serious ethnic cleavages tend to face political unrest, if not claims for secession. Thus, ethnic diversity must be a negative. Religion, on the other hand, manifests itself in various belief systems, where the logical link with democracy and its principles of government is far from evident. It may actually be the *practice* of a religion which determines how it relates to the democratic regime. And practice may change considerably over time.

A constitutional democracy respects the idea of freedom of religion and worship besides the other classical liberties – thought, conscience, the press, and so on. It also presupposes the formal equality of men and women as the foundation for voting. Now, which of the world religions endorses this idea of freedom of religion as a fundamental part of its doctrine as well as accepts and endorses the formal equality of men and women? We would suggest that only Protestantism does this. Thus, we would go further and dare to suggest that Protestantism is a sufficient condition for democracy. However, it is not a *necessary* condition.

Catholicism and Greek Orthodoxy do not exclude democracy. It all depends on how these religions are interpreted. Religious belief has changed considerably due to the ongoing process of secularization. Thus, Catholicism today endorses democracy, although this was not the case in the beginnings of the twentieth century. The religion which we would suggest is most adverse to democracy is Islam. Whereas Hinduism and Buddhism may be interpreted in such a manner that they do not contradict the principles of democracy, the doctrine of Islam can be regarded as being in collision with democracy, especially in terms of its attitude towards religious tolerance.

We thus predict that societies with a strong Protestant influence lean towards democracy, whereas the opposite is true of Muslim societies. But it should be pointed out that a number of countries which are identified as Protestant include very large groups of non-believers (atheists, agnostics), which is also true of the former Communist countries. Thus, the efficacy of Protestantism may not be large in reality. How religious belief is manifested in behaviour is the final test of whether this kind of culture affects democratic probability. It may also be mentioned that some Muslim groups try to combine Islam with democracy, as the Alaouites in Turkey and the Palestinians.

The traditional model of democratic requisites includes five conditions which either promote or reduce democratic longevity:

- modernization (% agricultural population)
- affluence (GDP)
- ethnic fragmentation (diversity index)
- Protestantism (% adherents)
- Islam (% adherents).

This basic exogenous model of constitutional democracy received support in earlier research on democracy. However, what needs to be researched is whether it explains the current situation equally well, when more data about more countries have become available. Perhaps the time has come to endogenize democracy, that is, to look for determinants of the variation of democracy among factors within the political system.

Conclusion

A democratic regime is appealing to those who believe that a people can govern itself somehow, creating its own law out of the entire mass of individual wills. Such a regime exists more or less now in almost 50 per cent of the countries of the world. Given a few major restrictions identified earlier in this Introduction, democracy is possible in many more countries. But how likely is democracy?

The probability of a stable democracy or the probability of democratic consolidation can be estimated from data about the countries of the world. One may distinguish between two sets of conditions: inside and outside conditions. The exogenous conditions include the outside factors which cannot be changed, at least not in the short term, whereas the endogenous conditions include the inside factors which can be changed such as the introduction of institutions. We will call the first set of conditions 'exogenous democracy' and the second set of conditions 'endogenous democracy'. The question is, which set plays a major role for the probability of democracy in a country? Perhaps both? If so, then we ask whether democracy is more determined from outside the political system or from inside it.

One may wish to turn the coin around and enquire into the consequences of democracy instead of looking at the factors that are conducive to it. The question of whether democracy affects affluence or economic growth has been much researched, although without arriving at a conclusive answer. Here we will focus on the link between democracy and outcomes such as equality, social protection and the environment.

We start in Part I with an overview of the research into the causes and consequences of democracy. Here we present the methodology to be employed for the evaluation of the key hypotheses. Part II then enquires into exogeneity in relation to the probability of democracy. In Part III we examine models of endogenous democracy and apply them in a few case studies of the consolidation of democracy in Eastern Europe, in Africa, in Asia as well as in Latin America. Finally, Part IV is devoted to the impact of democracy on outcomes.

The probability of a stable democratic regime is, we hypothesize, more endogenous than exogenous. It is true that the economic situation of the country, its culture and its institutions play a role, as all three kinds of factors impact on democratic probability. Moreover our basic theory is that the key political institutions in endogenous democracy include the rules of parliamentarism and the Ombudsman as well as the rules of economic freedom. Thus, the crucial social institution is the market economy. The chapters that follow substantiate this endogenous theory of democracy focussing on thin constitutionalism.

Part I

Methodology

Analysing democracy can be done in several ways. We need to decide what aspects of democracy we will study, as well as outline what methodology we will employ in the conduct of our enquiries. Part I is made up of two chapters seeking to answer a few key methodological questions concerning the study of democracy. Chapter 1 looks at the factual and normative questions about democracy, whereas Chapter 2 presents the methodology that will be applied in the empirical enquiry into democracy as a macro regime in many of the countries of the world.

Since the emphasis is on causality – the conditions and consequences of democracy – we argue that methodological positivism is the most suitable framework for investigating the degree of democracy in the countries of the world. A number of models of democracy will be derived from the literature and tested on a broad-based database comprising information about most countries that have a population of more than 1 million people. We classify the key models as either exogenous or endogenous models of democracy.

1 Democracy

Ideal or real?

Introduction

Democracy has been as well researched as capitalism. It is one of the two great institutional achievements of mankind, the second being the market economy (Fukuyama, 1992). The literature on democracy is so immense that we cannot make a complete overview of it here. In the 1950s, the Norwegian philosopher Arne Naess published an overview of the concept of democracy as used in the social sciences for UNESCO, which run into hundreds of pages (Naess, *et al.* 1956). Books and articles on democracy have continued to pour out over the last few decades.

Our focus on democracy is limited to the study of this political regime as a phenomenon that exists in space and time: real democracy. There is a cluster of questions that are always raised in relation to real-life democracy relating to stability, longevity, causes and consequences. However, it must be emphasized that the discourse on democracy is also normative. Thus, a large part of the literature discusses the pros and cons of democracy as an ideal. In the theories of justice, democracy has a significant place. We will not cover the normative debate *pro et contra* democracy. This is, though, an important scientific debate with implications for political reforms of existing democracies. We are thinking about the debate about communicative democracy (Habermas, 1984), deliberative democracy (Elster, 1998) and associative democracy (Hirst, 1994).

Our perspective is positivistic, meaning that we examine theories enquiring into real democracy and not ideal democracy. Thus, we are interested in understanding and predicting democracy as a macro political regime, dealing especially with its causes and effects. The purpose of this chapter is to indicate what questions the empirical enquiry into democracy entails.

Democracy and causality

Schematically speaking, the huge literature on democracy deals with two general questions, besides providing for numerous case studies of democracy in individual countries. Theorizing democracy concerns one or the other of these two general questions, as any answer to them requires a theory, that is, a set of interlinked hypotheses. The two key general questions are:

Q1 what are the conditions for democratic stability?
Q2 what are the outcomes of a democratic regime?

Q1 entails a search for the socio-economic and political conditions which enhance the longevity of a democratic system of government. The basic idea is that economic, social and political factors either increase or decrease the probability that a country has a stable democratic regime. Why is it the case that countries differ so much in their capacity to sustain democracy? A number of theories of democracy have suggested a list of factors which impact on how democratic a country's political system actually is.

Q2 looks at democracy from the other side of the coin, namely the effects from the operation of a democratic regime on society and the economy. Whether a country is democratic or not is of extreme importance for its citizens, as well as foreigners and the international community in general. It would be difficult to imagine that a country could offer liberty and the rule of law without acknowledging formally that it endorses democracy. Yet, the theories about the impact of democracy deal with the relationship between democracy and socio-economic outcomes. Does democracy promote affluence and quality of life? A set of such outcome hypotheses would comprise both allocation and distribution.

The scholarly debate on these two questions has resulted in a huge literature involving lots of disagreement and contentious opinions. One of the first important contributions to this discussion was made by Lipset (1959), who focussed on factors which were conducive for the rise of democracy. Some time later, the first serious studies on the impact democracy may have on economic and social development were published, including Adelman and Morris (1967) who were working within the quantitative research tradition. This was typical of a large part of the research literature addressing these two issues, and it is mainly this tradition that will be addressed in this survey of the research literature. Only in a few instances, and also less systematically, will case studies be approached.

This chapter sets out to examine the two central concepts in this debate, namely democracy and development. The chapter attempts to clarify the meanings of these concepts as well as to review various ways of measuring them empirically. Here we also map the variation over time and in space of democracy and development. Moreover, this chapter aims to survey the research literature dealing with both the issue of to what extent socio-economic conditions determines the variation in democracy and the issue of what impact democracy may have on various dimensions of development. Let us start with the classical problem of defining 'democracy'.

Definitions of 'democracy'

The meaning of the word 'democracy' and its usage has varied over time (Lively, 1975; Baechler, 1995; Cunningham, 2002). What was understood as democracy in classical Athens differs from what may be understood as democracy today. Not only the concept of democracy has changed, but there have also been differences in the valuation of democracy as well as differences in the conceptions of democracy. In this section we will briefly review the major concepts of democracy. Furthermore, some of the more frequently used indices constructed to measure democracy will be presented, and these will be employed to map the variation in the occurrence of democracy over time as well as in space.

Literally 'democracy' comes from the Greek words 'demos' and 'cratein', meaning 'rule by the people'. Thus, the concept of democracy comprises of at least two components: 'rule' and 'people'. The crux of the matter is that what should be meant by 'rule' and by 'people' may be interpreted in many different ways. One may therefore distinguish between at least two approaches to democracy: one based on the meanings of 'rule' and another on what may be included in 'people'. We will mainly focus on democracy as rule and only briefly deal with the inclusion problem.

When considering democracy as rule, one may identify two basic conceptions: one narrow, focussing on democracy as a system of government, and a broad conception suggesting that democracy is something more than just a system of government. In ancient Greece, democracy was understood to be a system of government. When Aristotle in his *Politics* presented an overview of current political constitutions, a democratic constitution was one of those identified. The two criteria he applied for characterizing democracy were number of rulers and the ends of ruling. Democracy was not the kind of system he preferred, but for him it was basically a system of government.

Yet, 'democracy' has for a long time been associated with demands for economic and social equality. And at the time of the French Revolution one may say that economic equality became 'a permanent part of the democratic creed' (Laski, 1931: 77). There are even claims that, up until the mid nineteenth century, democracy 'first of all implied social equality' (Naess *et al.*, 1956: 130). Prominent among theoreticians identifying democracy with social equality was Tocqueville. His use of basic concepts like democracy and equality was often ambiguous (Lively, 1962: 49), but there is no doubt that, for him, democracy was something more than a system of government. Particularly before 1848, one may find a 'rather strong association and even identification of social equality with what was called "democracy" and "democratic"' (Christophersen, 1968: 86).

This broader conception of democracy as equality is to be found more frequently in radical analyses of democracy. Thus, John Dewey noted that a 'democracy is more than a form of government; it is primarily a mode of associated living, of conjoint communicated experience' (1966: 87). This is also the gist of the concluding section of the overview of democracy written by Laski:

> That is why [the new democratic theory] refuses to confine the ideal of democracy to the purely political sphere. It believes that for the average man constitutional government is not less important in industry than in politics or any other sphere. (1931: 84)

A similar position is taken by MacPherson, who stated: 'Democracy in the broad sense requires not just equality but also freedom from starvation, ignorance, and early diseased death' (1966: 53). In political theory one often encounters the interpretation of democracy as equality. Let us quote again from MacPherson:

> As soon as democracy is seen as a kind of society, not merely a mechanism of choosing and authorizing governments, the egalitarian principle inherent in democracy requires not only 'one man, one vote' but also 'one man, one equal effective right to live as fully humanly as he may wish'.
>
>   (1973: 51; see also Cunningham, 1987)

A similar standpoint may also be deduced from Rawls in his deliberations about democratic equality (cf. Anglade, 1994: 234). It is obvious that most feminist and Marxist accounts of democracy adhere to this broad conception of democracy (Pateman, 1989; Doveton, 1994; see also Luckham *et al.*, 2000).

Yet, within mainstream political science, at least since the late nineteenth century, democracy has been understood as a system of government. In his survey of democracies Lord Bryce notes:

> Democracy – which is merely a form of government, not a consideration of the purposes to which government may be turned – has nothing to do with Economic Equality, which might exist under any form of government, and might possibly work more smoothly under some other form.
>
>   (Bryce, 1921: 76)

Ernest Baker wrote, in a similar vein:

> Democracy does not mean the well being or prosperity of the people, but a method of *government* of the people; and a democratic measure is a measure which originates from, or tends to promote, such a method of government – not a measure which tends to increase the amount or to rectify the distribution of prosperity or well-being.
>
>   (Barker, 1942: 315)

A more recent statement of a similar position is taken by Brian Barry who maintains that democracy is to be understood in procedural terms:

> I reject the notion that one should build into 'democracy' any constraints on the content of the outcomes produced, such as substantive equality, respect for human rights, and concern for the general welfare, personal liberty, or the rule of law.
>
>   (Barry, 1989: 25)

Varsheney argues that, from an analytical point of view, it is necessary to distinguish between democracy as a procedure and economic equality as an outcome. If not, 'it ends up conflating the explanandum and explanans, or to put it differently, the independent and dependent variables' (1999: 12). Prze-worski proposes a similar minimalist conception of democracy (1999: 23–4).

Let us now turn to the inclusion problem. What is to constitute the people or the 'demos'? Here we also find different opinions and practices over time. In classical Greece, only the free men were allowed to be included into the 'demos'. In most political systems, the inclusion of women occurred later than was the case for men. Today we have on the agenda the question of the inclusion of migrants and young people into the 'demos'. Robert Dahl is the political scientist who has dealt with this issue most systematically and, in his opinion, one may formulate the following categorical principle:

> Every adult subject to a government and its laws must be presumed to be qualified as, and has an unqualified right to be, a member of the demos.
>
> (Dahl, 1989: 127)

Dahl states that there are two difficulties with this principle. One has to do with the boundary between childhood and adulthood, and a second one with the presence of foreigners in a country – which of them to include or not include. And these difficulties may be treated differently in various contexts.

We have so far identified two conceptions of democracy, one broader and one narrower. There are pros and cons for each of these conceptions. It may indeed be attractive to associate democracy with the good society. But from a pragmatic point of view it may yet be more reasonable to characterize the political sphere as more or less democratic and let it be an empirical issue whether the good society is associated with a democratic government or not. This means that we adhere to the narrow conception of democracy, although we will research whether democracy as a set of procedures enhances affluence and equality.

Democratic procedures

Maintaining that democracy refers to a method of government where adult people are to be included into the demos has only vaguely delimited what may be meant by democracy. To arrive at a more precise understanding of what democracy stands for, there are a number of further issues concerning procedures that have to be dealt with. It is generally acknowledged that the concept of democracy is both diffuse and multi-faceted (Sartori, 1987: 1). Even if this is the case, most participants discussing democracy have attempted to contribute with their own version of what a concept of democracy may stand for. Defining democracy is important for discriminating between democratic and non-democratic political systems, but also for attempts to map a variation in the degree of democracy (Schmidt, 2000; see also Brooker, 2000).

When surveying more contemporary definitions of democracy, then, there are a few procedures that seem to be highlighted most often. Democracy means rule of the people, but to have a democracy there must be a set of procedures which enhance: (a) *contestation* between political alternatives, (b) citizens *participating* in political life, and (c) real guarantees for the existence of *political liberties.* Let us explain what is meant by democracy as a set of procedures by referring to one of the more prominent theoreticians of democracy – Joseph A. Schumpeter. In his study on *Capitalism, Socialism and Democracy* (1976), first published in 1942, he works with two definitions of democracy. One is attempting to capture the classical doctrine of democracy, while the other deals with what he calls 'another theory of democracy'. The classical definition reads like this:

> the democratic method is that institutional arrangement for arriving at political decisions which realizes the common good by making people itself decide issues through the election of individuals who are to assemble in order to carry out its will.
>
> (1976: 250)

The other definition reverses the role of the selection of representatives, and here Schumpeter defines the method of democracy as:

> that institutional arrangement for arriving at political decisions in which individuals acquire the power to decide by means of a competitive struggle for the people's vote.
>
> (ibid.: 269)

Robert A. Dahl stressed another dimension. In his *A Preface to Democratic Theory*, the core of democracy was the 'processes by which ordinary citizens exert a relatively high degree of control over leaders' (Dahl, 1963: 3). Mainstream definitions of democracy have followed the paths of Schumpeter and Dahl, identifying the three procedures: contestation, participation and political liberties. Typical here is the definition employed by Huntington:

> this study defines a twentieth-century political system as democratic to the extent that its most powerful collective decision makers are selected through fair, honest, and periodic elections in which candidates freely competes for votes and in which virtually all the adult population is eligible to vote.
>
> (1991: 7)

With some minor modifications we find that these three dimensions – contestation, participation, civil and political freedoms – occur in many of the definitions suggested for democracy or its synonyms, political democracy or liberal democracy (cf. Oppenheim, 1971; Therborn, 1977: 4; Pennock, 1979: 7; Powell, 1982: 3; Diamond *et al.*, 1988: xvi; Hadenius, 1992: 9; Sørensen, 1993: 13; Markoff, 1999: 662–3; Schmidt, 1999: 282). Even a scholar like Randall Collins, working in another discipline and starting from a Weberian approach, concludes by identifying the following three core dimensions of democracy: degree of collegially shared power, extent of the participatory franchise and political rights (Collins, 1998: 18).

There may also be other dimensions that could be included into a proper definition of democracy. The pragmatic view proposed here is, however, that the three dimensions most often included when defining democracy – contestation, participation, civil and political liberties – quite well captures what may be understood as democracy or its synonyms, political democracy and liberal democracy. Here we thus adhere to the core features of a democratic system suggested by Lipset:

> First, competition exists for government positions, and fair elections for public office occur at regular intervals without the use of force and without excluding any social group. Second, citizens participate in selecting their leaders and forming policies. And, third, civil and political liberties exist to ensure the integrity of political competition and participation.
>
> (1995: lv)

This means that it is an empirical issue whether democratic regimes tend to be more or less effective in their governance, whether a democratic regime is more or less compatible with a capitalist economic system (property rights, market economy), or whether democracies are more or less conducive for accomplishing social equality. Democracy may thus be conducive to the empowerment of various groups of people, but empowerment is not the same thing as democracy (cf. Beteille, 1999).

So far we have arrived at the understanding of democracy as a system of government adhering to the procedures of contestation and, participation, as well as civil and political liberties. These criteria may be employed not only to distinguish between democracies and non-democracies but also to go further and identify different types, or models, of democracy. In our next step we will proceed to enquire into ways of measuring democracy, which is also a way of distinguishing democracies from non-democracies.

Measuring democracy

Defining democracy is the first necessary step to take to enable us to measure democracy. But to measure democracy we need to do more than simply define it. As discussed by Bollen (1995: 817–21), there are a number of issues to deal with in order to arrive at satisfactory measures of democracy: categorical versus continuous measures, objective versus subjective indicators, individual versus panel judgements, single-time versus multiple-time measures.

There is a growing literature on how to measure democracy and there are nowadays a number of democracy indices in existence (Inkeles, 1990; Beetham, 1994; Lauth *et al.*, 2000). In addition, there are also a number of studies dealing with evaluating such measures (Bollen, 1986, 1990; Bollen and Paxton, 2000; Foweraker and Krznaric, 2000; Munck and Verkuilen, 2002).

One major issue when measuring democracy is whether one should consider it to be measured as a dichotomy or as a continuous scale. If democracy is a dichotomy then it is only possible to distinguish between democracies and non-democracies. If, on the other hand, it is considered to be a scale, then it will be possible to compare states with respect to their varying degree of democracy, or non-democracy. Basically this issue is about whether the difference between democracies and non-democracies is a difference of kind or a difference of degree. We may note that there are researchers arguing for these different standpoints and that there are measures developed on a nominal as well as an ordinal or interval level.

In his study, *The Third Wave*, Huntington preferred the dichotomous approach (1991: 11). An elaborate argument for employing a nominal classification is proposed by Przeworski *et al.* (2000: 57): 'We believe that although some regimes are more democratic than others, unless the offices are contested, they should not be considered democratic. The analogy with the proverbial pregnancy is thus that whereas democracy can be more or less advanced, one cannot be half-democratic: There is a natural zero point.' Their measure is based on the classification of five types of regimes, which are collapsed into either democracies (parliamentarism, mixed, presidentialism) or non-democracies (autocracy, bureaucracy).

Many researchers within the field do, however, employ some kind of continuous scale, be it on an ordinal or interval level. Bollen is a prominent advocate of employing continuous scales of democracy. He states that democracy is always a matter of degree: 'The concept of political democracy is continuous. We talk and think about the degree to which democracy is present' (1990: 15). This standpoint is strongly endorsed by Elkins who concludes a review of the discussion by stating: 'Democratization studies lead us to believe that there is substantial variation in the *degree* of democracy across both time and space' (2000: 299).

David Collier and Robert Adcock arrive at a more pragmatic conclusion in their survey of the discussion on democracy and dichotomies (1999: 562). They argue that whether a dichotomous or a continuous measure should be used depends on the research question addressed. For certain research questions, a dichotomous measure may be more appropriate, and for other research questions a continuous measure may be more appropriate.

Another issue concerns the use of objective or subjective measures. Objective measures may refer to number of parties standing for an election and the percentage of the population participating in such elections. These two indicators are the core components of the democracy index created by Vanhanen (2000) and, consequently, he is only using objective measures. In most other indices there are both subjective as well as objective measures employed. Examples of subjective measures may be ratings of civil liberties and political rights or judgements about the fairness of elections.

Measures may also differ with respect to whether they are building on the work of individual scholars, a group of scholars or a panel of experts. The democracy measures developed by Vanhanen, Bollen and, up to 1989, the Freedom House index designed by Gastil, were to a large extent contributions from individual scholars. The scores reported in the later Freedom House index (1990 onwards) rely on a panel of experts for the countries covered by the survey. The Polity measures (Gurr and Jaggers, 2000) and the classification of regimes reported by Przeworski *et al.* (2000) are the result of work from research groups and not from an individual researcher.

Some of the democracy measures report scores from multiple time periods, while others focus on single time periods. The Polity measure covers the longest range of time since it begins at 1800 and goes through the twentieth century; the Vanhanen measure covers almost the same period, starting at 1810. Przeworski's measure goes from 1950 to 1990 while the Freedom House measure begins in 1972 and has from that year been reporting yearly updates. The original Bollen measure covers the years 1960, 1965 and 1980 (Bollen, 1980 and 1993) and Hadenius (1992) focussed only on the year 1988 for Third World countries.

The dimensions included vary somewhat between the different indices. The dimensions we have included in our definition of democracy are contestation, participation and civil liberties. Considering six of the democracy indices reported in the research literature and their coverage of these dimensions, correspondences are presented in Table 1.1.

The most appropriate index would be Hadenius, but it only covers one year. The following three indices of these indicators will be used for mapping the variation in democracy: Freedom House, Przeworski and Polity.

Democracy will thus be understood as, and measured as, a system of government where adults are included in the demos and which meets certain criteria spelled out in these criteria. Democracy is thus not the same thing as system effectiveness or empowerment of people. These entities may go hand-in-hand, but whether this is the case is basically an empirical question. In fact, the conduct of empirical enquiry with these indices helps us answer relevant questions such as: is there a variation in the occurrence of democracy among the states of the world? Does democracy vary over time? Relying on three of the indices presented on page 30, we can map this variation in time as well as in space. Let us first look at the longitudinal variation.

Figure 1.1 contains mean-values for three of the indices starting with 1950 (Polity and Przeworski) and ending with estimates for year 2000 (Freedom House). It is obvious from the figure that the indices portray roughly the same picture, and this picture seems to agree with what Huntington called a second short wave of democratization (1943–62), a second reverse wave (1958–75) and a third wave of democratization (1974–) (Huntington, 1991: 16). The Przeworski scores are lower than the Polity scores but their patterns over time are strongly correlated. These indices all display a variation in democracy over time.

Table 1.1 Quantitative measures of democracy

Index	Contestation	Participation	Civil liberties
Bollen	✗		✗
Freedom House	✗		✗
Hadenius	✗	✗	✗
Polity	✗		✗
Przeworski *et al.*	✗		
Vanhanen	✗	✗	

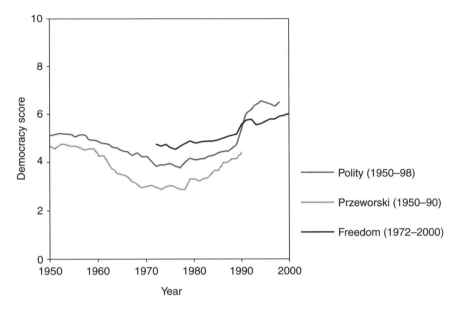

Figure 1.1 Variation in democracy over time according to three democracy measures (means).

Sources: see Appendix A1.

Note
The time period covered by the index is reported in parenthesis; the Przeworski index has been multiplied with 10 for this figure. Here the Freedom House index and the Polity index have been slightly adjusted. The Freedom House scores have been normalized so that a low degree of democracy scores 1 and a high degree of democracy scores 10. The adjusted Polity score has been arrived at by subtracting the original autocracy score from the democracy score and then normalizing the index to go from 0 to 10.

We may now establish that these three indices display a similar variation in space. The occidental countries achieve the highest scores while the lowest scores are to be found in Central and Eastern Europe during the period before 1989, as well as among countries in North Africa, the Middle East and in sub-Saharan Africa. Breaking down the data to these regions one may note that these indices tend to correlate quite highly, although there is no perfect match between them. In comparing how various indices score for particular countries over a period, there may be distinctive discrepancies between them (McHenry, 2000). Even if one may raise questions about the validity of particular scores, these are the major indices that are available and they give a general but still accurate picture of how democracy varies over time and in space. Table 1.2 shows the same variation in democracy across regions when measured with the three indices.

Table 1.2 Variation in democracy between major regions of the world (means)

Region	Przeworski					Polity						Freedom House			
	1950	1960	1970	1980	1990	1950	1960	1970	1980	1990	1998	1980	1990	1998	2000
Occident	9.1	9.1	8.7	10.0	10.0	9.0	9.0	8.8	9.8	9.9	9.9	9.5	9.8	9.7	9.7
Cee + Cis	0.0	0.0	0.0	0.0	5.0	1.3	1.4	1.4	1.5	6.6	6.7	2.1	6.1	6.0	6.1
C + LatAm	4.2	6.3	6.3	4.8	7.6	4.1	5.2	4.5	4.9	8.3	8.6	5.7	7.3	7.0	7.2
SubS Afr	0.0	1.4	1.4	1.1	0.3	4.1	3.6	2.7	2.6	2.4	5.5	3.1	3.5	4.9	5.0
NA + ME	0.0	0.0	0.0	0.0	0.7	3.9	1.5	1.6	1.0	2.3	2.6	3.4	3.2	2.8	2.9
So Asia	8.0	6.0	6.0	1.7	5.0	5.2	4.2	3.9	3.2	4.3	5.6	4.8	4.1	4.5	4.2
SE Asia	1.4	3.0	3.0	1.7	4.2	2.8	4.2	3.8	3.4	5.0	6.0	4.0	4.9	5.2	5.5
All	4.7	4.3	4.3	3.3	4.4	5.1	4.9	4.2	4.2	5.5	6.6	4.8	5.5	5.9	6.0
eta sq	0.55	0.49	0.48	0.58	0.59	0.51	0.43	0.43	0.58	0.60	0.41	0.61	0.46	0.46	0.45
N	73	98	116	121	121	81	98	120	122	123	146	133	132	150	150

Sources: see Appendix A1.

Notes

eta sq = amount of variation explained by region.

Summing up

It is meaningful to distinguish between two conceptions of democracy, a broader and a narrower one. In order to conduct empirical enquiries, there seems to be an agreement that democracy should be understood to refer to a system of government. Based on such an assumption it is possible to arrive at ways to measure the variation in scores of democracy across countries and over time. These indices may discriminate between countries, whether their regimes are more or less democratic. Using them it is possible to map a variation that is important for enquiring into the relation between democracy and development. Yet, when this is said, one must remember that those democracies that we have identified – scoring high on the indices – may vary among themselves. It is possible to distinguish between a number of democracy models with reference to a variation in their institutional set-ups. This will be examined later in this book. The issue to be dealt with now is about democracy and development in general.

Conditions for and outcomes of democracy

'Development and democracy' has often been the title for enquiries into the causes and effects of democracy as a political regime. Thus, one has discussed whether democracy requires a developed society, affluence being one precondition, as well as whether democracy promotes development, meaning whether it enhances economic growth and income equality. Yet, development is a concept that many would say defies any definition. The meanings of 'development' vary and the numbers of definitions attempted are quite numerous. Measuring development also faces a number of problems. Let us consider various ways to deal with the concept of development.

It is common knowledge that development may refer either to a process or the product of a process or, to put it another way, process versus condition (Nagel, 1957: 15; see also Riggs, 1984: 133). These processes may refer to different spheres where one distinction may be made between an economic sphere and the non-economic spheres. The economic sphere may refer to total income, per-capita income or the size distribution of the economy (Machlup, 1963: 270–3). In the years immediately after the Second World War, economists understood development as economic development, which was virtually equated with economic growth (Arndt, 1989: 51). This was also true for more orthodox Marxist economists (Dobb, 1963; Lange, 1963). Two decades later, in the early 1970s, the focus in the development literature had shifted to include items belonging to a non-economic sphere, such as employment, equality, poverty eradication and basic needs fulfilment (Arndt, 1989: 92; see also Huntington, 1987; Adelman, 2000).

According to Sen (1983), economic growth is not necessarily the same thing as development, but economic growth is a means to achieve some other important objectives like improvements in life expectancy, literacy, health and higher education. A similar approach to the goals of development is expressed by Goulet (1995: 41–6) when identifying the following three goals which, he suggests, are universal ones: life-sustenance, esteem and freedom.

In the current development literature, there seems to be a consensus that development may be understood as the achievement of a better life. This attempt to combine the economic and non-economic spheres of development is obvious in the construction of the human development index, which contains both economic and non-economic indicators. It is also striking that the concept of development will increasingly become broader to also incorporate gender (gender development) and environmental (sustainable development) dimensions, rather than going back to the narrower concept of economic growth. Such an approach to development is also evident with the World Commission on Environment and Development (WCED). For them, the objective of development is the satisfaction of human needs and aspirations and 'sustainable development is development that meets the needs of the present without compromising the ability of future generations to meet their own needs' (WCED, 1987: 43; see also Barraclough, 2001).

Sen has noted this change of direction in development economics clearly. There is now a 'focusing on the quality of life and of substantive freedoms, rather than just on income or wealth' (Sen, 1999: 24). And freedoms like the liberty of political participation or the opportunity to receive basic education or health care, Sen argues, are constituent components of development (ibid.: 5). Freedoms, or entitlements as they may also be called, are not only ends but also means to achieve these ends. And these freedoms are not fundamentally 'Western' values, but universal ones. In the article, 'East and West: The reach of reason', he forcefully argues that champions of freedom and tolerance are to be found among western as well as non-western authors (Sen, 2000: 36).

Thus one may conclude that it is hardly possible to arrive at one, and only one, satisfactory definition of development. Over time we may, however, note some important changes in the conceptions of development. From an early understanding of development as economic growth, meaning a narrow conception, development is today looked on more as including both economic and non-economic elements, suggesting a broad conception of what development stands for.

In our enquiries into the relationships between a democratic regime and social and economic factors, we will stay away from the vague term 'development' with its strong western bias. Instead we will target a few key models about the interaction between democracy on the one hand and economic and social factors on the other. Let us introduce the indicators on these macro economic and social factors, which will be approached as either conditions for democracy or as effects of democracy.

Indicators

If we accept that development is both a process and the product of a process, as well as covering economic and non-economic spheres, we may identify at least three different ways of measuring development (cf. Bunge, 1980; Offner, 2000). Let us start with the economic sphere.

The most common economic indicator employed to measure development is the national income expressed as GNP or GDP. Economic growth may then refer to changes over time in the value of GNP/GDP. It may be measured as the real growth or the growth per capita or per worker. Per capita income may also be used as an index of development – the level of development. There are a number of deficiencies associated with this measure (Henderson, 1996: 51), but it is still widely used because of the lack of better alternatives.

If the per capita measure is to be used for comparisons between countries, it is necessary to convert the local currency to the currency it is to be compared with, which in most cases is US dollar. There are then a number of options available as to which exchange rate to employ – a current or a fixed exchange rate. This may be qualified as the 'nominal' per capita GDP/GNP.

Even when employing correct exchange rates, there may be problems in comparing per capita incomes due to differences in purchasing power between rich and poor countries. One way of getting around this is to estimate the relation between the purchasing power of a specific country compared with the same one in USA and then estimate new per capita income values corrected for purchasing powers – arriving at purchasing power parities (PPP), or 'real' per capita GDP/GNP. The quality of these income measures has certainly improved and the estimates now reported by the Penn World Tables (Summers and Heston, 1994) as well as the World Bank (2000c) provide the research community with data covering a large sample of countries going back at least to the early 1950s.

The level of income is one thing, but it is another thing to say something about the distribution of the incomes within a society. In talking about income distribution, we are moving in the direction of indicators covering the quality of life. From a distributive point of view a more equal distribution of income may be prefererable to a less equal one. A widely used measure to capture the variation in income distribution in a country is the Gini-coefficient (Deininger and Squire, 1997; Milanovic, 1999; World Bank, 2000a; Milanovic and Yitzhaki, 2000); the Gini-coefficient goes from 0 to 1 and the lower the value, the more equal is the income distribution.

Another aspect of the distribution of incomes in a country is the presence of poverty (Fields, 1999). A number of attempts to measure poverty are reported in the literature. One standard applied by the World Bank is the percentage of a population living on less than $1 a day in 1993 PPP (World Bank, 2000b: 17). Another standard is suggested by UNDP, which has constructed a Human Poverty Index (HPI) that concentrates on 'deprivations in three essential dimensions of human life' – longevity, knowledge and a decent standard of living (UNDP, 1999: 163). These poverty measures focus mostly on the developing countries.

Moving from strictly economic measures to broader measures of development, it is possible to identify different approaches. One approach has been to conduct an analysis of socio-economic development through the employment of a system of indicators as practised by the team headed by Donald McGranahan at UNRISD in Geneva (McGranahan, 1971, 1995). In a report from 1985, they list nine indicators which were considered to be usable: infant mortality, life expectancy at birth, literacy, school enrolment, telephones per 1000 population, agricultural production per male agricultural worker, steel consumption per capita, energy consumption per capita and GNP per capita in US dollars (McGranahan *et al.*, 1985: 117–18); a similar approach has been applied by Estes (1984, 1996).

Another approach has been the employment of indicators strictly measuring quality of life. One of the first steps in establishing such an index was the construction of the Physical Quality of Life Index (PQLI) by Morris (1979, 1996). This index was constructed as the non-weighted average for life expectancy, infant mortality and literacy rate. One may see this index as one of a number of early predecessors of the Human Development Index (HDI) made available by the United Nations Development Programme (UNDP) from 1990 and onwards (Desai, 1991). The Human Development Index contains the following three components: life expectancy, adult literacy and the log of GDP per head (Anand and Sen, 1994, 2000). Over time, the index has been refined and the latest version differs in certain respects from the first one presented in 1990. There has also been an intense debate about the pros and cons of this index, and a number of proposals for changing and improving it have been suggested (Streeten, 1995; Hicks, 1997; Castles, 1998; Noorbakhsh, 1998; Henderson, 2000; Jolly, 2000). Still there is no doubt that the HDI today is recognized as the major quality of life index available, and it is now commonly employed in cross-country studies.

Within the framework of the research conducted by the UNDP, this quality of life index approach has been extended to cover gender dimensions. The *Fourth World Conference of Women, Beijing* in 1995 was the starting point for the construction of a Gender Development-related Index (GDI) and a Gender Empowerment Measure (GEM). The GDI takes into account differences in human development for men and women (Anand and Sen, 1995; see also Bardhan and Klasen, 1999; Razavi, 1999; Saith and Harriss-White, 1999). The GEM captures the position of women in various kinds of societal positions (Kabeer, 1999). One aspect of gender empowerment is female participation in parliament (WOM) (IPU, 2000). It should be noted that there has been a huge effort in the 1990s to make gender an important aspect of measuring development (Nussbaum, 1995; Razavi, 1997; Danner *et al.*, 1999).

In a similar vein, another UN-organization – UNICEF – has annually, from 1979, attempted to review the condition of the world's children. The measure they use as the principal indicator capturing the level of well being for children is the under-five mortality rate (U5MR) (UNICEF, 2001a; see also Jordan, 1993).

Other extensions of this approach to development relate to environmental dimensions including attempts to map changes in the human footprint on the ecosystems (WWF, 2000) as well as constructing an Environmental Sustainability Index (ESI) (World Economic Forum, 2001).

In addition to these more objective measures, a number of subjective measures on the quality of life are also available. These measures are based on worldwide surveys and most often they only cover a smaller sample of the countries of the world (Diener and Suh, 1997). To summarize, we may establish that development can be measured in a number of different ways. In this book, development will stand for an economic dimension as well as a non-economic dimension; furthermore, there will be a distinction between two states of development: development as growth and development as level. These deliberations may be summarized in a 2×2 table as presented below in Table 1.3.

In empirical studies of development, indicators like those listed in Table 1.3 are used. Some indicators capture economic or non-economic dimensions of development, and some focus on various states such as growth in or level of development. Together these indicators may, hopefully, capture relevant aspects of the multi-faceted concept of development. These are the main indicators that are employed in the research literature to be surveyed, and we will make use of them in both this chapter and subsequently.

Economic and social conditions

Let us look at the variation in the economic factors. First, we take the level of development as measured by per capita incomes. According to the IMF estimates reported in *World Economic Outlook*, Gross World Product per capita steadily rose from US$1186 in 1970 to an estimated figure of US$7200 in year 2000 (IMF, 2000). Yet, there is a huge variation across countries. Table 1.4 presents data for the 1990s for a few major regions of the world, based on different ways of measuring per capita income, expressed in US$.

Irrespective of which measures are employed, they all show basically the same thing for the 1990s. There is a huge variation between the different regions of the world. The western countries are the rich countries and countries of South Asia and Africa make up the poor areas of the world, while the South East Asian countries have risen to a position of second among the regions on display in Table 1.4.

In Figure 1.2 the focus is changed from the level of per capita incomes to displaying year-to-year changes in per capita incomes. The figure displays annual changes between 1971 and 2000 in the size of world population (POPUGRO) as well as in Gross World Product, and world economic growth is measured as real growth (PPPGRO) and as per capita growth (PPPCGRO). We then find that population growth is slightly declining, from a rate of more than 2 per cent in the early 1970s to a rate of less than 2 per cent in the 1990s. Economic growth also goes down where the per capita rate is less than the rate for real economic growth due to the impact of population growth. Further-

Table 1.3 Indicators

Dimension/state	Growth	Level
Economic	Real GDP, Real GDP/ capita, Population	Real GDP/capita
Non-economic	–	Gini, HPI, PQLI, HDI, GDI, GEM, FEM, U5MR, ESI

Table 1.4 Variation in per capita incomes in the 1990s by major world regions (different measures)

Region	PWT	MADD	GDP in PPP		GNP in PPP		GNP Atlas		GNP Constant	
	1990	1990	1990	1998	1990	1998	1990	1998	1990	1998
Occident	13,055	16,266	16,945	21,982	16,901	21,791	18,834	24,106	22,674	26,166
Cee + Cis	4804	5497	6492	5567	6515	5508	2380	2309	2721	2387
C + LatAm	3354	3865	3945	5219	3739	5079	1658	2813	2266	2787
SubS Afr	1282	1304	1668	1942	1610	1869	771	756	758	798
NA + ME	2717	4340	4625	5279	4757	5272	4307	3233	4024	3164
So Asia	1536	1266	1281	1804	1259	1780	373	458	361	453
SE Asia	5695	6089	6030	8085	5657	8116	5400	7517	6818	8560
All	5176	5586	6112	7463	6034	7381	5123	6216	5881	6686
eta sq	0.771	0.751	0.723	0.740	0.695	0.721	0.700	0.704	0.644	0.678
N	103	131	129	135	131	135	124	136	134	136

Sources: see Appendix A1.

Notes
PWT = Penn World Tables; MADD = Maddison; GDP = Gross Domestic Product; GNP = Gross National Product; PPP = Purchasing Power Parities; Atlas = World Bank Atlas method; Constant = constant prices; eta sq = amount of variation explained by region.

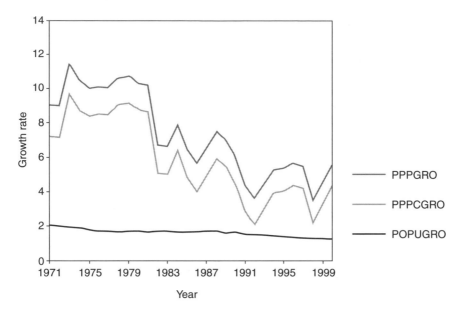

Figure 1.2 Variation in economic and population growth over time (1971–2000).

Sources: see Appendix A1.

Notes
PPPGRO = yearly growth in Gross World Product expressed in PPPs; PPPCGRO = yearly growth in Gross World Product/capita expressed in PPPs; POPUGRO = yearly growth in world population.

more, it is important to observe that economic growth hovers a lot over time, while the population growth rate follows a smooth linear pattern.

Breaking down these aggregate world data to a number of major regions on one hand and, on the other hand, averaging the yearly data to three periods (1961–73, 1973–90, 1990–8) we may identify a regional pattern, as portrayed in Table 1.5. It is obvious that economic growth varies over time. Having a high economic growth rate at one period does not mean that a country or a region may experience a high growth rate at another period. There is also a major variation in economic growth between the major regions of the world. South East Asia stands out as one of the major growth regions for the whole period, while the western region experiences lower rates of economic growth during the 1990s than was the case in the 1960s. Population growth also varies between regions – highest rates in North Africa and the Middle East, and lowest rates in the western region – but this regional pattern is not shifting over time.

It may be helpful to look at some of the variation in the social factors. First let us look at the changes over time in inequality between the countries of the world. There is no agreement about whether there has been an increase in inequalities or not. Estimates reported by Korzeniewicz and Moran (1997: 1021) for the period 1965–90 suggest a slight increase, while estimates made by Firebaugh (1999: 1613) for the same period indicate virtually no changes:

Table 1.5 Variation in population growth and economic growth by major world regions

Region	Population growth (POPGRO)			GNP growth (PPPGROW)			GNP/capita growth (PPPCGROW)		
	1961–73	1973–90	1990–8	1961–73	1973–90	1990–8	1961–73	1973–90	1990–8
Occident	1.0	0.6	0.7	5.2	2.8	2.6	4.1	2.1	1.8
Cee + Cis	1.5	1.0	0.1	6.8	3.1	−4.2	6.4	2.7	−4.2
C + LatAm	2.5	2.1	1.8	5.2	2.7	3.8	2.6	0.5	1.9
SubS Afr	2.5	2.8	2.6	4.6	3.3	2.5	2.0	0.4	−0.2
NA + ME	3.7	3.6	2.6	5.4	4.7	4.5	2.8	1.4	1.8
So Asia	2.2	2.2	2.2	3.4	4.5	4.7	10	2.4	2.9
SE Asia	2.4	1.9	1.8	7.4	6.3	5.2	4.9	4.3	3.3
All	2.2	2.0	1.7	5.2	3.6	2.4	3.1	1.5	0.7
eta sq	0.361	0.555	0.575	0.162	0.265	0.589	0.460	0.300	0.460
N	127	149	149	85	99	128	84	98	127

Sources: see Appendix A1.

Note

eta sq = amount of variation explained by region.

from 0.540 in 1960 to 0.543 in 1989. Later estimates presented by Milanovic (1999: 34) suggest an increase from a Gini coefficient of 0.551 in 1988 to 0.578 in 1993.

Data on poverty presented by the World Bank (2000b: 23–4) indicate that the proportion of people living under poverty has decreased from 1987 to 1998. The proportion living on a daily income of US$1 has decreased from 28.3 per cent to 24.0 per cent; using other indicators on relative poverty, the picture is similar: from 36.3 per cent in 1987 to 32.1 per cent in 1998. At the same time, we know that the number of countries classified as Least Developed Countries (LDCs) has increased from twenty-four in 1971 to forty-nine in year 2000 (UNCTAD, 2000).

The HDI measure indicates an increase over time. The non-weighted mean from a sample of countries numbering at the most 143 shows a slight but steady rise in human development over time. In 1975, the mean score was 0.596 and it had increased to 0.680 in 1998. Thus, one may conclude that there is no distinctive pattern of change over time for these indicators on non-economic dimensions of development, but some of the evidence suggests that the situation is not deteriorating.

Let us therefore continue to look at the spatial variation for some of these indicators on non-economic dimensions of development. As one can note from the data displayed in Table 1.6, there is again quite a large variation between the different regions, and these indicators do also go together strongly.

With the exception for the Gini indcx, thcsc indicators correlate strongly with each other. Unequal income distributions are thus not the same thing as the presence of deep poverty in a country. In general, the western world has a higher level of development, as suggested by these indicators, and in most cases, the sub-Saharan countries in Africa display the lowest level of development.

Summing up

'Development' may be given many different meanings, but there seems to be an agreement that development may be identified by a set of economic and social factors; thus we have concentrated on them. Cross-country comparisons indicate that the level of development, whether referring to economic or the non-economic dimensions, tends to display a similar pattern of variation in space. In both dimensions there is a deep divide between different regions of the world and this pattern seems to have been rather stable over time.

Let us now employ these findings in looking for relationships between these economic and social factors on the one hand and democracy on the other. As emphasized, one may approach this interaction from two sides, either searching for the conditions for the stability of a democratic regime or looking for the outcomes of the operation of a democratic regime.

Table 1.6 Variation in non-economic dimensions of development by major world regions

Region	GINIWDI	HPI (1999)	PQLI (1993)	HDI (1998)	GDI (1998)	GEM (1998)	ESI (2001)
Occident	31.5	–	92.1	0.912	0.907	0.690	65.7
Cee + Cis	31.9	–	86.4	0.762	0.767	0.497	50.0
C + LatAm	49.8	15.7	78.5	0.729	0.717	0.492	51.0
SubS Afr	45.5	41.2	48.7	0.450	0.452	0.353	42.2
NA + ME	37.3	24.7	67.1	0.679	0.653	0.306	38.6
So Asia	34.7	38.4	54.5	0.546	0.539	0.307	44.3
SE Asia	38.4	23.3	78.9	0.715	0.732	0.453	44.6
All	39.1	29.5	70.1	0.680	0.683	0.529	49.4
eta sq	0.515	0.486	0.731	0.744	0.739	0.728	0.571
N	107	81	116	143	126	63	121

Sources: see Appendix A1.

Notes

GINI = Gini index; HPI = Human Poverty Index; PQLI = Physical Quality of Life Index; HDI = Human Development Index; GDI = Gender-related Development Index; GEM = Gender Empowerment Measure; ESI = Environmental Sustainability Index.

Conditions: development and democracy

In political thinking there is a common understanding that there is a relation between the degree of wealth of a society and the kind of political regime that one may find there (Elgström and Hyden, 2002). This was obvious for Aristotle, who suggested that different kinds of political regimes – democracy or oligarchy – were to be expected in a society, depending on whether there were a large number of poor people or whether there were more affluent people (Aristotle, 1981: 271; 1289^{a}38). This view was taken over, more or less, by later mainstream political science. Thus, according to MacIver, one may expect that democracies will be more frequent in countries characterized by economic and cultural advancement. He states:

> The claim is not here made that countries of cultural advancement always develop some kind of democracy, but only that where democracy has developed it has been in such countries.
>
> (1965: 142)

The first empirical tests of the model suggesting that wealth has a positive impact on the presence of democratic regimes were conducted in the later part of the 1950s. The data employed and the techniques used were quite simple. Yet both Lerner (1964: 63) and Lipset claimed that they had been able to show a positive relation between wealth and democracy. In an often-quoted section, Lipset wrote:

> Perhaps the most common generalization linking political systems to other aspects of society has been that democracy is related to the state of economic development. The more well-to-do a nation, the greater the chances that it will sustain democracy.
>
> (Lipset, 1963: 48–50)

What Lipset was suggesting was a more or less linear relation between wealth and democracy. The mechanism linking wealth with democracy was education and the formation of a middle class. Growing wealth opens up the possibility to invest more in the social structure of a country. Education means an investment in human capital, but more education also fosters new orientations among citizens. More education and the rise of a new middle class is also conducive to less polarization in political life. A less polarized polity may find it easier to combat non-democratic political forces, thereby securing democratic stability. This was the approach of the modernization school in predicting a long-term rise in transitions to democracy as a consequence of rising wealth worldwide.

In a Festschrift in honour of Lipset from 1992, Diamond surveyed some of the major studies in the field from the 1960s to the late 1980s. It is striking that all of the studies quoted by Diamond suggest a positive effect of wealth on democracy (Diamond, 1992: 470). His conclusion of this survey indicates that Lipset was broadly correct in his assertion of a strong causal relationship between economic development and democracy and in his explanations of why developments promotes democracy.

(ibid.: 485)

The challenges against Lipset has been more about whether there is a linear or non-linear relation, or in the role of wealth when control for other determinants of democracy have been established, as well as whether a further stage of development really was conducive for democracy or rather would produce 'bureaucratic–authoritarian' regimes as was the case in Latin America in the 1970s (O'Donnell, 1979).

In two articles published in 1993 and 1994, Lipset and his collaborators addressed some of these challenges. In these studies more recent data and more refined techniques were employed. The democracy variable was based on the Freedom House rankings and they covered the period up to the late 1980s. In general they found support for the 'hypothesized relationship between economic development and democratization' (Lipset *et al.*, 1993: 158). Testing for the impact of other factors, the strongest impact recorded was for economic development. Their findings also suggested that the relation between wealth and democracy could be well described as an *N*-curve, meaning that there is an upper threshold of economic development where an increasing level of economic development does not affect a higher level of political democracy. In short, Lipset implied that these findings did support what was hypothesized in the modernization theory. But he was hesitant when it came to predicting future outcomes: 'The various factors I have reviewed here do shape the probabilities for democracy, but they do not determine the outcomes' (Lipset, 1994: 17). This is a thesis that claims economic development is the most important factor while, at the same time, it also acknowledges the importance of political culture, religious tradition, institutions and civil society.

In an attempt to test some of the hypotheses generated within modernization theory, Hadenius constructed a democracy index of his own, covering Third World countries for 1988. His finding here was that economic development was not unimportant, but other socio-economic factors were more important – namely, literacy and education. Or, in his own words:

> Yet, it is not primarily the economic factors – which have loomed large in recent research in this field – which are interesting in this context. The crucial point for a political change in the said direction chiefly comprises attributes which pertain to popular education.
>
> (Hadenius 1992: 90; see also Rueschemeyer *et al.*, 1992)

There are thus mediating factors operating between wealth and democracy. Muller (1995) suggested that income distribution might be such a factor. In some cases – as in Costa Rica – intermediate inequality may have been conducive for the establishment of a stable democracy (1995: 970). However, in general, income inequality may decrease the probability of democracies in some intermediate phases of economic development. His conclusion was that 'high levels of income inequality are incompatible with the development of a stable democratic system' (Muller, 1995: 981; see also Boix, 2000).

Another mediating factor that may reduce the impact of wealth on democracy is position in the world system. That is the conclusion drawn by Burkhart and Lewis-Beck (1994) analysing a set of 131 countries for the period 1972 to 1989, using the Freedom House ratings as measures for democracy. They conclude:

> On balance, it is clear that economic development substantially improves a nation's democratic prospects. However, the full magnitude of that effect depends on the location of the nation in the world system. As the nation moves from the core, to the semi periphery, to the periphery, the effect diminishes.
>
> (Burkhart and Lewis-Back, 1994: 907)

Barro's analysis of 'The determinants of democracy' broadly supports the hypothesis that 'a higher standard of living promotes democracy' (Barro, 1999: 182), but he also identifies a number of mediating factors among which one may name colonial heritage and religious affiliation. Some may disagree on the importance of the position in the world system (Glasure *et al.*, 1999) or the relevance of cultural beliefs and institutional inheritance (Clague *et al.*, 2001), but they agree that wealth is an important predictor of democracy.

Thus, most of the studies conducting a broad cross-country analysis of the relationship between wealth and democracy tend to find empirical support for this hypothesis. Still there are some challenges to this consensus. Enquiring into this relationship for Latin American countries, Landman (1999) finds no empirical support for such a hypothesis. There may be a number of reasons for this non-relation. One may be the fact that only a few countries in Latin America reach a critical threshold where this relation between development and democracy is expected to hold true. Another reason may be that there are other factors operating which, in the Latin American context, relaxes the relation between development and democracy.

The most recent and, so far, the most thorough study of this issue is *Democracy and Development: Political Institutions and Well-Being in the World, 1950–1990* by Adam Przeworski and his collaborators (2000). Their database covers a maximum of 135 countries for a period of forty years. They have constructed a democracy index of their own, and to measure well-being they rely to a large extent on the estimates of national incomes made available from the Penn World data project. What makes this study important is, however, not the database employed but rather the extremely sophisticated econometric techniques applied to this data set. What they do is establish controls for various factors which makes it possible to compare democracies and non-democracies in relevant aspects; these techniques probably make it possible to arrive at more reliable estimates than is possible with the application of conventional regression techniques (see also Feng, 2001).

Chapter 2 of their book deals with the impact of economic development on

political regimes. Their finding here is that the level of economic development as measured by per capita income is by far the best predictor of political
regimes. But they also add:

> Yet there are countries in which dictatorships persist when all the observ-
> able conditions indicate they should not; there are others in which demo-
> cracies flourish in spite of all the odds.
>
> (Przeworski *et al.*, 2000: 88)

This could be interpreted as a support for the modernization approach, but
this is not the case (see also Przeworski and Limongi, 1997b).

The reason that democracies are more common in countries with a high
level of economic development is not as a consequence of a process where, as
countries grow in wealth they also become more democratic. It relates to the
dynamics of regime changes; and the logic is not primarily about the change
from dictatorship to democracy, but, rather, with the change from democracy
to dictatorship. Democracies never die in affluent countries (Przeworski *et al.*,
2000: 117). In poor countries, democracies as well as dictatorships are vulnerable to economic crises; democracies even more than dictatorships. Why this is
so is not that clear and no mechanism is suggested, but in the long run this
implies that when poor countries are moving on to become wealthier, then
their probability of surviving as a democracy will increase, simply because in
wealthy countries democracies never die.

All of the studies referred to so far only cover the relation between development and democracy up to 1990. Therefore it may be appropriate to take a
look at the situation during the 1990s. After all, the process of the third wave
of democratization has continued during this time (Diamond, 1997a, b). Let
us first look at the overall picture of the level of economic development and
democracy in the late 1990s. As may be noted from Figure 1.3, there is no
strict linear relation between development and democracy. Actually, the best
fit is arrived at using a curve-linear approximation.

It is thus only among countries reaching a level of per capita income of
around US$10,000 that the level of democracy is high. Below that income
level, the type of political regime varies highly. Breaking down this relationship to various major regions of the world, it is noteworthy that this positive
relation between development and democracy only holds true for the western
industrialized countries, central and Eastern Europe and Africa, but not in
Latin America, the Middle East or Asia. Although there is an overall positive
impact of affluence on democracy, it is not so in each of the major regions of
the world. In particular, this has implications for the poor regions of the world
– the LDCs. In these regions, no countries reach the threshold of per capita
income around US$10,000. Here one may expect that factors other than level
of development may impact – income distribution may be an important intervening variable – on the variation in level of democracy.

From Figure 1.3, it is also obvious that there are a number of countries that
do not fit into the model. A few quite wealthy countries have a lower level of
democracy than would be expected from their level of economic development

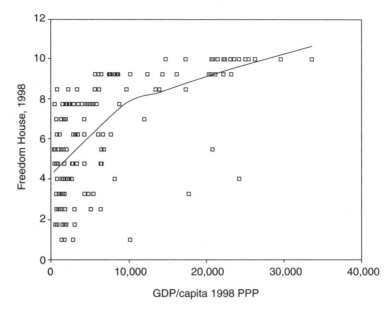

Figure 1.3 Affluence and democracy: the late 1990s.

Sources: Freedom House, 2002; World Bank, 2000c.

– the most glaring cases here are Singapore and oil-exporting countries like Kuwait and Saudi Arabia. On the other hand, there are countries which in the late 1990s score much higher on the democracy variable than would be expected from their level of economic development. Two such cases – among a number of them – that may be singled out are India and South Africa (RSA). Let us take a closer look at these countries and enquire into the relation between level of economic development and level of democracy over time.

The per capita income expressed in US$ PPP for 1998 differs markedly between these three countries. Singapore has a per capita income more than ten times that of India and three times that of South Africa. Going back to 1950, India was still the poorest country, with Singapore being only three times as rich, but at this time South Africa was the country with the highest per capita income. Therefore, it is Singapore that has experienced a most significant rise in the level of economic development over time, while the rise in per capita income has been quite modest for both India and South Africa.

Looking at the democracy scores – the Freedom House scores (DEM) are displayed in Figure 1.4 – India and South Africa come out higher in the 1990s than Singapore, while in the 1970s only India scored high on the democracy index. The clearly deviating case is thus Singapore, having experienced a prolonged period of high economic growth moving the country from a group of poor countries to the group of really wealthy countries. Why is Singapore not scoring higher on the democracy indices?

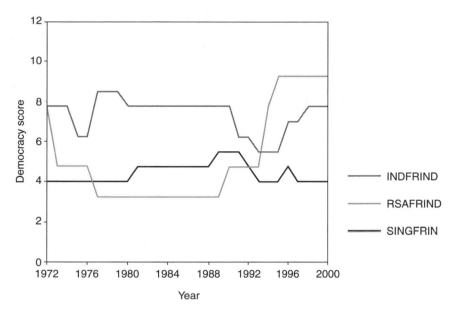

Figure 1.4 Democracy scores for India, Singapore and South Africa (1972–2000).

Sources: see Appendix A1.

Notes
INDFRIND = Freedom House Index for India, 1972–2000; RSAFRIND = Freedom House Index for South Africa, 1972–2000; SINGFRIN = Freedom House Index for Singapore, 1972–2000.

Singapore is sometimes classified as an illiberal democracy (Bell and Jaya-suriya, 1995; see also Means, 1996; Mutalib, 2000). Certain political rights are guaranteed and elections are conducted within regular intervals, but the political system has been even stricter with respect to various civil liberties which also include press freedom. Ever since Singapore gained independence in 1965, the People's Action Party (PAP) has governed it and, in the latest election in 1997, it received 65 per cent of the vote but secured 81 of 83 seats in the Parliament. This was, in fact, the best result for PAP since 1984 (Li and Elklit, 1999). No clear signs of political liberalization or democratization are as yet in sight (Khng, 1997). Although it is classified as partially free in the political arena, Singapore is ranked among the freest with reference to economic freedom.

As a matter of fact, Singapore is a most interesting case from the point of view of democracy theory. Given its high affluence, Singapore should score very high on the democracy indices. But Singapore only achieves a medium ranking. This ranking is all the more stunning as Singapore has put in place Rule of Law with a strong record on fighting corruption in government. When one reads the memoirs of Lee Kuan Yew, *From Third World to First* (2000), then one is constantly reminded of all the efforts he took as long-time premier to remove from his city-state all that would remind people of oriental despotism. Why, then, does Singapore not score high on the democracy indices? Religion could not be the decisive factor as the Muslim community (Malays and Indians) is small in comparison with the Gulf states. The answer is the election system, which gives the People's Action Party (PAP) a formidable advantage. When, as in Singapore, the plurality election formula is employed together with a strong natonalist ideology of handling conflictual matters within the ruling party, then the election technique may provide one party with virtual hegemony over the state. Perhaps Singapore confronting the twenty-first century could consider a move to a PR formula in order to make the emergence of opposition parties easier?

One explanation put forward is the presence of 'Asian values'. Countries exposed to a political culture characterized by 'Asian values' are supporting Communitarian orientations more than individualism, which stresses civil liberties. Singapore and other parts of South East Asia – it is claimed – has established a model of development of their own where a high level of economic development need not go hand-in-hand with political liberalization. This notion of 'Asian values' and its implications has been contested (cf. Fukuyama, 1995). Singapore is, however, interesting as a case where the link between development and democracy is explicitly questioned (Bhardwaj and Vijayakrishnan, 1998: 89–97).

Ever since it got independence, India has been classified as a democracy (Dahl, 1989: 253; see also Sørensen, 1991). The only major setback for Indian democracy was the period of a proclaimed state of emergency issued by Indira Gandhi between 1975 and 1977. Reasons raised in the literature for India's positive deviation suggest factors as different as the choice of political institutions and the quality of political leadership taking over at the time of independence. From the beginning, Nehru was very clear on the virtues of democracy, and these political beliefs were widely accepted by the Indian leadership at that time (Kaviraj, 1996: 118; see also Dahl, 1971: 200). The combination of traditional British institutions with federalism and consociational devices has probably been conducive for democratic stability in India (Lijphart, 1996).

South Africa's process of democratization started in 1989 after a process covering more than two decades, with deteriorating performance (Giliomee, 1995; Lodge, 1996). An enlightened leadership took the necessary steps for introducing a process of negotiated democratization. The first parliamentary election, held in 1994, was the beginning of a period of pacted democracy where the second election, held in 1999, could be seen as a test of whether democracy in South Africa was consolidating or not. There were, of course, a number of factors which were important for the process of democratization in South Africa, but there is no doubt that the leadership involved in this process – Nelson Mandela – mattered very much.

Summing up

Studies dealing with the impact of economic and social factors on democracy tend to focus on the impact of affluence and its social attributes. Other dimensions of development are not addressed as a determinant of democracy in the research literature. Most of these empirical studies agree that democracies are mainly to be found in countries with a relatively high level of economic development. There are, of course, other factors that are conducive to the rise of democracy, but not one that can really compete with affluence. It may be pointed out that the level of affluence and the level of democracy are rather stable over time. There are also a number of deviating cases that do not fit this general model. In poor countries, the quality of leadership and the political institutions implemented into the political system may be decisive. On the other hand, in wealthy countries, the non-existence of democracy may be due to the impact of a particular political culture, but it may also be the consequence of the system's ability to perform well in other non-political spheres of society.

Still, there is no real satisfactory explanation for why economic development should produce democracy if the modernization theory does not hold true. Democracies never die in affluent countries it is stated, but why is this so? Is it that democracies are more efficient and that they are more conducive to economic development? If so, then this could be the link between affluence and democracy. Let us move to the outcome perspective.

Outcomes: democracy and development

Analytically it is possible to distinguish between the impact of development on democracy and the impact of democracy on development, but in reality there are a number of reciprocities operating between development and democracy and many other factors. However, now the focus will be moved from the impact of development on democracy to the impact of democracy on development.

The issue raised here is thus whether political regime does matter for socio-economic development. This issue has probably been the focus of even more research than on development and democracy and was important for comparisons between economic systems during the Cold War (socialism versus capitalism), but it was only in the 1960s that more systematic studies were to be conducted. The studies dealt with in this section approach development as economic growth.

Economic growth

We have been able to identify at least six surveys of the research literature on democracy and growth or institutions and development in the 1990s (Sirowy and Inkeles, 1990; Przeworski and Limongi, 1993; Alesina and Perotti, 1994; Brunetti and Weder, 1995; Brunetti, 1997; Aron, 2000). Most of the research covered in these surveys studies the impact of democracy on economic growth. The conclusions reached in these surveys tend to be similar in that they are both cautious and not conclusive. Sirowy and Inkeles (1990: 150) summarize in the following way, writing that the studies 'would seem to suggest that political democracy does not widely and directly facilitate more rapid economic growth ... even the conclusion that political democracy does not facilitate economic growth is at best a tentative one.' Przeworski and Limongi were even more cautions in their conclusion: 'The simple answer to the question with which we began is that we do not know whether democracy fosters or hinders economic growth. All we can offer at the moment are some educated guesses' (1993: 63).

Brunetti and Weder affirm a sceptical view, stating: 'The survey has shown that the empirical links between the political regime and the growth performance of a country are highly controversial. One conclusion that could be drawn is that there is simply no systematic relationship between the political institutions of a country and its economic growth performance' (Brunetti and Weder, 1995: 129). Brunetti returning to the subject in a more recent survey from 1997 that reports basically the same finding: 'Considering the evidence of this survey, it can be safely stated that there is no clear relationship between democracy, at least as measured in these studies, and economic growth' (Brunetti, 1997: 172). Alesina and Perotti, however, reach some slightly different conclusions in their review: 'In summary, there is no evidence that, on average, a democracy with civil liberties is costly in terms of economic development. If anything, it may be the other way around, that a democracy with civil liberties promotes economic development' (Alesina and Perotti, 1994: 354).

The most recent survey written by Aron takes a more general approach to the relations between institutions and growth, but she also signals a sceptical view:

> Thus a definitive positive conclusion on the links between growth and institutions is difficult to pin down, suggesting that the claims for causality should be treated with caution.
>
> (Aron, 2000: 128)

These surveys cover research conducted up to the early 1990s making use of data up to roughly 1990. Their conclusions tend to be similar, most of them agreeing that there is no clearly positive impact of democracy on economic growth (see also Moore, 1995).

It may therefore be appropriate to present a survey of some more recent studies from the 1990s and a few from 2000 on the issue of the impact of political regime on economic growth. Table 1.7 attempts to give a systematic presentation of fourteen research articles published in different social science journals (or texts) from 1994 onwards. It is also obvious here that the chief findings differ between the various studies undertaken. Somewhat crudely we may distinguish between findings identifying a positive impact from democracy, no impact and a negative impact on economic growth.

There may be a number of factors influencing the findings reported. Therefore Table 1.7 also contains information on some important aspects of the research undertaken; some of this information refers to technical details of the research undertaken. How is democracy measured? How is development operationalized? Which period is covered by the study? And, finally, which findings are reported?

Table 1.7 Survey of studies of the relation between democracy and economic growth (the 1990s)

Author	Year	Democracy measure	Development	Period	Findings
Burkhart and Lewis-Beck	1994	Freedom	Economic development: level	1973–88	No impact
Mbaku	1994	Bollen	GDP/capita growth: average	1970–90	Varies with sample
Abrams and Lewis	1995	Freedom + Humana	GDP/capita growth: average	1968–87	Positive
De Haan and Siermann	1995	Gasiorowski	GDP/capita growth: average	1961–92	No impact
Goldsmith	1995	Freedom	GDP growth: average 1988–93	1980–90	Negative
Barro	1996	Freedom	GDP/capita growth: average	1960–90	Negative (weakly)
Feng	1996	Polity	GDP/capita growth: average + annual	1960–92	Positive
Leblang	1996	Polity	GDP/capita growth: average	1960–90	No impact
Bhalla	1997	Freedom	GDP/capita growth: average	1973–90	Positive
Feng	1997	Polity	GDP/capita growth: average	1960–80	Negative
Leblang	1997	Polity: initial level	GDP/capita growth: average	1960–90	Positive
Przeworski and Limongi	1997a	Przeworski *et al.*	GDP growth: yearly	1960–90	No impact
Nelson and Singh	1998	Freedom	GDP growth: average	1970–84	Positive
Gasiorowski	2000	Polity: two-year lag	GDP growth: yearly	1968–91	Negative

Let us look at some observable patterns from the survey in Table 1.7. The findings are quite evenly distributed between those reporting positive impact, no impact or negative impact. The most popular democracy index still seems to be The Freedom House scores, but the Polity measure is more commonly used in the studies published in the latter part of the 1990s. It is also obvious that economic growth is mostly measured as per capita growth averaged for a longer period of time than one year. Balanced samples are most common and they are almost equally divided between studies designed as a distinct cross-section or as a panel study; panel studies are, however, more common in the more recently published studies, indicating that panel-designed studies represents the state of the art within this research tradition. Applying a panel design on the study also implies that it is not enough to employ OLS as the estimation technique, and it is clear that most of the panel studies employ OLS together with other estimation techniques to arrive at reliable estimates. Finally, one may note that these most recent studies do not go beyond the period of the early 1990s.

The findings reported in the studies do not seem to be related to how they have been conducted with relation to data, sample, design or methods employed. Such a conclusion is confirmed from an analysis of some 45 articles/chapters devoted to the issue of the impact of democracy on economic growth: there is no systematic relation between the findings and the way research has been conducted.

This conclusion is broadly in agreement with what has been reported from other surveys of the literature. Research conducted so far has reached no firm conclusion about whether political regime has an impact or not on development when operationalized as economic growth; and if there is any impact, there is no conclusion as to whether it is positive or negative. Therefore, the next step in this survey is to report in some detail the theoretical considerations discussed in these studies.

The empirical findings differ, but which are the theoretical expectations linked to these findings? Are there reasons to believe that political regimes should have an impact on economic growth or not? Here we will try to follow the distinctions suggested by Sirowy and Inkeles (1990) distinguishing between a sceptical perspective (no impact), a conflict perspective (negative impact) and a comparability perspective (positive impact). Let us first look at studies suggesting no relations between democracy and economic growth.

Arriving at a certain empirical finding need not be in accordance with theoretical expectations. One may claim that the theoretical expectations are reasonable but note that empirical data or the estimation techniques employed are deficient in one way or another. To find no impact may therefore not be a theoretical expectation from the beginning. It would, however, be possible to also argue for no impact from a theoretical perspective, suggesting that there are other factors that are more important for explaining cross-country variation in economic growth than political regimes. Other factors expected to have an impact on economic growth are the ones well known within economic theory: physical capital and human capital; to these factors there is a growing interest in the impact of social capital (Knack, 1999; Woolcock and Narayan, 2000). Why, then, expect an impact from political regimes?

When these theoretical issues are addressed, which is not often, then it is argued that politics alone need not matter much and that the kind of policies pursued or that the nature of the party system matters more (De Haan and Siermann, 1995: 181). Or it may be stated that there are other factors that are indirectly fostered by democracy, like level of education (Helliwell, 1994: 246) or stronger property rights (Leblang, 1996: 21), but political regime per se need not matter.

A number of theoretical expectations on why democracies would have a negative impact on economic growth may be raised. First, there is a trade-off to be expected between democracy and economic growth: more democracy will be reflected in less economic growth, and vice versa. Among the mechanisms linking this relationship we have the propensity of democratic regimes to pursue policies that may generate popular support and lead to more emphasis on consumption (redistributive policies) and less on investment, and this would be a policy not conducive to long-term economic growth. Second, authoritarian regimes are also expected to have more suitable means to achieve the kind of discipline that may be needed to conduct policies resulting in a concerted action aiming at long-term development. This means that there may be a need for a strong developmental state that may not be compatible with a democratic state.

Common to all of these expectations is that a democratic regime – and this refers primarily to poor countries – may face problems implementing policies necessary to generate economic growth. It may be argued that such limitations need not apply to authoritarian regimes.

There are also reasons why democracy should foster economic growth. First, it may be argued that political pluralism opens up for other kinds of pluralism in a society – economic pluralism. Therefore, one would expect that property rights should be better protected in democracies than in non-democracies. Closely related to this argument is the expectation that there are more effective checks on government in a democracy which prevent government from implementing policies that may be harmful for economic growth. In a democracy there is also more transparency due to the existence of a free press, which may highlight problems in public policy-making, something that is not possible in non-democracies. Second, there are also a number of positive trade-offs to be expected from a democracy. Democracies would be more effective in reforming an economy. Since democracies may also be expected to pursue more equitable economic policies, they may also, in the long run, be conducive for a sustainable economic growth (see also Rodrik, 1997; Bhagwati, 1998).

The argument is thus that – in addition to the fact that democracy in itself represents a number of intrinsic positive values – in a democracy one finds a number of conditions that, at least in the long term, would be conducive to economic growth.

From a theoretical point of view, it is difficult to draw any conclusion about which kind of expectation is more appropriate than the other. It is obvious that empirical analysis is not a sufficient guide. It may therefore be tempting to adhere to the sceptical view. After all, it is the case that economic growth hovers quite extensively over time and this is not true of changes in political regimes to the same extent. It may therefore be reasonable to argue that political regime is not unimportant, but there may be other factors that have more impact, and political regime may operate in a more indirect way.

In the analysis by Przeworski *et al.* (2000: 217) of the impact of democracy on economic growth they are explicit about some major distinctions. Economic growth stands for: annual rate of growth of per capita income (G) = annual rate of growth of real GDP (YG) − annual rate of growth of population (POPG). Their analysis starts with what impact political regimes may have on the annual rate of growth of real GDP (YG). Establishing control for various factors, their finding is that political regimes have no impact on the rate of growth of total income. This also holds true for the comparison of regimes in poor and wealthy countries. In poor countries (LDCs) regime has no impact simply because 'whatever the regime, the society is too poor to finance an effective state' (Przeworski *et al.*, 2000: 162). This is also true for the wealthier regimes, but the patterns of growth and their strategies are different. They state:

> Dictatorships repress workers, exploit them, and use them carelessly. Democracies allow workers to fight for their interests, pay them better, and employ them better.
>
> (ibid.: 176)

Even if there is no difference with respect to economic growth, there are important differences between the regimes.

The next step is to deal with the other element in the equation – annual rate of growth of population (POPG). And here they have a finding: 'Indeed, the most surprising finding in our entire study is that regime matter more for the growth of population than for the growth of income' (Przeworski *et al.*, 2000: 217). Population growth depends on birth rates, death rates and migration. More children are born under dictatorships, i.e. the fertility rate and the rate of infant mortality are both higher under dictatorships. Death rates are also higher in dictatorships, but not large enough to change the overall differences in population growth. The interesting issue, then, is: why do political regimes impact on fertility rates? They suggest basically two kinds of explanations. One is related to policy stability and the other to the lives of women. Reproductive decisions are made with a very large time horizon and therefore depend on policy stability. Since dictatorships generally display less policy stability, there will be more of an incentive for 'reproductive units to hoard children' (ibid.: 255). Fertility rates are also conditioned by the lives of women. And the 'effect of political regimes on the lives of women is glaring ... under dictatorship women ... bear many more children, see more of them die, and are themselves more likely to die' (ibid.: 265). A similar argument is put forward by Sen, saying that lower fertility rates in Third World countries depend, to a large extent, on women's empowerment (Sen, 1997: 13).

Completing the growth equation means subtracting population growth (POPG) from the annual rate of growth of real GDP (G). The per capita incomes arrived at differ between the regimes because the differences in population growth is larger than the difference in the growth of total output. There is thus an impact of political regime on the growth in per capita incomes but it is through the impact on population growth and not on economic growth per se.

Their finding suggests that there need not be any direct causal links between a political regime and economic performance. Instead, political regime may have an impact on non-economic spheres of society, and these aspects of development will be dealt with next.

Quality of life

The causal relationship between the level of democracy and social dimensions of development may be difficult to establish since they are both reciprocally dependent on each other. The focus in this section, however, is the hypothesis that democracy may have an impact on such dimensions of development and not the other way. These dimensions of development mainly refer to the end of a process, i.e. levels of development, and not to changes in development, which was the case in the previous section. The social dimensions of development to be covered here are: income distribution, poverty, the physical quality of life, human development, various aspects of gender development and environmental sustainability. There has been less research focussing on the impact of democracy on social aspects of development when compared with the number of studies on democracy and economic growth. It is also the case that within this field more is done on the impact on income distribution and the quality of life than on gender development or environmental sustainability.

Let us first enquire into the impact of democracy on income distribution. This is an issue that has been considered since the 1960s but, due to the lack of good data on income distribution, the first serious studies on the subject date from the 1980s. Surveying some previous studies, Bollen and Jackman (1985) note in their conclusion that there were no consistent findings to report. From a theoretical point of view, one may expect positive as well as no impact from democracy on inequality, but neither finding is intrinsically more reasonable than the other. The finding reported by Bollen and Jackman from their own research is that there is no evidence to suggest a democracy–inequality linkage (1985: 450). Weede (1993: 188) supports this finding: 'Again, the idea that democracy (or absence of repressiveness) equalizes income distribution is not confirmed'. The reasons for this absence of linkage is that there is no mechanism operating in a democracy that makes it possible for votes to be translated into policies which may reduce income inequalities.

Other researchers have reported other findings. Muller (1988: 65) finds it plausible to state that the influence of democracy to reduce inequality is only valid if it is maintained for a relatively long time. Simpson (1990: 689) concludes that democratic rights and educational level are the best predictors and the proximal causes of income distribution. The relation between democracy and income distribution is, however, not linear but non-linear. Burkhart also notes this inverted U-curve effect of democracy on income distribution. His finding is that 'democracy at lower levels has an initial tendency to increase income inequality. This tendency lessens as the democracy score rises. After a certain point, democracy then acts to increase income equality' (Burkhart, 1997: 159). Gradstein *et al.* (2000: 35) concludes 'that it is not democracy per se that matters for inequality', but rather the impact of different societal values.

The conclusion that may be drawn from this survey is thus that there are no firm conclusions available. There appears to be a non-linear relation between democracy and income distribution, but whether it also holds true after controlling for the impact of other factors is less clear.

Sen is associated with a thesis saying that 'democracy prevents famine'. This thesis stems from his collaborative work with Jean Dréze (1989). This issue is again discussed in his book, *Development as Freedom*, where he comments: 'Indeed, no substantial famine has ever occurred in a democratic country – no matter how poor' (Sen, 1999: 51). The mechanism which links democracies to the prevention of famines is the presence of freedom which makes criticisms and publishing of all kinds of news possible in a democracy but not in an authoritarian regime. Early stages of a famine cannot be hidden in a democracy and the public will put pressure on the authorities to take steps necessary for preventing such an event. Testing this thesis is not easy, but Waal reaches a similar conclusion:

> In conclusion, more than just 'democracy' is required to prevent famine. In fact, liberal political institutions and popular mobilisation appear to be more important than simple electoral democracy.
>
> (2000: 17)

Neither are there many studies explicitly addressing the issue of democracy and poverty. One such study, by Varshney, finds that one cannot say that democracies perform better than authoritarian countries with respect to poverty alleviation. His conclusion states: 'In short, the wild authoritarian fluctuations contrast sharply with a certain middling democratic consistency. Democracies may not be necessarily pro-poor, but authoritarian systems can be viciously anti-poor. To repeat, democratic attack on poverty has simply been slow but steady' (1999: 17). Again there is reason to be a little cautious about the impact of democracy. Democracies prevent famines but one could have expected more from them with respect to poverty alleviation.

The construction of the Physical Quality of Life Index by Morris (1979) gave an impetus to conduct research on the relation between democracy and the quality of life (PQLI). Most studies dealing with this relation have, however, not yet made much use of the Human Development Index (HDI) as an indicator for quality of life. One of a few studies dealing with the impact of democracy on human development finds no support for such a hypothesis – other factors such as the quality of government are more important (Moore *et al.*, 1999: 9).

In general the conclusion has been that there is a positive relation between level of democracy and PQLI (Moon and Dixon, 1985; Shin, 1989). Frey and

Al-Roumi (1999: 91) also comes to the conclusion that there is a link between democracy and PQLI. They are then relying on estimates for the 1970s, 1980s and 1990s. The mechanism that they suggest links democracy and the quality of life is that, in a democracy, it is easier to centre the political agenda on issues that enhance life quality (see also Zweifel and Navia, 2000).

Not all agree completely with these findings. Gough and Thomas (1994) are critical of the employment of the PQLI as an indicator of human welfare and construct other measures, which they, do however, find go together with the extent of democracy and human rights of a country. Emizet (2000) states that there need not be a linear relation between democracy and PQLI. His finding suggests that the relationship between democracy and quality of life is best accounted for through an inverted U-shaped curve (Emizet, 2000: 1065). As the level of democracy increases, democracy itself may have a less positive impact on the quality of life.

There seems to be more of agreement in the findings from the research on this issue. Democracy goes together with the level of the quality of life, although there may be different opinions about the correct functional form of this relationship. This finding should come as no surprise, since the level of quality of life is strongly correlated with the level of economic development as this may be measured by the per capita income measure, which has an impact on democracy. What is difficult to establish is thus to say whether quality of life determines democracy or whether democracy fosters a better quality of life.

Gender equality

It is striking that there are as yet relatively few studies that focus on the explicit relation between democracy and gender development (cf. Razavi, 2000). Issues raised in this context have been more concerned with how economic development may impact on gender development or how gender development may be conducive to further human development. Gender development has, in other words, often been understood as the independent variable and not as the dependent variable. Ever since the study by Esther Boserup from 1970, there has been a knowledge that the position of women in society may be of great importance for development, not least in the developing countries (Dollar and Gatti, 1999; Seguino, 2000; see also Nussbaum and Glover, 1995). To this category we may also count studies researching the importance of the empowerment of women for various developmental outcomes. While, to begin with, there were high expectations about the impact of the empowerment of women (Goulet, 1989), one may now note contributions questioning certain aspects of empowerment (Botchway, 2001; Kabeer, 2001).

When, in the political science tradition, democracy has been used for explaining the variation in gender development, then the focus has been on female parliamentary representation worldwide. Democracy has not been used as a crucially important factor but, rather, it has been regarded as a general background factor. More importance has been given to cultural and institutional factors like what kind of electoral system is implemented in a polity. When empirical analyses have been conducted, it has been noted that female representation covaries with the level of democracy, but as soon as control for other factors are introduced, the impact of democracy is lost (Kenworthy and Malami, 1998: 259) or it takes a negative sign (Paxton, 1997: 453).

Thus we may conclude that, as yet, there are only a few studies that directly address the issue of the impact of democracy on gender development. When gender development is interpreted as female parliamentary representation, there are no firm conclusions indicating that democracy matters much in this respect, other factors probably being more important.

Environmental sustainability

One would expect a link between democracy and sustainable development, based on the definition of sustainable development made by the World Commission on Environment and Development. Participation was understood to be one important element for achieving this kind of development. From a theoretical point of view, one would also expect that democracies would do a better job of safeguarding the environment. Democracies are, in general, better as market places for ideas, have more responsiveness among the regimes and are also expected to have better abilities of political learning. These are all important capabilities for dealing with environmental issues (Payne, 1995: 43–52; see also Jänicke, 1996).

There are an increasing number of studies available that have made efforts to carry out empirical tests of the impact of democracy on the environment. One problem that this research has to deal with is the lack of measures of environmental sustainability that researchers would agree on. Indicators employed that measure environmental performance have included the degree of deforestation, CO_2 emissions or soil erosion. The findings are not always consistent, but at least they suggest that democracy is not harmful to the environment.

Didia (1997: 74) concludes that 'as a country becomes more democratic, we can expect a reduction in the rate of tropical deforestation'. However, in this study no control for the impact of other factors was introduced. Mather and Needle, also studying the process of deforestation, reached a similar conclusion: favourable forest trends 'are associated with high levels of economic, social and political development' (1999: 115). Midlarsky employed a wider set of indicators to measure environmental performance and his conclusion was more cautious: 'The first and most obvious conclusion is that there is no uniform relationship between democracy and the environment' (1998: 358). One reason why these findings differ is that Midlarsky controls for the impact of economic development and geographical location. Doing so, there is no longer a direct impact of democracy on the environment in its different manifestations. Doubts about the positive impact of democracy on the environment get some support from case studies carried out in southern Africa and reported by Walker (1999). The conclusion is again that 'there is no necessary relationship between the environment and democratization as it has been experienced in southern Africa' (1999: 278).

So far, there are relatively few studies reported that explicitly deals with the impact of democracy on the environment. The more rigorously conducted studies suggest little of a direct positive impact of democracy on the environment. Democracy in itself does no harm, but there are other factors operating that have more impact on the environment.

Summing up

In general, the performance profiles of the development dimensions studied here are better in democracies than in non-democracies. This is, however, not the same thing as saying that more democracy in itself will lead to better socio-economic performance. There may be other factors that have more importance than democracy and it may also be difficult to uncover whether democracy impacts on development or whether development impacts on democracy. Let us, however, present an empirical illustration from the 1990s displaying the relationship between democracy and those dimensions of development dealt with in this section. This illustration will be a brief case study of the Indian state of Kerala.

Empirical illustration: Kerala

India may be an interesting case to take a closer look at. India is generally considered to have been a democracy for most of the period since it gained independence. And it is indeed the case that India and parts of India have received a lot of attention from students of development. One of the Indian states very often addressed in these circumstances is Kerala, located in the southern part of India (Bhardwaj and Vijayakrishnan, 1998: 13–17; Sen, 1999: 21–4).

Kerala has received this attention for a number of reasons. Among the Indian states, Kerala has the best record for poverty reduction for the period 1960–94 (Ravallion and Datt, 1999: 13). Kerala also comes out highest on the Human Development Index. Kerala ranks highest among the Indian states with regard to infant mortality rates, life expectancy at birth, but also female literacy rates. Kerala also scores highest on measures of social capital in India (Morris, 1998; Mayer, 2001; Serra, 2001). This is achieved despite Kerala having a relatively low per capita income (Serra, 1999: 32). Kerala also sharply deviates from the general trend in India with a decreasing sex ratio for women. While the ratio of women to men is lower in India than in most other countries of the world, this ratio has fallen from 0.972 in 1901 to 0.927 in 1991 and slightly increased to 0.933 in 2001. Looking at the specific experience of Kerala, this ratio was 1.004 in 1901, increased to 1.022 in 1961, had risen to 1.036 in 1991, and increased again in 2001 to 1.058; from 1991, Kerala has had the highest sex ratio among all the Indian states and territories (Census of India, 2001). In other words, Kerala seems to be a case where quite a high level of human development is achieved at the same time as this is not a consequence of a high level of economic development. Kerala has therefore been singled out as one of a few successful cases of alternative ways of development. But there have also been problems associated with the Keralan experience.

Kerala has not been able to achieve the same high levels of economic growth as in the non-economic spheres. Yet it is noteworthy that, in the 1990s, Kerala has performed much better than most other Indian states (Ahluwalia, 2000). Another disturbing aspect of social life in Kerala is the very high rates of suicide. Overall, however, the Keralan achievements must be qualified as most impressive in a Third World context. Why is Kerala different?

There are a number of suggested explanations. It may be related to social structure, with historical and cultural traditions, but also with political choices made which are possible in a democratic society. Linguistically, Kerala is a quite homogenous state as, in 1991, more than 96 per cent of the population spoke Malayalam. The majority were Hindus (57 per cent) in 1991, but Muslims (23 per cent) and Christians (19 per cent) constituted two quite numerous religious minorities (Census of India, 2001; see also Chiriyankandath, 1996). These three religious communities have a tradition of living relatively peacefully together here. Therefore, one may conclude that communal strife has not been a major problem in Kerala.

One important feature of southern India has been the presence of a family system containing matrilineal elements. Such a family system tends to strengthen the position of the women in the household (Todd, 1985: 166–8, 1987: 81–4; see also Dyson and Moore, 1983). Although this is far from a system of matriarchy, it has less patriarchal elements than is the case in most other family systems. The tradition of such a family system may thus be important for explaining the relatively strong position women seem to have in Kerala.

Another important explanation put forward relates to the models of development employed in the state. Together with West Bengal, Kerala has been one of the strongholds of Indian communism. The communist parties in Kerala (CPM and CPI) have been able to mobilize less privileged social groups into political life to a large extent; in particular, this is true for the major low caste in Kerala – the Ezhavas (Nossiter, 1982: 30–2). Kerala is a state where the lower castes/classes have been strongly represented and where policies have also been pursued that includes redistribution and land reform (Harriss, 1999).

Let us here consider the support for the two communist parties at the elections to the State Legislative Assembly from 1957 and forwards. The CPI was split in 1964 and ever since the CPM has been the stronger party. Together they receive around 30 per cent of the vote, which makes it necessary to form alliances with other parties to gain political power. Table 1.8 therefore also contains information about the parliamentary support for the two major blocks in Keralan politics – the Communists and those close to the Congress party.

From the split of the old party in 1964 up to 1980, the CPM and CPI were bitter political rivals. CPI sided with the Congress party when in government while the CPM found their own allies. The first Communist government was in power between 1957 and 1959. Between 1965 and 1980 the two parties never sat in the same government. Between the years 1967 and 1969 the CPM had the position of Chief Minister in Kerala. From the 1980 election, the CPM has

Table 1.8 Electoral support for the communist parties in Kerala at state elections

Election year	Votes (%)		Seats (N)		
	CPI	CPM	Com + allies	Congr + allies	Total
1957	35.3	–	65	43	126
1960	39.1	–	29	94	126
1965	8.1	19.9	66	36	133
1967	8.6	23.5	117	9	133
1970	8.9	23.8	49	69	133
1977	9.9	22.2	29	111	140
1980	7.8	19.4	93	46	140
1982	8.4	18.8	63	77	140
1987	8.1	22.8	78	61	140
1991	8.3	21.7	48	92	140
1996	7.6	21.6	80	59	140
2001	7.3	21.4	40	99	140

Sources: Election Commission of India, 2001; Chiriyankandath, 1997; Kumar, 2001.

dominated the Left Democratic Front (LDF) which has also included the CPI, and they have been in power during the following three periods: 1980–1, 1987–91 and 1996–2001 (see also Isaac and Kumar, 1991). The election in May 2001 resulted in the return of the Congress-led UDF coalition to government.

To begin with the policies were strongly reliant on measures from the state, accompanied with the rhetoric of class struggle. In the 1990s this 'old' Kerala model was followed by a 'new' Kerala model having other aims – to achieve sustainable development – and using other means – democratic decentralization and popular participation through, for example, the 'people's planning campaign' (Heller, 1995; Törnquist, 1995; Parayil, 2000; Véron, 2001).

The achievements of the Kerala experience have also been widely recognized in the research literature (Prakash, 1999; Zachariah and Rajan, 1997; Heller, 1996, 2000). Yet, at issue is whether these achievements are the consequences of the policies associated with both the old and the new Kerala model or whether it is more due to favourable historical and cultural circumstances that have been present in Kerala. Ramachandran may be representative of those arguing that the Keralan achievements to a large extent are due to the public policies associated with the Kerala models first formulated by the communists: 'The first government of Kerala was a Communist government, and the major features of its agenda and of later communist ministries in the state were, among other things, land reform, health, education, and strengthening the system of public distribution of food and other essential commodities' (1998: 315).

However, not everyone agrees. Jeffrey argues in *Politics, Women and Wellbeing*, that the achievements were due more to a previous heritage:

There is no Kerala model – neither in the sense of coherent policies that have produced specific results, nor a desirable goal that other parts of

India or the world might wish to achieve. The remarkable social statistics that have intrigued scholars since the 1970s stem from the way in which public politics and the role of women took shape between the 1920s and 1950s amid the dissolution of the old Kerala.

(1992: 217)

A similar sceptical view of the importance of state action for the Kerala achievements is also put forward by Kanath (1999).

These interpretations need not contradict each other. It may indeed be true that historical and cultural traditions have been conducive to the formation of policies that have been positive for the development in the non-economic spheres achieved in Kerala. If this is so, then it also opens up a space for forming public policies that may have an impact on development. In that sense, one may say that democracy in India has been important for allowing the formation of alternative political experiences in the country, something that would probably not have been possible in a non-democratic India.

Democracy and development

There seems to be more empirical support for a thesis that democracy has a positive impact on non-economic dimensions of development. Yet, even here there are reasons to be a little cautious. First, looking at the pattern of changes over time, there are similarities between the scores on democracy and the scores on the non-economic dimensions of development. The spatial distribution of the democracy scores is rather stable over time, and this is also true for many of the indicators on the level of non-economic dimensions of development. Therefore we may expect more of a statistical co-variation between these two entities.

Second, there may be more theoretical expectations that democracy should foster social development. Democracies should be more open than non-democracies and the probability for non-privileged groups to gain access to the political power would be higher in democracies than in non-democracies; and, consequently, the possibility of forming policies that are conducive to development focussing on poverty alleviation or gender empowerment should be greater in democracies than in non-democracies.

Third, however, we have the fact that a high level of economic development seems to be conducive to more democracy, and a high level of economic development is also conducive to higher levels of social development. Since levels of development – economic and social – strongly go together, then there may be a reason to ask whether democracy really makes a difference. It is obvious that democracy does no harm to social development, but there may be factors other than democracy per se that matter. Some studies suggest that the quality of government or the institutional set up of a democracy matter more.

Thus, there is a huge scholarly interest in topics relating to democracy and development. This interest has been strengthened during the previous decades. To a certain extent this is due to the fact that data are now available that permits large-scale cross-country empirical analyses addressing these issues. One may certainly raise some doubts about the validity of the democracy indices employed, and there is a challenge to improve them, but new indices would probably not drastically change the picture we have presented. There is a deep divide between different parts of the world, and the level of democracy goes quite closely together with levels of various dimensions of development.

When the issue of the causal relation between democracy and development is addressed in research studies, most seem to suggest that a high level of development is conducive to a high level of democracy and not the other way around. It is, however, important to note that many of these relations do not hold for the very poorest parts of the world – the LDCs. One crucial reason for this is probably, as suggested by Przeworski *et al.*, that in the very poor countries there is no space for public policies and the kind of regime governing can only have a limited impact on development of any kind.

Democracy is correlated with levels of development, but it is less clear as to whether there is a causal impact of democracy on development. The many studies dealing with the issue of the impact of democracy on economic growth are quite cautious in their conclusions, and most of them suggest no direct impact of democracy. Most studies are hesitant in their conclusions about the direct impact from democracy per se on development. When this is said, it is important to add that democracy in itself is not harmful to development. Democracy may also, in a less direct way, impact on development through the effects on population policies or the set up of property rights. The less direct impact of democracy may also be due to the fact that democracies can vary quite immensely among themselves in terms of institutional choices and cultural traditions they may be associated with.

This is the general picture that comes out of the studies surveyed. But it is equally important to remember that there are always exceptions to the general pattern outlined. Affluence and democracy need not be closely related, as highlighted by cases like Singapore and India. And, from the Indian experience, the Keralan achievement has been singled out as an example where policies – and indirectly probably democracy – may make a difference for human development.

Thus it seems to be fair to conclude that democracy is important for development, but not in a straightforward way. Democracy in itself stands for a number of intrinsic values, which makes it preferable to non-democracy. Democracies may also indirectly be conducive for factors that may foster development. It is probably erroneous, however, to expect that democracy per se should create favourable conditions for more development.

And here we may have a policy implication. There is also a scholarly literature on the theme of foreign aid and about promoting democracy through foreign aid (Carothers, 1997, 2000; Crawford, 1997; Hook, 1998; Ottaway and Chung, 1999; Svensson, 1999; Knack, 2000). The findings reported there seem to be sceptical about the evidence of aid promoting democracy and of the promotion of democracy to generate development. To promote democracy need not directly have positive consequences for development, at least in the short term. Promoting democracy may have a value in itself, but there may be a risk in putting too much expectation in promoting democracy to achieve development. There are simply too many functions that may not be related to each other. And such an expectation also seems to gain support from the more general oriented research literature dealing with democracy and development.

Conclusion

There is a significant literature in the social and economic sciences dealing with democracy and development. To us the questions that are posed and the answers that are given in various models are all versions of the general theme of democracy and causality. The two key questions are:

Q1 what are the general conditions for democratic stability?
Q2 what are the main outcomes of a democratic regime?

One may reformulate them in the language of development theory, but the crucial thing is to conduct research which results in corroborated models stating either causes or effects of democracy as an existing macro political regime. The problematic nature of the concept of development – complex, value loaded (Myrdal, 1969) – leads us to simply focus on democracy and causality. Chapter 2 outlines a methodology that is highly suitable for the conduct of causal enquiry: methodological positivism. We will then return to the question of the conditions enhancing democratic vitality (Parts II and III) as well as to the problem of the outcomes promoted by democracy (Part IV). It is all a matter of probabilities, as the social and political reality is stochastic in its fundamental nature.

2 Methodological positivism
Its relevance for democracy analysis

Introduction

Understanding the causes and consequences of democracy is a knowledge-based enterprise involving the search for truth. True knowledge about the conditions and outcomes of democracy would consist of a body of 'true statements' in the sense of 'corresponding to reality'. Theoretical plausibility and empirical evidence can help us to make the best choice of these propositions we consider true of democracy. Methodological positivism (MP) outlines a strategy for making these choices so as to come as close as possible to the truth.

MP suggests a number of steps to be taken in order to avoid the two classical mistakes in human knowledge: the Type I error (accepting a false statement) and the Type II error (rejecting a true statement). We formulate our knowledge about the external world in the form of hypotheses, which we hope are 'true', in the sense of 'corresponding to reality'. We formulate a large number of hypotheses guessing at what the external world is like. Thus, we need some criteria or rules to be employed to distinguish between true and false hypotheses. In particular, we must avoid Type I and Type II errors.

The growth of scientific knowledge involves an incremental process of rejecting and accepting hypotheses where decisions are to be taken in accordance with scientific criteria of two kinds, namely theoretical coherence and empirical evidence. A scientific breakthrough involves a non-incremental jump in the growth of human knowledge, a new hypothesis replacing a whole set of older hypotheses.

In this chapter, we will argue that MP is the best strategy for making choices about hypotheses. Our argument can be split into two parts. First we deal with the criticism of MP which rests on invalid assumptions and allegations. Second we outline a positive argument for MP, stating that it is the best strategy if we wish to avoid Type I and Type II errors.

In the social sciences, MP has today been overthrown by various postmodernist frameworks such as hermeneutics. This is extremely unfortunate as postmodernism harbours the erroneous doctrine of subjectivism, or the notion that human knowledge about the external world is impossible. MP has, however, maintained its methodological position in economics, which, one may argue, is the main reason that much of economic science is more advanced than the social sciences.

Subjectivism

Modern social theory has a strong inclination towards subjectivism. Subjectivism is a philosophical position, consisting of a theory of epistemology for the social sciences, which is not only wrong but borders on nonsense. Modern subjectivism, or as it is somewhat ludicrously called, 'postmodernism' is basically the ambition to crush what is called 'objectivism', launching a theory about what social science knowledge is all about. Thus, subjectivism contains an argument for a new epistemology for any kind of social theory, replacing the major objectivist arguments in the twentieth century.

We will argue that political science should be based on some objectivist theory of knowledge. There are actually several schools to choose from: the various so-called positivist schools, the Cambridge School, the Popperian framework, the Weberian philosophy of the social sciences, one of the Scandinavian versions, e.g. the Uppsala School or the Oslo School, and, finally, American pragmatism (White, 1956; Wedberg, 1984).

The Cambridge school with its two leading personalities, G.E. Moore and B. Russell, stated a strong case for objectivism, which had an immense impact on twentieth-century philosophy. Moore never hesitated in his firm rejection of subjectivism (Moore, 1959, 1960). Interestingly, a major social theorist, Max Weber, developed a total rejection of subjectivism at the same time as Moore (Weber, 1949). Our objective is to pin down what positions subjectivism amounts to as it is expressed in modern social theory and then proceed to reject them one by one.

Social theory at the twilight of postmodernist thought focuses on something called the 'subject'. What is taking place is the deconstruction of subjectivity in the form of a conceptual or philosophical revaluation of it. To political science this is interesting partly because the discipline belongs to the general class of social theories and partly because it is argued that subjectivity and political agency are intimately connected. What, then, does theorizing subjectivity amount to? The key question is simply: what is 'subjectivity'? Three senses of this word can be distinguished.

First, in epistemology one starts from a distinction between the subject or the person who searches for true knowledge, and the object, which is that which is known or true. Thus, the social science researcher is a subject and what he/she researches is an object. Therefore a distinction may be introduced between the subject and the object in the epistemological sense of a subject reaching out to know the object, where the subject may commit two sins, a type I error or a type II error, accepting a false statement about the object or rejecting a true statement about the object.

The relationship between the subject and the object is far from a static one, or one involving a process of interaction where the object imprints its shape on the subject as a tabula rasa. Instead, the subject is active in numerous ways in researching the object through the construction of theory, concepts and hypotheses. Accepting false beliefs as well as rejecting true beliefs frequently occurs in the conduct of inquiry, as the interaction between the subject and the object involves an endless search.

Looking briefly at the history of epistemology, one may claim that there is either an emphasis on the subject or the object in this interaction. Whereas empiricism underlines the object, rationalism places the emphasis on the subject. Kantian philosophers may be placed somewhere in-between these two extremes.

Political science has a variety of objects to study, whether they are identified as micro (behaviour, action) or macro entities (political systems, democracies). The conduct of inquiry in political science is the process through which more becomes known about the object through the activities of the subject. There is no need for political scientists to side with either extreme, denying the subject or the object, but they could point to the balance between them.

Second, 'subjectivity' may mean some special attribute of a human being, perhaps the mind and its various states: attitudes, wishes, values, etc. The opposition between subject and object is now something entirely different from the epistemological opposition. What is an object is not something that is not the mind, i.e. *materia*. Subjectivity is that which involves the mind and objectivity is that which concerns matter.

Again, in the history of philosophy we find extreme positions denying either the existence of the mind or matter, idealists versus materialists, as it were. Political science need again not commit itself to any particular position, as it looks at both mind phenomena and matter phenomena. Thus, political science deals with attitudes, values and beliefs but also behaviour. It is impossible to say in a general way whether the part of the world that political science examines is more consciousness or behaviour. A subject can, of course, enquire into other people's minds, which then become the object of his or her enquiry. One must not confuse these two meanings of subject and subjectivity.

Finally, there is a third sensible interpretation of subjectivity as meaning that subjects are important, or people matter! Social theory has to struggle with the actor–structure problem, or the distinction between the micro and the macro perspective. Individuals or groups: what is most important? A classical question in social theory is the problem of holism, or whether a macro unit such as a society is more than simply the aggregation of the micro units – individual actors. On the one hand, there is methodological individualism, which rejects holism, and on the other hand there is a variety of doctrines which affirms holism, or the belief that the whole determines its parts and not the other way around. Subjectivism may harbour a commitment against holism, insisting on actors ahead of society. However, it is an open question as to whether there is any link between subjectivism and the much more extreme position that only individuals exist, social aggregates being secondary. Political science does best when insisting on a balance between the micro and macro perspectives.

To sum up: if subjectivity is an epistemological theory that underlines the activities of knowing subjects reaching out to understand objects, then all is fine. If subjectivity is an ontological theory that claims that people's attitudes, values and beliefs should be studied, then again all is well. Thus, 'subjectivity'

– as requiring a balance between subject and object in epistemology as well as insisting on an ontology which harbours not only matter but also mind phenomena, and using both micro and macro approaches to the study of individuals and society – is, as far as we can judge, a sound position to take, at least with regard to the concerns of political science as a social science discipline.

Subjectivist dogmas

Yet, subjectivity in social theory harbours much, much more extreme positions. We will list in this section some of the major beliefs of modern subjectivism (SB) as they are stated in modern social theory. The aim here is not the accuracy in rendering a variety of standpoints but merely focussing on widely held beliefs, formulated in one version or another. Thus, no attempt will be made here to be absolutely true to each and every statement of these beliefs with various authors. Such an exegesis would require a much longer treatise than is actually necessary for pinpointing the crucial beliefs. Thus, what follows below is a critique of a few ideas, stated in an ideal-typical way, and not a descriptively accurate account of the key authors in modern social theory.

Subjectivity has been denied by positivist philosophies (SB1)

The diamond in the subjectivist social philosophy is something referred to as 'positivism'. All opponents of subjectivism are called 'positivists'. And positivists are said to be adherents of a set of doctrines in epistemology, ontology and morals. More specifically, positivists are the scholars who adhere to objectivism in epistemology, materialism in ontology and functionalism, i.e. the doctrine that society is determined by needs that go beyond the wishes and preferences of its individuals. They are the villains of the twentieth century, the scholars who oppose progress, or who fight radical social thought, who claim that society is more important than individuals, etc.

Yet, in relation to (SB1) one may point out that this set of so-called positivists is empty. There is no philosopher or social scientist that has propagated these three beliefs at the same time. 'Positivism' has been used as a self-designating term by only two groups, on the one hand the logical positivists of the Vienna school of philosophy during the interwar years and a group of legal scholars on the other hand insisting on the study of law as an existing valid order, the legal positivists, who wished to separate themselves from natural law scholars. Not much unites these two groups, with the exception of the common core meaning of 'positivism', i.e. that there exists a reality that is positively given, whatever its nature may be, and which the scholar is actively researching. Some of these people, the legal positivists and the logical positivists, adhered to some of the extreme standpoints referred to above. But others did not, which is the essential point, as these two groups were in no way homogeneous.

It is unhelpful to label people as 'positivists' and attribute to them positions as if they all held these views. The group of scholars who did call themselves 'positivists' is very amorphous, but they all insisted on clear thinking, a respect for the distinction between the subject and the object, as well as separation between explanation of the world and moral analysis. Positivists have never denied the relevance of subjectivity, either epistemologically, ontologically or from the point of view of holism versus atomism. Modern social theory claims that positivistic social scientists use the concept of subjectivity, unlike objectivity, pejoratively and considers that it needs to be eliminated from the research process.

'Subjectivity' may cognitively mean a belief that is arbitrary, ill founded or capricious. Such beliefs have not only been rejected by positivists, but – we trust – by all scholars reflecting on human beliefs. 'Subjectivity' may also refer to a legal context where there is a lack of rules or, even more serious, a disrespect of the law. Such a form of subjectivity is usually considered as a threat against the rule of law, or the *Rechtsstaat*. However, 'subjectivity' meaning 'unwarranted' beliefs or decisions would hardly meet with much approval from anyone.

Whatever branch of analytical philosophy in the twentieth century that one consults – positivist or anti-positivist – all start from the subject–object distinction, and they respect that distinction either in the context of discovery or in the context of justification. How can one eliminate the subject from the relation of *someone* knowing *something*? The subject is active both in the process of discovery of the object and in the process of justifying his/her beliefs. Human knowledge, is a distinctly human enterprise, but in so far as it is true knowledge, it is knowledge about an object outside of the subject – 'true' meaning 'corresponding to the world'.

The talk about 'positivism' in modern social science is more confusing than illuminating. There are so many different schools that are ridiculed as 'positivism' that the word has no distinct meaning. (SB1) is nonsense.

Social reality is basically a subjective world (SB2)

According to modern social theory, objectivism considers social practices as objects that are exterior to the observer, similar to the phenomena that are studied by the natural sciences. However, a fundamental tenet of modern social theory is that the social sciences are radically different from the natural sciences, because they examine subjective phenomena. What can be meant by 'subjective' phenomena here? We must ask this question first, before we move to the conclusion drawn in modern social theory that since the object is subjective, then the object vanishes.

Now we enter something entirely different from (SB1), because (SB2) concerns only the social sciences. The question is now: what is the nature of social reality, that is, social life resulting from human interaction? (SB2) is not the same as the general epistemological problem of how a subject knows an object, which is also a problem for physics and the other natural sciences. (SB2) is not a question in epistemology (how can a subject know an object?) but raises a question of ontology (what is reality?).

For modern social theory, when approaching social reality, the main focus of study is the purposeful, reasoning human agent. Action, in this context, is

seen as the outcome of individual intentionality. This is an often used definition of the concept of action as involving two separate elements, behaviour or
movements in space and time on the one hand, and intention or motivation,
conceived of as mind phenomena or as the 'meaning' of the behaviour. In the
philosophy of the social sciences, this distinction between mere behaviour or
outer movements and action as involving an inner aspect has been the focus
of many prolonged methodological disagreements. The core disagreement
has been between two approaches that centre on two extremes: (1) beha-
viourism, or the denial of the existence of intention or motivation; (2) subjectivism, or the position that the essential aspects of action are its meanings or
motivations.

Political science should reject both of these absurd positions. It can very
well say that social reality is 'subjectively lived' but that it also consists of phenomena that are not 'subjectively lived'. If action is behaviour that is orientated in its course, then social reality would by definition comprise both
behaviour and intention, both physical movements and mind phenomena.
Much of social science is the analysis of mind phenomena, but it is not exclusively so. In micro analysis, it is true that one attempts to look at behaviour as
the maximization of interests, given existing knowledge and preferences, i.e.
mind phenomena, but in macro analysis there is no hindrance to focussing on
unintended or unrecognized states.

One must distinguish between the perspective of the actor and that of the
researcher. If one fails to distinguish the two, then modern social theory will
continually mix up SB1 with SB2.

From the perspective of the researcher, both behaviour and intention are
objects of study. That an intention of an actor is 'subjectively lived' by the
actor does not preclude that it is, at the same time, the object of study for a
researcher. Epistemologically speaking, a subject may face different methodological problems when attempting to get at knowledge about behaviour and
intention, because they are different kinds of entities, but one cannot draw
the conclusion that, because a researcher wants to know something about an
intention, the researcher cannot be objective. Equally erroneous is the claim
of modern social theory that the social world is not an external world.

There is no external world (SB3)

Social life stems from the interaction of human beings, ego and alter ego in
the most simple form of interaction. Ego's behaviour is orientated in opposition to alter ego's behaviour, which entails that there is both behaviour and
intention on the part of both. Surely, this is all part of an external world to the
researcher, in the same sense as objects epistemologically are external to the
subject, whatever the objects are made up of. But modern social theory states
that there is no external world. How come?

Subjectivism, like all so-called interpretative approaches, does not define
social reality as an exterior object, we are told. Social reality is seen, we have
noted, as a subjectively lived construct, from which it follows, modern social
theory claims, that the study of social reality as an 'external object' is in fact a

methodological impossibility. Here, we not only have the confusion of the two senses of 'subjectivity', established above; this is even worse, as it entails that other people's minds – 'subjectively lived' phenomena – are not the analysis of an external object. Surely, other people's minds are outside the mind of the researcher and do exist as an 'external object'. When one does attitudinal research about Swiss people – their behaviour as well as their attitudes – then surely these phenomena are outside of the researcher's mind and do exist in the external world.

Does 'external' mean 'outside of the researcher'? Or does it mean 'non-intentional objects'? Take the case of the most elementary type of social inter-action: ego versus alter ego. What is now internal and what is external? The question is meaningless, as one must specify: what is internal to whom and what is external to whom?

Clearly, both ego and alter ego have perceptions about each other, as well as intentions when they interact. These phenomena constitute internal worlds to ego and alter ego in the sense that their ideas and wishes remain purely private or secret if they are not disclosed. However, ego's behaviour as well as alter ego's behaviour make up an external world that is not private or secret. Even the most elementary form of social reality does not consist of merely internal worlds. (SB3) is fundamentally ambiguous, but in whatever manner it is interpreted it cannot carry the argument that there is no external world. External to whom?

Human existence is an internal world (SB4)

If subjectivism is a theory that emphasizes the importance of 'subjectively lived' phenomena for social life, then there is little cause for objection. Ideas, preferences, images, ideologies, religions, etc. are of fundamental importance in society. Such entities are examined in political science as well as in eco-nomics. We know of no objectivists in the twentieth century that have denied the existence of such phenomena or shown an awareness of the methodo-logical problems involved in studying them. However, subjectivism asserts much more extreme positions, claiming that such mind phenomena consti-tute a world of its own, a world that is neither an object world nor an external world, and that it cannot be analysed by the ordinary canons of scientific analysis. Is (SB4) true? Is the social reality only a set of mind phenomena?

How ideas, preferences and other mind phenomena are to be analysed ontologically is one of the classical topics of philosophy (Putnam, 1979) – the ghost in the machine question. Is mind radically different from matter? If so, in what sense of 'radically different'? Political science needs to get involved in the dispute between idealists and materialists, as it were. Political science can well accept a position that states that behaviour is different from intention and that intentions constitute an internal world, whereas behaviour is part of an external world. However, internal worlds do exist and can be the object of social science research just as well as external worlds. One can argue, as Ryle and Quine did, that one can explain thoughts, preferences and the like without assuming the existence of a separate ontological entity like awareness

(Hookway, 1988). Or one can claim that the concept of the mind is not reducible to behaviour or language, as Adolf Phalèn did (Marc-Wogau, 1968). What is, ontologically speaking, the difference between voting in an election and the intention to vote in an election? Can one have knowledge about the intention of an actor without knowing the behaviour of the actor?

For social science purposes these are interesting and profound but not quite relevant philosophical questions about what exists in the most fundamental sense of 'existence'. Similarly, one may ask: what is human existence? Modern social theory claims that human existence is 'subjectively lived'. By whom, we may ask: the actor him/herself or the researcher? If one accepts the Heideggerian interpretation of human existence as being 'in the world' in the ordinary sense of these words, then one fails to understand why social reality could not be an external object for the researcher. Even if one equates human existence with subjectively lived phenomena such as thoughts, interests and images, then the conclusion does not follow, since other people's minds can be researched as exterior objects. Yet, human existence involves not only subjectively lived phenomena but also entities which are not mind phenomena: behaviour, predicaments, situations, outcomes, etc., which define human existence.

One may argue that certain social phenomena like culture or religion carry a lot of semantic weight and thus such phenomena are subjectively lived ones. How can one understand the ethics of Calvinism without an interpretative approach focussing on how human behaviour was experienced and valued by the main authors in this tradition? Whether God is part of an external world or not, need not bother the researcher, as his/her interest is on how various writers looked at the relation between what is believed to be God and humanity. But other social phenomena – for example, the loss of millions of Jewish people during the Nazi period – are not merely a subjectively lived construct. Auschwitz, Dachau and Treblinka are exterior objects, as was the behaviour exhibited by the Nazis at those and other places.

Human existence is not only a subjectively lived world. And when it is such a subjectively lived world, then it remains an exterior object to the researcher. One can read and interpret Calvin in order to describe and analyse his religious thoughts (epistemological object). And when religious thoughts become pervasively accepted with many followers, then they certainly form exterior objects with major consequences for social life (alter ego's thoughts being exterior to ego). In a sense, all mind entities are interior ones, because they exist in somebody's consciousness. Take away the consciousness of a person, and the thoughts, wishes, interests, emotions, etc. of that very same person disappear. However, this interior nature of mind phenomena does not entail epistemological subjectivism in the sense that these objects cannot be studied. Nor does it entail that they are not exterior to other actors who definitely have to take into account the existence of other people's minds.

If one takes the absurd position that the fundamental structure of human existence is not an exterior object, then how is social science possible? What is the rationale of testing hypothesis? What does falsification amount to? 'Subjectivism' may mean a very extreme epistemological position according to which one can only know one's own mind – an epistemology impossible to accommodate within political science.

To see that one can be an epistemological subjectivist, emphasizing the role of the subject in relation to the object, and reject all forms of exterior worlds whether natural or social, one could examine the writings of Leibniz and his monadologie. Thus, one can be a subjectivist also in relation to the universe, or the world of the natural sciences. Of course, the extreme Leibniz position has had very few followers.

The methodology of the social sciences is radically different from that of the natural sciences (SB5)

Subjectivism is not only an epistemological theory or an ontological position. In addition, it harbours a special methodology, which – it argues – follows from the ontological standpoint.

Does the subjectivist ontological position entail that the social sciences must adopt a methodology that is different from the natural sciences? Suppose it is true that the social world consists only of mind phenomena; are we to conclude that this mind world can only be researched with methods that are entirely different from the methods employed to enquire into the material world? Before we can evaluate this radical claim, we must arrive at an understanding of what is meant by the methodological autonomy of the social sciences. What methods are, then, appropriate for the enquiry into mind phenomena?

It should be pointed out that we are not looking for just another version of the subjectivist epistemological position, claiming that it is irrelevant to adopt a perspective suggesting a neutral and objective study of social reality. We know already that subjectivism rejects such a perspective. What we wish to know is why the social sciences cannot or should not use methods that are similar to the ones employed in the natural sciences, or – as it is expressed – methods that are merely 'imported from the natural sciences'. What can be meant by this radical statement (SB5)?

Social reality can never be explained through generalizations (SB6)

Subjectivism favours an idiographic methodology while accusing objectivism for being nomothetic. Mind phenomena lie outside of the scope of generalizations, because they lack causes. One should distinguish between these two grounds for rejecting a nomothetic approach, one denying causality in social reality and the other stating the general irrelevance of any kind of generalization. One may debate whether the notion of causality entails the idea of a generalization or law-like statement, and vice versa. Yet, it is enough here to discuss whether probabilistic generalizations are relevant for the social sciences in general and political science in particular.

If (SB6) is correct, then subjectivism may move one step further, denying causality in the social reality. However, such an additional claim would have to be based on a Humean interpretation of causality as constant conjunction. If the social sciences cannot even use probabilistic generalizations at all, then how can it ever dream of arriving at invariant, universal generalizations lacking all time and space parameters?

Yet, it seems absurd to deny the legitimate use of statistical generalizations within the social sciences. Such propositions are employed all the time in economic and political science in order to move from a particular case to a statistical generalization covering a large set of cases. It is generally agreed that statistical tests allow for more certain conclusions than the findings in a case study. As long as no one can suggest an a priori argument against the use of statistical generalizations within the social sciences, then one would be foolish not to use them. It could well be the case that some of these statistical generalizations constitute errors resulting from spurious correlations or simply wrong measurements. However, why should one use statistical generalizations in order to describe and explain social reality?

Subjectivism, when confronted with this reasonable objection, does not answer on the methodological arena but goes back to its ontological position, claiming that social reality, being made-up of only mind phenomena, never recur but constitute only a unique flow of events. Suppose one accepts the ontological position of subjectivism, that is, suppose one starts from the assumption that the social reality is made up of mind phenomena. Then, why would one not engage in statistical research uncovering attitudes, beliefs, values, norms, etc. It seems simply arbitrary to argue that mind phenomena could not possibly display regularities. As a matter of fact, research into religious beliefs as well as non-religious values has resulted in lots of knowledge about mind phenomena that take the form of probability statements.

One does not need to decide whether probabilistic generalizations could constitute causal laws in order to argue that the social sciences may use statistical regularities to their benefit. It is an open question whether the universe has a deterministic structure or a probabilistic one. What is true of the social sciences, however, is that all the empirical research has only been able to corroborate statistical regularities. Thus, one need not commit oneself to the position that the social reality is subjected to universal laws in order to accept the relevance of statistical regularities. Whether these regularities contain some critical temporal or spatial parameter limiting their validity to some time period or some set of countries may be relevant to the question of whether they constitute law-like generalizations or merely temporal and spatial aggregations of averages. Yet, even such statistical generalizations that summarize averages are extremely helpful in social science research. Thus, (SB6) is untenable. We need to go to a stronger version of (SB5).

Intentions can never be the cause of human behaviour (SB7)

The rejection of generalization only makes sense if (SB6) is combined with (SB7). Under a Humean interpretation of causality, saying that A is the cause of B entails a probabilistic generalization at least, or a law-like statement at most. Thus, if the principle of causality does not reign in the social reality, then there would be no need for generalization. And, inversely, if generalizations hold in the social reality, then they could ground causal attributions, for instance a counterfactual statement to the effect that if not A, then not B, even though A actually occurred. We have rejected this close association between probabilistic generalizations and the concept of causality earlier in the chapter, as one may wish to use the information contained in a probabilistic generalization within a time and space parameter without making any claim about causality. Be that as it may, we must discuss (SB7) independently of (SB6).

In any action there is behaviour and intention. The subjectivists argue that only the intention is part of the social reality. This is wrong. Behaviour also enters the social reality. Admitting this, can we then conclude that an intention can be the cause of behaviour? Or one may pose the question in the following manner, if one claims that intentions are mind phenomena and all mind phenomena are radically different from behaviour: can a mind phenomenon be the cause of behaviour? We here face two major questions in philosophy, with many different answers but, as of now, no agreement:

Q1 what is the nature of an intention or a motive or a reason?
Q2 can an intention or a reason be a Humean cause of behaviour?

These two questions are no doubt extremely tricky, as the work of Donald Davidson shows (Evnine, 1991). We do not see that the social sciences are dependent on whether one answers 'Yes' or 'No' to one or both questions. The social sciences utilize statistical generalizations all the time in order to master their mass of knowledge. These generalizations take different forms, but they carry no implications for the resolution of the major problems in philosophy.

Statistical generalizations are employed at various levels of knowledge. And they cover both intentions and behaviour. Sometimes, it is a question of merely aggregating empirical findings. Sometimes, it is a question about testing hypotheses about relationships between factors. Rarely does one encounter a universal generalization. However, statistical generalizations are extremely valuable in organizing social science knowledge. They not only structure behaviour phenomena but also mind phenomena. They also formulate hypotheses about connections between mind phenomena such as religious beliefs and behaviour such as economic outcomes.

Thus, (SB7) does not entail that generalizations cannot play a role in the conduct of social research, whatever the cognitive status of (SB7) may be in itself. Probability statements fulfil a useful function not only in macro research, which is only indirectly related to intentions, but also in micro research about attitudes as well as behaviour. Whether our intention to vote is a Humean cause of our actual going to vote is an interesting philosophical problem, but the resolution of this question one way or the other has limited implications for the use of probability generalizations in political science research. One subjectivist dogma that is close to (SB7) takes an even stronger stance about social causality, as it completely denies its existence.

Social causality does not exist (SB8)

(SB7) may entail (SB8), only if one argues that intentions are the basic or important entities in social reality. However, one may arrive at (SB8) without (SB7). Suppose that one argues that social reality is basically random, then one could accept probability but deny causality as determination. One does not need a theory about intentions in order to deny causality in the social reality. If one starts from intentions, then one need not arrive at (SB8) in any case, since one may embrace a theory of intentions that allow that they can be so-called Humean causes. If, however, one denies that intentions can be Humean causes, then one could still argue that social reality includes causality, because intentions are not the only elements of social reality, comprising the outer aspects of behaviour (i.e. the actual physical movements) as well as the inner.

The argument about determination is thus different from (SB7), as one could arrive at the indetermination thesis without employing a theory about intentions. Taking a stochastic approach to causality, equating causes with probabilities, allows for a medium position between strict determination and strict indetermination. It seems highly capricious and extremely extravagant to deny the legitimate and frequent use of probabilistic associations in social sciences research. It is always an interesting question to pose, whether a probabilistic association could be interpreted as indicating a stable causal structure underneath the structure of appearance or whether it is a matter of an association which is time and space bound.

One may conduct a long philosophical discussion about whether the world behind the appearances is truly probabilistic in nature or whether probability is a measure of the lack of complete knowledge. In any case, probabilities derived from the analysis of data offer the materials for causal induction, resulting in theories about causal connections, with or without stochastic elements.

Objectivism implies the argument that society is more important than individuals (SB9)

Now subjectivism, when claiming (SB9), enters an entirely different terrain, namely ethics and normative discourse. The target of criticism is the so-called functionalist framework within the social sciences, or structural–functionalism. Here, one must separate two things. It is one thing as to whether the functionalist framework contains an explicit or implicit commitment towards a holistic ethics, giving priority to the needs of society ahead of the interests of single individuals. But it is another matter to question whether functionalism, whatever it may say about society and the individual, is a doctrine that is logically connected with objectivism. If one refutes the main bulk of the subjectivist dogmas – (SB1)–(SB7) – then must one adhere to functionalism?

This is not the place to embark on a lengthy discussion of functionalism in one version or another. It is enough to say that structural–functionalism has been discussed at length and it is perhaps not entirely wrong to assert that its appeal has diminished rather drastically, mainly due to a criticism of its basic beliefs launched by scholars adhering to some kind of objectivism (Black, 1961). A so-called functionalist explanation raises difficult questions about teleology which make a passage from biology to the social sciences problematic. There is a significant literature on the structure of a functionalist explanation, whether or not it is scientific, but there is no decisive result as yet.

If it is true that functionalism entails an ethical reasoning – we underline 'if' – and if it is also true that functionalism, containing a moral argument, implies that social needs are more important than individual interests, then functionalism is outside the domain of objectivism. Not only is the distinction between the *is* and the *ought* firmly entrenched within almost all major forms of objectivism. But even when objectivist scholars do engage in moral reasoning, then there is no tendency that they uniformly favour one set of values ahead of another set, except for a rejection of totalitarian philosophies. (SB9) is empirically false, as the major objectivist scholars of the twentieth century have opposed collectivism. And it is not likely that they are fooling themselves meaning that they adhere to a philosophy that implies positions that they would hate to endorse. We fail to see that objectivism along the lines suggested by scholars such as Moore, Hägerström, Popper, Hayek or the leading Americans (Goodman, 1972; Putnam, 1979) would endorse explicitly or implicitly functionalism, or any commitment to the societal oppression of individuals.

By insisting on the distinction between is and ought, *objectivism requires the impossible (SB10)*

In all forms of subjectivism, there is a strong tendency to argue that social theory is entirely different from natural social theory. We have already encountered one such line of argument, focussing on the so-called subjective nature of social reality, here meaning that social reality consists basically of something that is not matter: consciousness or mind. However, (SB10) adds another kind of dimension to 'subjectivism', as 'subjectivity' is now not ontological but pertains to the distinction between neutrality and partiality. Now it is not a matter of the values of actors, but the values of the scholar.

Actually, here we enter into another great debate in philosophy, about the relations between values and knowledge, how values enter the conduct of scientific enquiry – value premises – and condition the end results of such research – value loaded research or biased research. In order to discuss (SB10), one must make a sharp distinction between the values of the observer and the values of the actor observed (Nagel, 1961). 'Subjective' may mean that the actors of the social reality hold preferences and express values in their behaviour. Thus, how can social theory be value free, if values play an important part in shaping behaviour and values enter the mind world? 'Subjective' may mean something entirely different, namely that a scholar cannot describe, explain or analyse the world without evaluating it in terms of his own values. A value-free research would be a research that is neutral in relation to what it investigates or in relation to what it states as true about the world.

Take the case of a norm that is institutionalized in a society. One needs to separate between the norm and the analysis of that norm. Just as one can establish whether a norm is applied or not, one can also distinguish between a positive and a negative evaluation of the norm. Actually, all four possibilities are not only logical but occur frequently. To state that a norm exists or does not exist is independent of whether one claims that the norm is desirable or not desirable; the *is* and the *ought* can be separated. Thus, there is no logical connection between the following three sentences:

i   Julius Caesar acted against the Roman Constitution when he crossed the Rubicon River.
ii   Julius Caesar was a detestable tyrant.
iii   Julius Caesar was a great, noble man.

It is not only logically possible but also in reality quite feasible to distinguish between the values of the actors and the values of the analyst. Thus, the sentences i–iii are not entailed in the following sentence:

iv   Brutus and Cassius detested Caesar because he violated the Roman Constitution.

Refusing to distinguish between the values that one describes and one's own values is often the basis of a justifiable accusation of wrongdoing, as being 'subjective', meaning partial or biased. Impartiality may be difficult to achieve, but it is neither a muddled conception nor an impossible strategy. Social science need not be value loaded.

(SB10) is a fallacy. Understanding people's values does not entail that one must share these values oneself. One can describe and analyse norms in a neutral manner. 'Normative analysis' stands for two different things: the analysis of norms that exist and the recommendation of norms that one may wish exist.

We are witnessing the emergence of a general social science theory – subjectivism – which harbours a totality of views concerning the nature of knowledge about society (epistemology), the nature of social reality (ontology), the nature of social explanation (methodology) as well as the nature of social morality (ethics). It is true that the three sisters of ethnomethodology, phenomenology and hermeneutics have existed for some time as a kind of alternative to the main philosophies developing out of the Enlightenment, like, for example, also Marxism. They seek their sources among philosophers who reject the basic distinctions that Hume arrived at: between *is* and *ought*, between existence and possibility, between the particular and the general, between law-likeness and obligation, between reason and emotion, between deduction and induction. Among the subjectivists, one usually encounters deep admiration for philosophers who rejected either Occidental civilization (Nietzsche) or who suggested entirely different meanings for basic philosophical terms (Heidegger). Today, there is a reunion in the messages of the three sisters of subjectivism.

Subjectivism should not be adopted within political science, because its basic tenets – (SB1)–(SB8) – constitute one fallacy after another. A textbook on modern social theory presents the goals of 'speculative social science' in the following manner:

> Put rather abstractly, the idea of a speculative social science is informed by four basic principles: that Hegel's notion of 'spirit' is the recognition of the truth/finitude of its temporal forms; (2) that social science explanations recognize and abstract particular (and essential) forms from the totality of ethical life; (3) that this abstraction is acknowledged as the condition of social critique; and (4) that 'sociality' (ethical life) is recognized as formed through the differentiation (of the concept), not as the suppression of difference.
>
> (Abbinnett, 1998: 37)

Actually, in this programme declaration we can retrieve all the subjectivist dogmas criticized in this chapter. Drawing on the major achievements within twentieth century analytical philosophy, we would argue that all four of Abbinnett's standpoints are wrong. First, social reality involves more than spirit, and spirit is not the same as true knowledge; second, the social sciences cannot relinquish its generalizing methodology, not even when it tries to explain spirit or morals; third, the social sciences carry no logical commitment to social critique beyond what is entailed in the concept of truth; fourth, the social sciences must model not only altruism but also egoism if truth is to be approached.

We do not posit analytical philosophy as a compact framework where political science may find its proper epistemology, ontology and methodology. Although there has been a tendency towards reunion in analytical philosophy, the predicament today remains one of fierce competition between alternative schools in the philosophy of pure reason (Couvalis, 1997). Yet, the requirement of objectivity and what it entails for the conduct of enquiry stands as strong now as it did in the Enlightenment.

In favour of objectivism

The late Aaron Wildavsky raised a highly relevant question in relation to the so-called subjectivist disciplines: 'Has modernity killed objectivity?'. Critical theory and its various offspring as well as postmodernist philosophy harbour a basic tenet which involves a most drastic deviation from the conception of science, inherited from the Enlightenment, namely the distinction between belief and the world (Wildavsky, 1993).

Beliefs are either true or false, whereas the world is or is not. Science is the search for true knowledge, i.e. beliefs which correspond to the world. A belief about the world as so-and-so is true only if the world is such. From this irreducible relationship between a knowing subject and the known object follows a number of ethical rules guiding the conduct of enquiry: objectivity, neutrality and intersubjectivity (Scheffler, 1982). Modern social theory suggests that these rules are no longer relevant, that somehow the social sciences can do without them. Although Wildavsky was preoccupied with cultural theory right up to the time of his death, i.e. with the phenomena of the mind world such as values, attitudes and beliefs, he still would not relax the norms that regulate the conduct of enquiry (Thompson, Ellis and Wildavsky, 1990).

It must be repeated time and again that objectivism has stood strong in various schools within analytical philosophy, not only within logical positivism. One finds a basic objectivism within post-positivism (Pap, 1949; Nagel, 1961) as well as with the Harvard school (Quine, 1960; Putnam, 1979). The debate about the theory-loaded nature of observations or data (Hesse, 1974) is not a validation of the subjectivist positions, but it amounts to a serious reminder to the effect that all human knowledge involves both a subject and an object. Any reduction of the subject to the object is just as fallacious as the reduction of the object to the subject. In the conduct of inquiry, the subject plays a large role in being active against the object (Kaplan, 1964), but the object is not merely a figment of the subject's imagination (Quine and Ulliam, 1978).

The postmodernist approaches, however different they may be, all claim that social reality cannot be studied as an external world. Somehow there is a fundamental problem in the social reality or in the study of the social reality which entails that the ordinary canons of scientific research do not apply or suffice. We have examined these arguments earlier in this chapter and found them utterly confusing. The social world is an external world which one may study for the purpose of achieving objective knowledge. What does objectivism entail for the theory of democracy?

Modelling democracy: sorting the variables

When investigating the conditions for democracy, it is useful to make certain distinctions among the factors that one may wish to enter into an equation to express a relationship among variables. We classify the conditions or factors that impact on the probability of democracy in the following way:

- structural conditions: economic and social factors;
- cultural conditions: ethnicity and religion;
- institutional conditions: political, social and economic rules.

Our major research question is, which of these three sets of factors matter most for democratic probability?

We will transform these two sets of conditions and the factors they consist of into a set of variables measured by means of a set of indicators. This allows us to formulate a number of models linking these variables to be tested against a body of data consisting of all the countries of the world with a population larger than 1 million people. The estimation of a number of models results in *reduced form evidence* (correlation) and *structural model evidence* (multi-variate regression). We will employ both kinds of model evidence, as both have advantages and disadvantages.

Now, formulating a model of democratic probability can be done using two different kinds of languages, one used by social scientists and another employed by econometricians. The first group speaks about independent and dependent variables, whereas the second group talks of endogenous and exogenous factors. When these two discourses cross each other, there is a risk of confusion. Let us attempt to clarify what is involved here. Whereas the distinction between the dependent variable (democratic probability) and the independent conditions (structural, cultural, institutional) is clear and easy to put in place, the separation between exogenous and endogenous conditions is less transparent and could be a source of confusion.

In simultaneous equation models, variables are classified as endogenous and exogenous. The traditional definition of these terms is that endogenous variables are determined by the economic model and exogenous variables are determined from outside. Endogenous variables are also called 'jointly determined' and exogenous variables are called 'predetermined' (Maddala, 2001: 345). Thus, the following identities would hold.

1   exogenous variables = independent variables
2   endogenous variables = dependent variables

However, things are more complicated than that as two factors can impact on each other (which are then endogenous and exogenous?), as well as because 'endogenous variable' may mean that the variable can be affected by human agency, whereas 'exogeneity' implies 'outside human control'.

The definition of exogeneity as 'determined from outside the model' has been questioned in the econometric literature:

a   *the Liu critique*: the distinction between endogenous and exogenous variables may be arbitrary and is often incomplete as a model does not incorporate all relevant variables.
b   *the Lucas critique*: forecasting the values of endogenous variables from the values of exogenous variables presupposes that the coefficients in the model remain invariant. This presupposition cannot be validated within one and the same model, as the coefficients may be affected by the exogeneous variables.

These two objections amount to raising the same difficulty; namely, that a model linking cause and effect or condition and outcome is merely a hypothesis or a qualified guess which is in need of empirical confirmation and successive elaboration in order to approach verisimilitude. As Hume stated, causality is never certainty, as relationships may be spurious or instable and factors omitted.

However, there is another objection against speaking of endogenous and exogenous factors, in that the basic meanings involved are entirely different than that between 'determined inside a model' and 'determined outside a model'. A variable is sometimes referred to as 'endogenous' when it can be manipulated by an agent such as the government. The opposite of an endogenous variable would be a factor which is beyond the control of an agent, i.e. strictly determined by outside factors in the sense of 'beyond human control'.

Endogenous variables could thus be determined by an agent in order to have an impact on an outcome variable, such as when government takes a number of measures in order to enhance employment, reduce inflation or raise salaries. Here, we have the true source of confusion, as 'endogenous variable' now stands for the cause rather than the effect. The confusion is hardly reduced by the fact that 'instrument variable' often stands for an indicator variable, i.e. a variable that measures another variable or other variables. However, one often employs the concept of 'instrument variable' as meaning 'agency variable'. In order to avoid the confusion of an endogenous variable denoting both the effect and the cause, we will use exogeneity and endogeneity in the following senses:

- exogeneity: determined from outside of the political system;
- endogenous: determined from inside the political system.

Evidently, this separation requires a model of the political system which entails that exogenous democracy is democracy determined by factors that are fixed outside of a political model, such as economic and social conditions. Endogenous democracy is democracy determined by factors generated from within the political system, such as institutions.

Conditions for democracy: exogeneity or endogeneity?

Our key question is, which factors account the most for democracy: exogenous ones or endogenous ones? By this we mean whether the probability of a democracy is basically driven by factors which are beyond the control of agents such as the government of a country, or whether democracy can be affected by the introduction of factors which government has some control over, such as institutions.

If the probability of a democratic regime depends on exogenous factors, then the possibility of constitutional engineering is small indeed. On the other hand, if the variation in democracy around the globe is significantly affected by the occurrence of man-made rules, then democracy could be contrived by constitutional policy-making (Sartori, 1994).

Is democracy exogenous or endogenous? Perhaps it is both. But then we need to conduct an empirical enquiry into what matters the most:

- exogenous factors covered by structural variables and cultural ones;
- endogenous factors covered by institutional variables.

Answering the question of whether democracy is endogenous or exogenous requires the use of the best tools of MP, namely the test of a number of models which predict democracy from structural, cultural and institutional variables. We will employ both reduced form evidence – correlations – as well as structural form evidence – regressions. What follows in Part II is a broad enquiry into the conditions for democracy, either democratic viability or democratic consolidation, according to this key aspect of whether democracy depends more on exogenous factors than endogenous ones, or the other way around.

An enquiry into the conditions for democracy – exogenous as well as endogenous ones – must combine model building with empirical test. One starts from some set of hypotheses that makes sense in relation to the literature. Then one looks for a data set which comprises of a set of valid and reliable indicators on the concepts contained in the models. Finally, one runs the econometric tests in order to arrive at estimates of the model coefficients. Models are revised on the basis of the empirical findings, and so on. The conduct of scientific enquiry consists of the double confrontation: testing theory against data and making sense of data with theory, which is the perennial interaction between idea and observation in all kinds of human knowledge about the external world.

Conclusion

Understanding and explaining macro democracy requires a scientific methodology. We suggest that methodological positivism (MP) affords the answer here, building on its success in economics (Blaugh, 1992). Democracy as a political regime which enforces human rights and builds on open political contestation in free and fair elections: why does this regime vary among the countries of the globe? This is an example of an existence question which can only be answered by referring to generalizations about conditions.

Generalizations – hypotheses about cause and effect – may be true or false. Only empirical tests can help us decide between alternative models of social causality. In democracy theory the key questions are: (a) which conditions have an impact on democratic probability: democratic longevity as well as democratic consolidation? And (b): do exogenous conditions play a larger role than endogenous ones in stabilizing democracy?

MP suggests that we combine theoretical speculation resulting in model building with empirical tests in order to answer these two questions. To put the case even more strongly: only MP can guide us when choosing between alternative models of democracy, as it offers a systematic method for confronting hypotheses with empirical evidence, either reduced form evidence (correlations) or structural form evidence (regression). Although the Duheim–Quine position that no theory can be conclusively falsified or verified is correct, it remains true that the only way to choose between alternative models is to consult empirical findings and spell out their implications for model testing.

Part II

Exogeneity

A number of theories of democracy have sought to identify the external factors that enhance democracy as a political regime. Here we find a large number of hypotheses that attempt to account for the fact that democracy exists in very different forms around the world. When one examines data about democratic longevity since the end of the Second World War, one is confronted with a clear variation in democratic stability or the duration of a democratic regime. The problem is to account for this variation, once it is documented in a sufficiently reliable manner.

At first, democracy research concentrated on conditions that are uncontrollable, such as affluence, ethnicity and religion. Then the institutionalist approach arrived, which underlined the contribution of rules, i.e. endogenous conditions which a country may control to some extent. Political institutions play the role of instrument variables in the sense that institutional design may improve on outcomes by means of explicit institutional reforms. At the same time, institutions could be regarded as endogenous factors conditioned by exogenous factors.

Let us start the analysis of the conditions for democratic probability by means of the distinction between two sets of conditions: exogenous conditions or factors determined outside of the political system on the one hand, and endogenous conditions or factors determined inside the political system on the other. We will use both correlations and regression analysis in order to test the central hypotheses about the factors which enhance or reduce democratic longevity. We start with the exogenous economic factors as their role was hinted at early in the macro research on how democracy occurs differently around the world.

3 The economy

Introduction

Economic forces tend to be given a major role in explanations of macro political phenomena, as political systems must mobilize and allocate resources in order to have a capacity to act. The question is, how important is the economy in relation to the polity? Economic determinism renders a key role to the economy in shaping the polity. We will argue that that there is a set of economic factors which impact on democracy, but clarifying these relationships takes us beyond the simple theory of economic determinism, especially in Marxist-inspired approaches.

Theorizing the interaction between the polity and the economy, one may focus either on economic outcomes or on economic institutions. One may wish to argue that the actual state of the economy – affluence, inflation and unemployment – conditions democracy in one way or the other. Or one could claim that the rules of the economic game spill over into the institutions of the political game. We find both these perspectives in political economy, which is the discipline that researches politico-economic interaction. Here we will examine hypotheses about the economic foundations of democracy, whereas in Part III we will reverse the perspective and enquire into whether democracy impacts on economic outcomes, especially equality and public expenditures. Let us start by examining the basic exogenous model of democracy as determined by economic output.

Affluence

Democratic instability would be conditioned by economic difficulties. This is a sound idea that one finds in the work of several scholars, starting with Tocqueville. It is, however, much more difficult to turn such a vague statement into more precise models which link various economic outcomes with democratic longevity. Economic outcomes tend to fluctuate considerably over time, which makes it all the more important to specify models which identify long-term effects.

Economic difficulties tend to provoke calls for political change, yet it does not necessarily have to be a demand for authoritarian leadership to guide a country out of an economic crisis. There are several examples of economic difficulties undermining dictatorships. In general, however, the literature on democracy contains the following model (M1):

Democracy = f (affluence)

Much research has been conducted in order to confirm this model empirically. One may employ various indicators on democracy as well as different indicators on economic affluence. All the findings indicate that there is a stable positive relationship between these two variables and these findings change little if one examines one time period or another. The key question is to account for this relationship, that is, to identify the transmission mechanism between affluence and democracy.

In the Lipset approach, the position of the middle classes is the link between affluence and democracy. Economic prosperity forms the basis of a broad middle class, which demands political and civil liberties when economic success increases political consciousness. By implication, democracy will not prevail or it will not be stable when groups other than the middle classes dominate the social and political life of a country. In Marxist approaches, it is instead the working classes which explain the connection between affluence and democracy. Economic development – industrialization and urbanization – promotes a working-class movement, which demands democracy either as an end or as a means in the political struggle against the bourgeoisie. Typical of authoritarian regimes is that they suppress the rights of labour, especially outlawing or controlling trade unions.

Marxist scholars have suggested that the Lipset mechanism is flawed, as the middle classes are looked on as a potential source of authoritarianism (O'Donnell, 1979). Actually, one may find a similar idea in civil society theory, as Tocqueville, for instance, claims that people when hit by an economic crisis will call for a strong leader.

Thus, economic affluence increases the probability of democracy whereas poverty decreases it – this is the main implication of (M1). Table 3.1 presents reduced form evidence for (M1) using various indicators for different periods of time.

We find that the relationship between affluence and democracy is a robust positive one whether one looks at data for the 1970s, 1980s or the 1990s. It is generally the case that wealthy countries score high on democracy indicators whereas poor countries score low. The vast system transformation initiated in 1989 has not changed this pattern, as it is richer countries that have moved towards democracy in the 1990s whereas poorer countries have failed to initiate or complete this regime transformation.

Yet, (M1) does not identify a necessary or sufficient condition, as there are several exceptions to the rule that democracy needs affluence. There are rich countries which are authoritarian and the largest democracy on earth – India – is a very poor country. However, one would be wrong in jumping to the conclusion that (M1) expresses a spurious correlation. There is an impact of affluence on democracy, but other factors also play a role. The problem is to

Table 3.1 Affluence (GDPC in US$ PPP) and democracy (DEM) (correlations)

		DEM 1972–6	DEM 1981–5	DEM 1991–5	DEM 1995–2001
GDPC 1975	r	0.55	0.54	0.48	0.45
	N	94	96	98	98
GDPC 1985	r	–	0.65	0.61	0.58
	N	–	107	110	110
GDPC 1995	r	–	–	0.67	0.62
	N	–	–	135	136
GDPC 1998	r	–	–	–	0.63
	N	–	–	–	135

Sources: see Appendix A1.

Note
All correlations have a level of significance on 0.000.

identify these factors and estimate their strength in relation to the basic economic condition, which is affluence.

One may develop (M1) through an enquiry into the specific effects of various economic difficulties on democracy. As it stands now, (M1) is a very simple model which explains little about the link between affluence or poverty and democracy. A number of economic models of democracy seek to identify the complexity in this interaction.

Inflation and debt

One may suggest that democracy is threatened by various kinds of economic difficulties or crises phenomena such as hyperinflation and debt. The economic approach to democracy may be developed into a deterministic theory about the impossibility of democracy in the periphery of a system of global capitalism. The implication is that authoritarian countries or democratically unstable countries are to be found in the hinterland of the world economic system where countries are plagued by inflation, unemployment and massive debt, whereas the core countries in the global economy would be safe for democracy. Here, we have a most general theory – world systems analysis – which may be unpacked into a few specific models that can be tested empirically. They are highly relevant for understanding why economic difficulties or crises reduce democratic probability.

Thus, (M1) may be given more substance by testing the following models (M2):

Democracy = f (inflation)

as well as (M3):

Democracy = f (debt)

Hyperinflation creates the scenario that Tocqueville was the first to portray, namely that people become so desperate about losing their assets that they look for a quick fix by summoning a leader to the heights of political power. One example often mentioned is the ascent of the NSDAP after the German depression in 1922. Hyperinflation has been a typical economic difficulty in many poor countries after the Second World War, especially in Latin America and Africa. It may impact on democracy directly or through its negative impact on affluence, as it is known that hyperinflation reduces economic growth (Frieden, 1991).

Hyperinflation implies that the country's financial situation is unhealthy. According to the well-known Friedman model of inflation, it is the government which is the ultimate source of hyperinflation as it is the monetary authority. It all depends on what is regarded as the exogenous and endogenous variables. If a weak government is regarded as the cause of inflation, then one may object that government is weak because the economy is unhealthy. When governments print money to pay for their expenses because they lack other revenues, they are engaging in such self-defeating policies because they have no other option. In any case, hyperinflation may hurt democracy as it is conducive to political instability.

Actually, hyperinflation may bring down a democratic regime as people voice their discontent with deficits, an unhealthy economy and stagflation. However, hyperinflation may also shake an authoritarian regime which fails in its economic policies. If this occurs, then hyperinflation may pave the way for democracy, as people want more responsible leadership. We expect a negative association between democratic longevity and hyperinflation, but it will hardly be a strong one, as hyperinflation is more linked with political instability. The relationship between democracy and inflation during the 1990s displays no covariation.

Testing the debt model brings us into the network of hypotheses which constitute dependency theory. We cannot do justice to the many ideas that have been launched within this paradigm for analysing interaction between the core and the periphery of the globe, anticipating the globalization theme to some extent. We will concentrate on the model (M2), which captures the essence of the dependency theory linking the precarious predicament in many countries with their debt problems.

The debt problem of a country may be analysed using a few indicators, such as total external debt, the debt payment burden and the total state debt. Although these indicators tap different phenomena, there is a correlation between them, as countries with debt difficulties tend to display all three kinds of problems. We would be inclined to argue that debt is first and foremost a cause of political instability, meaning that debt problems may bring down both a democracy and a dictatorship. In general, however, one would expect democratic probability to be reduced by debt difficulties. Table 3.2 offers reduced form evidence for these two models, (M2) and (M3).

The chief finding in Table 3.2 is that, though democracy is affected negatively by economic disturbances like inflation or huge debt, the impact of such economic difficulties is nowhere in the range of the general impact of affluence on democratic probability. When a country is burdened by hyper-

Table 3.2 Democracy (DEM), inflation (INFL) and debt (TOTDEB, CGDEBT)
(correlations)

DEM and INFL		DEM and TOTDEB		DEM and CGDEBT	
1972–6 and 1961–73	$r = -0.16$ sig. $= 0.200$ $N = 64$	1972–6 and 1975 –	$r = 0.29$ sig. $= 0.016$ $N = 70$	1972–6 and 1975 –	$r = 0.02$ sig. $= 0.902$ $N = 44$
1981–5 and 1973–90	$r = -0.05$ sig. $= 0.667$ $N = 88$	1981–5 and 1980 –	$r = 0.21$ sig. $= 0.079$ $N = 72$	1981–5 and 1980 –	$r = 0.10$ sig. $= 0.481$ $N = 48$
1991–5 and 1990–8	$r = -0.05$ sig. $= 0.636$ $N = 64$	1991–5 and 1995 –	$r = 0.12$ sig. $= 0.213$ $N = 107$	1991–5 and 1990 –	$r = -0.20$ sig. $= 0.172$ $N = 50$
1995–2001 and 1995–8	$r = -0.16$ sig $= 0.078$ $N = 117$	1995–2001 and 1998 –	$r = 0.08$ sig. $= 0.437$ $N = 107$	1995–2001 and 1995 –	$r = -0.44$ sig. $= 0.001$ $N = 55$

Sources: see Appendix A1.

inflation or huge debts, either in terms of the country as a whole or in the form of continuous deficits by the national government, then democracy may suffer. However, inflation and debt does not entail the fall of a democracy or constitute a formidable hindrance to democracy.

Hyperinflation destabilizes a country. When people in a country such as Ecuador or Argentina begin to fear that the official money of the country will run into hyperinflation, then they start chasing US dollars. This is a bad outcome, as it shifts the daily attention away from production, investments and thrift towards hoarding and exchanging. However, it does not bring about the fall of democracy or signal the arrival of authoritarian rule.

The debt problem does not constitute an asset for a democracy, or for any government. When a country has huge external debts or the national government engages year by year in deficit spending, then political instability may be the outcome. But the relationship is not a decisive one, meaning that deficits or debts lead to the downfall of a democracy or the introduction of dictatorship. Some countries live comfortably with inflation and debts, remaining democracies. There is a negative relationship between democracy and debt measured as central government debt.

When national government debt reaches levels over 100 per cent of GDP, the country is certainly in a severe debt crisis. However, few countries face such an extraordinary debt burden. Countries with extreme debt burdens score low on the democracy index but, except for these extreme cases, there is hardly any interaction between debt and democracy. Many democratic countries have a national government debt between 50 and 100 per cent of GDP. Let us look at the impact of economic institutions on democracy. Economic rules may be modelled as either exogenous or endogenous conditions for democracy.

Economic rules

Economic outcomes have a specific but limited impact on democracy – this is the major finding from testing the three models (M1), (M2) and (M3). Affluence is positively related to democracy whereas hyperinflation and debt hardly matter at all. These models are too simple and they do not specify any mechanism that account for the interaction between economic outcomes and democracy.

When economic conditions were underlined in the 1960s, 1970s and 1980s, the focus was clearly on economic output, i.e. affluence. In the 1990s the research shifted perspective as the emphasis moved to economic institutions, or the economic regime. The basic idea is that economic freedom strengthens democracy, which is directly the opposite of what the Yale School of political economy argued in the 1970s and 1980s, linking political democracy with economic democracy. The theory that economic freedom is a condition for political democracy may be found in old economic institutionalism focussing on capitalism and democracy (Hayek, Friedman) as well as in new economic institutionalism (Williamson, North), although never explicitly formulated in a clear manner and subsequently tested empirically.

Discussing the impact of the economic system on the political system, one must sharply differentiate between the basic rules of the economic game on the one hand and the size of public expenditures on the other. We will argue that the rules of the market economy are not only in agreement with political democracy, but their institutionalization also increases democratic probability. Instead of capitalism enhancing authoritarianism, it is claimed that the market economy has strong affinities with democracy, both protecting human rights. Authoritarianism is to be found in countries which harbour a planned economy or practice economic nationalism, which both provide for immense state control over the economy and thus also society.

At the same time, the market economy hypothesis should be separated from the theory that minimizing the public sector increases democracy – the Friedman argument which builds on the Manchester conception of the guardian state. Several of the most stable democracies are to be found among the countries with large public sectors. The market hypothesis may be phrased in such a manner that it links only economic freedom with democracy (M4):

Democracy $= f$ (economic freedom).

(M4) bypasses the size of public expenditures and the debate about the pros and cons of the welfare state.

Thus, (M4) is not the same as the Hayek position that democratic decision-making intervening in market outcomes entails the road to serfdom. Yet it links the economy and the polity through the key economic institutions. Democracy will be firmly entrenched where there are rules that offer not only political freedom but also economic freedom. The exact nature of this link between economic and political rules has never been fully understood, as we lack a model for the full transmission mechanism between economic freedom and political liberty. Let us examine reduced form evidence for (M4).

Table 3.3 Economic freedom and democracy (correlations)

		DEM 1972–6	DEM 1981–5	DEM 1991–5	DEM 1995–2001
Fraser, 1975	r	0.45	0.43	0.39	0.41
	N	76	78	78	78
Fraser, 1985	r	–	0.53	0.50	0.46
	N	–	103	103	103
Fraser, 1995	r	–	–	0.64	0.63
	N	–	–	113	113
Fraser, 1999	r	–	–	–	0.64
	N	–	–	–	114
Heritage, 2000	r	–	–	–	0.76
	N	–	–	–	144

Sources: see Appendix A1.

Note
The Heritage index has been recoded so that the higher the score, the more economic freedom; the Fraser index is scored in such a way that the higher the score, the more economic freedom.

The reduced form evidence for the claims of old economic institutionalism or neo-institutionalism is strong, as one may have expected. It is true that the planned economies all score extremely low on all democracy indices, but that stems from the idea of democratic centralism or proletarian democracy. It is also true that several of the countries practising economic nationalism have leaned towards an authoritarian regime, but it is not entirely clear that this is merely an economic system effect, or whether it also depends on purely political reasons involving a rejection of democracy. Yet the finding in Table 3.3 is that economic institutions correlate strongly with democracy, thus suggesting that the market economy will increase democratic probability.

Given the institutional transformation initiated in 1989–90, it comes as no surprise that the correlations display stronger association between economic and political institutions in the 1990s. One can state on the basis of these findings that the market economy and democracy go hand-in-hand, as well as that the stronger economic freedom is entrenched in the economy, the more likely it is that the polity in a country will be democratic. There is thus a fundamental affinity between the market economy and democracy.

However, this finding concerning a positive relationship between the market economy and democracy cannot be interpreted as evidence for the main arguments by Hayek and Friedman that a small public sector is crucial for democracy. One cannot show that economic freedom is a function of the size of government, meaning that economic freedom is considerably reduced in a welfare state. Table 3.4 shows reduced form evidence of how economic freedom is related to measures of the size of the public sector.

In Table 3.4 one finds strong evidence for the compatibility of the market economy with the welfare state, characterized by big government financially (the 'tax state'). Economic freedom is high not only in the United States, Australia and Japan but also in the Nordic countries and Switzerland. Thus, we reject the hypothesis of Hayek and Friedman that democracy needs a guardian state or that a welfare state implies a risk for political authoritarianism.

Table 3.4 Economic freedom (FRASER, HERITAGE) and public sector size (GGEXP)
(correlations)

		Fraser, 1975	Fraser, 1985	Fraser, 1995	Fraser, 1999	Heritage, 2000
GGEXP	r	0.06	–	–	–	–
1975	sig.	0.607	–	–	–	–
	N	67	–	–	–	–
GGEXP	r	0.14	0.24	–	–	–
1985	sig.	0.249	0.027	–	–	–
	N	69	83	–	–	–
GGEXP	r	0.28	0.40	0.28	–	–
1995	sig.	0.019	0.000	0.007	–	–
	N	69	83	90	–	–
GGEXP	r	0.36	0.52	0.31	0.36	0.39
1999	sig.	0.010	0.000	0.068	0.002	0.001
	N	52	64	72	72	72
GOVSP	r	0.11	0.18	0.13	0.08	0.18
2000	sig.	0.471	0.191	0.328	0.536	0.184
	N	48	55	58	58	59
TOTOUT	r	0.05	0.16	0.06	−0.02	0.06
2000	sig.	0.749	0.253	0.683	0.889	0.652
	N	46	52	54	54	54

Sources: see Appendix A1.

There is a strong positive relationship between democracy and economic institutions. It is clearly the case that there is a strong positive correlation between these two variables, the market economy and political democracy.

There are two conflicting views about the market economy and democracy in the literature. One group of scholars argue that they tend to go together, whereas another group of scholars claim that they involve a contradiction. The first position is the correct one, but it cannot be interpreted in such a way that democracy requires the largest possible market economy, i.e. as denying the possibility that a welfare state can be a full democracy.

We suggest that there are *two* links between the economy and democracy. The first link is that between economic affluence and democracy, the second between economic and political freedom. The summary of this argument is that the market economy strongly stabilizes democracy when it produces affluence. If a market economy fails to produce affluence, then its contribution to promoting democracy is far weaker. Let us look at structural model evidence concerning how economic affluence and economic institutions interact to enhance democratic probability.

Which economic factors matter most?

We have seen that both the economic situation of a country (affluence, inflation, debt) and its economic institutions are linked with its democracy score.

Thus, the correlations between economic outcomes and economic regime on the one hand and political regime on the other are strong enough to warrant a search for an explanation for the link between economic conditions and political democracy. In a structural model one may attempt to separate the impact of economic outcomes from that of economic rules. Such a regression model is tested in Table 3.5.

The regression technique for carrying out empirical research allows us to draw a few stunning conclusions about the impact of economic conditions on democracy. According to Table 3.5, it is economic freedom which is a key factor, as economic institutions add as much if not more to democracy as affluence, i.e. production. Economic rules can be modelled as either exogenous or endogenous conditions for democracy.

The major finding in this chapter is thus that economic institutions are as important, if not more important, as economic output for political democracy. If a government wishes to enhance democratic probability, it could move to accept more of the institutions of the market economy and attempt to enforce such rules of the economic game. Economic affluence is much more difficult to fabricate, as it depends on many factors besides the economic regime.

The importance of both economic freedom and affluence for democracy appears when one tests a model consisting of affluence, institutions, inflation and debt – see Table 3.6. Here we test two models – Model 3 and Model 4, which combine these basic conditions identified in this chapter. Model 3 refers to industrialized countries while Model 4 mainly pertains to Third World countries.

The impact of economic conditions for democracy may be summarized as follows, on the basis of the structural model evidence in Table 3.6: economic affluence as well as economic freedom enhances democratic probability, whereas inflation and debt reduce it. The first two factors are more powerful than the last ones. Economic rules matter more for democracy in Third World

Table 3.5 Economic freedom, affluence and democracy (regression) – dependent variable: democracy (DEM) scores (1995–2001)

Independent variables	Coeffs	Model 1	Model 2
LN GDP/CAP 1998	coeff	0.872	0.525
	t-stat	3.95	2.50
Fraser, 1999	coeff	0.576	–
	t-stat	3.36	–
Heritage, 2000	coeff	–	2.093
	t-stat	–	6.25
Constant	coeff	−4.728	−2.236
	t-stat	−3.22	−1.66
rsq adj		0.47	0.53
N		109	132

Sources: see Appendix A1.

Table 3.6 Affluence, inflation and debt (regression) – dependent variable: democracy
(DEM) scores (1995–2001)

Independent variables	Coeffs	Model 3	Model 4
LNGDP/CAP 1998	coeff	0.924	0.484
	t-stat	2.25	1.90
HERITAGE, 2000	coeff	0.664	2.46
	t-stat	0.88	6.08
INFL 1995–8	coeff	−0.021	0.000
	t-stat	−2.44	0.15
CGDEBT 1995	coeff	−0.011	–
	t-stat	−1.78	–
TOTDEB 1998	coeff	–	−0.000
	t-stat	–	−0.10
Constant	coeff	−1.244	−2.40
	t-stat	−0.49	−1.35
rsq adj		0.56	0.47
N		49	83

Sources: see Appendix A1.

Note
Model 3 mainly refers to industrialized countries while Model 4 mainly refers to Third World
countries.

countries than affluence. This is an important new finding in democracy
research, which calls for an analysis of endogenous democracy.

In the research on the economic sources of political democracy, the key
model is affluence increasing democratic stability, i.e. an exogenous model.
We have shown here that even more important for democratic longevity in the
Third World is economic freedom, which is an endogenous factor to the
extent that governments can change their basic economic institutions.

Conclusion

Democracy has occurred much more frequently in wealthy countries than in
poor countries. Or it has been much more stable in wealthy countries than in
poor countries. The hypothesis that affluence affects democracy seems plausible, and it is the central idea in modernization theory, which was introduced
in the 1950s. Reduced form evidence indicates that affluence has a positive
impact on democratic stability. Affluence is basically the same as economic
output. When a country prospers economically, then the prospects for stable
democracy increase.

Given modernization theory, it remains a puzzle as to why some very rich
countries are not democratic (the Gulf) and some poor countries are democracies (India, Botswana, Mauritius). One may reply to this question by
consulting institutionalist theory, old or new. Economic institutionalism,
attracting much attention recently, claims that the economic regime not only

affects economic outcomes but also impacts on the political regime. Actually, one finds the hypothesis about a connection between capitalism and democracy with old institutionalism as propagated by Hayek and Friedman. In the new economic institutionalism, there is an emphasis on transaction cost saving mechanisms and their beneficial economic outcomes, mainly affluence. The evidence supports new economic institutionalism more than old economic institutionalism. The evidence shows that the economic rules of the market economy positively and directly effects democracy.

The main competitor to modernization theory has been the dependency theory also initiated in the 1950s, and flourishing in the 1960s and 1970s. According to dependency theory, democracy as well as economic development is much conditioned by core–periphery relationships in the world economic system. We find some evidence for this theory, as hyperinflation and huge debts reduce democratic probability.

If one argues that affluence is a key positive condition for democracy, then one must explain why the rich Gulf States are authoritarian as well as why India has maintained democracy for such a long period of time since independence. We will return to these anomalies in the following chapters, where more conditions are taken into account, such as culture and political institutions.

4   Ethnicity

Introduction

In this chapter, we will broaden the analysis of exogenous factors and enquire into the impact of one major cultural factor, namely ethnicity, on democracy. People are different in two major ways, besides the possession of economic resources. We will focus on two major sources of cultural differences among countries, namely ethnicity and religion. The ethnic and religious differences between people constitute macro distinctions as groups cluster according to ethnic and religious criteria. The social structure of a country consists of groups which are defined (and often define themselves) according to ethnic and religious criteria. The implications for democracy need to be spelled out. Let us start with ethnicity and democracy in this chapter.

Mainstream social science literature underlines the negative impact of ethnic diversity on democracy (Rabushka and Shepsle, 1972; Esman, 1977; Lijphart, 1977; Horowitz, 1985, 1993; Reilly, 2001; see also Collier, 2000). Ethnic cleavages in a country destabilize the polity and undermine democracy. Ethnic homogeneity on the other hand promotes democracy and political stability. Democracy is viable when it occurs in a nation-state. Thus, mainstream political sociology emphasizes the positive influence of ethnic homogeneity on democracy.

The purpose of this chapter is to unpack this theory of ethnicity and democracy, using a distinction between two central models. It should be emphasized that ethnicity and democracy could interact in two ways. One the one hand, there is the model of the nation-state, claiming that democracy is highly viable when it occurs in a homogenous nation-state. On the other hand, there is the theory of ethnic cleavages, stating that they are conducive to political instability, thus harming democratic longevity. We will examine both models, as they are highly relevant to understanding the prospects of democracy in the future, where societies will become more and more multicultural.

Nation-building and democracy

Several scholars have analysed the process of democratization of European countries as closely related to the emergence of nation-states. The replacement of traditional rule in empires by government by nation-states according to the principle of 'one people–one state' was conducive to the victory of democracy, although both fascism and communism scored temporary successes when traditional rule was abandoned in Europe. Perhaps Stein Rokkan more than any other scholar underlined the link between nation-building in the eighteenth and nineteenth centuries and the success of democracy in Europe around 1900. The nation-state is based on a foundation of egalitarian solidarity which is democratic in spirit (Rokkan *et al.*, 1970; Flora and Kuhnle, 1999). In the new world, the demand for democracy went hand-in-hand with a growing national consciousness, as colonial power was dismantled.

Yet the interaction between nationalism and democracy is more complicated than mainstream nation-building theory suggests. Nationalism has two faces, one humanitarian, the other aggressive. A nation-state may respect other nations and strive for the mutual recognition of and respect between the nation-states of the world. Or a strong nation-state may strive for the domination of peoples, either within their own borders or through the conquest of other territories. It is far from self-evident that the more compact the nation is, the more likely it is that it will adhere to democracy. Let us develop a few measures on nation-building and conduct an empirical analysis into the link between them on the one hand and democratic stability on the other.

Nation-states are the states where a huge majority of the population shares one common body of beliefs or values including a language, a cultural heritage or a myth of common ancestry. The nation-state shares with democracy a fundamental egalitarian emphasis as all people, both poor and rich, are invited to be part of the nation. Thus, a high level of national consciousness would be impossible without popular participation in politics, and government support for the empowerment of the population. This is why the rise of nationalism has been linked with the evolution of an industrial and urban society where mass participation is feasible (Smith, 1998). At the same time the belief within nationalism of a set of core myths about a compact nation or people has made scholars link nationalism with romanticism, populism or even extremism. Nationalism is a paradoxical phenomenon covering both democratic and non-democratic features. Here we will focus on a comparison between nationalism and nation-building.

The theory of the nation-state as the womb of democracy may be examined by looking at the relationship between nation-building and democracy. If one assumes that time is crucial for building a nation-state, then one could measure the strength of a nation-state by the length of time that has passed since a modern state was put in place. Often a crucial political transition, from traditional rule to a modern state, occurred at some point in time in the history of the country, when what is called 'modernized leadership' was introduced. The longer the time span since this major political event, the stronger one would assume the nation-state to be, all other things being equal. One key indicator on nation-building is the length of time of uninterrupted modernized leadership.

One could counter-argue against this factor – the length of uninterrupted modern statehood – by suggesting that it merely represents the peculiar history of a country. Thus, western countries will display early modern statehood and thus score high on nation-state compactness, whereas Third World countries cannot score high due to the often long period of colonial domination they had to endure. Yet, accepting this objection, one could still argue that the fact of colonialism only confirms what this factor is supposed to identify, namely the lack of national coherence or solidarity in many of the countries which became independent after the Second World War.

One may wish to add other indicators of nation-building which complement modernized leadership. Thus, we will measure the constitutional stability of the country which measures the state-building process in a country. The longer the time span of uninterrupted constitutional development, the stronger and more coherent is the state in a country, we argue. Young states characterized by excessive constitutional change are not likely to offer democratically stable government.

Let us look at reduced form evidence that may indicate whether there is a link between the nation-state or state-building and democracy. The relevant model would be (M5):

Democracy = f (nation-state, state-building)

Table 4.1 shows the correlation between length in time of a modern state as well as the number of constitutional revisions on the one hand and democracy on the other hand, corresponding to a test of the model (M5). All the indicators on nation-building and state-building correlate positively with democratic longevity.

Thus, there is ample empirical support for (M5) in Table 4.1. Nation-building in the form of 'a long time period since modernized leadership was introduced' as well as firm state-building in the form of 'constitutional coherence during the most recent decades' impact positively on democracy under moderately strong correlations of about 0.5.

In particular, we find that the early institutionalization of a modern state – nation-building – is positively connected with democracy. Countries which have been democratically stable over a period of almost fifty years, that is, from 1945, tend to be the countries where the transition to a legal rational

Table 4.1 Democracy (DEM) and the nation-state (STATEAGE, CONYR) (correlations)

DEM		STATEAGE	CONYR 1978	CONYR 1985	CONYR 1996
1972–6	r	0.54	0.54	0.48	0.57
	N	128	119	119	120
1981–5	r	0.57	0.49	0.40	0.55
	N	133	123	123	124
1991–5	r	0.55	0.40	0.33	0.40
	N	148	124	124	142
1995–2001	r	0.53	0.38	0.32	0.38
	N	150	124	124	144

Sources: see Appendix A1.

Note
All correlations are significant at the level of 0.000.

type of state, in the Weberian conception, took place in the eighteenth or nineteenth centuries. Early nation-building enhances democratic probability, as Rokkan would have emphasized (Flora *et al.*, 1999). And there is indeed a relationship between nation-building effort (the length of modernized leadership) and democracy.

Yet, we wish to underline that the past does not determine the present, as the correlations are hardly strong ones. One may interpret the findings in Table 4.1 as support for the theory that a compact nation-state enhances democratic probability through its emphasis on solidarity as well as on equality. Nationalism and democracy can be brought into harmony, supporting each other. This is the positive side of the ethnicity coin with regard to democracy. However, we must look at the negative side of the coin too, as compact nation-states are not easily found today.

Ethnic heterogeneity has been on the rise during recent decades. Societies that did create a modern state early are also now experiencing rapidly increasing ethnic heterogeneity with the arrival of the multi-cultural society. Migration on a massive scale increases ethnic fragmentation, especially in wealthy countries. If a compact nation-state is a positive for democracy, then perhaps ethnic fragmentation is a negative?

Ethnic fragmentation and democracy

The population of many countries is becoming increasingly ethnically diverse. Many scholars have pointed out that ethnic identity is an amorphous concept as it is difficult to specify in an unambiguous fashion what the core features of an ethnic group are. Max Weber pointed out that an ethnic group could be constituted by almost any kind of characteristic, but he drew the wrong conclusion when he argued that ethnicity is unimportant (Weber, 1978). What matters is how groups identify themselves and take action on the basis of commonly shared beliefs, whatever the nature of such beliefs or myths.

At the beginning of the twenty-first century, we have witnessed an ethnic revival, as groups have moved towards a stronger recognition of their ethnic characteristics. It has been much discussed as to whether ethnicity is based on real or imagined communities. We suggest that language is the core of ethnicity and that ethnic communities mobilize on the basis of characteristics that somehow relate to their various languages.

Ethnic communities are not the only kind of groups in the social structure of a country. There could be religious communities as well as racial ones. The link between ethnicity and race has been much discussed. In general, race and ethnicity is not the same thing. However, in some countries, racial communities and ethnic communities overlap, as in the United States and, to some extent, in Russia. Racial groups are notoriously difficult to specify, as the criteria employed have been much criticized. When a community identifies itself on the basis of racial criteria such as, for instance, the black community in the United States or the Tartar population in Russia, then racial communities are very much considered to exist. It is much more problematic to speak about racial communities when self-identification is virtually non-existent or the group in question does not engage in any activity to promote its common interests.

Some countries are characterized by sharp ethnic cleavages where language communities have mobilized politically to enhance their interests. In the literature, these countries are called 'divided societies' and a key question has been to come up with the institutional mechanisms which allow these societies to have a democratic system of government. The prevailing image of divided societies is that they tend towards political instability and that, thus, democracy is fragile in these countries. One could cite Northern Ireland, Lebanon and Sri Lanka as examples of divided societies where sectarianism has resulted in massive political instability.

Ethnic mobilization can occur to varying degrees. It is when ethnic consciousness turns to the use of violence that ethnic mobilization is conducive to political instability. It has been argued that ethnic cleavages are particularly prone to result in political instability, as ethnic conflict is less amenable to conflict management through bargaining techniques. Our focus here is on the link between ethnic fragmentation and democracy. If ethnic cleavages undermine political stability, then they would also constitute a threat to democracy. Table 4.2 shows the reduced form evidence for a model like (M6):

Democracy $= f$ (ethnic fragmentation)

Ethnic heterogeneity may be measured by various indices, and Africa is the most fragmented continent (cf. Scarritt and Mozaffar, 1999). We will employ three measures (ELF1–3) taken from the literature on ethnic fragmentation and ethnic cleavages.

The evidence suggests that ethnic fragmentation is a negative for democratic stability. As ethnic fragmentation is increasing in many countries, this fact constitutes a challenge to the democratic regime. Sectionalism can be

Table 4.2 Ethnic cleavages (ELF) and democracy (DEM) (correlations)

DEM		ELF1	ELF2	ELF3
1972–6	r	−0.29	−0.24	−0.28
	sig.	0.001	0.007	0.002
	N	125	125	118
1981–5	r	−0.32	−0.23	−0.30
	sig.	0.000	0.009	0.001
	N	130	130	123
1991–5	r	−0.32	−0.25	−0.30
	sig.	0.000	0.002	0.001
	N	148	148	124
1995–2001	r	−0.26	−0.20	−0.23
	sig.	0.002	0.014	0.009
	N	150	148	124

Sources: see Appendix A1.

handled or resolved in two main ways. Either a country breaks up as a minority group moves on to create its own polity – secessionism. Or the country in question devises mechanisms which allow for ethnic participation in decision-making through so-called consociational devices, including federalism, minority representation or the protection of special minority rights. We will analyse the impact of such institutions on democratic probability in Chapter 6.

What is the relationship between ethnic fragmentation and democracy as things stand today? The general pattern suggests that democracy is weaker in countries with more extensive ethnic fragmentation, but it is equally important to note that democracies are to be found in ethnically heterogeneous countries as well as in ethnically homogenous countries.

Ethnicity is a negative exogenous condition for democracy when it takes the appearance of ethnic diversity. This is the reverse side of the coin to the already-cited finding that compact nation-states are likely to be democratic (see p. 102). Yet, it must be pointed out that the strength of the association between ethnic fragmentation and democracy is not particularly strong.

Nation-building and multi-culturalism

The findings reported above (indicate that ethnicity and democracy interact in two ways. A long process of nation-building, enhancing consensus on the values of the nation is a positive. But ethnic fragmentation is a negative. And ethnic heterogeneity is increasing today due to the strong currents of multi-culturalism that began to occur at the end of the twentieth century, as manifested in increased immigration in the wake of globalization.

As Miller has pointed out (2000), multiculturalism poses a challenge to nation-building, if indeed the idea of nation-building still has relevance at all. The new theory of the politics of mutual respect is an attempt to reconcile democracy with the challenge of a multi-cultural society. Diasporas are rapidly spreading around the globe, where migrants look for jobs and opportunities in other countries. Many of these diasporas have an ethnic background. Constitutional democracy is often said to be the most accurate response to increasing ethnic fragmentation. However, a constitutional democracy cannot merely maximize the rights of various ethnic minorities, as it must also guarantee that democracy can function without too many hindrances. We will return to this dilemma when we argue in favour of majoritarian democracy.

Ethnicity is an exogenous condition for democratic stability, as the findings above (p. 104) show. A government cannot, in general, change the ethnic composition of the country. But it can promote nation-building by fostering a spirit of national unity and refrain from policies which harm constitutional continuity. As multi-culturalism advances, governments must find new tools for nation-building than just promoting ethnic homogeneity. Democracy today must find the institutions which combine the mechanism of majoritarian democracy with the implications of ethnic diversity.

Conclusion

Ethnicity, we have shown, works both ways both positively and negatively – in relation to democracy. Ethnicity may enhance democratic probability when there is a compact nation-state, with ethnic homogeneity strengthening democracy. On the other hand, ethnicity counteracts democracy when there is ethnic fragmentation. In divided societies democracy can only be maintained if the divisive implications of ethnic cleavages are balanced by a special institutional set up.

Although reduced form evidence exists for the ethnicity hypotheses about democracy – both (M5) and (M6) – it is actually difficult to conceive of the transmission link between the two entities. We suggest that ethnicity primarily impacts on political stability and secondarily on democracy. Thus, ethnic fragmentation may result in the break-up of a state or the change of the regime, which may have severe repercussions on a democracy. However, the negative link is not primarily between ethnic cleavages and democracy but ethnic fragmentation and political instability.

One may argue that democracy is the only regime that can handle ethnic cleavages in a manner that presents any hope of political stability in a country with strong ethnic fragmentation. Dictatorships often face fierce resistance from ethnic minorities, as they strive in vain to suppress demands from such groups. Ethnic conflict will have the same impact on the polity, whether it is an authoritarian or a democratic one, i.e. it increases political instability. Democracies can cope with only so much political instability, meaning that ethnic mobilization along different lines may damage democratic probability.

As the nation-state loses more and more of its relevance, democracies must consider institutional reforms which accommodate minorities. When compact nations no longer dominate the politics of a country, then nationalism and democracy must dissolve their marriage, forged in the late nineteenth and early twentieth centuries. Democracy, in fact, offers the best available regime for handling ethnic cleavages, although secessionism may constitute a better option than attempting to hold a state together at any price.

5 Religion

Introduction

Religion provides answers to the big questions of mankind, concerning the meaning of life and the existence of life after death. Religious behaviour is often contrasted with secular behaviour, as they can tend to differ and collide. Yet religious action is strongly linked with mundane considerations as, for instance, when religious belief is institutionalized. Thus, religion has powerful consequences on daily life and the organization of routines in the world.

Religion and democracy may be researched in two different ways. First, one may repeat the analysis of the consequences of ethnic fragmentation but focus on religious cleavages. Second, one may examine the implications of various religions on democracy when there is one dominant religion in the population. The second perspective is probably more interesting and rewarding than the first, which is merely another fragmentation which would link religion primarily with political instability.

It has been discussed whether ethnicity or religion presents most problems for political stability, as one kind of community could be more compact than the other or one kind of belief would be more politically explosive than another. Both ethnic and religious mobilization may result in large scale violence, as the civil wars in Kurdistan and India illustrate. When ethnic and religious cleavages combine, then civil war appears probable, as in Northern Ireland and Nigeria.

Religion and politics

The models which connect religion as a system of beliefs and values with democracy consider any contradiction between what a religion entails and what democracy requires. Thus, religions are seen as a hindrance on the institutionalization of democracy, a democratic regime being a secular type of government. The question then becomes: which of the world's religions could most easily accept democracy?

Democracy as a system of rules has one very clear implication for both religious belief and religious movements (Gill, 2001; Stepan, 2001a). Democracy requires religious toleration, if not the strict neutrality of the state in relation to various religious groups. The idea of religious tolerance was actually formed before the advent of democracy as a result of the fierce religious wars in Europe, as Christianity lost its unity due to the Reformation and the Counter-Reformation. The key statement was made by John Locke in 1699, *A Letter Concerning Toleration* (Locke, 1991). However, it is not natural to expect a religion to endorse toleration of other belief systems.

The world religions have of tradition taken action against phenomena that may threaten their position in society. Thus, all the world religions contain prescriptions about the following:

1   apostasy;
2   proselytism;
3   heresy.

The major world religions tend to reject all three forms of behaviour in this list, especially when these actions go against them. Sometimes the punishments against these behaviours have been severe, indeed extremely severe. All three forms of behaviour could threaten the existence or expansion of a religion. However, toleration requires that a religion accepts them.

It has been argued that toleration became a viable idea only when it was obvious to everyone that Christianity had split and no side could win a final and enduring victory. Thus, mainly Protestant-based sects advocated toleration as a form of self-defence and not as a principled cause. Yet, it was not long before several Calvinist sects, one of which Locke adhered to himself, endorsed toleration as a matter of principle.

Protestantism and Hinduism are today the religions that, perhaps, most endorse toleration. As a principle, toleration of other religions is hardly accepted within Islam or within Roman Catholicism or in Greek Orthodoxy, although pragmatism has also spread to these religions. Toleration is typical of the various brands of Buddhism today, at least when there is no major challenge to its place in society.

State neutrality is not the same as toleration, as Protestantism shows. In many countries where Protestantism is the dominant religion there is toleration but not state neutrality. The major exception is Northern America, where religious diversity, from an early stage, called for both toleration and state neutrality in religious matters. In Northern Europe, the Lutheran state Church is still in existence. The institutionalization of religion often meant that government or political authority was employed for regulating religious matters.

The use of the state for religious purposes, or the employment of religion for government objectives, is to be found in all the world religions. What we need to look at is whether some countries managed to put in place the principle of state neutrality during the twentieth century. One finds state neutrality explicitly endorsed in countries like the United States, France, and Turkey. The opposite is to be found in Muslim countries where Sharia Law is declared part of the constitution or *the* constitution of the state, as in Saudi Arabia or Pakistan. State neutrality in Catholic countries remains problematic, as in Italy or Ireland. In Greek Orthodox countries, the state is closely linked with religion, as in Greece.

When atheism is the official belief system of the state, then state neutrality may be put aside for the suppression of religious behaviour, as during the short history of the USSR. It seems that the Chinese state today accepts more state neutrality than before, although the status of Tibetan Buddhism remains precarious. Atheism may become a dominant belief system though, even if the state remains neutral in religious matters. This is what is slowly happening in several Protestant countries where secularization is proceeding smoothly.

State neutrality in religious matters has become a contested issue in India, where Hindu nationalism is challenging the neutral position of the Congress Party. Buddhism has always had close links with political power, as its way of life spread through support from powerful rulers. However, the spread of communism in East Asia has considerably weakened its official position.

Politics and religion may finally be examined from the point of view of the internal governance of a religion and its worldly business. Whereas Roman Catholicism explicitly favoured hierarchy in the form of a Church separated from the state, Islam fused political and religious authority in the Caliphate. Only the Protestant-based sects, including Calvinism, displayed a democratic spirit, calling for the rule of the congregation when internal matters were to be decided on. Priests have always demonstrated a strong tendency to distance themselves from laymen, favouring some form of hierocracy. In Greek Ortho-doxy and Hinduism, these tendencies were extremely successful, whereas Bud-dhism does not display the same extent of priest domination. In Judaism, religion and politics are closely connected as within Islam, although the state of Israel today respects diversity of religious beliefs.

Among the world religions, one may dare to suggest that Protestantism is most easily combined with democracy, whereas Islam would be the religion which could be seen as the least in agreement with democracy and its require-ment of secularization and religious freedom. Any such interpretation of the core meaning of a religion would, though, have to be substantiated by means of behavioural correlations. When theorizing the social and political con-sequences of world religions, one may wish to use Max Weber's mode of analy-sis, although he narrowly focussed on the economic implications of various religious belief-systems.

Why did Weber not examine the link between religion and democracy? One can only speculate about the reasons which led Weber to deal exclusively with the religious conditions for the rise of modern capitalism. In his sociology of religions, Weber displayed an acute awareness of the political implications of religious belief and religious movements. Thus, he portrayed the evolution of religion from animism and examined how religion and politics have been meshed in a variety of ways. In his short analysis of Islam, the political implica-tions of the prophecy of Muhammad are strongly emphasized. However, his main focus was on the economic consequences of religious doctrine and the behaviour of the *religious virtuousi*.

Weber's approach

Weber's argument about the economic implications of the different world reli-gions comprised both a logical interpretation and an empirical verification

(Weber, 1993). Weber started out by claiming that modern capitalism was essentially linked with economic rationality as manifested most clearly in the continuous calculation of the best means to obtain economic gain. Then he posed his basic question: where could one find the beginnings of this rationality?

Weber adheres to the traditional view that all the world religions originate in animism, which he regards as irrational belief or behaviour. The rationalization of religious belief within the world religions takes the form of the emergence of critical ideas about distinguishing between matter and spirit, determination and free will, this world and another world after death, etc. Such distinctions may involve the idea of one God as well as the strict separation between nature and spiritual matters. Weber never raised the question of whether religious belief, in whatever form it was presented, was not basically beyond the powers of human reason. Thus, his link between religion and economics was rationality. And he had to find one religion that took rationality to such an extreme that it got close to the rationality typical of modern capitalism or modern science. We all know his surprising answer: Protestantism.

Only religion, rather than race or language, makes people different from each other. Thus, only religion can be the source of modern capitalism, which may be seen as one aspect of the rationality of modernization. And the most rational religion was, according to Weber, Calvinism. We cannot discuss the Weber thesis here, as the debate about the origins of modern capitalism is a most extensive one. The market economy has been exported all over the world and there is hardly any principled difference between Occidental and Oriental countries in terms of their attitude towards economic rationalism. More interesting is to examine the political implications of the different world religions, especially what they imply for democracy.

Although Weber was very interested in political regimes and investigated them extensively in terms of his well-known typology of authority systems, it is astonishing that he never systematically theorized the relationship between religion and politics. Actually, Weber had little to say about democracy, as he focussed on legal or rational authority in general. Democracy belongs, of course, to this third category, although he also acknowledged that some democratic politicians employ charismatic talents. Yet he only dealt specifically with democratic regimes in his analysis of presidentialism and parliamentarism.

Is there any of the world religions which explicitly embraces the idea of democracy? Or, to put the same problem somewhat differently: is any of the world religions explicitly against the idea of democracy? One could investigate this problem by merely looking at reduced form evidence linking each of the world religions with scores on democracy. However, such an empiricist approach would not explain why it is that a country where the majority of the population adheres to a certain religious belief tends to be democratic or non-democratic. In other words, one would want to understand the *link* between religion and democracy.

Weber had such a link very much in mind when he argued that Protestantism was more in tune with capitalism than any of the other religions, namely rationality. Since capitalism was economic rationality writ large to

Weber, he set out to find the religions which in their belief systems were most rational. Thus, he argued that each of the major world religions except Protestantism in its Calvinist version had strong elements of irrationality, at least when judged from an economic point of view.

Weber used a very simple taxonomy, classifying religions as 'rational' or 'irrational' as well as 'innerwordly' or 'outerworldy'. He found the decisive belief system for modernity was the religion that was, at the same time, outerworldly and rational, meaning that the rational conduct of behaviour promoted salvation along the road to paradise. One may raise the question as to whether any religion is – strictly speaking – a rational one, as all kinds of religious belief except atheism or agnosticism entails metaphysical elements of one kind or another. Perhaps the mere belief in a world beyond the universe as it can be observed today is an irrational one, meaning that the innerworldly–outerwordly perspective is not entirely independent of the rational–irrational distinction?

World religions and democracy

How would one relate the world religions to democracy? Certainly, it could hardly matter much whether the religion in question emphasizes this world (innerwordly) or another world (outerworldy). In principle, no religion supports democracy, as they are two kinds of legitimation which are at odds with each other. When adherents of a religion claim tolerance, it could be claimed that they are acting out of strategic reasons, meaning that they consider that their own religion cannot prevail. Historically, none of the world religions has really had tolerance as a basic idea in its core beliefs. Tolerance may also be advocated from the point of view of scepticism, though this is basically outside of the religious perspective. Only when one turns to a syncretistic religion like the Bahai in the twentieth century does one find tolerance as a basic principle of the religion in question.

Theoretical deliberations

What counts, when a religion encounters democracy, is how strongly its adherents will insist on the integrity, hegemony and purity of the religion. Catholicism took a considerable amount of time before it endorsed the idea of democracy. Islam has still not accommodated the core ideas of a democracy, focussing on the right to choose as well as to reject a religion. Hinduism is such a flexible religion that it can easily accommodate democracy as long as one respects the restriction that only Indians can become Hinduists. Buddhism may certainly be the religion of peace and cooperation among men and women, but it favours traditional authority ahead of the power of people.

What is critical, we suggest, is whether a religion can accept the following elements: apostasy, proselytism and state neutrality. In the name of religious freedom, a religion must accept that believers leave it for another religion as well as that other religions may be actively attracting new believers. When religious freedom is not accepted, then the state is asked to impose rules which limit religious tolerance. Thus, government falls into the hands of one religion, which denies the possibility of a secular state.

Protestantism appears to be the world religion which has had the fewest problems in accepting the principles of a secular state based on, among other things, religious freedom. Islam has thus far given in to neither the secular state nor religious freedom. Hinduism and Buddhism have shown themselves more flexible, just like the Catholic Church and Greek Orthodoxy. Finally, Judaism has always been in the minority position except within Israel today. One allegation against Israel is that it is a theocracy of sorts. However, this allegation is debatable, as non-Jews may become citizens of Israel, including Arab Muslims.

The link between religion and democracy passes over individualism, we argue. When a religion underlines the importance of the individual person and gives a prominent role to individual judgement in religious matters, then it may accept democracy at the end of the day. This is what happened with Protestantism, but it took a considerable amount of time in several countries before even this religion accepted the principle of state neutrality. When a religion is more collectivist in spirit, such as Catholicism, Islam or Buddhism, then it will create resistance to democracy.

Thus, we would expect democracy to be less well institutionalized in countries where Catholicism, Islam and Buddhism stand strong. What complicates the test of such a model as the following (M7):

$$\text{Democracy} = f\,(\text{Protestantism})$$

is that the absence of Protestantism does not mean that democracy must be unstable or completely lacking. First, there is Hinduism, which is in conformity with democracy, given its syncretistic nature and its lack of a Church hierarchy. Second, more and more people adhere to no religion, meaning that they are atheists in theory or practice. Atheism is strong not only in Western Europe but also in the former communist countries including China. When testing the religious model, one should focus specifically on a few of the world religions such as, for example, Islam and Buddhism in order to find out whether there is any empirical support for the religious model. Thus, we will test two models (M8):

$$\text{Democracy} = f\,(\text{Islam})$$

and (M9):

$$\text{Democracy} = f\,(\text{Buddhism})$$

where we expect the estimation to show negative relationships. Here, both religious doctrine and religious tradition can have the same result of discouraging the acceptance of political democracy.

Arab traditionalism, especially its adherence to traditional political authority, has no doubt had the result that democracy has failed in many Muslim countries. However, the basic idea in Islam of a political community – *Umma* – has meant that religion and politics are difficult to separate. This applies to both Sunni and Shia countries, although a Shia heritage, with its focus on the role of the priests or *Ulema*, makes democracy even less likely than a Sunni heritage. Within Buddhism, it is tradition that counts the most, as this religion not only underlines obedience to authority but has also aligned itself through history with traditional or feudal authority. Recently the new doctrine of Asian values has presented the lenience of Buddhism–Confucianism towards stability and family authority in a new light, but has not been more favourable towards democracy than traditional Buddhism.

When we come to the other brands of Christian faith, i.e. not Protestantism or, specifically, Calvinism, then matters are more complicated. Here, contingencies will play a major role, we hypothesize. One may identify three kinds of orthodox Christian beliefs. First, we have the Roman Catholic tradition, which is basically anti-democratic, but the official stance of the Church has changed with the advancements of democracy. At first the Church maintained its hierarchical position and its insistence on a Catholic way of life in accordance with its official philosophy originating in Scholasticism. However, modernization called for a new response and the key papal encyclicals of *Rerum Novarum* and *Quadragesimo Anno* opened up an accommodation of democracy with Roman Catholicism.

According to the doctrine of subsidiarity, developed over the centuries and originating in Medieval Catholicism, political democracy has a place in society, like the market economy and the family. However, political democracy cannot prevail over the Church, or fail to respect the role that Roman Catholicism plays in daily life such as within education. This effort to accommodate democracy does not mean that the Church endorses complete tolerance or state neutrality, as it still strives for a Christian education and family life. One may expect the relationship between the Roman Catholic Church and the democratic regime to be complicated and, at times, conflictual.

To capture this uneasy balance between the Church and democracy, especially in Latin America, one may wish to use several points in time in order to get reduced form evidence for the model (M10):

Democracy $= f$ (Catholicism)

One needs to recognize that Roman Catholicism plays different political roles, often at the same time, in the same country. Thus, one part of the Church has, by tradition, been allied with the authorities, whoever they may happen to be, whereas another part has defended the interests of the poor. Nowhere has this confrontation between different layers and different philosophies within the Church been more apparent than in South America, Mexico and the Philippines. In contrast, in Africa, the Catholic Church quickly sided with democratic forces.

Second, there is Greek Orthodoxy, which dates back to the division of the Roman Empire into a western and eastern part. As long as the Byzantine Empire existed, the leader of the Greek Orthodox Church resided in Constantinople. After 1453, the Greek Orthodox Church has two centres, one in

Athens and another in Moscow. The role of the Greek Orthodox Church was no doubt enormously reduced by the victory of communism, first in Russia and then all over Eastern Europe. However, its importance has increased after the fall of communism in 1989. It was commonly stated that the Greek Orthodox Church was 'caesaro–papist', meaning that it fused with political authority. Can we find any link between democracy and Greek Orthodoxy today in accordance with the model (M11):

Democracy $= f$ (Greek Orthodoxy)?

Finally, we come to ancient Christianity, which is to be found in the Middle East. Here we have large Christian minorities adhering to Christian beliefs as they were interpreted before the establishment of the Catholic Church in the Roman Empire with Constantine. Here, we find the Armenians, the Maronites and the Copts, among others. Since they live mostly under Muslim domination, there is no way to test a model which links democracy with this kind of Christianity.

The connection between the political regime and a religion is so complex and so affected by circumstances and historical accidents that one would like to make the broadest test possible of the five models. Can we find traces of an interaction here when various points in time are examined? Just take the example of religion and politics in Africa after independence from colonial rule. Although the Christian movements have fought for democracy in countries like Kenya and Tanzania, these countries score low on democracy indices. However, one cannot conclude that the various Christian religions have been lukewarm in their support for democracy, which is actually what the lower scores on the correlations will indicate.

Empirical evidence

Let us first consult Table 5.1, which has the reduced form evidence for various versions of (M7)–(M9). Here, we focus on democratic longevity and its sources in Protestantism, Islam and Buddhism.

The main findings are clearly in accordance with the hypotheses introduced above (p. 112). The positive association between Protestantism and democracy is quite strong, which is also true of the negative association between Islam and democracy. However, the link between Buddhism and democracy is less clear-cut. There are, as a matter of fact, several countries where Buddhism is strong and which endorse democracy. One may cite Japan, South Korea, Taiwan and Sri Lanka.

The relationship between democracy and the spread of Protestantism in a wide sense around 1995, indicates that where Protestantism has a strong standing, i.e. more than 30 per cent of the population, there democracy generally scores high. But it is also true that democracy could score high where Protestantism is absent.

Here we may also note that democracy is negatively correlated in relation to the size of the Muslim population in a country. The relationship is slightly

Table 5.1 Democracy and religion: Protestantism, Buddhism and Islam (correlations)

		DEM 1972–6	*DEM 1981–5*	*DEM 1991–5*	*DEM 1995–2001*
PROT 1970	*r*	0.45	0.38	0.40	0.40
	sig.	0.000	0.000	0.000	0.000
	N	124	129	133	135
MUSL 1970	*r*	−0.34	−0.37	−0.50	−0.53
	sig.	0.000	0.000	0.000	0.000
	N	124	129	133	135
BUDD 1970	*r*	−0.02	−0.05	−0.015	−0.013
	sig.	0.851	0.545	0.086	0.134
	N	124	129	133	135
PROT 1995	*r*	–	–	0.39	0.41
	sig.	–	–	0.000	0.000
	N	–	–	148	150
MUSL 1995	*r*	–	–	−0.52	−0.55
	sig.	–	–	0.000	0.000
	N	–	–	148	150
BUDD 1995	*r*	–	–	−0.11	−0.09
	sig.	–	–	0.191	0.283
	N	–	–	148	150

Sources: see Appendix A1.

negatively non-linear. In countries where the Muslim population is numerous, i.e. more than 30 per cent, the average democracy score is lower than in countries where Islam has a very low presence. There are a few Muslim countries that score relatively high on the democracy score (Mali, Turkey), but most countries with a numerous Muslim population score low (Esposito and Voll, 1996; Lewis, 1996; Midlarsky, 1998; Abootalebi, 2000).

Let us now turn to the more difficult question of how Roman Catholicism and Greek Orthodoxy relates to democracy. Table 5.2 presents data about these two links using various kinds of data. First, we measure the strength of Catholicism for three different periods of time, namely early 1900, 1970 and 1995. Second, the democracy index we employ covers different periods of time for the post-war period, going from 1950 to 1998. Third, we report the correlation analysis for two different samples: one for a European sub sample and one for the total sample.

The correlations reported in Table 5.2 indicate that Roman Catholicism and Greek Orthodoxy are hardly any major sources of support for democracy. Today many countries where Roman Catholicism is strong endorse the democratic regime, but it has not always been so. Democracy does not stand strong in many Greek Orthodox countries.

Summing up

The findings here concerning the world religions and democracy confirm the hypotheses guiding this enquiry. Protestantism reinforces democracy whereas the position of democracy within Islam is precarious, to say the least. Matters

Table 5.2 Democracy (POLITY), Roman Catholicism and Greek Orthodoxy (correlations); Occidental and Central Eastern Europe and CIS as well as full sample within parenthesis

		POLITY 1950	POLITY 1970	POLITY 1990	POLITY 1998
RC 1900	r	−0.11 (0.01)	−0.07 (0.17)	0.21 (0.53)	0.13 (0.43)
	sig.	0.574 (0.934)	0.728 (0.06)	0.261 (0.000)	0.423 (0.000)
	N	31 (81)	31 (120)	31 (123)	39 (135)
RC 1970	r	–	0.03 (0.14)	0.33 (0.45)	0.22 (0.39)
	sig.	–	0.870 (0.129)	0.074 (0.000)	0.209 (0.000)
	N	–	31 (120)	31 (123)	35 (131)
RC 1995	r	–	–	0.28 (0.45)	0.38 (0.40)
	sig.	–	–	0.134 (0.000)	0.007 (0.000)
	N	–	–	31 (123)	50 (146)
ORTH 1900	r	−0.50 (−0.17)	−0.58 (−0.14)	−0.41 (0.09)	−0.47 (0.07)
	sig.	0.004 (0.131)	0.001 (0.130)	0.021 (0.347)	0.003 (0.444)
	N	31 (81)	31 (120)	31 (123)	39 (135)
ORTH 1970	r	–	−0.50 (−0.13)	−0.36 (0.08)	−0.43 (0.05)
	sig.	–	0.004 (0.173)	0.048 (0.410)	0.011 (0.590)
	N	–	31 (120)	31 (123)	35 (131)
ORTH 1995	r	–	–	−0.45 (0.08)	−0.22 (0.06)
	sig.	–	–	0.012 (0.386)	0.121 (0.489)
	N	–	–	31 (123)	50 (146)

Sources: see Appendix A1.

are more open with regard to the other world religions. Thus, Buddhism displays a slight negative interaction with democracy, whereas Roman Catholicism has changed to a slight positive relationship with democracy. How Greek Orthodoxy relates to democracy is more difficult to tell, as its role has been confined during the period of Soviet rule in Eastern Europe. We have not displayed any reduced form evidence for Hinduism and Judaism, as they occur mainly in one country, India and Israel respectively. One can only speculate on what Weber would have said, if he had lived to see democracy being implemented on a grand scale in India or on a small scale in Israel. He regarded both Judaism and Hinduism as inferior to Protestantism on his measuring rod, i.e. rationality.

The most stunning deviation from the Weber approach would be, we argue, India. How did democracy succeed in this giant country, although its two main religions – Hinduism and Islam – hardly score high on the Weber scale of modernization? In addition, there is the tension between these two world religions, which has often resulted in political violence. We will examine this question in Chapter 7. Democracy in Israel has been scrutinized in order to find out whether it hides a theocracy. Although the Zionist nature of the Israeli state is explicitly mentioned in the founding documents of Israel, one must point out that citizenship in Israel also encompasses a large minority of Muslims.

The strongest confirmation of Weber's theory of the social consequences of religious belief is to be found in the negative correlation of Islam with two key aspects of modernity, namely democracy and economic prosperity. However, Weber never really predicted these outcomes for Islam. As a matter of fact, Weber never wrote a full scale analysis for Islam, its evolution and spread from the Arab Peninsula to Mahgreb, the Middle East and onwards to South East Asia. It has been suggested that Weber left out Islam, one of the major world religions, while analysing the others at great length, because he had inherited the prevailing negative bias against the religion of Muhammad in oriental studies (Huff and Schluchter, 1999). Be that as it may, Weber clearly stated the relatively backward nature of the Arab society from an economic point of view and he linked this with Islam, but he did not raise the issue of democracy. Perhaps Weber did not fully realize the extent of Western colonialism against Arab countries as well as its dismal consequences?

Bypassing the issue of an Occidental bias in Weber's model of the world religions, we wish to emphasize the negative finding concerning Islam and democracy. The Muslim world must raise and debate the question of whether and in what combination Islam can host democracy. It is far from evident that religion is the key factor that reduces the probability of democracy in the Muslim world. It is all too easy to equate Islam with basic features of, for example, the Arab societies, such as traditionalism and patrimonialism. Let us look somewhat closer at democracy in the set of Muslim countries and ask which factors are at work.

Lack of democracy in the Muslim world

The Muslim world may be designated as such on the basis of the number of believers in Islam as a percentage of the entire population of a country. When a country has a predominantly Muslim population, then it can be classified as belonging to the Muslim world. Sometimes the state acknowledges Islam as the state religion or Sharia Law as part of the constitution of the country. In these cases there is little hesitation to designate a country as 'Muslim'. However, not all countries with a large Muslim population state explicitly that they adhere to Islam or practise Sharia Law. Actually, the country with the second largest Muslim population – India – is a secular state which does not recognize Sharia Law. One may divide the Muslim world into two groups:

- the Arab world: Mahgreb, the Middle East (except Israel) and the Arab Peninsula;
- the non-Arab Muslim world: Turkey, Iran, Mauritania, Mali, Senegal, Pakistan, Bangladesh and Indonesia.

In addition one may wish to mention a number of countries where the Muslim population is somewhere close to more than 50 per cent of the population: Nigeria, Sierra Leone, Chad, Albania, Malaysia and Kazakhstan. Here we will make use of a dummy variable discriminating between Muslim countries belonging to the Arab world or to the non-Arab world. The Arab society is the origin of Islam and one would expect to find the tension between Islam and democracy in the Arab world. Is that the case? One may pose an additional question to this one, namely: why is there so little democracy in the Muslim world? One could look at the Muslim world per se and compare the countries which have achieved some democracy with the others. Then we may establish that democracy and Islam are not impossible to combine. In countries like Mali, Bangladesh and Senegal the democracy variable displays quite high scores whereas countries that are part of the Arab region score low: Sudan, Saudi Arabia. Is there a special Arab factor at work?

To test this hypothesis, we suggest a model comprising three factors: religion (MUSL), a regional dummy (MUSLARAB), poverty (LNGDP/CAP) and traditional rule (ABSOLUT). We have already established that Islam and democracy do not go together in the world today. And we know that poverty is a strong predictor of authoritarian regimes or democratic instability. Traditional rule may be measured by the existence of real monarchies, or regimes which are based on royal power in one form or another, the most extreme form being the sultanistic regime (Chehabi and Linz, 1998). Here the presence of an absolutist regime captures traditional rule such as when a king, emir or sultan not only reigns but also rules. Now, which factor weighs the most within the Muslim world?

Table 5.3 tests a regression model where the variation in democracy in the Muslim world (thirty-nine countries with a Muslim population estimated to be more than 40 per cent, but, due to missing data, the analysis only covers thirty-one countries) is regressed on the percentage of Muslims, a regional dummy, the level of GDP and the extent of traditional rule in the state.

It is obvious that when we only consider the Muslim set of countries, there is no longer any relation between religion and democracy. In fact none of the models tested explains the variation in democracy. Absolutist rule does not matter, as it is only the regional dummy (MUSLARAB) which has an impact. Democracy in the Muslim world is more affected by region – the Arab legacy – than by the number of Muslim adherents.

We now turn to an entirely different aspect of the interaction between religion and democracy. It is no longer a matter of finding out whether a religion

Table 5.3 Democracy in the Muslim world (regression models)

Independent variables	Dependent variable: DEM 1995–2001					
	coeff	t-stat	coeff	t-stat	coeff	t-stat
MUSL	0.008	0.47	0.008	0.53	−0.000	−0.01
MUSLARAB	−1.293	−1.98	−1.175	−1.89	–	–
LNGDP/CAP	−0.277	−0.76	−0.188	−0.56	−0.439	−1.17
ABSOLUT	0.707	0.66	–	–	0.120	0.11
Constant	5.518	1.86	4.786	1.76	7.013	2.32
adj rsq	0.06	–	0.08	–	0.00	–
N	31	–	31	–	31	–

Sources: see Appendix A1.

can be interpreted so that it is in tune with democracy and its values. Instead we will focus on the consequences of religious cleavages for democracy.

Religious fragmentation

The argument about ethnic fragmentation and democracy may be replicated with regard to religious fragmentation. When different religions meet, then they tend to clash, at least until they find an understanding of their mutual borders. We would argue that what is at stake is not so much democracy but political stability.

There are speculations about whether ethnic fragmentation or religious fragmentation presents the worst threat to democratic stability. It is very difficult to say which kind of conflict – ethnic or religious – moves people the most. One finds instances of extremely violent confrontations in both ethnic and religious cleavages. According to one hypothesis, ethnic conflict is most prone to result in violence and political instability. However, religious cleavages in the Balkan, Sudan and in India do not display less intensity than ethnic cleavages in the Great Lakes area or in Spain.

The theory of cleavages and political stability must be made more precise in order to clarify the threshold where ethnic and religious tensions turn into ethnic and religious violence. It has been suggested that ethnic and religious fragmentation needs one more element to become a threat to political instability, but what this additional element is has never been identified. The hypothesis about mutually overlapping cleavages speaks of the coincidence of ethnic or religious fragmentation with economic disparities, or simply the combination of both ethnic and religious cleavages, as in Sri Lanka.

Yet, it must be pointed out that the link between religious fragmentation on the one hand and political instability or democratic instability on the other is far from a clear cut one. One finds several examples of countries where religious fragmentation has not resulted in a threat to the polity or the democratic regime, such as Switzerland, India and the Netherlands. However, one may wish to counter that religious cleavages present a formidable challenge to the stability of the polity in several countries, although the religious conflict is more latent than manifest: Lebanon, Egypt, China and Nigeria, for instance. Thus, we will test a model about religious fragmentation and democracy (M12):

Democracy = f (religious fragmentation)

We would expect a slight negative correlation between democracy and religious fragmentation. Religious fragmentation is measured in two ways. First, religious fragmentation (RELFR1) stands for the inclusion in the index of the major world religions, whereas the second measure (RELFR2) also includes the subdivisions of Christian denominations into the index. Table 5.4 has the reduced form evidence for the relation between religious fragmentation and democracy.

Table 5.4 Democracy (DEM) and religious fragmentation (RELFR) (correlations)

		DEM 1972–6	DEM 1981–5	DEM 1991–5	DEM 1995–2001
RELFR1 1970	r	−0.25	−0.33	−0.26	−0.21
	sig.	0.004	0.000	0.003	0.013
	N	124	129	133	135
RELFR2 1970	r	−0.09	−0.19	−0.05	−0.02
	sig.	0.318	0.032	0.543	0.781
	N	124	129	133	135
RELFR1 1995	r	–	–	−0.05	−0.04
	sig.	–	–	0.563	0.369
	N	–	–	148	150
RELFR2 1995	r	–	–	0.07	0.09
	sig.	–	–	0.369	0.255
	N	–	–	148	150

Sources: see Appendix A1.

Interestingly, the relationship between religious fragmentation and democracy is weaker than that between democracy and ethnic fragmentation. The low significance scores indicate that there are many countries which have religious cleavages but remain stable democracies. It is true, though, that high religious fragmentation is often accompanied by low democracy scores for a country. One observes from Table 5.4 how impossible it is to tell whether religious fragmentation is a necessary or sufficient condition for democratic instability.

The relationship between religious fragmentation and democracy is so weak that one must question the entire theory of the divided society. This theory singles out a special kind of social structure and attributes heavy negative consequences to it for political stability. A divided society is a country with either deep-seated ethnic or religious cleavages. While there is evidence to the effect that ethnic fragmentation affects democracy negatively (Chapter 4), there is virtually no evidence at all concerning a negative impact on democracy from religious fragmentation.

It is obviously the case that there are religiously homogenous countries which are non-democratic as well as religiously heterogeneous countries which are democratic.

The theory of the divided society does not offer a sufficient or necessary condition for the absence of democracy. As a condition reducing democratic probability, religious fragmentation is far weaker than the nature of religion itself. Many countries have religious cleavages but they remain democratic. Perhaps a democratic regime is the only one that can cope with religious diversity, which would entail that the relationship between religious fragmentation and democracy need not be negative at all.

What makes the theory of the divided society less plausible is the fact that religious diversity is on the increase. Multi-culturalism turns many countries into so-called divided societies through immigration and globalization. Thus, there is hardly a sharp separation between societies that are religiously homogenous and those that are religiously heterogeneous.

Conclusion

In this chapter we have examined the evidence for the argument that religion conditions democracy. There are two basic versions of this argument in the literature. One argument focuses on religious heterogeneity whereas the other emphasizes the nature of the religion when there is religious homogeneity. The evidence suggests that the type of religion is more important for democracy than religious cleavages. In a sense, Weber was right in underlining the differences between the world religions, but he neglected entirely one aspect of modernization, namely democracy.

In his analysis of modernity, Weber only dealt with the market economy, and his theory emphasized the implications of the essences of the various world religions. Similarly, we wish to underline that religion matters, but religious fragmentation does not. The core of a religion as understood by the *religious virtuosi* of the same religion may be at odds with the idea of democracy. To Weber the essence of a religion was to be found with the ascetics who, in each religion, drove its core beliefs to their limit – *the virtuosi.*

The key actors in the Protestant-based sects accepted the idea of democracy early on, both for society (tolerance, state neutrality) and with regard to internal matters (congregation). On the contrary, in Islam, the religious *virtuosi* explicitly rejected democracy, calling for charismatic leadership, as within Shiism, or traditional authority, as within Sunni. Roman Catholicism and Buddhism have proved highly adaptable to contingencies, sometimes supporting authoritarian rule but at other times endorsing democracy. Both Judaism and Greek Orthodoxy display theocratic tendencies. Finally, one may mention that Hinduism has shown a surprising capacity to support democracy, at least as long as Hindu nationalism does not become a dominant force in Indian society.

The theory of the divided society should be revised in the light of the multicultural society (Kymlicka, 1995). There is very little evidence for a negative impact of religious fragmentation on democratic stability. Most societies have religious cleavages today, but even when societies are homogenous, from a religious point of view, they can still be non-democratic.

Part III

Endogeneity

From the previous part, we have learned that exogenous factors have an impact on the variation in democratic consolidation. Thus, we know that the economy, ethnicity and religion impact on democracy. These factors arc largely determined from outside the political system. To the extent that such exogenous factors impact on democratic longevity, governments will have to accept this democratic exogeneity.

This third part will now examine the role of endogenous factors, and here the focus will be on institutions. Governments may enhance democratic prospects by choosing the 'correct' political institutions. What needs to be researched, though, is which political institutions enhance democracy the most. Whether an institution is endogenous or not depends on whether it is modelled as being determined inside the political system or not. Whereas political institutions can be introduced by means of constitutional policy-making, it is far less obvious that economic or social rules are as easily introduced and enforced.

In Part III we first look at the link between political and social institutions on the one hand and democratic outcomes on the other. Second, we enquire into the role of political institutions in processes of consolidating democracy during the 1990s after the major global political system transition was initiated in 1989. Third, we look in particular at whether democracy in a few key Third World countries is exogenous or endogenous, that is, whether the differences in the implementation of a democratic regime in countries like India, South Africa and Singapore are linked by outside or inside factors. We start by examining the general links between political institutions and democracy in order to isolate those political institutions which best promote the stability of a democratic regime – the perspective of Tocqueville again.

6 Political institutions

Introduction

Rules frame behaviour. Of the two major determinants of action – preferences and institutions – it is an open question as to which carries the most weight. In each specific situation preferences would outweigh rules, but from a macro perspective, institutions may explain more than preferences. Institutional approaches in the social sciences all argue that rules matter for behaviour by restraining or facilitating action.

This chapter will test a number of well-known institutional models of democracy (Lijphart and Waisman, 1996). Such models are especially important when they link institutions which are not self-evidently linked with democracy as an outcome, such as presidentialism, proportional election techniques, bicameralism and the Ombudsman. It would be almost true by definition to claim that parliamentarism fosters democracy, as the very idea of a parliamentary system of government excludes authoritarian rule. But not all countries with a parliamentary regime score high on the democracy indices, for instance with Singapore.

One may widen the scope of enquiry and include not only political institutions but also social institutions. If the rules of the most basic unit in a society – the family – are not in agreement with the idea of democracy, then political democracy may not be supported by the society in question. In this chapter we examine the contribution of both political and social institutions to democracy.

If the notion of endogenous democracy is a valid one, then political institutions must have a major impact on democratic longevity. Countries can, to a certain extent, frame their political institutions through constitutional policy-making. Which institutions should they choose, if they wish to enhance democratic probability? Besides rules, political culture may matter for democracy. Thus, countries could also enhance the probability of democracy by successfully fighting corruption in their practices. Later in this chapter we will attempt to identify a few key elements in endogenous democracy after testing a few key institutional models.

Political rules

Most countries of the world are modern states based on legal–rational authority, governed by means of a written constitution. The constitution contains a basic formal outline of the political system, which is more or less implemented in practice. Thus, the constitution provides information about whether the state is unitary and federal as well as how the executive, legislative and judicial functions are to be carried out. It is true that constitutional practice is not always in agreement with the formal constitution. In some countries, the written constitution has been suspended, as military rule is practised. In other countries constitutional practice has developed in a manner that has made the written constitution obsolete in several ways (Gallagher *et al.*, 2000). Here we focus on the real political institutions of a country independently of whether they have been codified or not. Which of the key political institutions promote democracy strongly?

Presidentialism

The structure of the executive is clearly a relevant topic for a discussion about the conditions for democracy. It seems obvious to state that frequent military coups destroy the prospects of democracy. Similarly, a communist executive is not in agreement with the idea of democracy. However, for all other alternative ways of structuring the executive, it is an open question as to whether one or another promotes democratic stability.

Weber argued that premiers promote democracy better than presidents. He clearly saw that German democracy was better served by a parliamentary system of government than a presidential regime, as presidentialism entails double legitimacy, one stemming from elections to the legislative assembly and another from the direct election of a president. Linz has presented a modern version of this idea of double legitimacy with the intent of accounting for the failure of presidential democracy in Latin America during the twentieth century (Linz, 1994; see also Shugart and Carey, 1992; Mainwaring, 1993; Stepan and Skach, 1993; Mainwaring and Shugart, 1997a, b; Cheibub, 2002).

Yet, one could launch a counter-argument stating that presidentialism would be the executive regime that is most appropriate for democracy. After all, presidentialism is in perfect agreement with the Montesquieu model of the three powers of government being strictly separated. In theory, presidentialism should be conducive to democracy, because the president is elected by the people and the regime separates the three competences of any government – the *trias politica*. The hypothesis that parliamentarism is more conducive to democracy than presidentialism is also to be found in Lijphart's well-known theory of democracy, which will be examined later in this chapter. Here we just note a kind of contradiction in the Lijphart conclusion that parliamentarism should do better than presidentialism on democratic longevity.

The key to understanding Lijphart's two models of democracy – two ideal-types, in the Weberian sense – is the concept of politics as a cooperative game with constant sum outcomes, where all players share in the distribution of benefits (pacts, oversized coalitions). When all the major stakeholders get a piece of the pie, then political stability is enhanced. In this view, politics is a process of bargaining where all players are brought on board supporting the final negotiated solution which will be Pareto-optimal as well as acceptable from the point of view of each player. This kind of democracy is sometimes called 'amicable agreement' or '*Konkordanzdemokratie*'.

One would expect a presidential regime to promote this kind of democracy, as the existence of the president would result in bargaining between the executive branch and the legislative as well as in the diffusion of power among all stakeholders, including the judicial branch of government. Perhaps democracy in the United States operates on the whole according to this model prediction, although one may add that American democracy has received a strong plutocratic bias recently, as the costs of campaigning have risen to staggering levels. Yet, what goes wrong when one after the other of the presidential regimes makes democracy unstable or even transforms democracy into dictatorship?

Let us first look at whether presidential regimes promote or demote democratic longevity. Executive power can be structured in three ways:

- traditional authority or charismatic authority: kings, queens, sultans, military juntas, war lords, etc.;
- premiers;
- mixed premiers and presidents;
- only presidents.

The first category comprises a number of different executives, but they have in common that they are not based on legal–rational authority in the Weberian sense. One may discuss whether any ruler really possesses much charismatic authority, especially military juntas that take power by force, but to simplify matters we have placed all executives that are not legal–rational in this category. Executives in communist countries have been classified according to the formal state structure of the country in question, although the real executive of many of these countries used to be the central committee of the party – at least before the 1989 system transition.

Many countries employ mixed executives, under which a president and a premier share power (Duverger, 1980; Elgie, 1999). One would assume that such a system would be conducive to instability, but this kind of executive is actually more and more prevalent around the world. In Europe semi-presidentialism is the only presidential system in operation, but one also finds examples of it in Africa and Asia, but less so in Latin America. Table 6.1 presents the reduced form evidence for the hypothesis that the structure of the executive, here measured as presidentialism, for three different periods of time correlates with democratic probability.

The evidence supports the negative hypothesis about presidentialism, but it hardly constitutes strong evidence. Two interpretations are possible given the findings in Table 6.1. Either there is a tendency within presidentialism towards authoritarian rule, as Linz claims, or it happens to be the case that countries

Table 6.1 Democracy (DEM) and presidentialism (PRES) (correlations)

		DEM 1972–6	DEM 1981–5	DEM 1991–5	DEM 1995–2001
PRES(A) 1970	r	−0.24	−0.21	−0.20	−0.21
	sig.	0.008	0.018	0.024	0.022
	N	122	123	124	124
PRES(A) 1984	r	–	−0.23	−0.21	−0.15
	sig.	–	0.018	0.018	0.092
	N	–	129	129	129
PRES(A) 1995	r	–	–	−0.15	−0.09
	sig.	–	–	0.077	0.277
	N	–	–	147	149

Sources: see Appendix A1.

Note
Presidentialism (A) = coding based on information from Encyclopaedia Britannica.

characterized by democratic instability have opted for presidentialism. To decide between these two interpretations, one needs to do have structural model evidence.

Parliamentarism, on the other hand, is strongly associated with democracy, as Table 6.2 shows. When looking at reduced form evidence, there is the risk that the functional form of the estimated link between variables plays a role. Here, one may wish to consider only parliamentary and presidential regimes, as all other kinds of executives tend to be non-democratic. Thus, Table 6.2 includes only countries with a presidential or parliamentary executive where semi-presidential regimes have been classified as a category in-between parliamentary and presidential executives.

The evidence strongly indicates that parliamentarism supports democracy better than presidentialism. Countries have a choice when structuring the

Table 6.2 Democracy and parliamentarism (correlations)

		DEM 1981–5	DEM 1991–5	DEM 1995–2001
PARL 1980s	r	0.64	0.48	0.42
	sig.	0.000	0.000	0.001
	N	74	76	76
PARL (mid) 1990s	r	–	0.48	0.43
	sig.	–	0.000	0.000
	N	–	109	111
PARL (late) 1990s	r	–	–	0.42
	sig.	–	–	0.000
	N	–	–	114

Sources: see Appendix A1.

Note
The parliamentary variable is coded in the following way: 2 = parliamentarism, 1 = semi-presidentialism, and 0 = presidentialism.

executive branch of government. They should opt for a parliamentary system of government. How about the legislative assembly?

Bicameralism

The legislature plays a major role in a democratic system of government, as it provides for both legislation and finances. It has been argued that a legislature with two chambers is more prone to defend democracy than a legislature with only one chamber. Tsebelis provides an explanation for this link between bicameralism and democracy by suggesting that a second strong chamber reduces political instability and enhances a spirit of bargaining between the executive and the legislative branches of government (Tsebelis and Money, 1997). Table 6.3 examines reduced form evidence in relation to the bicameral hypothesis.

As the evidence suggests, the bicameral hypothesis is a plausible one. Although there are many one-chamber legislature countries which are firmly democratic, bicameral legislatures enhance stable democracy as spelled out by the positive correlation coefficients. Bicameralism can in special cases and circumstances critically enhance democracy, promoting a close scrutiny of legislation and delaying rushed decisions which will encounter fierce resistance when implemented. Its impact is strong enough to make bicameralism a serious option in constitutional reforms aiming to enhance democratic stability.

The costs of bicameralism may be smaller than its benefits, Table 6.3 suggests. A double chamber legislature may appear superfluous in a stable democracy, but if the country has a federal state framework, then, in theory, there must be symmetrical bicameralism. Does federalism promote democracy more than unitarism?

Table 6.3 Democracy (DEM) and bicameralism (BICAMER) (correlations)

		DEM 1972–6	DEM 1981–5	DEM 1991–5	DEM 1995–2001
BICAMER 1970	r	0.35	0.30	0.31	0.29
	sig.	0.000	0.001	0.001	0.001
	N	116	121	122	122
BICAMER 1980	r	–	0.42	0.34	0.33
	sig.	–	0.000	0.000	0.000
	N	–	123	125	125
BICAMER 1990	r	–	–	0.38	0.37
	sig.	–	–	0.000	0.000
	N	–	–	146	148

Sources: see Appendix A1.

Consociationalism, federalism and the election system

Constitutional democracy can employ a large number of rules that disperse political power – thick constitutionalism. Two theories are relevant when it comes to rules which disperse power, federalism and consociationalism. In federalism, power is divided between the central government and provincial governments in a dualist framework involving a division of competences. Consociationalism focuses on the grand coalition or rules which allow all groups to be brought on board. Is federalist or consociational democracy more stable than other kinds of democracy?

Arend Lijphart has argued in several persuasive analyses that consensus institutions promote democratic probability, identifying consensus democracy with both federalism and consociationalism (Lijphart, 1984, 1999; see also Lijphart, 2002a, b; Steiner and Ertman, 2002). He has used ever-larger data sets to back up his conclusions about the performance record of consensus democracies. According to Lijphart, it is better than the performance record of Westminster democracies. There are two difficulties with the Lijphart theory of democracy, which is the most systematically developed framework for analysing comparatively democratic institutions and their consequences.

First, what are the characteristics of consensus democracy? Initially Lijphart suggested the pact between elites, then the grand coalition or the oversized government, then proportional election methods, federalism and even corporatism, in order to end up with almost any mechanism that promotes constitutional democracy such as legal review against a codified constitution. Westminster democracy is, of course, also one form of constitutional democracy, although it favours an adversarial style of politics and policy-making. Whichever institution Lijphart has concentrated on, it still remains true that its specific attraction has waned rather quickly. Thus, grand coalitions or oversized governments are not often employed today. Majoritarian election methods retain their attraction, at least in combinations with proportional methods. Federalism is feared because it invites secessionism and corporatism is hardly a viable option, even in the Nordic countries.

Second, one must ask whether federalism or consociationalism offer institutions that promote democracy under special circumstances or whether they can be applied generally. According to one line of thought, federalism and consociationalism offer plausible institutions when the country is internally divided – ethnic or religious cleavages – or there is an external threat – military occupation or war. Under normal circumstances, there would be no need for the complicated framework that federalism or consociationalism entails. This was Lijphart's original position (Lijphart, 1977). According to another line of thought, corresponding to Lijphart's position today, federalist and consociational institutions always make democracy work better than Westminster rules (Lijphart, 1999; Crepaz *et al.*, 2000).

The key problem with the theory of consociationalism is this: it is difficult to identify which mechanism is the crucial one for enhancing democracy. On the one hand, the first versions of consociationalism focussed on the institutions which bring about supermajorities. Here we have the idea of the *consoci-*

atio – the pact (Althusius) – as well as the notion of *Konkordanz* – the grand coalition. However, it is not easy to build a general theory of democracy on these two concepts, the pact and the oversized government, because they occur rather infrequently. Thus, pacts are mainly concluded when a polity changes from dictatorship to democracy. And grand coalitions are employed in an institutionalized manner only in one country, Switzerland. This version of consociationalism has little relevance as it captures so little.

On the other hand, the latest versions of consociationalism include all kinds of institutions which disperse power in the polity, from a proportional election system to the power of judges to exercise constitutional review. This version of consociationalism appears to capture too much, as almost all democracies now adhere to constitutionalism. When India is classified as a consociational democracy, despite its Westminster legacy, then it may be pointed out that it is a federal state that allows for legal review (Lijphart, 1996). But how about the key Westminster features of India: a majoritarian election system and one-party governments?

We suggest that the election system is taken as the crucial criterion when making a judgement on whether a democracy is majoritarian or consensual. Electoral formulas differ from one country to another (Nurmi, 1987; Powell, 2000) but they may be classified in a reliable manner according to three categories:

1   Majoritarian;
2   Mixed;
3   PR.

We will retain the concept of consociational democracy for a polity where a grand coalition is institutionalized. As very few countries employ grand coalitions on a regular basis, this type of democracy is mostly to be found under special situations such as when a country faces or returns from civil war. The grand coalition as a model of government is fundamentally at odds with basic concepts in game theory. Including all players in an oversized coalition does not make sense in general, as it is more rational to create minimum winning coalitions that are minimum sized. The requirement of policy coherence may stimulate players to deviate from the so-called size principle for coalition formation, choosing either a minority coalition or an oversized coalition. However, in general, governments are not grand coalitions in the democracies of the world.

Presidential systems, whether democratic or dictatorial, tend to employ majoritarian election techniques, although countries which have a presidential system of government can employ PR techniques. Parliamentary systems could use any of the techniques 1–3. When a country endorses PR, then it strongly indicates that it wishes to avoid the power concentration that is typical of non-democratic presidential systems. PR is a consensus mechanism. However, the opposite is not true, namely that all countries with majoritarian election formulas tend towards authoritarian rule. As emphasized several times, Westminster democracy, with its strong endorsement of majoritarian techniques, is constitutional democracy too.

Let us make a short empirical enquiry into whether consociationalism or consensus institutions have an impact on democracy. Table 6.4 has the reduced form evidence, and it does not confirm the strong claims made by Lijphart that Westminster institutions are inferior to consensus institutions. Federalism has problems of its own as the many federal states that have not succeeded in developing stable democracies shows. What remains clear and positive evidence for consociationalism is that proportional election systems promote democracy better than majoritarian election techniques. However, the use of PR election techniques is not systematically related to the occurrence of grand coalitions or oversized coalitions, which is the essence of consociationalism. It is the election system that matters (Lijphart and Grofman, 1984; Lijphart, 1994a).

Table 6.4 does not confirm the strong claims made in favour of federalism – that it is the bedrock of democracy (Elazaar, 1987; see also Dahl, 1986; Linz, 1997; Stepan, 2001b). However, the evidence reported in Table 6.4 suggests that PR methods enhance democracy more than majoritarian techniques. This impact may, though, be the same as the impact already stated above (p. 128), namely presidentialism reducing democratic probability, as presidential elections employ some majoritarian election formulae.

If one equates consensus democracy with constitutional democracy, then one could argue that this kind of democracy, mixing federalism and consociationalism, promotes democratic stability. But how could one claim that Westminster democracy, is not constitutional democracy? In Westminster democracy the codified constitution may be lacking, but this is only true of a very small set of countries, namely the UK, New Zealand and Israel, two of which are very stable democracies.

Although Westminster institutions underline majoritarian or even adversarial politics, it remains true that they are completely at odds with a permanently dominant position for one party in the politics of a country, a so-called state party, which always recruits the government. The indicator 'Largest Party' (LGSTPTY) in Table 6.4 measures the extent to which the country is a one-

Table 6.4 Democracy: consociationalism (ELSYS, LGSTPTY) and federalism in the 1990s (correlations)

		DEM 1991–5	*DEM 1995–2001*
ELSYS	r	0.47	0.50
	sig.	0.000	0.000
	N	142	144
LGSTPTY	r	−0.80	−0.79
	sig.	0.000	0.000
	N	145	147
FEDER	r	0.19	0.16
	sig.	0.022	0.056
	N	147	149

Sources: see Appendix A1.

party state, formally or informally. This variable is strongly associated with a lack of democracy. When there is a dominant party that scores more than 50 per cent of the votes, then democracy is at risk. This tends to occur in one-party states and in states with a government-institutionalized predominant party which wins one election after another (for example, Mexico, Singapore, Taiwan). It does not occur in Westminster democracies where the government party tends to be balanced by the opposition party/parties.

What remains of the theory of consociational or consensus democracy in Table 6.4 is, in reality, the contribution of the PR election system to democracy (Powell, 2000). This should be the core of this model, and not the almost irrelevant idea of oversized coalitions or the grand coalition. Only Switzerland adheres consistently to the *fomule magique* (Lane, 2001).

One may employ the finding concerning the significance of the electoral system to build a regression model which incorporates a few consociational practices but leaving the grand coalition outside, which is not really in agreement with basic coalition strategies derived from game theory (Laver and Shepsle, 1994, 1996). Consider Table 6.5, which distributes democracies and non-democracies as well as presidential and non-presidential systems onto various election systems.

Democracies tend to employ PR whereas non-democracies use plurality or majoritarian techniques. This is a most interesting finding, which may be interpreted in terms of a consociational or consensus conception. Democracies are more willing to allow a multiplicity of political parties which expect fairness in representation. Non-democracies aim at scoring one winner, not bringing all political groupings on board. However, there are some very

Table 6.5 Regime and electoral system

		Electoral system (ELSYS)				
		PR	Semi-PR	Plurality	Majority	Total
Przeworski, 1990 (number of countries)	Democracy	35	4	12	2	53
	Non-democracy	17	9	26	11	63
Freedom House (scores)	DEM 1990	7.27 ($N=55$)	5.07 ($N=14$)	4.50 ($N=42$)	3.75 ($N=15$)	5.68 ($N=126$)
	DEM 2001	7.94 ($N=59$)	5.74 ($N=19$)	4.87 ($N=43$)	4.00 ($N=23$)	6.10 ($N=144$)
PRES (A)	Presidential	26	3	15	6	50
	Non-presidential	33	15	28	17	93
PRES (B)	Presidential	30	15	20	18	83
	Semi-presidential	7	1	2	2	12
	Parliamentary	20	1	14	1	36
PRES (C)	Presidential	34	13	13	15	75
	Parliamentary	20	1	14	1	36

Sources: see Appendix A1.

important exceptions to this generalization, as there are democracies which rely on plurality and majoritarian methods such as the USA, United Kingdom and France.

Table 6.5 also shows that presidential regimes tend to employ plurality or majoritarian techniques whereas parliamentary regimes tend to use PR techniques. Since some of the presidential systems are non-democracies, this is the same finding as the one stated above (p. 134). However, there is again no perfect match. Some parliamentary regimes favour plurality (Westminster model) and a few presidential regimes use PR.

In the consensus model of democracy created by Lijphart, there is an emphasis on power sharing mechanisms. But, in deleting the idea of oversized coalitions, what remains? First, we have the election system where PR ensures the participation of all, or the most relevant, groups, securing fairness in representation. Second, there is federalism which, when it really works, decentralizes power from the central government to regional and local government. The problem is that formal federalism is often far from real or true federalism. Finally, there is presidentialism. In theory presidentialism is a power-sharing device, as political power is to be shared among the three branches of government in an equilibrated manner (checks and balances, countervailing powers). In reality, presidentialism may degenerate into dictatorship or semi-authoritarian rule – *decretismo* (Nwabueze, 1974; Mainwaring and Shugart, 1997b). Table 6.6 tests such a revised consociational model with structural model evidence.

The finding in Table 6.6 is that consociationalism thus defined matters. All the factors receive confirmation according to model expectations. Thus, PR strongly enhances democracy, federalism weakly promotes democracy and presidentialism constitutes a strong negative. This is as far as we can get in

Table 6.6 Consociational democracy (regression)

Independent variables	Dependent variable: DEM 1995–2001					
	coeff	t-stat	coeff	t-stat	coeff	t-stat
FEDER	1.178	1.90	0.550	0.97	0.114	0.218
ELSYS	2.928	7.10	2.125	5.64	1.928	5.27
PRES(A)	−1.295	−3.05	–	–	–	–
PRES(B)	–	–	−1.259	−5.91	–	–
PRES(C)	–	–	–	–	−1.800	−4.56
Constant	5.133	17.55	8.335	14.02	9.063	12.303
adj rsq	0.29	–	0.39	–	0.32	–
N	143	–	131	–	111	–

Sources: see Appendix A1.

Note
PRES(A) = coding for 1999 based on Encyclopaedia Britannica; PRES(B) = coding (presidential, mixed, parliamentary) for the late 1990s based on Derbyshire and Derbyshire, 1999; PRES(C) = coding (presidential, parliamentary) for the late 1990s based on Derbyshire and Derbyshire, 1999.

corroborating the Lijphart theory, but the goodness of fit is hardly impressive. Thus, one may wish to look at other institutions, as consociationalism is not enough. The institutional implication of constitutional policy-making in the world is, however, crystal clear: choose a parliamentary regime based on some PR technique, all other things equal.

Legal review and the Ombudsman

When a country has a codified constitution, then there exists the possibility of legal review, meaning that a court may test the constitutionality of laws and actions. However, one cannot say that legal review is necessary for democratic stability or that it is an essential element in constitutional democracy. Let us explain why. Consider Table 6.7 which has the reduced form evidence for the impact of legal institutions on democracy.

Table 6.7 suggests that the hypothesis of judicial power enhancing democracy is basically correct. However, the evidence concerning one form – legal review – is positive but hardly strong. The explanation may simply be that there are other forms of judicial power than legal review, such as, for instance, the Ombudsman. Again we wish to emphasize that constitutional democracy comes in many shapes. Legal review is one key institution in constitutional democracy, but it is certainly not the only form of judicial power or check by the judicial branch on the executive and the legislature.

The Scandinavian contribution to democratic institutionalism focuses on the Ombudsman. It has become more and more prevalent around the world, especially in countries which lack legal review. Thus, it offers a substitute to legal review, accomplishing much the same effect, namely a judicial check, ensuring that democracy proceeds according to the rule of law. More and more countries employ the Ombudsman as a complement to legal review, as it is an attractive mechanism for handling complaints and offering remedies.

The Ombudsman differs from legal review in that it is not, strictly speaking, a judicial mechanism. It is the little man's procedure for enhancing rule of law, offering the possibility of investigations into the bureaucracy resulting in criticism of administrative decisions as well as suggestions for changing practices. The Swedish version of an Ombudsman includes a strong element of

Table 6.7 Democracy and legal review (correlations)

		DEM 1991–5	DEM 1995–2001
LEGREV 1990s	r	0.23	0.25
	sig.	0.000	0.000
	N	144	146
OMBUDS	r	0.59	0.62
	sig.	0.000	0.000
	N	148	150

Sources: see Appendix A1.

legal action, as the Ombudsman is also a prosecutor, whereas the Swiss form underlines only mediation between the plaintiff and the bureaucracy. Table 6.7 suggests strong evidence for the hypothesis that an Ombudsman office promotes stable democracy. It is an excellent mechanism for promoting the rule of law.

We have enquired into the link between executive, legislative and judicial rules on the one hand and democratic probability on the other. We will end this chapter by testing the hypothesis that democracy requires congruence between its rules and the basic institutions of society. The family is perhaps the most fundamental institution for an individual in any society. Do alternative ways of structuring the family impact on democracy?

Social institutions: individualism versus collectivism

Political institutionalism has researched the outcomes of many separate institutions, as reported above (pp. 126–35). One may ask, however, whether it is not the general spirit of the institutions of a country that matters the most, remembering the emphasis by Montesquieu on not the *specifics* but the *spirit* of the laws. There is one interesting hypothesis about the sources of democracy in the overall nature of the institutions of a country, stating that democracy requires parallelism between political institutions and social institutions. This is the well-known argument that political democracy expresses individualism, which can only prevail if civil society harbours the same kind of individualism (Eckstein, 1966).

This argument focuses on the negative impact of a contradiction between political individualism and a lack of social individualism. There must be congruence between political and social institutions. One may examine this hypothesis more closely by looking at the family structure in a country, whether it expresses individualist or collectivist values. The Todd taxonomy over family structures may be employed in the comparative research on preconditions for democracy (Todd, 1985). Its eight detailed categories may be reduced into a one-dimension scale of individualism as against collectivism in the family system of a country. Table 6.8 has the reduced form evidence linking democracy and family structure.

The empirical analysis in Table 6.8 supports the congruence hypothesis linking political democracy with personal freedom in social life. The correlations between individualism and democracy are strongly positive whatever time period one investigates. One may argue, however, that social institutions

Table 6.8 Democracy and family institutions (correlations)

		DEM 1972–6	DEM 1981–5	DEM 1991–5	DEM 1995–2001
FAMSYST	r	0.61	0.65	0.64	0.62
	sig.	0.000	0.000	0.000	0.000
	N	125	130	148	150

Sources: see Appendix A1.

like the structure of the family system constitute exogenous conditions for democracy as governments cannot alter them at will. Instead, family structures develop slowly over time in response to major social change.

Rules, culture and democracy

A set of institutions securing democracy as the rule of the people must satisfy three conditions:

- channel the will of the people;
- prohibit majoritarian excesses, such as a one-party state;
- reduce the likelihood of immobilism such as ethnic or religious stalemate.

These conditions constitute necessary requirements for democracy, but it is an open question as to which political institution secures these requirements. Montesquieu launched the first modern theory of government suggesting *trias politica* as the safeguard for constitutional government. Today presidentialism comes closest to his preoccupations. But why, then, does presidentialism not work, as it fulfils the three preconditions in the list?

Presidentialism displays contradictory outcomes. In some countries it has worked out well, as it has been successfully married to both political stability and economic affluence. In other countries, presidentialism has been a failure as it has not secured democracy nor has it been combined with economic and social development. Is this merely an unfortunate result or is there a problem in presidentialism itself?

To shed light on these matters we will carry out a regression analysis testing a model which predicts democracy from presidentialism, corruption and poverty. Almost all of the countries where presidentialism has not worked out are characterized by corruption and poverty, which – we know – constitute negative conditions for democracy. If presidentialism in itself reduces democratic probability, then Table 6.9 would capture this partial effect as the impact from corruption and poverty is held constant.

What Table 6.9 shows is that the negative association between presidentialism and democracy is considerably reduced when one takes the impact of poverty and corruption into account at the same time. Presidentialism is very sensitive to the political culture, as it degenerates when there is massive corruption and a lack of social trust. Thus, the failure of presidentialism in Africa and Asia cannot only be attributed to institutions. In the African context, the concept of prebendalism is crucial (Joseph, 1987, 1999), whereas in East Asia one can cite crony capitalism (Kang, 2002).

This finding is actually strong evidence against Linz's interpretation of Latin American politics, suggesting that presidentialism is the main cause of the failure of stable democracy in this part of the world (Linz and Valenzuela, 1994). All of the Latin American countries are characterized by poverty and corruption. The level of corruption distinguishes the political culture of a country, and its impact should be taken into account in a model of endogenous democracy underling institutions.

Table 6.9 Presidentialism and democracy (regression)

Independent variables	Coeffs	Dependent variable: Democracy 1995–2001		
		Model 1	Model 2	Model 3
LNGDP/CAP 1998	coeff	1.118	0.960	1.021
	t-stat	3.77	3.43	4.03
NEWCORR	coeff	0.256	0.244	0.242
	t-stat	1.85	1.87	2.05
PRES(A)	coeff	0.166	–	–
	t-stat	0.43	–	–
PRES(B)	coeff	–	−0.289	–
	t-stat	–	−1.33	–
PRES(C)	coeff	–	–	0.044
	t-stat	–	–	0.12
Constant	coeff	−3.86	−1.610	−2.605
	t-stat	−1.84	−0.74	−1.30
adj rsq		0.47	0.51	0.54
N		104	100	91

Sources: see Appendix A1.

Note
PRES(A) = coding for 1999 based on Encyclopaedia Britannica; PRES(B) = coding (presidential, mixed, parliamentary) for the late 1990s based on Derbyshire and Derbyshire, 1999; PRES(C) = coding (presidential, parliamentary) for the late 1990s based on Derbyshire and Derbyshire, 1999.

Conclusion

This chapter has tested a few models which make democracy endogenous, or determined from within the system. Political institutions can be changed by government in order to further democratic stability. Endogenous democracy is, the findings here suggest strongly, dependent on parliamentarism and the Ombudsman. These two institutions enhance the probability of constitutional democracy, parliamentarism avoiding the confrontation between the executive and the legislature with the Ombudsman Office promoting the Rule of Law.

One may see the findings in this chapter in the light of the classical book by Walter Bagehot, *The English Constitution* (1993), first published in 1867. Bagehot saw the operation of a modern liberal regime as a government that permits the people civil liberties, but does not permit the people to abuse those liberties. There was here a system of government that rules by the consent of the governed, yet doing so by restraining the vices of those who ought not to rule. The English government was moderate and decent because of a division of government into the 'dignified' and the 'efficient' parts, and a 'noble lie' about the relationship between the two ('the monarch reigns but does not rule'). It was this noble lie that permitted the government to operate without the interference of those who would turn it away from the public good.

We suggest that parliamentarism and the Ombudsman offer such Bagehot-efficient institutions for practising democracy, promoting government which flows from popular will at the same time as fundamental rights are respected. Presidentialism is hardly a positive for democracy, although the purportedly negative impact of presidentialism on democracy may have been exaggerated in the Linz model which neglects the impact of corruption. There is little support for strong constitutionalism seeking protection for a fragile democracy by the creation of a complex of political institutions such as federalism, bicameralism and legal review. Although these institutions enhance democratic stability, it is not correct to claim that they are necessary.

Consociationalism in its classical statement must also be interpreted as a theory about a sufficient condition for democracy, namely the grand coalition. When interpreted as a theory about a necessary condition for democratic longevity, then it is the use of PR which must be considered as the essence of consociationalism. However, a country may employ PR without going to the grand coalition format, as well as employing majoritarian techniques without endangering its democracy. Thus, the strong claims by Lijphart in favour of consociationalism are hardly corroborated. Power sharing devices such as PR, federalism and bi-cameralism enhance democracy, but other factors matter more. Majoritarian democracy and unitarism, in the form of Westminster institutions may work perfectly well, which is also true of presidentialism as long as it does not degenerate.

Modelling the conditions for democratic stability, one may focus on exogenous or endogenous conditions. In the literature on the sources of democracy, the emphasis has been on exogenous democracy. In this chapter we have reported on findings supporting such a perspective, such as the role of affluence and the impact of individualism. Yet, the most interesting findings in this chapter relate to endogenous democracy. Not only is it the case that parliamentarism and the Ombudsman contribute considerably to democratic stability; what is decisive is that the largest party in the political system does not achieve a hegemonic position, whether formally or in reality. Thus, what is crucial is not only the protection of human rights but the existence of real competition among the political parties or leaders, i.e. the acceptance of majoritarian politics where the government faces strong opposition. As Tingsten underlined, democratic vitality results from both adversial politics between government and opposition, as well as a consensus on shared values, protecting both government and opposition (Tingsten, 1965).

7 Democratic consolidation
The fate of Eastern Europe and the CIS countries

Introduction

The long-term perspective on democratic stability – democratic longevity – gives a probability assessment of the macro factors that impact on whether a country has a democratic regime which implements civil and political rights. The findings show that both exogenous factors, or big social forces, and endogenous factors, institutions, condition this probability. Thus, it is also the case that individual countries have ample space to manoeuvre in relation to these macro forces by choosing the correct institutions. What happens in a country in the short-term matters too. Let us analyse the short-term influences on democracy by means of an enquiry into some of the countries that began a system transition in 1989/90 – this has been the theme of democratic consolidation in Eastern Europe (Crawford and Lijphart, 1995; McFaul, 2002). Later in this chapter we will also deal with the question of which factors have impacted on economic growth in these countries during the same period of time – the period of system transition taking place in the last decade of the twentieth century.

An examination of the consolidation record of these countries is relevant from two theoretical perspectives: the new institutionalism claims that getting the institutions right is crucial for political stability as well as for positive economic development; transition theory claims that the way a country changes from one set of political institutions to another makes a great difference for outcomes (O'Donnell, Schmitter and Whitehead, 1986). The literature on democratic consolidation takes a short-term perspective of democracy and underlines what various elites in the country do to strengthen or undermine the new institutions. The impact of institutions is thus a suitable perspective when it comes to explaining the differential fates of many of these countries.

In this chapter we focus on the variation in democratic stability in Eastern Europe during the 1990s, enquiring into whether exogenous or endogenous conditions are most important when accounting for the national differences in democratic consolidation. The purpose is to explain why East European countries differ on the average score of democracy for the 1990s, i.e. its human rights rankings over a ten-year period. More specifically, we wish to find out whether the factors identified in Part I help us to understand why some European countries have succeeded and others failed in consolidating constitutional democracy. It could well be the case that democratic consolidation is conditioned more by institutional conditions, that is endogenous factors.

Consolidation of democracy: exogenous or endogenous factors?

Countries may shift from authoritarian rule to a democratic regime. What explains the differences in the success of democratic consolidation? An institutional approach to explaining performance variations as in Chapter 6, should be combined with alternative explanatory schemes, such as, for example, a socio-economic or a cultural framework. In the consolidation literature dealing with the process of transition to democracy in the 1990s around the world – Eastern Europe, Latin America, Africa and Asia – the standard analysis of country experiences with democratic consolidation points to the success or failure of the endeavour to consolidate democracy being linked with three key factors:

- structural factors: poverty, illiteracy, religion and ethnic cleavages;
- institutional factors: presidentialism, legal system, structure of parliament, constitutional volatility;
- behavioural factors: the making of pacts, consensus building, like temporary grand coalitions, the granting of amnesties.

In terms of our approach, democratic consolidation theory may focus on endogenous or exogenous conditions. In the literature we find both a deterministic and an indeterministic approach towards democratic success in the short-term (Linz and Stepan, 1996; Geddes, 1999; see also Gunther *et al.*, 1995). The literature on consolidation successes or failures often contains case studies or so-called narratives where the interaction between various elites is emphasized, in particular the constitutional policies of the government. As there is ample room for indeterminacy in these narratives or case studies, the outcome – consolidation or not – depends on contingencies including, for instance, the peculiar actions of people like the presidents of Belarus, the Ukraine and Kazakhstan as well as of key players in countries such as Ecuador and Indonesia. We will bypass the human factor – the skill or the errors of specific persons or personalities – and target the role that structural factors (exogeneity) and institutions (endogeneity) play. Which matters most for short-term democratic consolidation, the endogenous conditions – choice of suitable rules – or the exogenous conditions – poverty, ethnic or religious fragmentation?

Democracy in Eastern Europe from 1990

The logic of democratic consolidation can be studied in the countries that experienced a profound regime transition in 1989 or 1990. Has there been a successful transition or unsuccessful transition to democracy in Central and

Eastern Europe as well as in the former Soviet Union? Why do some countries succeed in consolidating their transition to democracy and others not? We will examine this question through an investigation into the fate of democracy in Eastern Europe after 1989. Eastern Europe is here taken in its widest meaning, covering all the countries from the German border to Mongolia, including the Khanates, all in all covering some twenty-seven countries (Dawisha and Parrott, 1997; Holmes, 1997).

During the years that have passed since the fall of the communist regimes in Eastern Europe, all of these countries have attempted to introduce some form of democracy. But only half of the former communist countries have succeeded in establishing firm constitutional democracy. Why? Table 7.1 documents the variations in democracy after the fall of the Soviet Union. We have employed an indicator on the performance of democracy which allows for annual measures. Thus, by calculating the average democracy scores for a series of years in the 1990s, we arrive at the overall assessment of democratic stability in Table 7.1 (Freedom House, 2002).

What has happened is that several countries hover between dictatorship and democracy (Karatnycky *et al.*, 2001a, b). The democratic institutions outlined in the various new constitutions do not function well in several East European countries. In some countries political stability is a major concern, as there are tendencies towards anarchy or civil war. However, in a few East European countries democracy has been put in place. What factors account for the variation in democratic consolidation in the vast area covering Central and Eastern Europe as well as the former Soviet Union?

The countries in Eastern Europe have developed differently since the great institutional change around 1990, when the communist rules of the game for the polity and the economy were abandoned. As pointed out in the many studies of institutional change in Eastern Europe, the institutions of both the economy and the polity were radically transformed within a few years (Bunce, 2001). On the one hand, the rules of democratic centralism were abandoned in an attempt to create democratic regimes. On the other hand, the rules of the planned economy were given up and many market institutions put in place. One set of countries look more and more like Western Europe in achieving a democratic society with a market economy that can deliver goods and services, raising the prosperity of the population. Another set of countries appears to fall behind, hovering between democracy and dictatorship and suffering from a 'Mafia economy', which is not really a very efficient one in the sense of delivering economic growth. Can we find structural or institutional effects that account for this distinction between the two sets of countries?

The introduction of democratic rules around 1990 involved a most profound transformation of the East European polities. Many countries created new states in the wake of the collapse of the USSR. Thus, new statehood and the making of democratic constitutions went hand-in-hand. Actually, no country has maintained the Leninist rules for the state, involving the one-party state format as well as the principle of centralization and parallelism. However, not all countries have been successful in implementing their formally democratic rules of the political game.

Table 7.1 Democracy ratings (1992–2001): Freedom House ratings – scale from 1 to 10

Country	DEM92	DEM93	DEM94	DEM95	DEM96	DEM97	DEM98	DEM99	DEM100 = 2000	DEM101 = 2001	DEM9201 = 1992–2001
Czech Rep.	8.5	9.25	9.25	9.25	9.25	9.25	9.25	9.25	9.25	9.25	9.18
Hungary	8.5	9.25	9.25	9.25	9.25	9.25	9.25	9.25	9.25	9.25	9.18
Slovenia	8.5	9.25	9.25	9.25	9.25	9.25	9.25	9.25	9.25	9.25	9.18
Poland	8.5	8.5	8.5	9.25	9.25	9.25	9.25	9.25	9.25	9.25	9.03
Lithuania	7.75	8.5	8.5	9.25	9.25	9.25	9.25	9.25	9.25	9.25	8.95
Estonia	7	7.75	7.75	8.5	9.25	9.25	9.25	9.25	9.25	9.25	8.65
Latvia	7	7	7.75	8.5	8.5	9.25	9.25	9.25	9.25	9.25	8.5
Bulgaria	7.75	8.5	8.5	8.5	7.75	7.75	7.75	7.75	7.75	8.5	8.05
Slovak Rep.	8.5	6.25	7.75	7.75	7	7	8.5	9.25	8.5	9.25	8.05
Romania	5.5	5.5	6.25	6.25	7.75	8.5	8.5	8.5	8.5	8.5	7.38
Macedonia	6.25	7	6.25	6.25	6.25	6.25	7	7	6.25	5.5	6.4
Ukraine	7	5.5	6.25	6.25	6.25	6.25	6.25	6.25	5.5	5.5	6.1
Croatia	5.5	5.5	5.5	5.5	5.5	5.5	5.5	5.5	7.75	8.5	6.03
Moldova	4	4	5.5	5.5	6.25	6.25	7	7	7	7	5.95
Albania	6.25	7	6.25	6.25	5.5	5.5	4.75	4.75	4.75	6.25	5.73
Armenia	6.25	6.25	6.25	5.5	4.75	4.75	5.5	5.5	5.5	5.5	5.58
Russia	6.25	6.25	6.25	6.25	6.25	6.25	5.5	4.75	4	4	5.58
Georgia	4.75	4	4	4.75	5.5	6.25	6.25	6.25	5.5	5.5	5.28
Kyrgyzstan	7	5.5	6.25	5.5	5.5	5.5	4	4	3.25	3.25	4.97
Belarus	6.25	4.75	5.5	4	2.5	2.5	2.5	2.5	2.5	2.5	3.55
Bosnia and H.	2.5	2.5	2.5	2.5	4	4	4	4	4.75	4.75	3.55
Yugoslavia	3.25	2.5	2.5	2.5	2.5	2.5	2.5	4	5.5	7	3.48
Kazakhstan	4	4	3.25	3.25	3.25	3.25	3.25	3.25	3.25	3.25	3.4
Azerbaijan	4	2.5	2.5	2.5	3.25	4	4	4	3.25	3.25	3.33
Tajikistan	2.5	1	1	1	1	2.5	2.5	2.5	2.5	2.5	1.9
Uzbekistan	2.5	1	1	1	1.75	1.75	1.75	1.75	1.75	1.75	1.6
Turkmenistan	1.75	1	1	1	1	1	1	1	1	1	1.08

Sources: see Appendix A2.

Note

The countries are sorted from highest to lowest according to the average score for the period 1992–2001.

The contrast between rules and reality has become considerable in some parts of Eastern Europe. It is not the case that the old type of dictatorship has re-emerged, but in some countries elites have taken power more or less permanently, skilfully manipulating the democratic rules of the game. Thus, there is an institutional deficit in several East European countries, meaning that rules and reality do not match. Table 7.1 pinpoints this deviation between hopes and reality in relation to democratic consolidation. The old nomenclature has resurfaced in many countries, showing great skill in winning semi-democratic elections and directing enterprises in a semi-market type economy. Putin is, after all, a former KGB officer.

Democracy, affluence and economic growth

The countries in Eastern Europe wanted to achieve two outcomes when they initiated the system change of 1989, namely democracy and affluence. Let us see how they have done so far on these two performance indicators. There is no doubt that, as things stand at the turn of the century, there is an immense annual variation between countries in both democratic stability and economic prosperity, and that this variation has been accumulated into sharp national differences.

There is thus a large spectrum of variation between countries. A few are still to be characterized as authoritarian but many have reached democracy scores at a level close to those of Western European countries. Several countries are to be found in the middle of the scale, for which one may still have some fear of an authoritarian reversal. Affluence among the East European countries also varies; the richest country, Slovenia, being many times more affluent than the poorest ones, Tajikistan, Uzbekistan and Turkmenistan. There is a clear geographical pattern, as countries that were parts of the Soviet Union lag behind the others, with the exception of the Baltic countries. Perhaps economic development is the key factor behind the variation in democratic consolidation?

It is also the case that there is a huge variation in average annual growth rates for the last decade of the twentieth century. One may again note that the immediate period after the system change was extremely difficult for the countries that had been parts of the former USSR.

The variation is almost entirely on the negative side, with reductions in output reaching in excess of 10 per cent. A few countries display a moderate positive economic growth – Poland and Slovenia in particular. In general, democracy and affluence are quite strongly correlated and the correlations between democracy and affluence is $r = 0.72$, and that between democracy and economic growth rates amounts to $r = 0.43$. These results are in agreement with the models discussed in Chapter 3.

We may also notice that there is a considerable variation in how successful the East European countries have been in achieving these two outcomes, human rights and economic growth. A priori, one would look on the country variation as the reflex of historical legacies, which always had Central–Eastern Europe more advanced than Eastern–Eastern Europe. What we wish to enquire into is if there is an institutional effect involved: do the country differences at the turn of the century reflect not only how thorough the system transition was made in the early 1990s but also the special impact of certain institutions? What we wish to enquire into is if there is an institutional effect involved: do the country differences reflect not only the interaction between democracy and affluence (economic growth) but also how the system transition or the institutional transformation was made in the early 1990s?

There are, of course, other conceivable and competing explanations for the events in Eastern Europe after the dismantling of the communist institutions, including both the rules about the dictatorship of the proletariat and the command economy. Let us list these alternative explanatory approaches systematically in order to contrast them with a set of institutional hypotheses – all to be tested against evidence from the 1990s. We will look at both the political and the economic transformations in Eastern Europe, as one may assume that they are linked. When the market transition goes well, then the prospects of successful polity transformation increase. Let us systematically list the alternative hypotheses that purport to explain the variation in democratic consolidation.

However, these findings may be accounted for by means of alternative theories, starting from different assumptions and containing alternative hypotheses about causality in social life. The only procedure available to make a correct choice of a theory is to use the regression tool, applying the theories onto data, and interpreting the findings against the predictions from the theories.

Alternative explanations of democratic consolidation

Which are the main contending approaches to the explanation of democratic consolidation? Let us first identify the chief alternative frameworks employed to understand democratic consolidation and then use data on all the East European countries to evaluate these models (Baylis, 1996; Frye, 1997, 2002; Ishiyama, 1997; Bunce, 1998; Elster *et al.*, 1998; Fish, 1998a; Ishiyama and Velten, 1998; Kopstein and Reilly, 2000; Shvetsova, 2002). We have already touched on the economic perspective of democratic consolidation, linking democracy with economic development. Thus, we have:

a   an approach underlining exogenous factors could refer to geographical location such as the distance from Brussels, i.e. an east–west dimension, or to various historical legacies containing past economic and political performances, i.e. the peculiar history of Central and Eastern Europe during the twentieth century.

b   an economic approach would explain democratic stability with the level of affluence. An economic explanation could also relate to socio-economic variables capturing the living standard in these countries.

c   a sociological explanation could focus on the homogeneity or heterogeneity of the East European societies, where ethnic and religious conflicts have tended in the past to be more divisive and violent than in Western

Europe. In the Khanates, the confrontation between Christians and Muslims appears to be on the rise.

d   a cultural approach would deal with another kind of legacy, namely religion. It has been argued that the confrontation between various kinds of Christianity has had a profound and long lasting impact on Eastern Europe, involving especially Roman Catholicism versus Greek Orthodoxy, involving a difference between two kinds of Slavic cultures, western and eastern. Such an approach could also refer to historical legacies, for example, the late modernization of Eastern Europe, at least in comparison with Western Europe.

e   an institutional approach should select those institutions which, when in operation, have a tendency to bring about democratic stability, such as presidentialism versus parliamentarism. It is an open question as to whether institutions such as the election system, a one-chamber system versus a two-chamber system, unitary versus federal states, and independent and strong judiciaries really matter for democratic consolidation. The institutional perspective should be widened to also include the economic system and the transformation of the rules for the economy – this is especially relevant for Eastern Europe where market economies have more or less replaced the planned economy.

Faced with such a list of alternative approaches, the question becomes how to evaluate different explanations derived from approaches a–e: why has one set of East European countries succeeded (the set of stable democratic countries) whereas another set has not (the set of democratically unstable ones)? At least we wish to identify certain factors or conditions that have a bearing on why some have managed to introduce a stable democratic polity and others have not made it thus far. In essence, this is the same as the consolidation perspective. Many countries initiated a transition to democracy in 1989–90, but not all of them have consolidated their democratic regimes ten years after. Which are the conditions at work in the East European consolidations of democracy?

One can single-out a set of countries that have consistently faced problems with democracy and political stability, including not only the former Khanates, but also a few Central European countries like Romania and Bulgaria, as well as of course, the war-torn former Yugoslavia. On the other hand, we have the success cases such as Estonia, Poland, the Czech Republic and Hungary, as well as Slovenia. What, if any, systematic factor accounts for this distinction between two sets of East European countries? Or is it all randomness, lucky leadership or just bad fortune? Surely the economy must be a very important factor conditioning democracy, but does it explain everything about the variation in democratic consolidation?

What matters for democratic consolidation?

The information available on East European countries increases continually. We have assembled a data file containing information about the factors listed above (p. 141) in the hypotheses to be tested. Appendix A2 gives a concise presentation of the variables, indicators and sources employed. The reliability of some of the data is not always as high as one would have wished. This is especially true of the information concerning the Khanates. In some cases, there is simply no information available. Next we report on the findings from a systematic test of the above-mentioned hypotheses.

Let us start with the exogenous factors. It is not difficult to find evidence for the impact of exogenous factors, as Table 7.2 has ample reduced form evidence that democratic consolidation in Eastern Europe is related to enduring factors which governments cannot change or control, such as the historical legacy of these countries. At the present stage of consolidation, there is no doubt that there is a sharp cleavage between countries located in the west (closer to Brussels) and those located in the east. Countries in the north also tend to be more consolidated than those in the south. Historical legacies, such as previous political traditions and earlier economic performance, also correlate with the democracy scores or democratic consolidation.

We continue with the structural explanations of the differential degrees of success with transition to democracy in Eastern Europe. Thus, Table 7.3 contains the reduced form evidence for structural models predicting the degree of democratic stability from socio-economic factors.

Table 7.2 Democratic consolidation and exogenous conditions (correlations)

Exogenous variables	Correlation	DEM 1992–2001	DEM 2001
BRUSSELS	r	−0.72	−0.79
	sig.	0.000	0.000
	N	27	27
LATITU	r	0.53	0.43
	sig.	0.005	0.024
	N	27	27
LONGITU	r	−0.58	−0.73
	sig.	0.001	0.000
	N	27	27
CIS	r	−0.68	−0.81
	sig.	0.000	0.000
	N	27	27
GDP/CAP 1973	r	0.47	0.40
	sig.	0.013	0.038
	N	27	27
GDP/CAP 1985	r	0.62	0.56
	sig.	0.001	0.003
	N	25	25
DEMOINTER	r	0.67	0.76
	sig.	0.000	0.000
	N	27	27

Sources: see Appendix A2.

Table 7.3 Democracy and socio-economic structure (correlations)

Socio-economic variables	Correlation	DEM 1992–2001	DEM 2001
U5MR	r	−0.78	−0.81
	sig.	0.000	0.000
	N	27	27
GINIA 1996–9	r	−0.51	−0.51
	sig.	0.017	0.016
	N	22	22
GINIB 1996–9	r	−0.45	−0.43
	sig.	0.041	0.050
	r	21	21
GDP/CAP 1998	r	0.73	0.67
	sig.	0.000	0.000
	N	24	24
INTERNET 1999	r	0.64	0.61
	sig.	0.000	0.001
	N	27	27
GDPINDEX (1989 = 100)	r	0.41	0.40
	sig.	0.041	0.048
	N	25	25

Sources: see Appendix A2.

The evidence in favour of a strictly economic model of democratic consolidation is strong indeed, as Table 7.3 indicates. One could hardly find stronger empirical support for the Lipset model of democracy, relating the success of the democratic regime to the state of the economy in accordance with the civil society conception of Tocqueville. The evidence for Eastern Europe holds that economic affluence is a very powerful predictor of democracy. The economy is an exogenous factor in the short-term, but one may wish to endogenize this factor by enquiring into which factors impact on economic development in Eastern Europe as well as whether some of these can be controlled by government. But let us first test a few other hypotheses derived from the list of alternative approaches above (pp. 145–6).

The standard sociological and cultural models of democracy are clearly relevant for understanding the consolidation of democracy in Eastern Europe. They cover not only ethnic fragmentation but also the tension between Catholics and Greek Orthodox as well as the Christian–Muslim opposition. The ethnic diversity of Eastern Europe and its strong religious cleavages reduce the prospects of consolidating democracy in this part of the world. The findings concerning democratic consolidation follow the findings concerning democratic probability in general – see Chapters 4 and 5. The relevance of religion is clear from the test of the cultural models in Table 7.4, with a large element of either Muslim or Greek Orthodox people in the population lowers the probability of democracy; the former having a more negative impact on democratic consolidation than the latter. With regard to the strong association between the civil society index and democracy, it should be pointed out that the civil society and the democracy scores more or less measure this same variation (analyticity).

Finally, we report on the test of institutional factors in Table 7.5, covering both political and economic institutions. The institutional approach receives support, as presidentialism is a negative, which implies that parliamentarism is a positive. Interestingly, the election system also matters, as majoritarian techniques constitute a negative whereas proportional techniques are a positive. Political institutions constitute the core of endogenous democracy, as governments can choose between alternative institutional arrangements and attempt to enforce them. Thus, political institutions are not decided outside of the political system, or to be taken as 'givens'. The number of veto-points provided for by the constitution is crucial when democracy is to be consolidated; this finding supports the claim of thick constitutionalism.

Thus, there is quite substantial support for an institutional approach to democratic consolidation. Several of the institutional factors correlate highly with democratic consolidation. Thus constitutions with many veto-points go hand-in-hand with the consolidation of democracy. Another finding in Table 7.5 is that a higher turnover among governments is positive for democratic consolidation, whereas the only negative correlation coefficient refers to the presence of a one-party type of government. It is true that political institutions which enhance the rule of law, like the occurrence of veto-points and the Ombudsman institution, facilitate the consolidation of democracy. One must

Table 7.4 Democracy and cultural factors (correlations)

Cultural factors	Correlation	DEM 1992–2001	DEM 2001
ELF	r	−0.35	−0.41
	sig.	0.078	0.035
	N	27	27
RELFR	r	−0.31	−0.30
	sig.	0.120	0.129
	N	27	27
MUSLIM	r	−0.76	−0.77
	sig.	0.000	0.000
	N	27	27
ORTH	r	−0.10	−0.11
	sig.	0.631	0.601
	N	27	27
RC	r	0.62	0.64
	sig.	0.001	0.000
	N	27	27
CIVILSOC	r	0.93	0.94
	sig.	0.000	0.000
	N	27	27

Sources: see Appendix A2.

Table 7.5 Democracy, politics and institutions (correlations)

Institutional variables	Correlation	DEM 1992–2001	DEM 2001
PRESIDIND	r	−0.69	−0.70
	sig.	0.000	0.000
	N	25	25
ELSYS	r	0.58	0.69
	sig.	0.000	0.000
	N	27	27
VETO	r	0.88	0.82
	sig.	0.000	0.000
	N	25	25
TURN	r	0.72	0.72
	sig.	0.000	0.000
	N	25	25
NOGOV	r	0.38	0.34
	sig.	0.051	0.086
	N	27	27
TYPEGOV	r	−0.68	−0.78
	sig.	0.000	0.000
	N	27	27
OMBUDS	r	0.30	0.28
	sig.	0.134	0.164
	N	27	27
ECFREE 1999	r	0.90	0.86
	sig.	0.000	0.000
	N	25	25
ECFREE 2001	r	0.83	0.77
	sig.	0.000	0.000
	N	27	27

Sources: see Appendix A2.

also note that economic rules for the economy display strong correlations with successful democratic consolidation.

Legacy, social structure, religion or institutions?

The findings from the tables on pages 148–50 are such that one would be interested in testing a mixed model where democratic consolidation is regressed on structural, cultural and institutional factors at the same time. Interestingly, all the approaches receive support when models derived from them are tested empirically. When establishing these findings from Tables 7.2–7.5, one must recognize that there is so-called multi-collinearity among the conditions that have an impact on democratic stability. Among the twenty-seven East European countries, it is, generally speaking, the CIS countries (Commonwealth of Independent States) which score low on the democracy index whereas the others do better, the exception being Albania. And the CIS countries display this very background that the correlations reported on above (pp. 149–50) disclose: poverty, negative growth, religious fragmentation and ethnic cleavage, weak institutionalization of rule of law and the market economy. But which of these factors matters most?

When the explanatory factors are highly intercorrelated, then the regression estimates may become affected. In Table 7.6, we estimate a few models combining factors from the different approaches already mentioned. By putting one institutional factor together with non-institutional ones in a mixed model, we hope to get an indication of which factor has the strongest impact, the institutional one or the economic, social or cultural factors. Table 7.6 has a few regressions predicting democracy from institutional and non-institutional factors.

The baseline model in Table 7.6 only contains exogenous variables. Adding institutional variables in models 2 to 4, we may note that the amount of explained variance increases in models 2 and 3 where veto-points and a presidential index are added. The fourth model, containing the electoral system variable, does not, however, increase the amount of explained variation.

We may draw the conclusion that political institutions matter for democratic consolidation in the new Eastern Europe. A negative impact on democratic consolidation from presidentialism stands out very clearly, which means that parliamentarism has a more positive impact. It is also true that veto-points in a constitution positively impact on democratic consolidation. This finding supporting thick constitutionalism indicates that processes of transition from authoritarian rule to democracy may be highly vulnerable to reversals or protracted delays, where the existence of veto-points may assure that democratic consolidation proceeds despite all kinds of difficulties. These institutional factors not only play a role when other major factors such as affluence and the size of the Muslim population are taken into account, but in some instances they even outweigh them.

Table 7.6 Democratic consolidation (regression models)

Independent variables	Dependent variable: Democracy 1992–2001 (average scores)							
	Model 1		Model 2		Model 3		Model 4	
	coeff	t-stat	*coeff*	t-stat	*coeff*	t-stat	*coeff*	t-stat
BRUSSELS	−0.000	−0.18	−0.000	−0.61	−0.000	−0.05	0.000	0.07
LN GDP/CAP 2000	1.174	2.87	0.706	2.82	0.571	1.62	1.037	2.39
MUSLIM	−0.032	−2.42	−0.013	−1.65	−0.036	−3.11	−0.033	−2.48
VETO	–	–	1.290	5.77	–	–	–	–
PRESIDIND	–	–	–	–	−0.199	−2.97	–	–
ELSYS	–	–	–	–	–	–	0.694	0.96
Constant	−1.612	−0.47	−0.759	−0.35	5.186	1.64	−1.074	−0.31
adj rsq	0.69	–	0.90	–	0.81	–	0.69	–
N	27	–	27	–	25	–	27	–

Sources: see Appendix A2.

This is all about political development in the form of the introduction and consolidation of constitutional democracy. Evidently, the economic development in a country in political transition is one crucial factor affecting political development. Let us therefore turn to the analysis of economic development in order to find out what factors play a role for affluence and economic growth. Perhaps institutions are again critical?

Economic development in Eastern Europe

The system change initiated with the fall of the Berlin Wall brought hopes of not only human rights (democracy) but also the search for better conditions of living in general. Material well being had become more and more of concern in Eastern Europe, as the command economies were lagging behind the market economies in Western Europe in an increasingly apparent manner. The East European countries, however, chose different strategies for introducing the institutions of the market economy (Przeworski, 1991; Åslund, 1992; Sachs, 1993). We wish to look into whether the differential implementation of the market economy rules has made any difference in the economic outcomes of these countries during the 1990s.

Economic affluence results from strong annual economic performance. Thus, a number of years with high or fairly high rates of economic growth translate into a substantially higher standard of living, whether measured by the GDP indicator or by the broader human development index. What, then, explains economic growth, which, after all, may vary from extremely negative numbers to extremely high positive numbers?

According to the theory of sustained balanced economic growth, the output expansion is dependent on the input of labour as well as capital in fixed proportions. Besides, there is the contribution of innovations or technological change, which alters the efficient mix of input factors, sometimes in a revolutionary fashion (Solow, 2000). Economic growth may be fuelled by access to huge economic rents, as with large exploitable oil reserves. Empirical research on economic growth has singled out a number of factors that influence the occurrence of a long-term process of economic expansion:

a   unemployment;
b   inflation;
c   trade; and
d   education.

Scholars disagree as to the relative importance of these factors in promoting economic growth, but our focus is not on issues in economic research but on the impact of institutions.

Short-term factors will always account for some of the fluctuations in the annual growth rates of an economy. Thus, external events in the general international business cycle play a major role when growth rates hover. Similarly, single shock events coming from outside can destabilize an economy for quite some time. Focussing on a long period, such as a decade, for example, allows one to cancel out these short-term effects and deal with the seminal trend of the economy of a country.

It seems as if the great debate between capitalists and socialists about which economic system delivers the most goods and services has been resolved in favour of the former, as the market economy appears triumphant at year 2000, as the institution that the process of globalization cherishes. What is now an issue is whether more or less markets matter; that is, whether the strength and size of the market economy affects economic growth. Thus, the transparency of market institutions may matter in the sense that the more clearly institutionalized the market rules are, the stronger the contribution of the market economy to economic expansion. Similarly, the smaller the public sector, the larger the scope for efficient markets to have a positive impact on economic growth.

Indices are available that measure the extensity and intensity of the market reforms in each of the East European countries. Two things are important when calculating the market economy score of a country:

1   the scope of the institutional transformation; that is, whether all the major sectors of the economy are involved – real and financial economy sectors;
2   the depth of the reforms, i.e. whether the intended changes have really been effectuated, or whether, after the command economy, comes a lack of institutional transparency.

We arrive at the following list of hypotheses that we wish to test in relation to the large differences in economic prosperity or average economic growth among countries in Eastern Europe during the 1990s:

i   the stability hypothesis: economic development is seen as reacting negatively on economic instability as manifested in high inflation or hyperinflation and huge public sector budget deficits which would hamper economic growth.
ii   the private sector hypothesis: economic growth would first and foremost be generated in the private sector where productivity gains would generate a larger output. Thus, countries which have managed to bring down their public sector size will reach higher growth rates than countries which rely on high public expenditures.
iii the investment hypothesis: output is basically a function of the input of capital. Thus an investment boom will bring about a sharp rise in output, which could stimulate new investments according to the accelerator mechanism. This hypothesis entails that countries plagued by capital flight will have negative growth rates.
iv   the human capital hypothesis: economic growth is becoming more and more dependent on the other factor input besides physical capital, namely the labour force. What is at stake today is not so much the quantity of labour available but its quality, which is intimately connected with the innovative capacity of industry. Education, especially tertiary education, is a good proxy for the human capital potential of a country.

v   the institutional hypothesis: output over a longer time span will depend on the rules that govern the economy, especially if these rules allow for private initiatives and their reward in a predictable manner. Thus, economic growth will react very positively on the introduction and implementation of the rules of the market economy.

When it comes to understanding how economic prosperity has developed after 1990 in Eastern Europe, then these hypotheses may help us account for the variation in affluence or economic growth during this decade among East European countries (World Bank, 1996; Fish, 1998b; Fisher *et al.*, 1998; Stark and Bruszt, 1998; Dethier *et al.*, 1999; Kitschelt, 1999; Fisher and Sahay, 2000; World Bank, 2000d; UNICEF, 2001b; World Bank, 2002). A first test of these hypotheses is conducted in Table 7.7, where reduced form evidence is employed.

From the table we may establish that most of the hypotheses seems to be corroborated in the correlation analysis. In fact, only two of the correlation coefficients arrived at seem to be at odds with what would be expected from the hypotheses. First we may note that a large public sector in the 1990s is positively related to economic growth during this decade. Second, there are no real indications suggesting that more foreign direct investments (FDI) would be conducive for economic growth in the longer term. Otherwise the findings in the table support typical claims that high inflation and huge deficits harm economic growth, while high investment rates, growth in labour productivity, higher rates of tertiary enrolment, as well as western economic institutions implementing or enforcing transparent rules for a market economy, strongly stimulate economic growth.

To further corroborate our interpretation concerning democratic consolidation in Eastern Europe as critically linked with economic development, we test a few regression models, displayed in Table 7.8. These models focus on the explanation of short-term economic development in Eastern Europe since 1990; that is, economic growth. In new institutional economics, there is a strong emphasis on the contribution of rules to economic development. However, the impact of institutions will take a long time to work itself out. In the short term, economic growth may be more dependent on the factors mentioned in non-institutional growth theories, such as, for instance, investments, including foreign direct investments.

Table 7.8 contains the results of a test of a few economic growth models in relation to data concerning average growth rates between 1990 and 2000. The impact of economic rules are measured in these regressions, namely the overall degree of economic freedom, the level of privatization and the starting-point in time of the use of new economic institutions. However, we also include political institutions like the level of democracy in an effort to test whether there is also reversed causation in Eastern Europe, meaning that political development impacts on economic development.

In Table 7.8 there is support for a classical growth model underlining investments, labour productivity and the absence of huge public deficits which promote monetary stability or the absence of inflation. The base-line model

Table 7.7 Economic growth and systemic variables (correlations)

	Correlation	*GROW 1990–8*	*GROW 1990–2000*
LNINFLA 1990–6	*r*	−0.77	−0.73
	sig.	0.000	0.000
	N	25	25
GGBAL 1993–8	*r*	0.31	0.34
	sig.	0.130	0.097
	N	25	25
PRIVSHARE 1991–8	*r*	0.64	0.56
	sig.	0.000	0.000
	N	25	25
GGEXP 1993–7	*r*	0.69	0.59
	sig.	0.000	0.002
	N	25	25
INVEST 1994	*r*	0.18	0.33
	sig.	0.422	0.121
	N	23	23
FDI 1997–2000	*r*	−0.25	−0.14
	sig.	0.220	0.491
	N	25	26
LABPROD 1993–7	*r*	0.86	0.73
	sig.	0.000	0.000
	N	24	24
TERTIARY 1993	*r*	0.45	0.28
	sig.	0.024	0.170
	N	25	25
INTERNET 1997	*r*	0.53	0.46
	sig.	0.006	0.020
	N	25	25
REFYEAR	*r*	−0.77	−0.61
	sig.	0.000	0.001
	N	25	25
ECFREE 1998	*r*	0.56	0.42
	sig.	0.004	0.043
	N	24	24
PRIVIND 1994	*r*	0.79	0.71
	sig.	0.000	0.000
	N	25	25
DEM 1992–2001	*r*	0.66	0.44
	sig.	0.000	0.025
	N	25	26

Sources: see Appendix A2.

Table 7.8 Economic growth (regression analysis)

Independent variables	Dependent variable: economic growth (GROWTH) 1990–2000									
	Model 5		Model 6		Model 7		Model 8		Model 9	
	coeff	t-stat	coeff	t-stat	coeff	t-stat	coeff	t-stat	coeff	t-stat
GGBAL	0.328	2.57	0.272	1.92	0.305	2.12	0.208	1.51	0.288	1.99
LABPROD	0.638	5.85	0.556	3.99	0.649	5.36	0.505	3.98	0.602	4.83
INVEST 1994	0.142	2.43	0.155	2.57	0.146	2.39	0.129	2.32	0.155	2.46
REFYEAR	–	–	-0.004	-0.95	–	–	–	–	–	–
ECFREE	–	–	–	–	0.084	0.09	–	–	–	–
PRIVIND	–	–	–	–	–	–	0.221	1.79	–	–
DEM	–	–	–	–	–	–	–	–	0.178	0.63
Constant	-5.456	-3.56	34.297	0.82	-6.118	-1.47	-9.667	-3.50	-6.975	-2.42
adj rsq	0.73	–	0.73	–	0.73	–	0.76	–	0.72	–
N	22	–	22	–	21	–	22	–	22	–

Sources: see Appendix A2.

(Model 5) explains roughly two-thirds of the variation in economic growth, but, although a large public sector correlates positively with economic growth, it has no impact in the regression model. Adding various institutional variables to the baseline model does not add the explanatory powers of the new models. These institutional variables strongly covary with economic growth. But when one controls for classical growth variables such as investments, labour productivity and public sector deficits, then they lose their impact. If one argues that it takes time before new institutions can have a positive impact on economic development, then it is understandable that we only get this weak institutional finding in Table 7.8.

Conclusion

The consolidation of a democratic regime is a process that occurs after the initial transition from an authoritarian regime has started. It has its own logic involving great risks of setbacks or even reversals. After the transition from dictatorship to democracy has been initiated there may come a period of political instability, leaving the country in-between authoritarianism and democracy. Several countries find themselves today in this grey zone between dictatorship and democracy, where it is difficult to tell which direction they will take in the future.

Which conditions, then, promote democratic consolidation? What we set out to discover was whether the large variation in democratic consolidation and economic growth in Eastern Europe was conditioned by exogenous or endogenous factors. The findings indicate that economic development is of critical importance, but political institutions matter. Thus, we have found evidence in the East European developments since the early 1990s of the occurrence of institutional effects. Eastern Europe is a vast area, covering many countries, and ranging from the River Oder to the Ural mountains. These countries have had rather different fortunes after their political, military and economic connections with the Soviet Empire were dismantled. Why have some succeeded with the double system transition typical of Eastern Europe, from authoritarianism and the command economy to democracy and the market economy? Because, we find in our quantitative analysis, they put in place institutions that enhance the accomplishments of the goals of the system transition, namely parliamentarism, the Ombudsman and veto-points, as well as western economic rules.

The institutional effect is very clear in relation to the political outcome, namely democratic stability. It is less strong in relation to the economic outcome, namely economic growth. These findings confirm the general impression that it is easier to accomplish political results than economic results, at least in the short term. A major factor explaining the differential success of democratic consolidation is economic development, where high levels of economic growth are more dependent on factors underlined in the neo-classical growth model than on factors emphasized in the neo-institutional models.

8 The impact of institutional conditions in Third World countries

Introduction

Various institutionalist schools in the social sciences emphasize the role of rules in shaping outcomes. We have found in the earlier chapters of this book that rules may indeed impact on democracy. Thus, if the existence of rules in advanced countries increases democratic probability – endogenous democracy – then would the introduction of new rules help consolidate democracy in the Third World? Yet, the existence of institutional effects does not entail institutional determinism.

We find in the recent transition and consolidation literature on democratic regimes and processes an overbelief in the efficacy of institutions. Here we wish to research the argument that the framing of a set of restrictive institutions results in predictable outcomes. This is the core of thick constitutionalism: the more of rules, the better the results. We wish to argue that rules play a key role, but one cannot neglect the impact of economic conditions or social preferences such as ethnicity and religion. The theory of consociational or consensus democracy is far from the only version of thick constitutionalism. One finds similar ideas within federalism, the judicialization of politics and the argument concerning veto players. We will argue that certain rules, when successfully institutionalized, make a difference to outcomes, but thin constitutionalism may work as well as thick constitutionalism.

The purpose of this chapter is to apply a special methodology in order to estimate which is the most important: rules, culture or economic conditions. We will focus on a small set of countries, including Argentina, Chile, South Africa, India and Singapore. This chapter suggests a method for discussing how key macro conditions either increase (positives) or decrease (negatives) the likelihood of democracy. It relies on regression analysis comparing estimated, or predicted, democracy scores with observed scores.

Thick constitutionalism

The theory of consensus democracy argues that democracy as a political system requires a heavy set of strong constitutional guarantees – 'thick constitutionalism'. The theory of thick constitutionalism entails that a country is safe for democracy only if it enshrines its democracy in a constitutional fabric comprising checks and balances or countervailing powers. An inclusive democracy which brings all on board or which includes numerous blocking steps functions better than a democracy where the majority rules. 'Thin constitutionalism' it is argued, favours majoritarian democracy or populist democracy.

Democratic theory offers two contrary theories about the outcomes of thick constitutional democracy. On the one hand, there is the favourable argument, stating that the greater the number of institutions, the better democracy works. Institutional complexity furthers democracy. On the other hand, there is the negative argument which sees a clear opposition between thick constitutional democracy and popular sovereignty. Although we cannot enter into all the ramifications that a debate about the pros and cons of consensus democracy and populist democracy entail, we will state some reservations concerning thick constitutionalism. A general discussion of the virtues and vices of populist democracy would take us into core themes in contemporary political philosophy. However, here we will only emphasize a few themes.

First, consensus democracy such as thick constitutionalism embraces legal review, or the capacity of judges to act as a third chamber in Parliament, destroying legislation and executive acts which are considered unconstitutional. Legal review may be practised by two alternative institutional set-ups. According to the American model, legal review is handled by each and every judge, which means, in the last resort, the Supreme Court of the country, with the rulings of individual judges able to be tested in higher courts. According to the Austrian–German model, constitutional review is entrusted to one single court, the Constitutional Court, which only handles matters concerning the respect for the rules of the constitution or the constitutionality of laws.

One may surmise that legal review is an institution that promotes democracy. If this belief is questioned, then one may point at a few successful examples such as Germany, Italy, Spain, Poland and Hungary. However, this is too simple. Several countries, for instance in Latin America, have had provisions for legal review but it did not work out as the framers of the constitutions in these countries imagined. It is not enough to have legal review outlined in the formal constitution. What matters is the extent to which there is a real rule of law in a country. Why is legal review sometimes so ineffective?

Thin constitutionalism argues that legal review is not necessary for democratic politics. It may even have severe negative repercussions on the capacity of the population to guide politicians and public policy, offering a huge role to lawyers and judges. What is crucial in a democracy is the rule of law, and it may be accomplished without the paraphernalia of legal review. Thus, many democracies safeguard the proper functioning of the state through checks on the implementation of public or administrative law, without recourse to legal review or the operations of a constitutional court. Here, we wish to underline the contribution of the Ombudsman Office to the achievement of rule of law – the special Nordic contribution to democratic institutional development around the world.

Second, thick constitutionalism implies a contradiction concerning presidentialism. In theory, presidentialism implies thick constitutionalism, as political power is to be divided between the executive, the legislature and the judiciary, which requires elaborate rules about checks and balances between these three branches of government. On the other hand, consensus theory states that parliamentarism is to be preferred to presidentialism, as presidentialism has an inherent tendency to degenerate into authoritarian practices. Yet, parliamentarism is, in theory, closer to thin constitutionalism than to thick constitutionalism, as it entails a fusion between the executive and the legislature. Parliamentarism is also hesitant about legal review, as it underlines the principle of the sovereignty of Parliament, which is hardly favourable to the judiciary exercising a veto in the form of surveillance over legislative decision-making, testing laws and regulations for constitutionality.

One difficulty with thick constitutionalism is that many countries have several rules about checks and balances but they are simply not enforced. Thus, merely having a thick constitutional document with lots of formal rules about counterveiling powers is not enough. However, the follow-up question concerning when institutions about checks and balances really hold cannot be answered within the institutional framework, as long as it merely looks at the formal organization of the state.

Thus, we face a paradox: thick institutionalism is said to be better than thin institutionalism but, at the same time, parliamentarism is stated to be safer for democracy than presidentialism. Yet, it is generally true that parliamentary systems of government are based on thin constitutionalism whereas presidential democracies tend to adhere to thick constitutionalism. In presidential systems there is a clear separation of powers between the executive, the legislature and the judiciary – that is, in theory. In reality, presidential systems are considered as constituting a potential threat towards constitutional democracy, as the power of the president may increase beyond what the constitution entails. If parliamentarism is thin constitutionalism, then perhaps thin constitutionalism enhances democratic longevity better than thick constitutionalism?

This paradox sets up our two research questions. Let us look at a few country-specific examples which involve either institutional failures or successes. Can one detect an impact from the institutions on democracy when the influence of other conditions is also taken into account? When there are several forces at work, for example, institutions of various kinds and different kinds of social forces, then we ask which factor decreases or increases the probability of democratic success the most? If institutions matter for democratic success in the Third World, then is it thin or thick institutionalism that is decisive? There is no established research technique for arriving at such an overall assessment of the contribution of various factors, although it would be useful to be able to weigh positive and negative factors. Let us employ the regression technique.

Latin America: institutional failure?

When one asks the classical question of why North America is so different from Latin America in terms of democratic longevity, then one faces a truly difficult problem in causal analysis. One may wish to mention the general requisites for democratic longevity laid down in Part II: modernization, affluence and Protestantism, but they do not tell the whole story. To understand democracy in Latin America, or better, to understand how fragile democracy has been in Central and South America, one needs to add more factors.

There is no dearth of hypotheses suggested in the literature:

a   failure of presidentialism;
b   excessive income inequalities;
c   high economic instability;
d   dependency on the USA;
e   Spanish or Portuguese legacy;
f   the role of Catholicism.

The methodological difficulty with each of these hypotheses is that they really do not confront the key problem about the special nature of Latin America. Thus, they merely beg the same question: why is there this impact in Latin America?

In addition to the economic and cultural factors, it has been suggested that the main institutions favour democracy much more weakly in Latin America than in North America, as the constitutions in Latin America are less well protected and enforced and thus easier to suspend by means of a coup d'etat. Constitutions in Latin America are less able to protect human rights as it is easy to apply them in a non-democratic manner. Some scholars point to presidentialism and its vices (Linz, 1994; cf. Mainwaring and Shugart, 1997b), but one would then merely ask: why can Latin America not capture the virtues of presidentialism?

The cultural argument about the Spanish legacy and its negative consequences is close to the economic system argument, focussing on too much state involvement in the economy – state-capitalism (Haber, 2000, North *et al.*, 2000). Again, one would like to know why Latin American countries could not rectify a negative Spanish heritage or undo economic nationalism when its disastrous consequences became obvious. One may even question whether a Spanish tradition is such an overall negative influence on a country, remembering that several South American countries had reached high levels of development around 1900, less than 100 years after independence was claimed from Spain. What, then is the explanation of 'Latinamericanization', or the many shifts between democracy and authoritarianism during the twentieth century?

Measured over a period of roughly thirty years, average democratic scores are not high for most countries in Latin America. Table 8.1 shows the difference between North America, Central America and South America, where we have placed Mexico with Central America. Understanding these differences in democracy on the American continent requires that one takes into account both the general conditions for democratic longevity and the special factors that apply to Latin America.

Democratic probability is a function of economic conditions, culture and institutions – this is the lesson from Part II. In relation to Latin America, this

Table 8.1 Average democracy scores (1972–2001): North, Central and South America

North America	Demscore	Central America	Demscore	South America	Demscore
Canada	10.00	Costa Rica	9.78	Argentina	6.85
United States	10.00	Cuba	1.58	Bolivia	6.65
		Dominican Republic	7.78	Brazil	6.58
		El Salvador	6.60	Chile	5.55
		Guatemala	5.60	Colombia	7.10
		Haiti	2.75	Ecuador	6.85
		Honduras	6.65	Paraguay	4.90
		Jamaica	8.20	Peru	5.65
		Mexico	6.08	Uruguay	6.80
		Nicaragua	5.08	Venezuela, RB	8.23
		Panama	5.28		
		Trinidad and Tobago	9.07		

Note
Based on Freedom House estimations; see Appendix A1.

entails that the continent's general poverty is a negative, its strong orientation towards Roman Catholicism hardly a positive and its presidentialism a further negative. In addition, one would like to take the following conditions into account:

- land ownership or the *latifundia* regime: a negative.
- sharp income inequalities: a negative.
- a high level of perceived corruption: a negative.
- the political involvement of the military: a negative.
- the absence of an Ombudsman: a negative.
- the low level of social trust: a negative.
- the weakness of currencies or hyperinflation: a negative.

Table 8.2 presents reduced form evidence in relation to these factors, drawing on as large a set of countries as possible. One may object that experience of military rule (coup d'etat) must always affect democracy negatively. Since we are predicting the average democracy score which takes into account a long

Table 8.2 Conditions for democratic longevity: average democracy scores (1972–2001) (correlations)

	r	*sig.*	N
FAMFARM	0.32	0.000	124
GINIWB	−0.28	0.008	91
COUPS	−0.28	0.001	125
NEWCORR	−0.74	0.000	86
OMBUDS	0.70	0.000	125
TRUST 1990–5	0.51	0.000	47
INFL 1973–90	−0.03	0.763	87

Sources: see Appendix A1.

period of time, the military coup is merely a transient regime which will be replaced in due course by civilian rule. However, once a military coup has occurred, it may take place again, initiating a long period of 'Latinamericanization'.

The failure of democracy in Latin America appears to be an overdetermined outcome, as there are so many negatives which happen to occur simultaneously on this continent. All the general relationships between various factors and democracy in Table 8.2 shows that Latin American countries constitute negative cases. Thus, there is immense poverty in some of these countries, enormous income disparities in all of them, not much independence for peasantry, a succession of coups d'etat in some as well as a general economic instability in all, besides the Spanish or Portuguese colonial heritage which is regarded as conducive to corruption. Yet Latin America has seen affluence, constitutionalism, democracy and economic development, one may wish to counter-argue. The concept of 'Latinamericanization' involves that democracy and authoritarianism alternates, and not that dictatorship reigns all of the time. What, then, makes democracy unstable in Latin America despite the fact that democratic regimes were introduced at the beginning of the twentieth century?

Latin American politics is often described as having a culture that reduces the probability of democracy, namely clientelism, corporatism, *caudillos*, racism, populism, etc. It is difficult to capture this spirit of politics that characterizes Latin America, at least according to prevailing stereotypes. Perhaps culture accounts for the difference between the predicted score from a most general structural model of democracy and the actually observed scores? Let us focus on a few countries in South and Central America.

Table 8.3 shows the difference between the predicted score and the observed score for a selection of countries on the South American continent, Chile, Brazil and Argentina, as well as Costa Rica and Mexico. We employ a few regression models predicting the democracy scores for the period 1972–2001.

The structural model evidence indicates that neither presidentialism nor the occurrence of coups d'etat have a strong impact on the democracy scores. The variables displaying more of an effect are the perception of corruption and a tradition of the Ombudsman institution, where Latin American countries tend to score high on the former and low on the latter – i.e. negatives. Comparing the observed and the predicted scores, it is only Chile that has a lower observed score than the ones predicted. In the Mexican case the predicted scores are very close to the observed score. In the Latin American context, Model 1 (coups d'etat) displays a slightly better fit for Argentina than for Chile, whereas the best fit for countries like Costa Rica and Mexico is achieved with Model 2 (no coups d'etat). Given its institutions and the level of corruption in the political culture, democracy should actually be even more fragile than it tends to be. What supports the shaky level of democracy that one finds in Latin America? It could hardly be the economy, according to the dependency school.

One may contrast the findings of the test of our specific model for Latin

Table 8.3 Democracy in Latin America: average democracy scores (1972–2001)
           (regression models)

Predictor variables	Coeffs	Model 1	Model 2	Model 3
FAMFARM	coeff	0.003	0.005	0.000
	t-stat	0.44	0.68	0.10
NEWCORR	coeff	−0.663	−0.628	−0.592
	t-stat	−7.22	−7.27	−6.96
PRES(A)	coeff	0.601	0.685	−
	t-stat	1.52	1.76	−
OMBUDS	coeff	0.973	0.959	1.012
	t-stat	4.04	3.98	4.18
COUPS	coeff	0.160	−	−
	t-stat	1.11	−	−
Constant	coeff	8.432	8.233	8.477
	t-stat	10.20	10.19	10.51
adj rsq		0.62	0.62	0.61
N		86	86	86

	Observed score	*Predicted scores*		
Argentina	6.85	6.25	5.91	5.65
Brazil	6.58	6.10	6.21	5.95
Chile	5.55	7.61	7.47	7.01
Costa Rica	9.78	6.47	6.60	6.26
Mexico	6.08	5.94	6.09	5.78

Sources: see Appendix A1.

America with the test of a pure exogenous model, such as, for instance, following the theory of Latin American political and economic instability developed by the dependency school of scholars started by Prebisch. Raúl Prebisch was an Argentinian economist at the United Nations Commission for Latin America (UNCLA) and later at UNCTAD, who developed the 'dependency' theory of economic development in the late 1950s. Prebisch argued that international trade had not furthered economic development in former European colonies. Rather, it geared production and the socio-economic structure of a country towards the economic needs of the First World. Thus, colonialism and its aftermath had created a unique set of structural problems in Latin America such as export-orientation and unbalanced growth. Third World countries were not 'underdeveloped' but rather 'badly developed', which, at the end of the day, led to unstable governments, weak state institutionalization and the occurrence of coups d'etat.

International trade reinforces this 'bad development' path. With distorted national institutions and economic structures, Third World countries were defenceless to the distortion development implied by trade-induced interaction with heavily financed First World monopolistic capitalism. As a result,

Third World countries were pulled into a state of 'dependency' on the First World, becoming the producers of raw material for First World manufacturing development. This was the crux of the matter: the 'centre-periphery' relationship. Prebisch argued that protectionism in trade and import substitution strategies were acceptable, indeed necessary, if these countries were to enter a self-sustaining development path. His ideas were developed by, *inter alia*, Frank and Cardoso.

Understanding 'Latinamericanization' – the fragile nature of democracy and the threat from authoritarianism – one cannot simply add more and more hypotheses. Perhaps there is something special about Latin America, captured by Prebisch and the dependency scholars? Or should we go back further into history to the cultural heritage thesis, reiterated today by North (1990)? This argument claims that Spanish or Portuguese colonialism left its negative imprint on Latin America to such an extent that the past determines the present. There is surely something special about South America, namely the Spanish or Portuguese culture as manifested in language, literature and general ways of life.

Presidentialism works well in some countries but fails in others. To explain this, one cannot simply say that presidentialism has a tendency towards authoritarianism, which when unchecked manifests itself. Why were there no effective checks and balances operating in Latin America? Income inequality is high in many countries, especially if they are poor, a factor that is covered by the term 'affluence'. Economic instability has been characteristic of Latin America with its experience of hyperinflation. But why is there hyperinflation in Latin America, with all of its resources? The dependency school in Latin America used to underline the core–periphery model, which analysed the developments in Latin America as the continuous underdevelopment of one part of the continent, reflecting the steady advances of the other part. Yet, why could Latin America not break out of dependency as South East Asia did? Colonial legacies affect many Third World countries, it is true, but Latin America became independent so long ago that negative colonial traditions could have been rectified. Finally, the impact of the Catholic Church on politics has been ambiguous in the twentieth century, sometimes supporting authority and sometimes supporting oppostion. Why, then, was the Catholic Church mainly a repressive force in Latin America?

Let us see how far a model combing Prebisch and North may take us in understanding democracy in Latin America, using the same methodology as above (p. 163). Table 8.4 shows the structural model evidence for such an exogenous model of democracy.

These two models suggest that in all but one country – Costa Rica – the predicted scores are higher than the observed ones. For the five Latin American countries, Model 4 performs somewhat better than Model 5.

We find that an institutional model (Table 8.3) performs better than a model which combines Prebisch and North (Table 8.4). Actually, the dependency school suffers from a major problem, as the empirical evidence is weak for its key factor, namely external dependency explaining political underdevelopment. The weight of the cultural factor of North is hardly stronger. Our

Table 8.4 Democracy in Latin America (regression models)

Predictor variables	Coeffs	Model 4	Model 5
CENTPERI	coeff	1.009	1.950
	t-stat	2.50	12.03
TOTDEB	coeff	0.021	–
	t-stat	1.23	–
IBERLEG	coeff	2.633	2.232
	t-stat	6.90	5.10
Constant	coeff	4.233	4.908
	t-stat	14.84	26.22
adj rsq		0.39	0.57
N		81	118

	Observed score	*Predicted scores*	
Argentina	6.85	7.20	7.65
Brazil	6.58	6.68	6.66
Chile	5.55	7.21	7.43
Costa Rica	9.78	6.27	5.68
Mexico	6.08	6.78	6.65

Sources: see Appendix A1.

model in Table 8.3 also offers hope for Latin America as institutional reforms would increase the probability of democracy, despite the core–hinterland interaction.

In Latin America, the threat to democracy during the twentieth century came mainly from the military, with the exception of Cuba, where a communist regime was put in place in the late 1950s. Authoritarianism in Latin America may have its roots in the European experience in the inter-war years – an imitation of Franco and Salazar, when authoritarian politics were introduced in several West European and East European countries. Authoritarianism in Latin America is driven by a peculiar constellation of forces which reinforce one another: charismatic politicians, the prestige of the army, the hierarchy of Catholicism and the family, and the socialist or anarchist threat against the established order, especially large-scale agrarian property. The special atmosphere of politics in Latin America – high stakes, win or lose, repressive structures, weak social trust – is at the core of this phenomenon: 'Latinamericanization'.

'Latinamericanization' is first and foremost the experience of military rule. A military regime will not last long, as it is an *ad hoc* institution right from the beginning. Thus, military rulers introduce emergency powers that will last until the normal constitution can be restored, at least according to their view. However, even if democracy is restored after a few years, the experience of military rule stays in the minds of people, as a coup d'etat could be repeated in the future. Once the constitution has been suspended, democracy has received lingering damage, which makes it less capable of resisting authoritarianism.

India: institutional success

If Latin America scores below what one may expect on democratic longevity, then India certainly scores above expectation. India has maintained its constitutional democracy since the creation of the modern state in 1948, with the exception of a few years of emergency rule by Indira Gandhi in the 1970s (Jayal, 2001; Kohli, 2001). Where does the vitality of democracy in India come from, given that the country is not very modernized, extremely poor and adheres to Hinduism, a religion that Max Weber, in his comparative analysis of religion and modernity, linked with traditionalism? If it is the case that affluence is such a strong determinant of democracy, then how is it that the largest democracy in the world displays such stunning stability and vitality? In addition, India is sharply heterogeneous in terms of ethnicity and religion.

Lijphart suggests that India has a stable democracy because it practises consociationalism, i.e. thick constitutionalism (Lijphart, 1996). This may be questioned. India practises parliamentary democracy on the basis of a majoritarian election system, as it has never employed the grand coalition or PR. Its politics are extremely adversarial, involving fierce opposition between the major parties, the Congress Party, the BJP and the Communist Party in certain states. It is doubtful whether India adheres to full-scale thick constitutionalism, although its federalist system of government is effective in dispersing power.

India practises constitutional democracy in combination with its majoritarian parliamentary executive. In addition, the country has a federal system of government which is not merely a façade but actually decentralizes power to the various states. It has a double chamber legislature and there is a constitutional court which engages in legal review. However, the Indian political system does not operate according to the logic of a consensus democracy like, for example, Switzerland. Political power is concentrated in the hands of the Premier, despite the immense size of the country and its enormous ethnic and religious diversity, which is often reflected in different political traditions at the state level.

Poverty in India, as well as its cultural diversity, should make the country democratically unstable, as these are the general relationships which apply to all countries around the globe – see Chapters 3, 4 and 5. However, Indian democracy appears far more stable and vital than democracy in any other Third World country. Can we conclude that the key political institutions of India counteract the negative impact from the lack of basic social and economic requisites of democracy?

To explain democratic performance in India, one cannot use the standard factors outlined in Part II, i.e. modernization, affluence, cultural homogeneity or an individualist and rationalistic religion. India has none of these attributes. One must search for the sources of democratic stability and vitality in India elsewhere than in a standard exogenous model of democracy. Clearly India must be seen as a case of institutional success, but which institutions have maintained India as a democracy? The solution is that one either searches for the roots of Indian democracy in the historical legacy of the country as a British colony, or one focuses on the combined effect of its institutions. There one may debate as to whether it is a matter of thick constitutionalism, as with consensus democracy, or merely thin constitutionalism, for instance, parliamentarism and the Ombudsman. Let us first look at correlations and then at regression models.

Table 8.5 contains a general estimation of the impact of a variety of political institutions on democracy. The Indian version of these institutions can hardly do better than the average scores reported on here, at least not in the long term.

The evidence reported in Table 8.5 hardly supports the claims that thick constitutionalism protects democracy better than thin constitutionalism. The key institution is parliamentarism, which, in India, comes in the clear form of British adversarial politics. Perhaps democracy is best served when two or more groups do not make up an elite separate from ordinary people, but interact in a vigilant manner in order to make all players respect the rules of the game? The second most important institution for promoting democracy is the Ombudsman. Again, this is what thin constitutionalism in India provides for: majoritarian politics and the rule of law.

Let us proceed to an analysis of the difference between predicted scores from a plausible regression model to the actual scores for India. In the difference between these two scores – predicted and observed – lies what remains to be explained, although we can only guess about what factors may be involved. Thus, Table 8.6 presents an analysis of India focussing on the role of its institutions in preserving constitutional democracy, while acknowledging the negative impact of poverty and ethnic diversity on democratic stability.

In this model, affluence and the political institutions of parliamentarism and the Ombudsman clearly have a positive impact on democratic performance when measured as the average score for the period 1972 to 2001. Yet, although the model suggests a good fit with an explained variation close to 75 per cent, it is obvious that, in India, the observed score is higher than the scores predicted by the models. India is, after all, one of the poorest countries in the world. Thus, there are factors operating in India which are conducive

Table 8.5 Democracy (average scores for 1972–2001) and institutions (correlations)

	r	*sig.*	N
FEDER	0.27	0.002	124
PARLIAM	0.60	0.000	125
BICAMER	0.40	0.000	123
LEGREV	0.25	0.007	121
OMBUDS	0.70	0.000	125
ELSYS	0.42	0.000	120
BRITLEG	0.09	0.309	125

Sources: see Appendix A1.

Table 8.6 Democracy in India: average scores (1972–2001) (regression models)

Predictor variables	Coeffs	Model 6	Model 7
LNGDP/CAP	coeff	0.930	0.950
	t-stat	5.83	6.17
ELF	coeff	−1.065	−0.988
	t-stat	−2.13	−1.99
FAMFARM	coeff	0.007	−
	t-stat	1.09	−
OMBUDS	coeff	1.269	1.124
	t-stat	6.56	3.31
PARLIAM	coeff	1.026	1.296
	t-stat	2.93	6.74
Constant	coeff	−3.446	−3.348
	t-stat	−2.60	−2.53
adj resq		0.73	0.73
N		112	112
	Observed score	Predicted scores	
India	7.35	6.82	6.81

Sources: see Appendix A1.

for the democratic performance of the country other than parliamentarism and the Ombudsman. We suggest that it is the British legacy of rule of law which framed the mind of India to a considerable extent.

South Africa: institutional engineering

The transition to democracy in the Republic of South Africa (RSA) was a typical example of institutionalism, or the belief that creating a state with rule of law with a plethora of institutions is a sine qua non for enhancing the probability for a successful transition to democracy. Yet, the developments in South Africa raise a few questions concerning the limits of constitutional engineering for democratic transition in Third World countries (Ake, 1996; Haynes, 2001). However critical it is for constitutional institutions to be established in a written constitution, the prospects of the South African regime transition will depend just as much on the social and economic forces at work (Southall, 2000).

On the African continent, the distinction between constitutional theory and constitutional praxis could hardly be more relevant. Outcomes depend not only on the framing of constitutional documents, but also (or even more) on the way in which the various political elites manoeuvre in relation to the institutions. It is how the constitutional provisions are interpreted and implemented that is decisive for the consolidation of democracy.

Constitutional engineering, or the agreement on a public law framework introducing both democracy and the rule of law, may be a necessary condition for democratic success, but it could hardly be a sufficient one, as institutions, however important they may be, operate in an environment where various forces impact on democracy and its stability. A constitutional state may be outlined on paper, but how institutions operate is decided by ongoing practice. There are many instances of formal constitutions or institutions on paper never being implemented, showing that blunt institutionalism simply does not work. Besides institutions, the probability of successful democratic transition depends on social structure and elite behaviour. How the political elites interpret the institutions is critically important for the implementation of public law articles, as opportunistic behaviour may lead elites towards confrontation concerning the implementation of the constitution.

There are certain macro relations between society and democracy, as well as between political institutions and democracy, that one may employ in trying to pin down what the prospects for a single country are. It is a matter of probabilities, because no deterministic relations are known, meaning that there are many exceptions. But, when several factors are relevant for one and the same country, then what is the overall judgement that one can make? If one could arrive at techniques for somehow adding correlations into probabilities, then it would advance our knowledge about democratic transition quite considerably. Let us here employ regression analysis as a tool for looking into how a specific case (RSA) fits into the general pattern identified for macro relations between various factors and democratic stability.

The political transformation of South Africa focussed on institutions (Jung and Shapiro, 1995; Koelble and Reynolds, 1996). What was attempted was the introduction of a strong constitutional state with numerous institutions, safeguarded by judicial bodies including the Constitutional Court, the Supreme Court, various commissions and an Ombudsman. At the same time, political transformation took place in relation to the strong social forces of the country, including sharp social heterogeneity along classical cleavage lines – mainly ethnicity, but also class and religion. The behaviour of the political elites was highly influential in shaping the short-term outcomes, including the arrival of a multi-party system with one dominant party (Johnson and Schlemmer, 1996). South Africa is a medium income country with an economy where market institutions play a considerable role. Now, taken one by one, what do these factors entail for the long-term success of democracy in South Africa?

Evidently, the RSA can do no better than an average country does. For some period of time, a country may achieve extraordinary outcomes, but exceptionalism is hardly possible in the long-term. Any judgement about the probability of democratic success in the RSA must, we argue, consider and take into account the known macro relationships concerning the effects of various social factors and institutional items, each having an impact on democratic stability. There is no doubt that the level of democracy has increased in the Republic of South Africa, employing some standard indices on civil and political rights.

Employing a scale of democracy which ranges from 1 to 10, the RSA must be said to have reached a very high level of democracy as a result of the fundamental regime change, initiated by De Klerk in 1990. One may actually question the validity of the high scores for the period around 1995, as the RSA had severe problems with political violence not only in this year but also during the early 1990s. One could characterize the situation in rural parts of KwaZulu Natal as a low-scale-intensity civil war, but the tribal factor has also been at work besides political antagonism between two of the political parties: the ANC and the Inkatha Freedom Party. The existence of political antagonism may provide various groups with ample opportunities for settling old scores dating back into the history of tribal and racial conflict in the complex ethnic mosaic of the RSA.

Yet, this is not the place to debate the merits of various international scales on democracy, as we focus on the likelihood of democratic stability (see Chapter 1). Focussing on the occurrence of political violence, one could argue from a short-term perspective that the RSA was, in 1995, a semi-democracy with a great potential for democratic deepening. However, even if one frames the research question in this manner, one faces the very same problem about long-term probabilities: could the RSA reach and maintain these high scores of democracy? Let us consider the macro forces that impinge on the probability of democratic longevity and relate the RSA to these macro forces.

What now follows is an examination of the Republic of South Africa, based on a number of well-known social science models, picturing associations between macro properties and democracy or democratic stability (Lipset *et al.*, 1993; Lipset, 1994; Przeworski *et al.*, 1996, 2000). We start with the major factors that impact on democracy. Then we estimate the macro relations between these forces and the degree of democracy on the basis of data from the late 1990s (1995–2001). Finally, we place South Africa in relation to these macro forces by means of comparing estimated scores of democracy with the observed ones.

For instance, it is certainly not enough to suggest that democracy in South Africa faces a difficulty due to ethnic or religious heterogeneity, because one needs to know in the first place whether heterogeneity is associated with democratic instability or authoritarian rule, generally speaking. Estimating the probability of democratic success in the RSA involves two things: (a) positioning the country in relation to macro forces, and (b) selecting those macro forces that matter according to well established social science models. With this in mind, we will proceed according to this two-step procedure. The analysis starts from the social and cultural factors that affect democratic longevity. To these factors we can then add institutional ones. The dependent variable in Tables 8.7 and 8.8 (pp. 172 and 175) is the average democracy score for the years 1995 to 2001. The predicted democracy scores for the RSA have been estimated through the employment of regression analysis.

If there is a divergence between the predicted score, using the bi-variate regression, and the observed score, then the country will have a higher or lower value of democracy than is actually warranted by the condition in question. What is critically important, besides the direction and strength of the macro relationship is, however, also the position or value of the country on the predictor variable.

Economic, social and cultural factors

The structure of society is relevant for the probability of democratic success. One may focus on either modernization or cleavages. Table 8.7 has the information about correlations, bi-variate regressions and the predicted democracy scores.

The population of South Africa may be classified according to race or according to ethnic community, as defined mainly but not exclusively by language. The population has increased sharply over the past decade and is expected to continue to grow to 60 million people by 2010. The rapid population growth among blacks has changed the numerical proportions between the four races in South Africa. At the same time, South Africa has received a large number of illegal immigrants, the exact number of which is not known.

There is little to suggest any correlation between race and democracy, simply because race is a very difficult concept to measure. Even if the composition of the population of South Africa is increasing most in the black community, there is nothing to suggest that this is a negative for democratic likelihood. Racial diversity could be a negative for democratic stability, especially if the racial distribution of the population varies considerably from one part of the country to another. It is true that the regional distribution of the Asian and Coloured populations is highly uneven, the first concentrated in KwaZulu Natal and the second in the Western Cape, but there is a substantial white population in the provinces of Gauteng, the Western Cape, the Northern Cape as well as around Blomfontein and Durban. The most densely populated province is that of KwaZulu Natal with some 8.5 million people, whereas about 6.8 million live in Gauteng.

Instead of race, one should focus on ethnic diversity in relation to the RSA. Diversity in the social structure of South Africa is based on the existence of several ethnic communities. It can readily be seen that the Zulu speakers constitute the largest ethnic community in South Africa, living mainly in KwaZulu Natal. But the political implications of the language divisions are far from straightforward, because the Zulus include several different tribes. One political party, the Inkatha Freedom Party, has attempted to mobilize Zulu

Table 8.7 Structural factors: observed (average 1995–2001) versus predicted democracy scores for the RSA

Predictor	r	rsq	Observed score	Predicted score
ELF1	−0.26	0.065	9.25	4.68
RELFR1	−0.04	0.001	9.25	5.76
PROT	0.41	0.168	9.25	7.19
GINIWB	−0.23	0.051	9.25	5.42
LNGDP/CAP	0.63	0.402	9.25	7.32
HDI	0.54	0.296	9.25	6.33
AGREMPL	−0.52	0.274	9.25	7.22
IMPEX 1975–98	0.06	0.003	9.25	5.92

Sources: see Appendix A1.

nationalism, but nonetheless the African National Congress (ANC) received widespread support in the province of KwaZulu Natal during the local government elections in 1996, especially in the urban areas. Thus, the ANC attracts not only the votes of the Xhosa, Sotho, Tswana and Venda tribes, but its electorate also includes many Zulus.

In addition, it should be remembered that many South Africans speak more than one language, and also that some of the African languages are closely related. For example, Siswati, Zulu and Xhosa are all Nguni languages. In addition, the compactness of the major ethnic communities is far from tight, as they include groups with different orientations. Thus, even the whites are to some extent divided along Afrikaans-speaking and English-speaking communities, reflecting their different historical pasts as well as the political struggles in the RSA since 1910. The Coloured and the Asian communities also have special historical roots, the former identifying with an indigenous population and the latter arriving in South Africa at the end of the nineteenth century.

Ethnic cleavages are very often claimed to be a major problem for democratic stability in the RSA, but there is little support for this argument when one examines macro correlations. It is true that the RSA scores very high on the index on ethnic heterogeneity (ELF1 in RSA = 0.87), but the association between ethnic heterogeneity and democracy is based on a weak, though negative, correlation, or $r = -0.26$. There are many democracies that are ethnically divided yet still work well; and there are several dictatorships that operate in homogeneous countries. Per se, high ethnic diversity is a slight negative reducing the probability of democratic success in South Africa somewhat, as one can see from the distance between predicted and observed scores. But what is the importance of religion?

Religion could constitute a powerful source of cleavage in the deeply divided society of the RSA. Yet religion has not been the rallying point of political mobilization to any great extent, although there is an African Christian Democratic Party. Among many rural and even urbanized people, traditional animist religious practices still occur. Religious heterogeneity (RELFR1 in RSA = 0.453), however, hardly constitutes a major drawback for democratic stability in South Africa, because the macro association between religious diversity and the extent of democracy is close to zero. The impact of religion on democracy stems much more from the kind of religion practised in the country, where there is a general positive association between the strength of Protestantism and the likelihood of democracy, or $r = 0.41$. This is a clear positive for South Africa, because various kinds of Protestant creeds have a strong position (PROT 1995 in RSA = 33.8) in the country among the various ethnic groups.

How about class? A major concern has been the unequal income distribution with a high Gini coefficient (GINIWB in RSA = 0.59), one of the highest in the world. There has been considerable discussion about whether the new government's policy should emphasize growth or redistribution, given a trade-off between efficiency and equity. It appears that the major new policy for development, the Reconstruction and Development Programme, attempts to promote both objectives, but the accomplishments have been meagre thus far. What are the implications for democratic viability of sharp income inequalities?

The cross-sectional evidence indicates a negative correlation between income inequality and democracy, but it is not strong, $r = -0.23$. Yet the RSA has such an extremely unequal distribution of income that we here have a negative, and there is also a sharp distance between observed and predicted score. It remains to be seen whether income differences will decrease now that legal restrictions in labour and capital mobility have been removed. If South Africa embarks on a process of sustained economic growth, then the income differences will decrease, whether the RDP programme is successful or not.

Now, let us see what the modernization models imply about South Africa's chances of reaching a stable democracy. Among the modernization forces that impinge on the likelihood of democratic success, one should distinguish between affluence on the one hand and its social correlates – industrialization, third sector size and quality of life – on the other.

South Africa has an industrialized and urbanized economy – this is a major positive. The overall urbanization rate is 65 per cent, yet the literacy rate stands at only 62 per cent, whereas life expectancy is 63.4 years. For a very large number of people, urbanization has taken place only recently. There are signs of the emergence of a post-industrial economy, although the state remains a Third World country as measured by gross domestic product (GDP) per capita. The contribution of the tertiary sector to GDP in 1993 was larger than that of the combined primary and secondary sectors.

Having a pronounced population growth, it is vital that the economy should have a growth rate which at least matches the population increase in total output. However, the growth rate in the economy has barely matched that of the population increase in the early 1990s. Economic growth rates have fallen dramatically over the last decades. Between 1960 and 1969, the average growth rate was 5.6 per cent. From 1970 to 1979 it was 3.3 per cent and between 1980 and 1989 it amounted to 2.0 per cent. In the 1990s, economic growth during the period 1990 to 1998 has swung to being negative, with a growth of -0.1 per cent. This means that the growth in total output is insufficient to offset population growth, which amounts to about 2.3 per cent a year during the same period of time.

The positive macro correlation about economic conditions for democracy indicates that the level of affluence is a most powerful condition for the likelihood of democracy ($r = 0.63$). Since average GNP per capita in South Africa is not high (GNP in PPP 1998 = US\$8295), the RSA receives a predicted score below its observed score on democracy. Thus, in the long-term, there must be economic growth in order to take full advantage of the positive connection between affluence and democracy. At the same time, it must be pointed out that the RSA is not a poor country. The size of agricultural employment affects democratic viability, $r = -0.52$, but this is hardly a negative for the RSA (AGREMPL 1990 for RSA = 13 per cent), since its population is concentrated mainly to industry and the third sector. Yet, the economic conditions for democracy in South Africa are somewhat weak, as the predicted score for quality of life indicates. There is a strong positive correlation between human development and democracy ($r = 0.54$), but the low score on the HDI for the RSA (HDI 1998 = 0.717) implies a distance between observed and predicted scores.

The critical question becomes, then, if the level of affluence can be maintained and hopefully augmented during the next decades. After all, South Africa is placed at the lower end of the scale of the medium income countries which could worsen, if economic growth does not pick up substantially, compensating for the immense increase in population.

In addition, one would want to take into account the macro relationship between the openness of the economy (imports and exports/total output) and democracy. Here we have a positive for South Africa as the country has considerable openness (IMPEX 1975–98 = 50.0), but the macro correlation is not particularly strong, although positive. Let us now look at economic and political institutions.

Institutional factors

Since South Africa is running a sharp deficit on the social and economic factors impacting on democracy, one may wish to look at the impact of either economic or political institutions on democracy. The basic kind of economic system a country has is as relevant as the kind of government institutions a country operates. Table 8.8 displays the information about macro correlations, bi-variate regressions and predicted democracy scores.

One may consider South Africa as a market economy, but such a general classification fails to take into account the many forms of state intervention that characterized the apartheid economy. What has taken place after the regime transition is a considerable liberalization of the economy. A widely debated question is whether affirmative action programmes should be employed in the recruitment of people to new positions in the public and private sectors. What should be done with the parastatal corporations? Transnet and Telkom, as well as other public corporations, employ large numbers of people. There has been much public discussion about the

Table 8.8 Institutional factors: observed (average 1995–2001) versus predicted democracy scores for the RSA

Predictor	r	rsq	Observed score	Predicted score
HERITAGE	0.76	0.573	9.25	6.53
FEDER (RSA = 0)	0.16	0.025	9.25	5.72
FEDER (RSA = 1)	0.18	0.031	9.25	7.21
PRES(A) (RSA = 0)	−0.11	0.011	9.25	6.10
PRES(A) (RSA = 1)	−0.09	0.008	9.25	5.53
PARLIAM (RSA = 0)	0.49	0.239	9.25	5.06
PARLIAM (RSA = 1)	0.50	0.253	9.25	8.38
LGSTPTY	−0.79	0.617	9.25	5.78

Sources: see Appendix A1.

introduction of privatization as the new government tries to undo many of the restrictions on the South African economy put into place in the past. Thus, trade barriers have been lowered substantially in order to increase competition in the economy. The economic policies of the new government need to take account of South Africa's connections with the international economy because the South African economy is an open one. The new government has lifted some of the restrictions on the currency, abolishing the two-currency system that used to prohibit capital flight. The rand, however, has depreciated over several years, as South Africa's foreign liabilities are larger than its foreign assets while, at the same time, the deficit on the state budget is substantial.

The increased openness of the South Africa economy is thus a positive. The same judgement can be made for the development of the economic institutions (HERITAGE 2000 for RSA = 2.10), which is clearly more in the direction of a market economy. The less the state control of the economy, the higher the probability of democratic success, or $r = 0.76$. State-capitalist systems perform badly on democracy, which is the kind of regime that apartheid would be classified under. What about the political institutions?

Constitutional engineering has no doubt changed the mode of political interaction from confrontation and large-scale repression to bargaining and mutual respect. Despite the erection of a strong constitutional state, there is no solution in sight to the problem of the interpretation of the nature of the South African state itself: unitary or federal, centralized or decentralized. Federalist and unitarist forces have confronted each other not only over the interim and definitive versions of the national constitution, but also over the possibility of regional constitutions. There is clearly a case for more federalist institutions in South Africa, as some of the regions include different cultures and past memories. Yet, it must be underlined that a move towards federalism would not dramatically improve the likelihood of democratic success in the long-term, because federalist institutions are not a necessary or sufficient condition for democracy, the macro correlation between federalist institutions and the extent of democracy being weak ($r = 0.16$). More important for South Africa and its future democracy is the structure of the executive, where the low degree of parliamentarism is a major negative.

Thus, whether the RSA is to be interpreted as a federal or a unitary state does not, per se, matter for democratic viability. The macro correlations for political institutions and democracy show that federalism is only marginally important for democracy. But more important are the government mechanisms, especially the structure of the executive. First, there is, among the macro correlations, a slight negative impact of presidentialism on democratic stability, as well as a clear positive impact of parliamentarism, $r = 0.50$.

The peculiar feature of the RSA is that it is both presidential and parliamentary (this is why we have made estimates for RSA as (non)parliamentarian as well as (non)presidential), as Mbeki has the presidential position with considerable prerogatives, although he was indirectly elected, but both he and his cabinet reflect a Premier system, dependent on the support of the Parliament. It would have enhanced democratic prospects if the new Constitution had more transparently endorsed parliamentarism, as appears from the large distance between predicted and observed score on this factor.

If constitutionalism is the first major feature of regime transition in South Africa, then consociationalism has been the second. The key players from the large social groups, in Lijphart's (1977) interpretation, shared executive powers during the transition period, from May 1994 to May 1996, as recommended for the RSA by Lijphart himself (1985; see also Lijphart 1994b, 1998, 2002a). But consociationalism is, at the moment, only partial, as only the ANC and the Inkatha Freedom Party share power (Connors, 1996). Ethnic mobilization of the different zuilen, or camps, although strong, is far from complete, as both Mandela and de Klerk tried catch-all strategies, whereas Buthelezi mainly attempted to attract the Zulu vote. Two of these three players have now withdrawn, and it is interesting to see how the new generation of leaders (Thabo Mbeki, Tony Leon, Martinius van Scahlkwyk) position themselves in relation to consociationalism, or the making of concurrent majorities in the early 2000s, which the new and final constitution neither rules out nor recommends.

Of critical importance, however, is the potential for true competition among the political parties, given their support among the population at large. The constitutional solution, negotiated in the early 1990s, underlined the importance of having oversized coalitions, i.e. the theme of consociationalism. However, what temporarily remains of the broad government of national unity, set up in 1994, is a coalition between the ANC and the Inkatha Freedom Party. The macro correlation shows that a hegemonic position for one of the parties is no good for democracy, or $r = -0.79$ for party size and democracy, meaning that the larger the electoral support for the largest party, the less the democratic prospects. Actually, the dominant position of the ANC constitutes a future threat (LGSTPTY 1995 = 62.7), as the party could develop along the lines of other dominant parties such as the Mexican case, the Singapore case or the Indian case.

One obtains much the same finding when one examines the institutional residuals as in the analysis of the structural residuals. The general impression is that the actual democracy score is at a very high level, which is hardly supported by the social and political conditions that either negatively or positively impact on the probability of democracy.

One could argue that the combined democracy score for the period 1995 to 2001 does not measure the real predicament, because the democratic procedures operate less smoothly than the score indicates. However, one could also argue, accepting the high democracy ranking, that democracy in the RSA lacks a strong structural and institutional foundation. Looking at the distance between predicted and observed scores in Table 8.7 and Table 8.8, one may enquire into the combined effect of the conditions impacting on democracy as it works out for the RSA. It could be the case that the whole is more than the sum of its parts, a combination of social and political conditions pushing up the probability of democratic viability in South Africa.

The social deficit is not that large, because South Africa fulfils to some extent certain macro conditions for democracy referring to modernization. It is a positive that agricultural employment is rather low, that Protestantism has a strong position as a religious creed and that the RSA is a medium income country, although the income distribution is a negative. Whether South Africa can maintain its rather favourable socio-economic background characteristics for democracy is uncertain, because the sharp population growth will depress GNP per capita. In the long-term, and if economic development does not match the population explosion, there will be a serious socio-economic deficit. However, Table 8.8 indicates that the political deficit is higher than the social deficit, at least for now.

Despite the emphasis on the creation of a constitutional democracy with transparent political institutions, it is not clear whether the executive in the RSA is presidential or parliamentary. This is a negative. The same applies to the dominant position of the ANC, which not only controls the national government with its extensive powers, but the ANC is a dominant force in all regions except the Western Cape Province. The transition to a market economy is a positive, because economic freedom tends generally to support democracy, but the transformation of the South African economy is not yet complete.

Theories of democratic transition underline either short-term (O'Donnell and Schmitter, 1986) or long-term conditions (Lipset *et al.*, 1993; Lipset, 1994). The spectacular regime transition in South Africa, initiated in 1990 and completed in 1996, is clearly a case of Schmitter's pact negotiated type of regime transformation from dictatorship to democracy. This is the short-term perspective. But one may also pursue the long-term perspective and pose the question about the probability of democratic stability or, simply, democratic viability.

However bright the prospects may appear at the moment, we wish to point out that when one looks at the macro conditions that tend to impact on democracy, either structural or institutional conditions following the literature, then a reservation may be made. Neither the social conditions nor the political conditions at place in South Africa at the moment are strong enough to carry the democracy in the long-term perspective. Although there are several positives, it is undeniable that economic prosperity is fragile, especially when one takes the enormous population growth projected into account. Similarly, the combination of semi-presidentialism with parliamentarism on the basis of informal one-party dominance constitutes a negative.

Both the socio-economic deficit and the political deficit raise worries about democratic stability in the decades to come. The socio-economic deficit could worsen if the economy does not expand in pace with population pressures, whereas the political deficit could be improved on by institutional reform (parliamentarism) and successful opposition politics at both the national and regional levels of government.

South East Asia: slow democratization

The exceptionalism of South East Asia has long been a research theme that has attracted many scholars. The focus has been to explain why several of these countries managed for such a long period to close the gap to the Occidental countries in terms of economic affluence. Our question is on the contrary: why is democracy so weak in this part of the world where affluence is common, given the modernisation effect?

The so-called tigers – Hong Kong, Taiwan, South Korea and Singapore – started on a path of stunning economic development in the 1960s, which, together with the Japanese miracle, made this part of the world the third economic centre of the world. There are different opinions as to the causes of South East Asian economic transformation. The alternative explanations include almost every conceivable factor, from purely economic, to cultural or institutional factors. We will not enter this controversy concerning the extent of economic exceptionalism in South East Asia.

Let us instead ask the political question of why democracy has been so slow in spreading in a stable manner in Far East Asia. Economic affluence has spread to other countries in the area – Malaysia, Thailand and China – but democracy has not really got a firm footing in any country except Japan (Iqbal and You, 2001). This presents a clear challenge to the Lipset model of democracy as a function of affluence.

It is true that democracy has been introduced in Taiwan and South Korea during the 1990s and that these countries will stay democratic in the future if nothing unforeseen occurs to change their situation. However, democracy is not firmly entrenched in Singapore, Thailand, Indonesia or Hong Kong. Why is there this political exceptionalism in the Far East?

To answer this question we must change our basic model somewhat. In South East Asia the prevailing religion is a variety of brands of Buddhism with the exception of Malaysia and Indonesia which are chiefly Muslim. Buddhism is hardly a source of individual rights against the state, which is why one may suggest the hypothesis that it reduces the probability of democracy, all other things being equal.

To understand the resistance to democracy in Asia it is not enough to focus on religion, especially Islam according to our basic model, but we must also include the special institutions that have dominated the economies of Asiatic countries. Here we will mention two: tenancy in agriculture (sharecropping); and economic nationalism in the industrial sector. Neither of these institutions promote democracy, for different reasons.

Let us focus on Singapore, using a model consisting of affluence, ethnic heterogeneity, Buddhism and economic freedom. Table 8.9 has the regression values as well as containing both predicted and actual scores. It is obvious that, in these two models, Singapore is a deviant case. The observed democracy score is distinctively lower than the scores predicted from the models. There are other factors operating in the case of Singapore that may explain the low democracy score, such as the election formula used. The presence of 'Asian values' may be one such factor. It may also be a consequence of a successful economy which delivers goods and utilities to such an extent that there is no real demand for individual freedoms and liberties.

Table 8.9 Democracy in Singapore (average 1972–2001) (regression model)

Predictor variables	Coeffs	Model 8	Model 9
LNGDP/CAP	coeff	0.824	0.967
	t-stat	3.79	4.83
ELF1	coeff	−0.931	−
	t-stat	−1.62	−
BUDD	coeff	−0.015	−0.014
	t-stat	−1.99	−1.94
HERITAGE	coeff	1.688	1.637
	t-stat	4.85	4.69
Constant	coeff	−4.240	−5.703
	t-stat	−2.78	−4.61
adj rsq		0.640	0.645
N		110	110

	Observed score	Predicted scores	
Singapore	4.40	8.92	9.09

Sources: see Appendix A1.

Conclusion

In this chapter we have examined the sources of democracy or the reasons for the lack of stable democracy in Third World countries which have received much attention. How can one explain the following anomalies?

1 Why is there 'Latinamericanization'? Many Latin American countries had male and female suffrage introduced at the same time as European countries. But democracy never stabilized in South America except Costa Rica – why?

2 Why is India a stable democracy when its lacks the economic and social requisites of democratic stability? Anarchy and authoritarianism in the Third World is often explained by merely referring to the dismal poverty characteristic of countries in Africa, Asia and Central America. How is it, then, that in India, where almost 50 per cent of the population struggles every day to survive, there is a vibrant democracy?

3 Will South Africa (RSA) remain a consolidated democracy well into the twenty-first century despite all of the political instability in sub-Saharan Africa?

4 Why is Singapore not a democracy? Affluence enhances democratic probability according to Lipset and the modernization scholars. Here we have a city-state which is as affluent as the richest OECD countries. It should be a democracy, which one may also expect for South Korea, Taiwan and Hong Kong (i.e. the Special Administrative Region in China).

We are, in a sense, looking for an answer to the same question in all of the case studies in this chapter, namely: which affects democracy the most – economic and social conditions on the one hand and rules on the other? This problem is critical in relation to the future of democracy in South Africa and South East Asia, but it also surfaces in relation to explaining the different paths of democracy in Latin America compared with South Asia. The overall finding is again that stable democracy is a function of economic, social and institutional conditions, where the latter weigh at least as heavy as economic and social conditions. Thus, one needs both exogenous and endogenous models of democracy to explain what Tingsten called 'the vitality of democracy', as measured by its probability. In an endogenous model, the key institutions for accomplishing stable democracy are parliamentarism and the Ombudsman, i.e. thin constitutionalism is enough. Thick institutionalism may offer contributory, but not necessary, or sufficient conditions of democratic vitality.

Swedish political scientist Herbert Tingsten argued early in the debate on how democracy becomes vital that this political regime feeds on both conflict and cooperation. *The Problem of Democracy* (1965) links the vitality of democracy with the opposition to government and the respect for mutually agreed upon rules of the game. Democracy in the Third World fails when there is too little conflict, too much conflict or no shared understanding of institutions.

Part IV

Outcomes of democracy

When the people govern, then one would expect to find outcomes that are in accordance with the preferences of ordinary citizens. Democratic politics operates through the policy cycle which transforms policy outputs into policy outcomes although not always in a perfect and predictable manner. Tocqueville suggested that democratic policies would emphasize either liberty or equality as well as have to trade-off these values against each other to a certain extent (Tocqueville, 1990, volume II). Since a democracy always achieves a certain amount of freedom for its citizens, we will focus on how equality is related to democracy as a political regime. Was Tocqueville right in predicting that a democratic society will promote equality more than a non-democratic society? If 'yes', then how does a democracy enhance equality?

What people want in a democratic society is some elementary form of equality. A democratic society is different from all other forms of societies to the extent that there is some degree of equality institutionalized in the organizations of society. In an aristocratic society, people are born unequal under the law. In a democratic society, people can live under very different economic and social conditions, but there will still be some form of formal equality recognized by the key institutions. A key question in democratic theory is how much equality there will or should be.

It is readily recognized that complete equality is not feasible given human incentives and the necessity to reward different contributions to society. Democratic countries harbour a market economy which distributes economic output in an unequal fashion. Yet societies vary considerably, displaying different degrees of macro inequality. Thus, the adherence to traditionalism supports inequalities whereas the spread of civic republicanism enhances equality. Similarly, an agriculturally based economy tends to establish immense inequalities, whereas an industrial market economy does not display inequalities to the same extent. Finally, governments may attempt to reduce inequalities through the making and implementation of public policies.

To scholars who emphasize democracy as equality, it must be an urgent research task to find out which conditions promote equality in society. First, one would wish to know whether democracies are more egalitarian than non-democracies. Second, one would want to know whether some democracies promote more equality than other democracies; and if so, why? In Chapter 9 we will analyse these two questions with reference to two kinds of inequalities, namely income inequality and gender inequality. Chapter 10 looks at other outcomes of public policy-making – the environment and corruption – in order to illuminate whether democracy matters.

An enquiry into democracy and equality shifts the focus towards the outputs and outcomes of democracy. Policy-making in a democratic regime will always, Tocqueville predicted, target equality. And the democratic state may accomplish real equality, or equality of results, by expanding public programmes. Thus, when examining democracy and equality, we must deal with the welfare state, or the tax state, the emergence of which Tocqueville also predicted.

9 Equality

Introduction

One need not accept the concept of democracy as equality in order to enquire into the link between the democratic regime and various egalitarian outcomes. Even if one does not accept the identity between democracy and equality, it would still be true that a democracy could not survive or flourish in an aristocratic society building on social inequalities institutionalized in law. Democracy requires a minimum of equality under the law. The key question is, though, whether democracy also promotes, or *should* promote, egalitarian outcomes over and beyond the mere legal requirement of one person, one vote.

Democracy may, in theory, have a strong egalitarian ring to it, but it was given an elitist interpretation early on when macro democracy was endorsed in constitutions in the early twentieth century. Although the so-called Neo-Machiavellians – Pareto, Mosca and Michels – were ambivalent about the blessings of democracy (Burnham, 1987), they clearly saw that the democratic regime would be run by the big mass political parties which could not operate without a society based on political and economic organization, including hierarchy. Modern democracy, they argued, needed political organization which would render democracy bureaucratic. Democracy could not operate without party government, state bureaucracy and an advanced market economy, which all restrained the possibility of radical egalitarian democracy. In a similar vein, Schumpeter went so far as to equate democracy with the competition between political elites, given an institutional framework of Rule of Law including the free entry and exit for political parties.

This neo-Machiavellian manner of thinking bypasses the fundamental point of modern democracy, namely that the people as a group has the capacity to eliminate elites which it does not like and elect new leaders. Thus, political elites in a democracy cannot neglect public opinion and govern in accordance with their own interests. Democracy and democratic elections are a sequence of principal-agent games. Perhaps this interaction between elites and citizens is conducive to a democratic responsiveness which leads to egalitarian policies which, in turn, result in more equality of outcomes? It all depends, at the end of the day, on which preferences the electorate demonstrates in their choice of political elites. Thus, the question of a close link between democracy and equality is an open one, where the answer depends on the shifting contingencies in various countries.

Let us first establish whether democracy as a macro regime tends to go together with real egalitarian outcomes such as income equality and gender equality. Then we will discuss one key causal mechanism involved in the relationship between democracy and equality – big government – and focus on how democracy would promote equality by supporting the welfare state. Two kinds of equality are central in this outcome enquiry, namely income equality and gender equality.

Income equality

Countries differ on the macro scores on income inequalities, as there will always be differences in income and wealth in a country, reflecting the natural variation in capacity and energy between individuals. The market economy tends to distribute income in accordance with the marginal productivity criterion, which entails sharp income differences. And heritage gives much to some and little to many, which again is conducive to major income differences among individuals or households. Why, then, are countries not all similar in terms of differences in income and wealth?

A variety of indicators have been developed to measure income differences. This research particularly looks at income differences and not the inequality in wealth, because wealth is looked on mainly as a result of income differences. If one understands the mechanisms that generate income differences, then one would also have understood much of the variation in wealth. All of these indicators of income inequality are relative measures which estimate how much of the total income generated one year ends up in the pockets of the households with the highest and lowest incomes, respectively. Here we will employ the Gini index as it has been estimated by the World Bank in various contexts.

What is problematic in the study of income inequalities is the access to reliable information. This problem may be resolved in relation to a few countries in the world, mainly those entering the OECD-set of countries. However, for many Third World countries, there is simply no data available. Thus, conclusions about income inequalities will have to be based on a small number of cases. Yet the overall picture is rather clearly indicated in the available data such as the data series on income inequality in Table 9.1. We apply these data to the following groups of countries: Nordic countries, Post-communist Europe, Continental Europe, countries with an Anglo-Saxon model and Third World countries.

The 'eta' scores in Table 9.1 indicate that there are significant differences between these sets of countries, although these differences in mean Gini scores have declined somewhat over time. Income inequality tends to be most pronounced in Third World countries but less conspicuous in Post-communist societies, although it is on the rise there after the system transformation initiated in 1989. Despite the fragility of the data, one would dare to suggest that both Anglo-Saxon countries and Continental Western Europe are character-

Table 9.1 Income distribution: Gini index scores 1970 onwards

Country group	GINI 1970	GINI 1980	GINI 1990	GINIWB	GINIMIL	GINILIS
Third World	0.453	0.423	0.444	0.437	0.426	0.386
Anglo-Saxon	0.333	0.353	0.371	0.354	0.368	0.333
Cont. Euro.	0.343	0.319	0.316	0.306	0.319	0.287
Post-com	0.251	0.269	0.281	0.304	0.317	0.307
Nordic	0.317	0.312	0.306	0.255	0.241	0.228
Average	0.394	0.378	0.393	0.391	0.385	0.299
eta sq	0.538	0.412	0.447	0.395	0.282	0.322
sig.	0.000	0.000	0.000	0.000	0.000	0.074
N	61	74	63	107	104	26

Sources: see Appendix A1.

ized by more income inequality than the countries which practise the Scandinavian model with its strong commitment to equality. Could democracy be one of the factors which explain the variation in Table 9.1 in overall income scores?

Gender equality

Social equality is no longer seen as only a matter of income and wealth. It is true that questions concerning gender inequality have lately become as much discussed as the issues in income inequality, at least in the democratic countries. The formal and real status of women is now considered an essential aspect of social equality. Gender inequality and income inequality overlap in countries only to a small extent, as they constitute different dimensions of the social structure, although not completely separated, as men tend to have a higher income than women, *ceteris paribus.* The equal recognition of women in society involves more than simply income and wealth.

In order to capture the gender dimension in society, the UNDP has, since the mid-1990s, presented two measures, one measuring a gender-related development index (GDI), and one measuring a gender empowerment measure (GEM). However, in addition to these two measures, one may employ a so-called proxy, namely a political indicator such as the proportion of women in parliament (WOM). This indicator does not reveal much about the social position of ordinary women, as political elites may co-opt women to a limited extent, a strategy that does not change the overall situation for ordinary women. However, in an indirect manner, it gives us an indication about the future direction of society, as women gaining access to political power can be employed for policy-making to empower women in general. The problem with the indicators on gender equality is thus rather validity than reliability, as data is available for many Third World countries. Table 9.2 states the overall country variation in the gender equality scores, using the same country classification as in Table 9.1.

We find a most substantial variation between these sets, as the 'eta' scores in Table 9.2 confirm. Interestingly, the differences in female empowerment are

Table 9.2 Gender equality: gender development, empowerment and representation
(1990 and 2000)

Country group	GDI 2000	GEM 2000	WOM 1990	WOM 1998
Third World	0.598	0.426	7.8	10.7
Anglo-Saxon	0.911	0.673	11.0	19.3
Cont. Euro.	0.899	0.659	16.7	21.1
Post-com	0.778	0.497	7.3	10.7
Nordic	0.923	0.792	37.6	38.5
Average	0.683	0.529	9.4	13.0
eta sq	0.490	0.605	0.430	0.366
sig.	0.000	0.000	0.000	0.000
N	126	63	141	128

Sources: see Appendix A1.

more pronounced than the variation in female representatives, as it is, after all, easier to co-opt women than to change the overall social predicament of ordinary women. The general picture is that the Nordic countries display the highest gender equality scores followed by the Anglo-Saxon and the Continental European ones, whereas the Third World countries have the lowest scores. Gender development is considerably higher in Post-communist countries than in Third World countries, reflecting an ideological heritage. At the same time, it must be underlined that women representation is lower in Post-communist countries than in western countries. Does democracy matter for the various gender equality scores?

Inequalities: economic and political factors

Our purpose here is not to suggest a complete model which explains income and gender inequalities in the countries of the world. First, our selection entails that less than half of the countries of the world are covered. Second, the reliability and validity of the information is not as high as is desirable. Third, when modelling inequality we only wish to identify whether democracy has an impact or not. Other factors may be assumed to play a role, including affluence, historical legacies, redistributional policies, etc. Thus, our explanatory effort has limited range and scope.

Table 9.3 tests a regression model linking both kinds of social inequality with affluence and democracy. What matters most for equality: affluence or democracy?

The major finding here is that affluence favours equality, both income equality and gender equality. A democratic regime has no independent impact on income distribution, but gender equality is positively affected by such a regime. Table 9.3 indicates that affluence promotes equality. Thus, economic development is crucial for reducing both income and gender inequalities. Do democratic policies not matter at all for the promotion of equality? They do, but the crucial thing is the size of the public sector.

Table 9.3 Inequality, affluence and democracy (regression analysis)

Independent variables	Dependent variables							
	GINIWB		GINIMIL		GEM00		WOM98	
	coeffs	t-stat	coeffs	t-stat	coeffs	t-stat	coeffs	t-stat
DEM 1995–2001	0.447	0.87	0.383	0.71	0.025	3.86	1.088	3.18
LNGDP/CAP	−4.404	−3.88	−3.292	−2.73	0.103	6.20	2.013	2.55
Constant	73.166	9.78	63.863	7.70	−0.603	−4.88	−11.058	−2.02
adj rsq	0.17	–	0.07	–	0.70	–	0.27	–
N	105	–	101	–	63	–	123	–

Sources: see Appendix A1.

Society generates inequalities but government may be the source of equality. We suggest, in the spirit of Tocqueville, that the size of government, or the public sector, is the key intervening factor between the democratic regime and egalitarian outcomes. Here we have the strong present relevance of Tocqueville and his prediction of the growth of government in the industrial society based on the market economy. Equality is promoted by extensive public policies funded by large public expenditures. As democracies differ in their acceptance of 'Big Government', some democracies favour equality more than others.

We will discuss the link between democracy and the size of government in two steps. First, we will enquire into a link between democracy and the size of government in general, that is, for all kinds of countries. Second, we will examine the occurrence of the welfare state in the set of stable democracies.

Democracy and 'Big Government'

According to one theory, democracy under-performs. This theory says that democracies are not capable of producing much in the way of outcomes. In a democracy there will be much debate about what to do, but little action. Democracies are ridden with conflict among various groups, meaning that consistent policy-making will not be forthcoming. In addition, there will be collective action difficulties, as groups in society free-ride on each other in attempts to avoid the costs of public policies.

According to another theory, democracies will over-perform. There is, some scholars argue, a persistent drive among democracies to engage in too many policies, trying to please each and every pressure group. Thus, there will be budget deficits and huge debts. The logic of democratic decision-making is basically that of log-rolling, meaning that minorities make endless *ad hoc* coalitions in order to secure their selfish interests at the expensive of silent majorities. Whether log-rolling can be done without corruption is an open question, but one would predict from this theory that democracies have big budgets and sustain a plethora of public policy programmes, including environmental protection.

Whether one accepts the theory of 'democracy as indecisiveness' or 'democracy as excessive spending', one would predict from these two theories that democracies fail to take proper action. Thus, there would be either too little policy or too much, but never just enough. Can we find any evidence that shows that democracies fail to take action in relation to, for example, the environment or that it overspends, dragging the state into deficits and huge debts? Actually, both of these theories of democratic decision-making imply that democracies would have a problem with honesty. But are democracies really more corrupt than authoritarian regimes?

One may throw some light on these two theories concerning democracy and the size of the public sector by means of a comparative evaluation of a few major outcomes in democratic and non-democratic countries. Let us start with the size of the government budget and then move on to examine environmental outcomes.

It is hardly a curiosity that public choice theory predicts two alternative budgets for the democratic government. First there is the Downs' prediction that the government budget will be too small (Downs, 1960, 1998) due to collective action failure to coordinate. Second, there is the Buchanan prediction that democratic governments are revenue-maximizing Leviathans spending on everything until deficits and debts stop them (Brennan and Buchanan, 1980). One may call the first theory the '*ex ante* hypothesis' and the second theory the '*ex post* hypothesis' of the size of a democratic government. Otherwise it is difficult to understand why one framework – rational choice – would comprise two contradictory conclusions about government.

The public budget in a market economy targets goods and services which complement the market and its typical mechanism of interaction: exchange. Thus, the public budgeting is orientated towards criteria such as public goods, economies of scale, externalities, essential facilities, public necessities and justice in distribution. *Ex ante*, a government which provides these goods and services will be short in forthcoming as no one has any incentive alone to provide for them or contribute voluntarily towards their allocation. Thus, the government budget will be small, as a result of coordination failures resulting in collective action difficulties such as free riding. This is the position of Downs, predicting an undersupply of collective goods and services, that is, goods and services that are allocated to all and can be used by all. Governments may attempt to allocate such collective goods and services but the various groups in the electorate will refuse to contribute voluntarily or will not reveal their true preferences, attempting to free ride (Olson, 1965).

Ex post, a government can use the immense tax power of the state to extract resources from society to such an extent that 'Big Government' can be put in place. However, the support for 'Big Government' will only be forthcoming when government concentrates favours to special interests and spreads out the costs on the silent majority. Once the tax and spending powers of the state are in place, there is no limit to the number of policy programmes government may wish to introduce or attempt to implement. If the taxation capacity of the state in relation to society is not limited through constitutional restrictions, then the spending proclivities of the Leviathan will keep increasing the public sector, if necessary through massive borrowing. This is the position of Buchanan. Which theory is correct?

The size of government can be measured in several ways. Thus, we employ a number of indicators on the size of the public sector, ranging from financial measures to regulatory or legislative measures. Here, we will use financial indicators in order to test the hypothesis that democratic governments are somehow different to non-democratic ones, either in having too small or too big budgets. One could include other measures as well, such as the number of public enterprises, the ownership of land, and so on. However, financial measures are enough to make a decision in relation to these two theories of democratic governments, as we only want to know whether democracy is somehow linked with big spending, big deficits and debt. Our measures include the following: CGCON = Central government consumption (World Bank); CGEXP = Central government expenditure (World Bank); GCON = Government consumption (Economic freedom of the world); TAXREV = Tax revenue (World Bank); GGEXP = General government expenditure (Economic freedom of the world); TRANS = Transfers payments (Economic freedom of the world); TOTOUT = Total outlays (Economic freedom of the world); GOVSP = Government spending (Global competitiveness report); DEFICITS = Central government deficits (World Bank); CG DEBT = Central government debt (World Bank), and TOTAL DEBT = Total debt service (World Bank).

Table 9.4 presents an initial picture of democracies and the size of the public sector. This reduced form evidence clearly indicates that budgets tend to be big in a democratic regime, as the correlations are all positive and sometimes strongly so.

The main finding in Table 9.4 is that democracy tends to be strongly associated with a large public sector. Can we, then, conclude that Buchanan is more right about the effects of democracy than Downs? Almost, we would say. Buchanan not only predicts that democracies expand public programmes and expenditures. He also claims that democracies are irresponsible, the democratic regime being conducive to budget deficits and debt. There is, however, little evidence of such an impact, as there is no systematic relationship between democracy and debt.

Perhaps the public sector is large in a democracy because the electorate so wishes – a normal Downsian effect if one applies his general theory of democracy as the median voter outcome (Downs, 1957). This would entail that Downs was wrong in his special theory of democracy as being conducive to an undersupply of public programmes, but right in his general theory of democracy as the capacity of the electorate to give correct direction to democratic decision-making.

One must, though, take a closer look at the interaction between democracy and the public finance indicators. In a second step, one would want to know whether it is really the democratic regime which increases public expenditures or revenues. Other possible factors that may account for the findings in Table 9.4 include affluence as well as the strength of the left in politics (TUD 95 = Trade Union Density in 1995).

Table 9.4 Democracy and public finance (correlations)

		DEM 1991–5	DEM 1995–2001	DEM 2000	DEM 2001
CGCON	*r*	0.18	0.17	0.17	0.16
	sig.	0.037	0.048	0.048	0.065
	N	134	135	135	135
CGEXP	*r*	0.40	0.36	0.34	0.34
	sig.	0.000	0.001	0.001	0.001
	N	89	89	89	89
GCON	*r*	0.43	0.39	0.37	0.37
	sig.	0.000	0.000	0.000	0.000
	N	113	113	113	113
TAXREV	*r*	0.56	56	0.55	0.54
	sig.	0.000	0.000	0.000	0.000
	N	89	89	89	89
GGEXP	*r*	0.62	0.60	0.58	0.56
	sig.	0.000	0.000	0.000	0.000
	N	72	72	72	72
TRANS	*r*	0.71	0.66	0.63	0.61
	sig.	0.000	0.000	0.000	0.000
	N	40	40	40	40
TOTOUT	*r*	0.49	0.40	0.35	0.31
	sig.	0.000	0.002	0.009	0.023
	N	54	54	54	54
GOVSP 1999	*r*	0.58	0.48	0.42	0.40
	sig.	0.000	0.000	0.000	0.000
	N	59	59	59	59
GOVSP 2000	*r*	0.63	0.56	0.52	0.48
	sig.	0.000	0.000	0.000	0.000
	N	59	59	59	59
DEFICITS 1995	*r*	0.04	0.08	0.10	0.10
	sig.	0.729	0.489	0.371	0.360
	N	81	81	81	81
CGDEBT 1995	*r*	−0.38	−0.44	−0.47	−0.44
	sig.	0.004	0.001	0.000	0.001
	N	55	55	55	55
TOTDEB 95	*r*	0.12	0.05	0.04	0.04
	sig.	0.213	0.643	0.696	0.721
	N	107	108	108	108

Sources: see Appendix A1.

This is not the place to enter into the literature on public expenditure determinants, which comprises a host of alternative approaches and hypotheses (Clark, 1998; Persson and Tabellini, 2002; Wilensky, 2002). Here, we only wish to probe for evidence that democracy as a regime has an impact on revenues, expenditures, deficits and debts. Table 9.5 presents a few regression models which have findings that are relevant here.

The regression models support the earlier positive finding that democracy is conducive to a large public sector as well as the earlier negative finding that democracy is not conducive to budget deficits and a huge public debt. The well-known Wagner effect, that affluence leads to higher public expenditures, is also confirmed in Table 9.5. Interestingly, affluence (resources), the posi-

Table 9.5 Democracy and public finance (regression models)

Predictors	Coeffs	Dependent variables					
		GOVSP 2000	TOTOUT 2000	GGEXP 1997	DEFICITS 1995	CGDEBT 1995	TOTDEB 1995
LNGDP/CAP	coeff	3.122	4.528	5.266	1.402	−0.946	−3.489
	t-stat	1.53	2.35	2.35	1.69	−0.09	−1.71
TUD 95	coeff	0.182	0.280	0.213	−0.081	0.057	−0.020
	t-stat	2.77	4.25	2.48	−2.40	0.16	−0.27
DEM 1995–2001	coeff	1.870	0.500	2.461	−0.601	−4.262	0.286
	t-stat	2.59	0.67	2.66	−1.75	−1.14	0.39
Constant	coeff	−14.123	−18.053	−41.568	−8.988	93.423	34.336
	t-stat	−0.91	−1.21	−2.384	−1.59	1.15	2.41
adj rsq		0.42	0.45	0.50	0.08	0.00	0.02
N		55	52	49	63	40	59

Sources: see Appendix A1.

tion of the trade unions (political will) and the democratic regime carry about the same weight when accounting for the size of the public sector. When it comes to budget deficits and debt, then poverty explains the most.

The link between democracy and a large public sector in the form of public expenditures may be interpreted in two different ways. Either one argues that democracies caring for their populations make a considerable effort to provide citizens with public services and income security; or one argues that democracies are likely to be invaded by redistributional coalitions which employ government taxation and spending for rent-seeking purpose (Olson, 1982). The evidence examined supports the first theory much more than the second.

Thus, we conclude that democratic government primarily use public expenditures to promote development objectives, such as education, healthcare and social assistance. The Human Development Index employed by the United Nations to measure social development around the world presents a picture not only of the national differences in affluence, or economic development, but also how social objectives are achieved. Does the democratic regime matter for social development? Table 9.6 displays how the overall level of human development in a country is linked with democracy as measured by the Pearson correlation coefficients. From the correlation analysis we may establish that democracy goes hand-in-hand with human development. It is, however, noteworthy that the size of the correlation coefficients is slightly weaker around year 2000 than was the case in the 1970s, reflecting, of course, that many new democracies, initiated after 1989, have not yet had enough time or resources to promote quality of life in their societies.

The association between the democratic regime and quality of life, documented in Table 9.6, may be interpreted as a historical reflex of the fact that most of the world's wealthy countries are democracies. However, in countries with an advanced economy, the tendency of democracy to support a large public sector may be restrained by the Tocqueville paradox, which states that democracy produces two outcomes, freedom and equality; advanced democracies face

Table 9.6 Human Development Index and democracy (correlation analysis)

	HDI 1975	HDI 1980	HDI 1985	HDI 1990	HDI 1995	HDI 1999
DEM 1972–6	$r = 0.73$	–	–	–	–	–
	$N = 90$	–	–	–	–	–
DEM 1981–5	$r = 0.76$	$r = 0.69$	$r = 0.68$	–	–	–
	$N = 90$	$N = 98$	$N = 104$	–	–	–
DEM 1991–5	$r = 0.72$	$r = 0.69$	$r = 0.68$	$r = 0.66$	–	–
	$N = 92$	$N = 100$	$N = 104$	$N = 117$	–	–
DEM 1995–2001	$r = 0.69$	$r = 0.66$	$r = 0.64$	$r = 0.62$	$r = 0.63$	$r = 0.58$
	$N = 92$	$N = 100$	$N = 106$	$N = 117$	$N = 118$	$N = 141$

Sources: see Appendix A1.

Note
All coefficients are significant at the level of 0.000.

a choice between liberty and equality. Let us explain this paradox in relation to the stable democracies of the world, that is the group of OECD countries.

The welfare state and the welfare society

In the group of stable democracies we find two pure types of government: small government (or the welfare society) and big government (or the welfare state). The welfare state – its size and format – is nothing but a version of the main problem in political economy, namely: state or market? After having reached a certain level of affluence countries may favour the use of markets in allocating resources or they may wish to employ government. The welfare state draws a considerable part of its support from solidarity. Thus, it emphasizes redistribution much more than the welfare society. Resource allocation and income redistribution are the two decision parameters in the debate on the pros and cons of the welfare state. There used to be a third dimension, namely labour market policies and macro economic policy-making. However, the difference between various schools in this area seems not to matter that much any more, as most governments accept labour retraining schemes of one sort or another and most governments cling to a modified version of monetarism, favouring low inflation as their first and most important target. Let us concentrate on resource allocation and redistribution.

Here, we have two polar types of societies. And today's realities may be analysed by means of the distinction between the welfare state and the welfare society. These two models – the welfare society and the welfare state – constitute two systems of policies and institutions. The policy package identifies the outputs of government whereas the institutional set up delivers the rules that guide the actions of bureaucrats and the expectations of citizens. Both elements must be specified, as the policies give us the size of the welfare state measured in terms of GDP, whereas the rules indicate how citizens are treated. The two welfare state models may be assessed in terms of a few performance criteria such as economic growth, income equality, and gender equality, as well as social solidarity.

A number of countries will be found between these two polar types, as they are mixtures. In the future they have a choice of either reducing their welfare state towards the welfare society model or increase their welfare state. The classical three-model distinction in the literature on the welfare state between the liberal, corporatist and social democratic welfare state models is not in accordance with realities today, if it even ever was. The changes in the welfare state in the 1990s have been so vast that it is time to reconceptualize it. In order to capture the essential features we suggest that one employs the Max Weber method of ideal-type concept formation. What is a welfare state today in the sense of an ideal-type?

Limits of classical welfare state analysis

Welfare state analysis still employs the conceptualization suggested by Esping-Andersen in *The Three Worlds of Welfare Capitalism* (1990). If the Esping-Andersen system focussing on three kinds of welfare states was correct for the period 1960–90, then it still holds true that reality has changed during the 1990s to such an extent that his three categories typology is now more confusing than illuminating. Let us explain why, and give a telling example of a country which does not fit this typology, namely Switzerland.

Classical welfare state analysis focuses on three types, which go under various labels. We will use the labels that are employed by Goodin *et al.* in their book *The Real Worlds of Welfare Capitalism* (1999). It may be pointed out that we agree with Goodin in his insistence on an empirical examination of the performance record of alternative models of the welfare state. In fact, the Goodin study is interesting from the perspective of institutional assessment, as it draws on a new kind of evidence, namely panel data on income and living standards. Following Goodin *et al.*, we have:

1   the liberal welfare regime;
2   the corporatist welfare regime;
3   the social democratic welfare regime.

These labels – 'liberal', 'corporatist' and 'social democratic' – are truly confusing. This is not accidental, as there is a heavy dose of politics in welfare state research. People who use these categories have a clear political preference in favour of heavy welfare state commitments, called 'social democracy'. In fact, these labels serve no other purpose than in signalling the political position of the researcher. If you believe that scientific objectivity is possible, and that it is connected with neutrality between various political opinions in accordance with the philosophy of Weber (1949), then this is no good at all.

Goodin chooses the Netherlands as an example of the social democratic model, but the Netherlands have never been ruled by social democracy, at least not in the majoritarian position typical of the Scandinavian countries. Why would the Dutch import a Scandinavian model? He lists Germany as an example of the corporatist model. Again, this is totally misleading. Corporatism has been strongly entrenched where social democracy is predominant, that is, in the Scandinavian countries and in Austria. In the past Germany has practised a social corporatism in a modest manner, but less and less so. Finally, the favourite of Goodin – the social democratic model – was never an invention of the Social Democratic Party. In the Scandinavian and Finnish contexts, the welfare state resulted from broad political consensus. Thus, the 'Scandinavian' or 'Nordic' model was supported not least by the centre parties, among which we find the liberal parties. There is no 'social democracy model', as all parties in the Nordic countries except Iceland supported the idea of a large public sector.

The approach comprising of three welfare state models mixes two analytical dimensions: size of public expenditures in terms of total societal resources; and the degree of universality in the rules covering various groups of citizens. The welfare state combining allocative and redistributive expenditures may range from a low 30 per cent of the GDP to a high 60 per cent of the GDP in advanced countries. This is the quantitative dimension, or welfare state ambition, as measured by the size of public expenditures, which may be low or high. On the other hand, we have the qualitative dimension, which refers to how the rules are framed. More specifically, the key question is whether the welfare rules apply equally to all citizens or whether separate groups have their own rules.

It is impossible to find concrete examples of the welfare state which combine low effort with universalism. Perhaps the idea of a universal allocation that has been much debated recently is an example of such a combination? It makes sense to make distinctions between various groups of citizens when there is a low welfare state effort. If only so much money can be used, then one may wish to use it to target the groups who need the resources the most.

The question that must be raised in relation to the typology in Table 9.1 is whether the separation between two generous models – the Continental and the Nordic models – really makes sense, especially after the reforms of the welfare state in the 1990s. All the Nordic welfare states have accepted so-called status distinctions in at least some of the redistributive programmes. Thus, the Scandinavian countries also link pensions and unemployment as well as sickness benefits with income earned and earlier job experience. In addition, one may say that there was always a universal element in the Continental model as healthcare or education was free to everyone, at least in some countries.

The distinction between a 'Social Democratic model' and a 'Corporatist model' is based more in ideology than social science. In many West European countries there is a high level of welfare state effort and in all of them there is a mixture of universal rules and rules with status distinctions. There may be differences in degree between various countries, reflecting historical legacies and so-called path dependencies. However, all of these countries with a high welfare state effort combine universalism and status distinctions. In reality, we are left with two basic models, one based on the market and the other on public expenditures. There are two polar types, the welfare society relying on a neo-liberal approach, and the welfare state, trusting politics and public administration. A number of countries are to be placed somewhere between these two polar types. Thus it is welfare state effort that is the key dimension.

The choice between two ideal-types of welfare states, the neo-liberal and the comprehensive, is very much linked with the resolution of the mix of the private and the public sectors. The neo-liberal model gives more space for markets to allocate resources and it limits redistribution to the needy. The comprehensive welfare state employs more public resource allocation and it engages in extensive income maintenance. The essential difference between the two ideal-types is the role of government. Thus, the public sector tends to stay at around 30 per cent of GDP in the neo-liberal model whereas the comprehensive welfare state tends towards 50 per cent or even 60 per cent. There are many countries that hover between these two polar types.

There are two distinctive features of the comprehensive welfare state. First, we have the tax state. Since the public sector is large, taxes must also be so. Sometimes social security charges are separated from proper taxes. However, in a comprehensive welfare state, all the charges paid by the employees are in reality taxes, as they cannot be avoided as long as one earns income. The average income tax including the obligatory charges tends towards 50 per cent in the comprehensive welfare state. Matters are entirely different in the neo-liberal model where people dispose of much more of their income, for instance by buying into pension plans or taking insurance against the risks in life. Average tax rates tend towards 25 per cent in the neo-liberal state. Thus one has here a very sure test of where a country is to be placed: look at the overall tax pressure, including in the taxes the *obligatory charges*.

Second, there is the set of *entitlements*. In a comprehensive welfare state, the set of rights is truly large, as it includes not only income maintenance in a number of different situations but also public services. The citizens may right-fully claim access to all kinds of education as well as healthcare. He/she may also claim by law a number of different transfer payments, some of which he/she is entitled to even when having contributed nothing. Some transfers require that people have paid charges during some time, but the system is still obligatory and the transfers constitute entitlements. In a neo-liberal model, the set of entitlements is small and targets special groups besides a modest general pension for all citizens. They tend to be means-tested entitlements, i.e. they are conditional on proving need.

If one believes that people can contract out almost everything to the private sector, then one adheres to the neo-liberal model. On the other hand, if one distrusts markets, then one favours the public sector. These beliefs tend to be ideological, but they may of course be evaluated. Thus, one asks: what are the pros and cons of the two polar types of welfare state?

It should be emphasized that the clear-cut separation between the private and the public sectors has become blurred lately due to the emergence of New Public Management (NPM). If people can contract efficiently in the private sector using market mechanisms, then government should employ similar techniques when it provides welfare. When a comprehensive welfare state engages massively in NPM, then it employs contracting – contracting out as well as in, but it does not privatize the decision about the allocation of services to ordinary citizens. Actually, a comprehensive welfare state may use all kinds of state–market mixtures when it engages in full line supply. However, if it is a comprehensive welfare state, then the overall tax pressure will be high, and the set of entitlements will be huge and generous. A comprehensive welfare state may rely on insurance companies as well as private supplies. As long as the charges are obligatory and the services are arranged by government, it is not a voluntary system.

In order to show how essential it is to underline these two characteristics of a comprehensive welfare state – obligatory solutions to welfare problems and the size of the tax state – we will briefly examine the Swiss public sector. It has always, in classical welfare state analysis, been identified as a neo-liberal example. Nothing could be more erroneous.

The Swiss 'outlier'

Correctly estimating the exact size of the public sector in Switzerland has become an issue in social science research. The problem is that the OECD in its comparative statistics has given numbers which are not comparable to the data for the other countries. And the cause of the problem is that Switzerland has not employed the same framework for its National Accounts as the other countries. Correcting for the OECD mistake may imply two alternative:

1   refraining from estimating the public sector in Switzerland while waiting until Switzerland implements the now standard manner of putting up National Accounts;
2   estimating public sector size using original Swiss data without any ambition to create a comparable measure.

Here we will discuss one effort to create comparability. But we will suggest that the most important question is what the Swiss data says about the public–private distinction, irrespectively of the question of comparability. The debate about the Swiss welfare state – its size and orientation – is characterized by a peculiar ambivalence. Of course, one wants to have the correct numbers for a central European country with an advanced economy and a spectacular presence on the world market. If it were true that Switzerland had a small welfare state like Australia or Japan, then it would constitute a peculiar exception in Europe – a true 'outlier'. If, on the other hand, Switzerland is like any other West European country when it comes to social ambitions, then the country would reinforce the image of the continental European welfare state. Which leg to stand on?

This ambivalence in comparative research – Switzerland as the major outlier or Switzerland as the confirmation of Wagner's Law – has a counterpart in a Swiss internal contradiction. On the one hand, it is strongly affirmed that Switzerland has a social state, i.e. the country takes care of its citizens through large public programmes, of both allocative and insurance types. Switzerland is not a miser country, that is, one with tested support programmes, social stigmatization and economizing on social welfare. On the other hand, it is strongly denied that Switzerland would harbour an expensive welfare state which does not control its costs and provide excessively generous programmes. Which leg to stand on?

Perhaps it is somewhat astonishing that no one in Switzerland knows the exact size of its public sector? In several countries, such measures are calculated as part of the ongoing budget process and enter into arguments about the pros and cons of public policy. However, the public–private separation is difficult to identify in Switzerland due to the complexity of the institutions of the country. There are three sources of this organized complexity: Swiss federalism which harbours a real decentralized state; Swiss public insurance, which is a thick patchwork of different programmes; Swiss public enterprises which come in many different ownership forms.

We will not bring up the public enterprises or the many private–public mixes that exist here, as for example, the cantonal banks and the new Swiss airline. Here it suffices to analyse the complexity in the free service provision – public resource allocation ('depenses publiques') as well as the complex structure of social insurance ('protection sociale'). Switzerland definitely has a welfare state and its size is quite comparable to nearby countries such as Germany, Austria and Italy. If one is in doubt about the existence of 'Big Government' in Switzerland, then one should consult a recently made estimation by two Swiss experts.

Chardonnens and Saurer state that different criteria can be employed for estimating the size of the public sector: the tax ratio; total expenditure; the National Accounts' criteria; the OECD criteria. They show how Switzerland scores on these different criteria, which is useful information. Let us repeat the essentials of this exercise in Table 9.7 following the separation between government provision of goods and services on the one hand and public insurance on the other.

One gets lower estimates on both the income and the expenditure side if one deletes certain items such as the PP (*provoyance professionnelle*) partly or wholly, the sickness insurance (*assurance maladie*) partly or wholly, etc. One may wish to use the same criteria as the OECD employs, in which case the income side is reduced to 34.4 per cent of GDP and the expenditure side goes down to 42.5 per cent. There is no certainty, though, that the OECD correctly applies their criteria onto the various OECD member countries, as it is quite arbitrary whether several social insurance items are to be classified as public or private in accordance with the OECD framework.

What is important to emphasize is that the goal of getting a picture of the overall size of the public sector in Switzerland is a worthwhile effort, independently of the sub goal of making international comparisons. If we start from this ambition, then one is interested in the upper-range numbers for both the income and the expenditure side. And they all indicate the same phenomenon, namely 'Big Government' in Switzerland.

The numbers calculated by Chardonnens and Saurer must be considered as the most accurate thus far, given their expertise and experience with such calculations. However, a puzzle remains to be settled given Table 9.7: why is the income column so different from the expenditure column? Swiss governments have certainly engaged in deficit spending, building up a state debt of about 50 per cent of GDP over the years. But deficit spending is not of such a dimension that it could account for the difference between the tax ratio at 42.7 and

Table 9.7 Switzerland: different criteria on the public–private separation in 1999 (million CHF)

	Income side	Expenditure side
Government	85,711	119,442
Insurance	79,403	79,022
Other	959	–
Total	166,073	198,464
% of GDP	42.7	51.1

Source: Chardonnens and Saurer, 2002.

Table 9.8 Public resource allocation ('Total après deduction des doubles imputations')

	Billion CHF 1999
Administration	7.7
Justice, police	6.5
Defence	5.4
Forcign rclations	2.2
Education	22.0
Culture	3.7
Health	15.1
Social welfare	23.1 (possible double-booking)
Traffic	12.1
Environment	4.8
Subventions	6.7
Financial costs	10.1
Total	119.4

Source: Adminstration fédérale des finances, 2001.

the expenditure roof at 51.1, i.e. in per cent of GDP. Something has been left out in Table 9.7. Let us try to figure out how much is missing and what it is.

The three levels of government – the Confederation, the cantons and the communes – offer an impressive list of public services – *full line supply* without any doubt. Next we will report only on the core government functions, meaning that we leave out the entire business side with the public enterprises. Here we find the Swiss welfare state when it comes to the provision of services *gratuit* (see Table 9.8). What costs are involved?

The only source of double-booking here is 'Prevoyance sociale' which contains certain costs amounting to 12.7 billion CHF for the following social welfare items, listed under social security categories: AVS: 5.7 (billion CHF); AI: 4; AM: 2.6. These costs could be deducted from the estimation of the costs for social security. In Table 9.9 we rely on the most recent series for social security.

Table 9.9 Social security expenditures (1999)

	Billion CHF
AVS (pensions)	27.4
PP (pensions)	28.7
AI (invalidity)	8.4
AM (sickness)	18.4
AA (accidents)	6.0
AC (unemployment)	5.1
AF (family)	4.3
APG (loss of revenue)	0.6
Ami (military)	0.2
Total	99.1

Source: Bundesamt für Statistik, 2001.

The list in Table 9.9 is a most impressive one. Probably no other West Euro-pean country pays the same cash amount to each client in real money – a question for research, no doubt. What is to be emphasized here is that, when we add social security to public administration, deducting the possible double-booking of the above 12.5 billion CHF, then we arrive at a total public sector size of 206 billion CHF – amounting to 53 per cent of GDP (388,568 million CHF). Thus, we are above the 51 per cent established by the two Swiss experts. Yet, a public sector size of 53 per cent is too low a figure when we move to the income side.

We have to proceed in the same manner on the revenues side, first looking at the income of the three governments while eliminating double-bookings; and, second, examining the revenues of the social security system in its entirety. It should be pointed out at once that tax and revenue are far from the same thing here, as both public administration and social security are financed by other kinds of income items besides taxes. The list of revenue items in Table 9.10 does not contain any social security charges. One may con-clude by comparing Table 9.10 with Table 9.11 that the entire system of public administration – all governments – ran with a deficit of about 2 billion CHF in 1999. However, matters are entirely different when we look at figures for the revenues in the social security system (payroll taxes) – Table 9.11. By compar-ing Table 9.11 with Table 9.9, we realize that there is a huge public savings components in the Swiss social security system, amounting to some 20 billion CHF in 1999. It is often emphasized that the Swiss social security system is basi-cally sound, as lots of annual savings have added up to a comfortable buffer from which to pay a population as the proportion of elderly and long-term sick increases. However, collective savings also have to be paid for. In terms of revenues, the social security system takes 31 per cent of GDP, to be redistrib-uted back to Swiss people mainly in the form of cheques. Some of it goes to pay the administration of the system and some is kept as savings in various institutional forms.

If we now add up the revenues for government with the revenues in the social security system, then we arrive at the highest number so far. Total public revenues would stand at 238.6 billion CHF – or 61.4 per cent of GDP. We would not be surprised if this total public revenues ratio is the highest one in

Table 9.10 Government revenues 1999 ('doubles imputations non comprises dans le total')

	Billion CHF
Current revenues	115.2
Taxes	85.7
Regalia	1.0
Charges	27.3
Capital revenues	2.6
Total	117.8

Source: Adminstration fédérale des finances, 2001.

Table 9.11 Social security revenues (1999)

	Billion CHF
AVS	27.2
PP	49.5
AI	7.6
AM	18.6
AA	6.2
AC	6.4
AF	4.2
APG	0.8
Ami	0.3
Total	120.8

Source: Bundesamt für Statistik, 2001.

all OECD countries. In Switzerland one has believed the wrong OECD message – that the country had a small public sector – for too long. Perhaps the confusion about the correct numbers was also due to the peculiar terminology used in classical welfare state analysis, as Switzerland could hardly be classified as 'social democratic', 'corporatist' or 'conservative'. Yet, no matter how the orientation of its welfare state is to be described, it is true that the country has expanded its public sector rapidly during the last twenty years.

The classical three categories typology for analysing welfare states is less applicable today than when it was launched. The choice is now between a welfare state or a welfare society, or the continental European model against the Anglo-Saxon model. A democracy may choose either one of these ideal-types.

Performance of the welfare state and the welfare society

The question about which welfare state model – the mixed economy or the decentralized market economy – performs the best is today as controversial as was the problem of the market and the state in the early twentieth century – the so-called 'Great Debate'. Goodin *et al.* (1999) present an outcome assessment that is unusual in terms of the methodology employed. In earlier studies one has compared welfare state regimes cross-sectionally, on the basis of macro data. Goodin and associates use panel data, which would increase the reliability of the findings, as the same group of people are followed over a period of years. The positive assessment of the welfare state by Goodin and associates should be contrasted with the findings of Tanzi and Schuknecht in *Public Spending in the 20th Century* (2000), which argues that welfare states perform worse than other kinds of politico-economic regimes.

Tanzi and Schuknecht state both that 'possibilities for reducing public spending now exist in many areas from the provision of pensions ... to the provision of educational and health services and infrastructures in general' (2000: 251) and that 'governments will become more efficient and public spending (and taxation) will decline in the future in spite of demographic trends that will tend, under existing policies, to increase public spending' (ibid.: 253). How are we to test which argument is the correct one?

Tanzi and Schuknecht use macro data over long periods of time. Thus, they compare a large number of countries with regard to public expenditure and taxation patterns on the one hand and their economic and social performance on the other. First, they make comparisons between OECD countries in relation to outcomes such as economic growth, inflation, unemployment, educational achievements, healthcare standards and income inequality. Second, they compare the OECD countries with a few of the newly industrialized countries in Asia and Latin America (Chile). The finding is that, when a country goes beyond about 35 per cent of GDP in public expenditures, then it makes no difference on economic and social outcomes, at least not a positive one.

Goodin and associates employ micro data from huge panel surveys of individuals in certain OECD countries, aggregating the data to country scores. Yet, using panel data, although more reliable than macro data, does not solve the basic difficulty in welfare regime evaluation, which is separating the impact of the regime from other factors which also impinge on the outcomes. Also, when one only examines three cases, let alone for a long period of years – a decade – one still faces the same problem of causal induction, meaning that the findings could be explained by the influence of factors not taken into account in the model. One could even argue that a cross-sectional approach is not inferior to the panel data framework, because cross-sectional analysis covering numerous cases allows for semi-controlled experiments. Thus, we will use the cross-sectional approach and attempt to maximize the number of cases. The evaluation of welfare state models tends to focus on two key outcomes: affluence, and equality of income. We would like to add a third one, which becomes more and more politically relevant, namely: equality of sexes.

We will focus on these three outcomes and try to estimate whether the welfare regime has a positive or negative impact on them. This strategy is in accordance with the key theory linking a politico-economic regime with outcomes, namely the Okun model of a trade-off between economic efficiency, that is maximizing total production, and the degree of equality in the distribution of resources, or income (Okun, 1975). The Okun model of an equity–efficiency trade-off entails that the neo-liberal welfare state would display more affluence but less income equality. Correspondingly, the comprehensive welfare state would be characterized with less affluence but more equality, especially income equality. This is a perfectly testable hypothesis, which ranges over all advanced countries with a market economy and a democratic system of government.

There is no single mechanism that explains why a welfare state would be less economically dynamic than a welfare society. Actually, economists are divided on the issue. Some would claim that the pros of the welfare state compensate for the cons, and thus that it is an open question as to whether a neo-liberal state does better than a comprehensive welfare state in terms of economic growth, short-term as well as long-term. Others would argue that, on the whole, the negative consequences of 'Big Government' tend to outweigh the positive ones, meaning that a welfare society would grow faster. All seem to be in agreement with the position that more of the public sector leads to less income inequality. However, this positive outcome comes with a price tag, as the size of the cake will be smaller, the more one attempts to divide it equally. This is the basic idea in the Okun model. Yet, it remains to explain what mechanisms link growth in output with equality in distribution. On the negative side we have the following key links.

Mechanism 1: the tax problem. The welfare state can only be financed by means of a considerable tax pressure. It does not matter whether these costs are covered by ordinary taxes or charges. They still have to be paid by obligatory payments. A high level of taxation, whether in the form of income taxes, sales taxes or labour charges, leads to the problem of *excess burden.* In addition to the cost of the tax, there is the loss in production from the behavioural response of the people who have to pay. Thus, they reduce consumption when goods are taxed, they reduce work when labour is taxed and they reduce investments when capital is taxed.

Mechanism 2: the crowding out problem. When government builds up a large public sector, then it often needs to borrow substantial amounts of money in the bond market, either for investments or for covering deficits. This leads to higher interest rates, which reduce private sector borrowing and, accordingly, investments. Again, there is an additional cost to the economy from 'Big Government'.

Mechanism 3: the incentive problem. A large welfare state offers various things – services as well as money checks – gratis or almost so. If people are driven by very mundane motives, or egoism even with guile, then various welfare state programmes change the behaviour of people and leads them to the overconsumption of these programmes. Thus, people will look for subsidized goods and services (housing, healthcare, etc.) or abstain from trying to get back into the normal job market (long-term illness, etc).

If only these three mechanisms were in operation, then the Okun hypothesis would hardly be controversial or difficult to confirm empirically. The difference between a welfare society and a welfare state would essentially be that the second regime would involve various inefficiencies that the first regime would avoid, relying on markets which tend to be both efficient and incentive compatible. However, we must also take into account the positive mechanisms of the comprehensive welfare state. Thus, we have the following mechanisms.

Mechanism 4: the human capital argument. Public education benefits the community at large. A country needs a well-educated labour force, and public money for schools and universities constitute investments in the future which pay handsomely. Educational spending may be suboptimal if left to individuals, as they tend to be myopic, focussing on short-term costs and failing to realise long-term benefits. Thus, government may just as well provide all kinds of education free of charge, stimulating demand. Free education probably promotes social equality strongly.

Mechanism 5: the infrastructure argument. Investments in the physical environment – roads, railway, airports, telecommunications, water, sewage – promotes economic growth by facilitating production. This is a classical argument for the role of government in the economy. Actually, few if any would deny its correctness. It is only recently that some economists have argued in favour of radical privatization of the infrastructure on the basis of efficiency considerations relating to the industry itself. However, no one questions the positive externalities of a good system of infrastructure.

Mechanism 6: the solidarity argument. A comprehensive welfare state promotes nation-building which is essential for peace and social order. A well-structured society requires a comprehensive welfare state in order for groups to come together and accept each other. Thus, welfare states are more viable than welfare societies where possessive individualism reigns. A high degree of solidarity between classes and communities may affect economic activity positively by increasing social capital. That solidarity goes with equality is evident.

To sum up: some mechanism in the neo-liberal model may enhance allocative efficiency and spur growth, but the same is true of the comprehensive model. How these six mechanisms work themselves out in practice is impossible to predict theoretically – only empirical evidence can tell which effects prevail. One would assume that the comprehensive model performs better on equality, but the key question is whether such an advantage must be traded off against a less vibrant economy. The evaluation of alternative welfare regimes should be made without entering into macro economic concerns. It is true that the welfare state used to be linked with Keynesianism, but this link is now effectively uncoupled. A country may practise monetarism and still endorse the tax state, as for example, is the case in Switzerland with its independent central bank.

Is the welfare state a complement or a substitute for the market? Some look on the public sector as a way to handle market failure. Thus, basically it does not interfere with the market economy. It is residualist. Others see the public sector as replacing the market economy in several important respects. It offers a mixed economy where one part of the GDP is generated in the markets and another part is forthcoming through government.

A large public sector, typical of the comprehensive welfare state, affects the market economy but it does not replace it. It is not correct to see the so-called 'Social Democratic model' as the first step towards another kind of economy that is not, so to speak, 'capitalist' in nature. All advanced economies are market economies, but they differ in terms of the size and scope of the public sector. A large public sector affects the market economy in two ways. First, it leads to reduced allocative scope for markets, as many services will be allocated by the budget or through some other public sector device. Thus, there will be less market allocation as education, healthcare and social care, as well as various forms of insurance, is allocated by means of a state bureaucracy. The critical question is whether this leads to allocative inefficiencies. Second, a big public sector involves a sharp difference between pre-tax and after-tax income, as the market distribution of income and revenues will be changed through the tax state and the income maintenance programmes. This will not reduce the size of the market much as the money that the government takes in will be handed back to the consumers. The critical question is whether this redistribution involves considerable excess burden to the economy or not.

It must be emphasized that it is an open question as to whether a welfare society performs better or worse than a welfare state. State provision is not per se inefficient production and redistribution may stimulate demand. Let us look at the empirical evidence in Table 9.12.

The evidence about the performance of the two welfare state models on economic and social criteria indicates a weak Okun effect, as welfare societies tend to perform slightly better on economic criteria whereas welfare states tend to perform a little better on social criteria. However, the differences between the outcomes of the two models are minor ones according to the 'eta' scores. Thus, strictly speaking, neither Goodin and associates nor Tanzi and Schuknecht are correct. Neither regime has a clear overall advantage when evaluated on economic performance indicators.

Thus, among the stable democracies of the world, we find the Tocqueville tension between freedom and liberty in the two basic models of a welfare society and a welfare state. However, when we contrast the democratic regime in general with the non-democratic regimes, then we find that democracy is associated with a large public sector.

Table 9.12 Welfare society and welfare state: comparing means for a set of OECD-countries ($N = 23$ at most)

Indicator	Welfare society	Welfare state	eta sq	sig.
GDPC 1975	5925	5700	0.007	0.707
GDPC 1980	9540	9197	0.007	0.713
GDPC 1985	12,423	11,797	0.013	0.607
GDPC 1990	17,432	17,091	0.002	0.834
GDPC 1995	21,518	20,890	0.005	0.744
GDPC 1998	22,889	21,895	0.012	0.617
GROWTH 1960–73	3.9	4.5	0.026	0.459
GROWTH 1973–85	1.4	1.6	0.010	0.646
GROWTH 1985–94	1.7	1.6	0.001	0.889
GROWTH 1990–8	2.3	1.6	0.084	0.181
INFL 1961–73	5.5	4.7	0.046	0.327
INFL 1973–90	12.5	8.9	0.059	0.263
INFL 1990–8	2.8	3.6	0.034	0.397
GINI 1970	0.331	0.335	0.002	0.859
GINI 1980	0.344	0.315	0.126	0.114
GINI 1990	0.358	0.312	0.243	0.073
GINIWB	0.355	0.288	0.315	0.007
GINIMIL	0.337	0.301	0.073	0.250
GINILIS	0.332	0.266	0.462	0.002
GDI 2000	0.917	0.904	0.122	0.103
GEM 2000	0.679	0.692	0.004	0.793

Sources: see Appendix A1.

Conclusion

This chapter started out by posing the question of whether democracy promotes equality. This is a classical problem in democracy theory, because, to some, democracy is only valuable if it enhances equality between people. Some democracy theorists have suggested that the core concept of democracy is equality (MacPherson, 1966; Pateman, 1970), with the implication that broad citizen participation is necessary. This is basically the Marxist approach to democracy, but it also figures prominently with Rousseau. We have examined whether democracy actually tends to promote income equality as well as gender equality. The evidence suggests that democracy as human rights is connected with equality, albeit not as strongly as the conception of egalitarian democracy requires. Thus, democracy matters more for gender equality than income equality.

The democratic regime tends to support 'Big Government'. A large public sector offers democracy the possibility of supplying a number of vital services to the population. Perhaps this is the simple reason why we find that democracy and the public sector go together? However, among the stable democracies there is a crucial choice between a society with a smaller public sector – the welfare society – and a society with a larger public sector – the welfare state. When one opts for the latter, then one trades off equality against economic efficiency – Tocqueville's paradox that a democracy cannot maximize both freedom and equality.

Democracy is linked with human development or quality of life. Could this regime also be linked to other outcomes such as environmental protection and a low level of corruption? Let us, in the next chapter, look at comparative data concerning the external state of the environment as well as the internal state of government in various countries and relate them to the political regime of the country.

10 Democracy, pollution and corruption

Introduction

The democratic regime has perhaps never met with more sympathy than today. It stands unchallenged, as there is no longer any competing model for how to govern a country. When democracy is rejected, then it is argued that it expresses the values of a particular culture – Occidental values, which are not in agreement with the beliefs of other civilizations. This is the basic idea behind the criticism of democracy within Islam and the Arab or Muslim world, as well as among the adherents of so-called 'Asian values'. But the critiques of democracy fail to come up with a competing paradigm that could claim to have a minimum universal appeal or legitimacy.

Democracy appears attractive because it endorses the rule of law as well as formal equality. Whether this political regime also enhances egalitarian outcomes such as equality in the distribution of income is far less obvious, as Chapter 9 showed. Democracy and gender equality are closely linked, though. In this chapter, we will broaden the outcome analysis and ask whether democracy promotes outcomes such as a low level of corruption as well as environmental protection. There is nothing inherently democratic about these outcomes, as an authoritarian regime may also decide to pursue them. However, it would be interesting to find out whether democratic regimes have a tendency to favour these desirable results more than non-democratic regimes. This question sets up a problem for regression analysis, as one needs to separate the impact of democracy from affluence, knowing that affluence is a most general predictor of several outcomes, including democracy itself.

Policy-making in a democratic country is always more responsive to citizen preferences than authoritarian policy-making. A democracy may display a better performance record than an authoritarian regime on environmental issues, because it reflects citizen preferences better. The openness of democratic politics makes it easier to politicize environmental problems and mobilize support for New Politics than in a dictatorship, where environmental concerns must be part of the rulers' agenda in order to become salient. Whether many or few citizens in a democracy always display an environmental consciousness is, however, a contingency. The connection between democracy and a low level of corruption does not reflect citizen preferences as much as a vital requirement for the functioning of democracy. A low level of corruption is a necessity for the vitality of democracy.

Democracy and the environment

The distinction between policy outputs and policy outcomes is crucial when examining the impact of democracy. Democratic decision-making may have a specific profile resulting in policies with an egalitarian orientation, but it remains an open question as to whether equality will increase in society. Public finance items are mainly a set of outputs, which government can control to a considerable extent. In Chapter 9, we found that democracies support public spending more than non-democracies, but the extent of income inequality is hardly less in democracies than in non-democracies. Whenever one enquires into outcome measures, then the impact of government ambitions and policies is always an open question. Whenever one looks at outcomes in society, it is an open question whether policies matter, as other factors play a role too, besides the efforts of governments. Let us take environmental outcomes as our example.

Most governments have become aware of the dangers to the nation's environment that industrialization and globalization present. Thus, environmental effort has been increasing for more than one decade. The key question, however, is whether environmental policies or regulation are enough to stem the pollution of the environment, which tends to increase every year, at least according to one opinion. Although the threat to the environment is a contested matter in both the scientific community and among social groups, it remains a valid question to enquire into whether the environment is in a better condition in one country than another. What we wish to find out is whether the democratic regime matters for environmental outcomes.

One may assume that there would be two forces operating in democracies. On the one hand, democracies tend to be industrial nations with advanced economies, meaning that their economies produce heavy pollution. Since non-democracies tend to be poor countries and poor countries do not pollute as much as rich countries, one would predict that democracies have more environmental problems than authoritarian countries. On the other hand, democracies are more responsive to citizen needs than dictatorships, meaning that democracies would be more inclined to put into place anti-pollution policies and environmental standards. To decide between these two hypotheses, we need to look at comparative measures of pollution.

It should be emphasized from the outset that the overall environmental condition of a country depends on both the actual production of waste and the capacity of nature to receive it. It is well-known that pollution increases with affluence, as industrialization produces, at the same time, both wealth and waste. However, environmental degradation also depends on the state of the environment before industrialization, as some parts of the world are more vulnerable than others. Thus, how polluted a country is depends on two factors, namely waste on the one hand and environmental fragility on the other. Given such a complicated equation, where environmental condition depends on both waste production and waste reception, it may be difficult to show that a democratic regime performs better than a non-democratic one. Let us look at the indicators; we may wish to employ a few different ones in order to measure both pollution and the actual state of the environment.

Indicators

When a field of research has matured, thanks to the research efforts over a long period of time, then the theoretical insights achieved tend to be accompanied by advances in the development of measurement variables. Within environment studies today there is hardly a set of established measures corresponding to the actual situation within economics and the measurement of output, for instance. We rely here on a few indicators which measure different aspects of the state of the environment and pollution. The World Wide Fund for Nature (WWF) has been highly instrumental in suggesting new indicators on environment and pollution in one of its key publications: *Living Planet Report 2000.*

Let us first point out that the WWF is an independent foundation registered under Swiss law, where the city of Gland is the home of the WWF International comprising the secretariat. Its role is to lead and coordinate the WWF network of offices around the world, working as a team towards the goal of halting the destruction of the globe's natural environment, engaging in activities such as developing policies, fostering global partnerships, coordinating international campaigns and providing supportive measures to make the global operations of the WWF run smoothly. It may be pointed out that the WWF emphasizes that its various offices carry out local conservation work within national boundaries, including practical field projects, scientific research, advice to local and national governments on environmental policy, promoting environmental education and raising awareness of environmental issues. In addition, the WWF has five Associate Organizations that are independent non-governmental bodies that work closely with the WWF in countries where the WWF has no independent office. Thus, the WWF has offices and friends in over forty countries around the world.

The main conclusions of the *Living Planet Report 2000* are based on two new indices, the Living Planet Index (LPI) and the Ecological Footprint (EF). This report first aimed at quantifying changes in the state of the Earth's natural ecosystems over time. Second, it set out to measure the human pressures on the natural environment arising from the consumption of renewable resources and pollution. Here an analysis of the geographic pattern in these ecological pressures was presented, which may be employed for describing the country variation in environment and pollution.

According to LPI, the state of the Earth's natural ecosystems has declined by about 33 per cent over the last thirty years. According to the EF, the ecological pressure of humanity on the Earth has increased by about 50 per cent over the same period, which exceeds the biosphere's regeneration rate. This is not the place to discuss the correctness of the conclusions of the WWF concerning the ecological state of the Earth. It is striking how scholars arrive at different conclusions about the state of Mother Nature (Wildavsky, 1995; Lomborg, 2001). We wish to employ the various indices the WWF suggests for the purposes of comparative analysis of the outcomes of alternative political regimes.

Measuring environmental outcomes is a contested area of research, where opinions tend to differ, to say the least. For example, the WWF states in its report that they have used more data to calculate the LPI in the hope of making the index more reliable. Because the volume of data used in the LPI is much larger than before, it is now calculated regionally, or by ocean in the case of marine ecosystems. According to the WWF, the overall conclusion remains unchanged: the natural wealth of the world's forests, freshwater ecosystems, and oceans and coasts has declined rapidly, particularly in freshwater and marine ecosystems. The WWF also suggests another index to estimate the pressure on the Earth resulting from humanity's natural resource consumption: the ecological footprint (WWF, 2000; see also Wackernagel and Rees, 1996; Costanza, 2000). It measures a population's consumption of food, materials and energy in terms of the area of biologically productive land or sea required to produce those resources and to absorb the corresponding waste. The WWF underlines that this index calculation of the footprint leaves out some kinds of ecological pressures for which data are incomplete, such as water consumption and the release of toxic pollutants, the results thus underestimating humanity's full impact.

The WWF has calculated the Ecological Footprint for individual countries in 1996, as well as for the world from 1961 to 1997. The ecological footprint method allows for estimates of the human pressures on the Earth, based on comparisons between humanity's demands on nature and the capacity of the Earth to supply resources and assimilate waste. In 1997, the ecological footprint of the global population was at least 30 per cent larger than the Earth's biological productive capacity, the WWF states. Highly controversial is the WWF's proposition that, at some time in the 1970s, humanity as a whole passed the point at which it lived within the global regenerative capacity of the Earth, causing depletion of the Earth's natural capital as a consequence. This could have occurred locally many times and in many places throughout human history. However, here we would have the ultimate cause of the decline in the natural wealth of the world's forest, freshwater, and marine ecosystems, as indicated by the LPI.

The WWF suggests that the steepest declines in all ecosystem types have taken place in southern temperate and tropical regions (WWF, 2000). This does not necessarily mean that the state of southern temperate and tropical ecosystems is worse than that of northern temperate ecosystems, but simply that the relative decline has been greatest in tropical ecosystems over the past thirty years. By comparing the resource consumption patterns of different countries, the analysis of the ecological footprint index leads to the conclusion that an average consumer in the industrialized world had an ecological impact four times that of an average consumer in the lower income countries. This implies that rich nations located mainly in northern temperate zones would primarily be responsible for the ongoing loss of natural wealth in the southern temperate and tropical regions of the world (WWF, 2000).

To measure the national ecological situation we rely on two sources of data. First, from the WWF sources we derive a few relevant indicators:

1 *Index on ecological footprint*: our first measure is based on the estimates of the ecological impact of humanity on the environment made by the WWF in their *Living Planet Report 2000* (WWF, 2000).

The ecological footprint measures how much productive land and water a country requires to produce all the resources it consumes and to absorb all the waste it generates. This measure thus says something about the size of the ecological pressure in a given country. High scores indicate heavy pollution. In addition to this measure, the WWF also calculates measures of biological capacity:

2 *Biological capacity index*: it measures the biological production capacity within a country. High scores indicate good environment.

The interesting thing with these two indices – ecological footprint and biological capacity – is that a country may score high on both indices at the same time. This happens when you have a country where there is heavy pollution at the same time as the country has a large capacity to sustain pollution. Employing the two indices, one arrives at the following combined measure which takes both pollution and biological capacity into account:

3 *Ecological deficit index*: it measures how much the Ecological Footprint exceeds the 'biological capacity'. High scores indicate non-sustainability.

The second kind of data is based on estimates available from, and supported by, the World Economic Forum (WEF, 2002):

4 *Environment system index (ESYSI)*: a component of the composite index measuring environmental sustainability (ESI), this set of indicators captures the environmental system of individual countries.

This set of measures (ESYSI) targets the current status of a nation's biophysical environment (air quality, water quantity, water quality, biodiversity and land). Low scores indicate low sustainability.

The World Economic Forum, based in Geneva, is an independent organization committed to improving the state of the world. Funded by the contributions of 1000 of the world's foremost corporations, the Forum acts to further economic growth and social progress. The Forum serves its members and society by creating partnerships between and among business, political, intellectual and other leaders of society to define, discuss and advance key issues on the global agenda. Incorporated in 1971 as a foundation, the World Economic Forum is impartial and not-for-profit, and is tied to no political, partisan or national interests. The Environmental Sustainability Index (ESI) is based on a collaborative project between the Forum and Yale Center for

Environmental Law and Policy and the Center for International Earth Science Information Network at Columbia University. 2002 is the third year that the ESI has been released. Let us see how different countries are ranked on these four indices, allowing for a certain amount of uncertainty in all of these measures.

Country scores

Since environmental indicators have been available for a relatively short period of time, the scoring of countries reflects considerable uncertainty. Yet, we list four measures for a number of countries in Table 10.1 in a tentative manner. What is important is not the exact score of a country but the relative position in relation to other countries. Looking at averages on these four indices, can we conclude that democracies are different from non-democracies?

These four indices do not measure the same thing. Total ecological footprint is an index that measures pollution whereas biological capacity stands for the robustness of a country from an environmental point of view. The scores of these two indices need not be related to each other. The indices on ecological deficits and environmental system target a similar phenomenon, namely Nature's sustainability. It cannot be sufficiently underlined that these measures on the health of the environment and the amount of environmental protection *do not* measure the same phenomenon. Countries may score both high and low on two of these indices, namely pollution and biological capacity. If there is an ecological deficit, then the environmental sustainability tends to be low.

One may wish to consult the details in Table 10.1 in order to come to grips with these environmental measures. It presents the country rankings for the ten highest and lowest scoring countries around 2000.

Examining the listings in Table 10.1 opens up a broad overview of the environmental situation of the globe. One must thus distinguish between *pollution* and the *capacity to endure pollution*. It is when countries has heavy pollution and, at the same time, a low capacity to receive it that there is a great danger to its environment, or a severe ecological deficit and lack of sustainability.

In Table 10.1 one observes that the top scoring countries when it comes to environmental pollution or pressure on the environment include mainly advanced countries, whether they are democratic or non-democratic: UAE, Singapore and the United States. On the other hand, countries where there is a very small ecological footprint include mainly extremely poor countries: Afghanistan, Namibia and Congo, Kinshasa. Ecological footprint is pollution which comes with modernization and it is mainly derived from industrialization. Countries that are highly vulnerable to pollution include an almost entirely different group, namely countries with a special environment such as Hong Kong, Taiwan and Singapore (islands), Yemen and Saudi Arabia (desert) as well as Bangladesh (flooding). The robust countries, from an environmental point of view, include the countries with a high biological capacity to receive

Table 10.1 State of the environment around 2000

ECTOTAL: total ecological footprint		BIOCAPA: existing biological capacity		ECODEFI: national ecological deficit		ENVSYS: environment system index	
Low ten	High ten	High ten	Low ten	Ten best	Ten worst	Ten high	Ten low
Afghanistan	United Arab Emirates	Gabon	Hong Kong	Gabon	United Arab Emirates	Canada	India
Bangladesh	Singapore	Papua New Guinea	Bangladesh	Papua New Guinea	Singapore	Gabon	United Arab Emirates
Namibia	United States	Congo, Brazzaville	Singapore	Congo, Brazzaville	Kuwait	Finland	Belgium
Yemen	Kuwait	New Zealand	Taiwan	Central African Republic	United States	Norway	Korea, Republic of
Congo, Kinshasa	Denmark	Central African Republic	Jordan	Bolivia	Hong Kong	Venezuela	Madagascar
Lesotho	New Zealand	Bolivia	Yemen	Brazil	Saudi Arabia	Botswana	Jamaica
Sierra Leone	Ireland	Brazil	Haiti	Peru	Japan	Congo, Brazzaville	Philippines
Chad	Australia	Canada	Iraq	Laos	Korea, Republic of	Namibia	Korea, Dem. Rep.
Burundi	Finland	Finland	Afghanistan	New Zealand	Israel	Iceland	Kuwait
Mozambique	Canada	Australia	Saudi Arabia	Congo, Kinshasa	United Kingdom	Argentina	Haiti

Sources: see Appendix A1; see also Appendix 10.1.

pollution: Gabon, Congo, Central African Republic and Brazil, for instance, as well as Bolivia, among the poor countries of the world. There are also, however, a few rich countries, such as Canada, Finland and Norway.

To understand sustainability, one needs to take account of how a country ranks on both these two indices: ecological footprint and biological capacity. Thus, one may suggest that the key index is the deficit indicator, which takes into account both pollution and robustness by subtracting the latter from the former. In essence, a country would face a threat to its environment when it is in minus on this indicator, meaning that it cannot compensate for pollution by robustness. Here we have both democracies like the United States, Japan, South Korea, Israel and the UK and undemocratic countries such as UAE, Kuwait and Saudi Arabia. These are the vulnerable countries including Singapore and Hong Kong, although the latter is now only a province in China.

The countries with an ecological surplus – robustness compensating for pollution – would likewise include both democratic and undemocratic countries. Here we have both giant Brazil and tiny Laos, mountainous Peru and Bolivia and a large island like New Zealand. Perhaps the ranking of Brazil will change in the future as the destruction of the Amazon Basin continues?

Finally, let us look at the scores on the index of the environment system, which comes from an entirely different source. Do these scores concerning sustainability correlate with the scores on environmental deficit? To a considerable extent these two independent country rankings do tend to go together ($r = 0.48$). The countries that face no problem with the environmental system include both democracies – Canada, Finland, Iceland, Botswana – and non-democracies or semi-democracies: Gabon, Congo, Venezuela and Argentina. On the other hand, environmental sustainability tends to be low in countries such as India, South Korea and Belgium (democracies) as well as in UAE, Kuwait and Madagascar (non-democracies). We may conclude that environmental deficit or sustainability must be largely independent of the nature of the political regime.

Reduced form evidence

Table 10.2 corroborates this conclusion concerning the impact of the political regime. It reports on how these alternative environmental measures corresponding to the different indices discussed above (p. 213) go together with the nature of the political regime. Democracy matters little for the variation in any of these indices.

The correlation analyses in Table 10.2 suggest that democracy is related to only one of the environmental outcome indicators, namely total ecological footprint. That democracy correlates positively in regard to the amount of total ecological footprint reflects the basic fact that most democracies are countries with an advanced economy. At the same time, democracy correlates weakly with biological capacity, which entails that there is some compensation involved. Thus, democracy has nothing to do with the amount of ecological deficit of a country. It even seems to be the case that democracy is weakly associated with the sustainability index, which could be interpreted as evidence

Table 10.2 Democracy and the environment indices (correlations)

		DEM 1991–5	DEM 1995–2001	DEM 2000	DEM 2001
ECOTOTAL	r	0.50	0.46	0.43	0.44
	sig.	0.000	0.000	0.000	0.000
	N	146	148	148	148
BIOCAPA	r	0.23	0.19	0.18	0.19
	sig.	0.004	0.019	0.026	0.018
	N	148	150	150	150
ECODEFI	r	−0.03	−0.06	−0.05	−0.04
	sig.	0.686	0.503	0.548	0.606
	N	148	150	150	150
ENVSYS	r	0.29	0.25	0.23	0.25
	sig.	0.000	0.003	0.006	0.003
	N	138	140	140	140

Sources: see Appendix A1.

that democracies operate environmental policies that reduce the consequences of the strong ecological footprint in these industrialized countries.

Structural model evidence

Given the weak interaction between democracy and the environmental indicators used here, one may wish to explore another framework for accounting for the national differences in environmental outcomes stated in Table 10.2. We suggest that the environmental scores should be related to the following factors in a regression model:

- GDP: increasing pollution;
- area: decreasing vulnerability;
- closeness to the Equator: increasing vulnerability;
- access to fresh water: decreasing vulnerability.

Table 10.3 reports on such a regression model. The findings indicate that GDP is a major cause of pollution and determinant of total ecological footprint. Interestingly, GDP does not have the same impact on ecological deficit, which shows that there is more to the condition of the environment than pollution. What needs to be taken into account is biological capacity, or the receptor capacity of a country. Ecological deficits occur when the environment is fragile, as when it is placed in a tropical environment with reduced access to fresh water resources. These regression models also include the democracy variable, thus controlling for the impact of democracy. But political regime is only significant for total ecological footprint, increasing and not decreasing the pressure on the environment.

It may be pointed out that only the model with total ecological footprint as the dependent variable arrives at a reasonably high degree of explained

Table 10.3 Environmental outcomes (regression analysis)

Dependent variables:	ECTOTAL		BIOCAPA		ECODEFI		ENVSYS	
Independent variables:	Coeffs	t-stat	Coeffs	t-stat	Coeffs	t-stat	Coeffs	t-stat
LANDAREA	0.000	3.71	0.000	1.09	0.000	0.26	0.000	2.14
LNGDP/CAP	1.437	7.76	2.160	2.60	0.723	0.85	4.075	1.79
LATITU	1.972	3.83	−4.053	−1.75	−6.025	−2.55	−9.192	−1.43
WATER	−0.011	−1.39	−0.098	−2.57	−0.086	−2.21	−0.124	−1.18
DEM 1995–2001	0.160	2.92	0.173	0.70	0.013	0.05	0.779	1.18
Constant	−9.600	−9.30	−6.932	−1.50	2.668	0.56	23.858	1.88
adj rsq	0.75	–	0.10	–	0.12	–	0.10	–
N	102	–	102	–	102	–	99	–

Sources: see Appendix A1.

variance. It is obvious that the level of the ecological footprint is highest among affluent societies and these are mainly found in the regions distant from the Equator. Therefore we may also expect a positive impact of the democracy variable on ecological pressure. Finally, the other three environmental models have some interesting findings. Land area impacts on the environmental system index, whereas ecological deficit is highest in areas close to the Equator. All in all, these models suggest that the index capturing the general stress on the environment (total ecological footprint) is influenced by mainly GDP, but that ecological deficit increases with proximity to the Equator. The total ecological footprint index captures the impact on the environment of the affluent industrial or post-industrial societies, among which many adhere to the democratic regime.

Thus, one cannot state that democracy promotes environmental sustainability. One could actually state that the limited set of data analysed above (p. 218) indicate rather that many democracies operate economies which threaten Mother Nature and ecological sustainability. But when one adds biological capacity to the equation, then it appears that other factors besides affluence play a role. An ecological deficit or a low level of sustainability occurs in countries where there is both a strong ecological footprint and a low biological capacity, which has nothing to do with democracy.

Corruption and democracy

Turning to the internal pollution in a country, we focus on the occurrence of corruption. According to one theory of democracy, the democratic regime should be immune towards this form of degeneration. In populist democracy the people are looked on as incorruptible and always correct when it takes decisions through the participation of all – Rousseau's approach. On the other hand, there is also the opposite theory of democracy, claiming that this regime can be invaded by special interests making coalitions with politicians in order to reap the benefits from rent-seeking. The public choice school has supported this framework (Olson, 1982), but it can also be found within Chicago School regulation theory (Stigler, 1988).

If 'corruption' stands for bribery and the illegal remuneration of public officials, then democracy as constitutional government cannot tolerate this phenomenon. When an authoritarian regime strongly emphasizes bureaucracy, then it also ends up fighting corruption. If 'corruption' refers to any form of money contribution by the private sector to politicians, then matters are different. Now let us focus on corruption as illegal bribery.

One would expect constitutional democracies to score lower on corruption in government than non-democratic countries, because modern democracy is committed to the promotion of the rule of law – at least in theory. According to rule of law conceptions, democratic government must fight corruption in government and its bureaucracies. Authoritarian regimes should be less resistant to this kind of private interest invasion, as their mode of operation is less well institutionalized. Many authoritarian regimes involve traditional rule which leans towards patrimonial or prebendal relationships. Yet one may find countries which are not considered fully democratic but fight corruption strongly, such as, for instance, Singapore.

In theory, one would expect the spread of corruption to reflect not only the political regime in operation in a country but also social and economic realities. The demand for and supply of corruption will be high, first and foremost, in poor or middle income countries. Along with economic factors, culture also matters. In some societies, corruption is looked on as unavoidable, whereas in others there is a strong ethic against the taking or offering of bribes. Such a spirit of anti-corruption may be fostered by a religion like Protestantism or by the spread of values such as interpersonal trust. Thus, how much corruption there is in any country will depend on more factors than merely the nature of the political regime.

In practice, measuring corruption in public administration and government is far from an easy task, especially if one wishes to make a comparative assessment. How can a macro index of corruption in government be developed? First, there are many conceptual questions concerning what is to count as corrupt practices or as behaviour which is either intentionally or unintentionally to be classified as an attempt at corrupting another person. Each legal system has its way of defining corruption and identifying criteria that detect attempts at corruption. Typically, both the person offering the bribe and the person receiving the bribe are considered guilty of an attempt at corruption. A 'bribe' may be a pecuniary reward or any kind of personal favour. Similarly, the service supplied for the bribe may include a public contract, a job or any form of special treatment. Practices vary significantly in how well corruption is identified, reflecting the fact that corruption laws are very differently enforced.

The stereotype is that corruption is widespread outside of Occidental countries. Poverty is, of course, a significant force in stimulating the demand for bribes. But it is also true that some countries have managed to fight corruption successfully, although they are not Occidental; for instance, Singapore and Hong Kong in South East Asia, and Oman and Qatar in the Gulf. These countries are rich, though. It is generally stated that corruption is omnipresent in poor Sub-Saharan Africa as well as in Latin America and South Asia. Corruption in poor countries often takes very concrete forms, as the offer for bribes is often quite visible. However, more subtle forms of corruption are involved when a whole country or culture is described as 'clientelistic'.

It is sometimes stated that corruption exists also in Occidental countries but its manifestations are different and less contrary to law. Thus, money is also transferred from the private sector to the public sector in Western Europe and the United States as well as in Japan, but these money transfers are more institutionalized and less personal in nature. In Western Europe, the phenomenon of corporatism could involve certain practices which involve – at least to some extent – gifts from private individuals to people in public positions or the other way around. In the United States the entire system of election campaign financing and the PACs (political action committees) appears to be very difficult to control and institutionalize completely in a just manner (Gais, 1996). Perhaps the entire funding of election campaigns in the US, with its extreme costs, has developed into an Achilles' heel for American democracy, favouring the influence on policy-making for big business? In several West European countries considerable public support for political parties has been introduced at various levels, together with a ban on explicit campaign contributions from private sources to the parties. Economic support for political parties may sometimes be chanelled to the newspapers of these parties.

The demand for corruption reflects people's view of politicians and bureaucrats. If the state is looked on as inefficient and unaccountable, then people will employ bribes to get the actions they need from the authorities. The supply of corruption depends again on the behaviour of politicians and bureaucrats. When they lack the resources necessary for the accomplishment of their tasks, then they see corruption as another source of revenue. One cannot state that democracy is always immune against the invasion of corruption or that dictatorships must be inclined towards corruption, as the demand and supply of corruption can be high or low in both types of political regimes depending on other factors.

Thus, an authoritarian regime could be successful in combating corruption if its government really wants to be, as the capacity to control and clamp down would be immense. At the same time, the lack of transparency and accountability in an authoritarian regime would make it vulnerable to the simple logic of demand and supply of corrupt practices. On theoretical grounds it is impossible to predict whether democracies or non-democracies perform better or worse on corruption. Both will suffer from the occurrence of various forms of corruption. Democracies are, in theory, to be immune to corruption but, in practice, their institutions may not be sufficiently enforced to stem it. Authoritarian regimes have, in theory, the control necessary to fight corruption but they may lack the will power to do it in practice. A macro index measuring the occurrence of corruption may clarify how often corruption tends to occur in democracies as against non-democracies.

Let us see how various countries score on a recently constructed index on the lack of corruption. We here rely on the index on perceived corruption generated by the Transparency International (TI). This index goes from 0 (high levels of perceived corruption) to 10 (no perceived corruption), and it is based on expert surveys directed to business people. This TI index seems to covary with other measures of corruption. Still, one may not be sure whether the TI index measures the real presence of corruption or it is the *perception of the image of corruption* that it targets. Here we simply make the assumption that the TI index is the best measure available, measuring a phenomena that may be labelled 'the presence of the perception of corruption' (Mauro, 1995; Treisman, 2000; Montinola and Jackman, 2002).

Thus, in Table 10.4, Corr 1998, 1999, 2000 stand for the perception of corruption, where low values entail more corruption, and high values imply less. The table also contains a rescaled variable (New corrupt) where high scores stand for a high level of perceived corruption and low scores for a low level of perceived corruption. Table 10.4 presents the reduced model evidence concerning the connection between democracy and the perceived level of (or lack of) corruption.

Table 10.4 Democracy and (lack of) corruption (correlations)

		DEM 1991–5	DEM 1995–2001	DEM 2000	DEM 2001
CORR 1998	*r*	0.67	0.63	0.59	0.58
	sig.	0.000	0.000	0.000	0.000
	N	85	85	85	85
CORR 1999	*r*	0.70	0.67	0.64	0.62
	sig.	0.000	0.000	0.000	0.000
	N	97	98	98	98
CORR 2000	*r*	0.74	0.68	0.64	0.62
	sig.	0.000	0.000	0.000	0.000
	N	90	90	90	90
NEWCORR	*r*	−0.69	−0.65	−0.62	−0.62
	sig.	0.000	0.000	0.000	0.000
	N	105	106	106	106

Sources: see Appendix A1.

Note
CORR 1998 to 2000 measure the perceived lack of corruption; NEWCORR is rescaled so that the higher the score, the more perceived corruption – this variable also adds information from the scores reported for the period 1998 to 2001.

The evidence reported in Table 10.4 indicates that democracies perform better than authoritarian regimes when it comes to lack of corruption. The correlation coefficients suggest a quite strong correlation between perceived corruption and democracy. However, we must check whether it is democracy that matters or whether there is not a common background factor: affluence. In an affluent society the bureaucracy would be paid decent salaries, which reduces the supply of corruption. Similarly, the demand for corruption would be lower, as people could get more of the services they need through the private sector.

Table 10.5 suggests a regression model with some relevant structural model evidence. In the regression models tested, we employ the rescaled corruption variable (new corrupt) as the dependent variable, meaning that high scores stand for high levels of perceived corruption. The background variable afflu-

Table 10.5 Democracy and perceived corruption (regression model)

Dependent variables: Independent variables:	NEWCORR Coeffs	t-stat	NEWCORR Coeffs	t-stat
DEM 1995–2001	−0.217	−2.76	−0.198	−2.53
HDI 1998	−7.148	−6.33	−7.498	−6.73
PROT	−0.029	−4.35	−0.028	−4.19
BUDD	−0.011	−1.58	–	–
Constant	12.671	19.54	12.714	19.48
adj rsq	0.63	–	0.63	–
N	104	–	104	–

Sources: see Appendix A1.

ence is here measured with the Human Development Index (HDI) estimated for 1998.

The estimates reported in Table 10.5 suggest that affluence (HDI 98) and religion (PROT) have the strongest impact on the level of corruption. Controlling for these two factors, we note though that democracy has an impact on the dependent variable. The size of the impact is, however, reduced through the control of affluence and religion. Democracy, we conclude, reduces the level of perceived corruption, but there are other factors that are operating and they have more of an impact on corruption than the political regime.

Democracy, private interests and the public interest

The question of corruption in politics raises a number of issues concerning how democracies handle the balance between private interests and the public interest. In principle, there are two alternative ways of interpreting democracy and interests. On the one hand, one may deny the existence of any public interest, admitting only that all players pursue their private interests. According to this view it becomes crucial that democracy delivers rules which prohibit that any interest prevails to the extent that it can dominate over all other interests. This is the pessimistic view, which focuses on counter-veiling forces, checks and balances as well as the possibility to use institutions to turn private interests into public interests according to the well-known formula suggested first by Mandeville.

Mandeville's *The Fable of the Bees: Or, Private Vices, Public Benefits*, first published in 1714, became highly controversial as it was accused of denigrating religion and virtue and recommending vices. His idea that self-interests may be conducive to public benefits initiated a whole framework of interpreting the role of interest in society, culminating in the idea of spontaneous order with Hayek (Barry, 1982). Mandeville suggested a theory of human development from an 'animal existence' to 'civilization', where human sociability and virtue followed from self-love and self-liking. Civilization was based on the vile characteristics of people, because humans could suppress their initial impulses and be manipulated into large cooperative societies by means of praise and blame. Although Mandeville assigned this task to 'skilful politicians', language, society, arts and sciences would result from a long-term development in this direction (Goldsmith, 1985).

On the other hand, there is the positive doctrine that public interests do exist and that rules can be devised which protect them from invasion from private interests. Thus, a polity has certain objective interests that it protects, such as the distinction between public and private and the 'cleanness' of politics, including the fight against corruption. Here, the definition and implementation of the public interest becomes the central preoccupation for the polity. This task may be made more difficult when the institutional set up allows many players to obstruct the public interest, for instance, by using their veto power. In the populist theory of democracy as the expression of the general will of the people, the idea of the public interest looms large.

The question of the nature of interests in politics has been long debated. Whether one adheres to the pessimistic or optimistic view, one can hardly accept the famous dictum: 'private vices = public benefits'. The pessimistic view also realizes that private interests may hurt the polity, if unchecked by rules that disperse power and invite citizen complaints and redress. Thus, institutions are a necessary complement to interests. When democracy is regarded as a mere prolongation of the market into the area of politics, then one wishes to point out that markets also need a set of transparent rules about fair play. Very few economists would take the position, that for example, insider trading poses no problem or that accounting failures do not disrupt the ordinary functioning of enterprises and financial markets. Similarly, corruption hurts the fairness of the political game (the pessimistic view) and it is entirely at odds with the view that democracy is a mechanism to reveal the true interests of people or the objective interests of a nation (the optimistic view).

An authoritarian regime may commit itself strongly to stamp out corruption, as it cannot accept the democratic view of the polity as a mechanism for the transformation of politics into a market game. An authoritarian regime believes that it harbours some general interests that democracy would pervert. Right-wing authoritarian regimes tend to adhere to interests connected with the nation, whereas left-wing authoritarian regimes focus on the interests of the people, i.e. the working classes. Corruption could threaten these interests, which is why some authoritarian regimes have extremely harsh punishments for attempts at corruption. Usually, such attempts make both the donor and the receiver of a bribe a criminal. In practice, however, authoritarian regimes tend to be invaded by special interests. Let us consider the presidential regimes of the world.

Presidentialism occurs frequently in poor Third World countries. Since most of these countries have failed in supporting a stable democracy, it is suggested that presidentialism is a negative for democracy (Linz and Valenzuela, 1994). One could, however, argue that the theory of the failure of presidentialism does not take corruption into account. When presidentialism fails, then it may be a matter of corruption destroying the credibility of government. When presidentialism is a success, then corruption may be under control. Let us look at the interaction between the structure of the executive and corruption – see Table 10.6.

Presidentialism correlates positively with higher levels of perceived corruption, whereas the opposite is true for parliamentarism. Thus, executive institutions covary with levels of perceived corruption, where two interpretations are

Table 10.6 Presidentialism and corruption (correlation analysis)

	PRES(A)	*PRES(B)*	*PARLIAM*
NEWCORR	$r = 0.29$ sig. $= 0.003$ $N = 106$	$r = 0.55$ sig. $= 0.00$ $N = 102$	$r = -0.49$ sig. $= 0.000$ $N = 93$

Sources: see Appendix A1.

possible. Either presidentialism is conducive to corruption or a society with lots of corruption prefers presidentialism to parliamentarism. Perhaps both interpretations are valid, as there could well be a vicious circle between presidentialism and corruption, one sustaining the other, etc.

Democracy and low levels of corruption go together. This interaction may again be looked on as both condition and effect. High levels of corruption reduce the probability of a democracy, and democracies try to stem corruption, not without success. Democracies elaborate a number of institutional practices which restrict the occurrence of corruption. It has been suggested that democracies also place certain kinds of policy-making at arm's length from government. Thus, independent authorities can be trusted with the making and implementation of policy in areas such as regulation and monetary policy, including the supply of money for the economy. Such policy devolution would, the argument claims, enhance the public interest and remove policy from the negative impact of self-seeking politicians acting with myopia and guile. Independent authorities prevent vital policy areas from becoming invaded by egoism and self-interests. Is there any evidence to support the theory that democracy should auto-limit itself through the support for independent authorities at arm's length from government?

Will independent bodies improve outcomes?

When the democratic regime is said to have a tendency to conduct bad economic policies resulting in deficits and debts, then one remedy is suggested. Economic policies are better decided by independent bodies, such as an independent central bank. Independent public bodies at arm's length from politicians seeking selfish short-term advantages would take a long-term perspective on the economy, engaging in policies which are in the best interests of the country. Such independent bodies would be staffed by high-profile experts who combine considerable authority to do what they consider best with an orientation towards the public interest. The conclusion of this argument is that democracies should employ decentralization to stem the consequences of myopia, rent-seeking and opportunism (Brennan and Buchanan, 1985, 1989).

Let us test this public choice argument by looking at the status of Central Banks and economic outcomes such as inflation and economic growth. Independent public bodies with which democracies entrust policy-making and implementation are mostly to be found in the economic area. Thus, independent public bodies often handle economic regulation such as anti-trust policy-making and harmonization policies. One may regard the EU Commission as one giant independent body to which the democracies in Western Europe have delegated much, if not most, of their economic legislation.

Let us focus on Central Banks here and test the hypothesis that their independence improves on important economic outcomes such as low inflation and low unemployment. The theory of Central Bank independence would, if true, restrict the attractiveness of democracy as a regime. It calls for constitutional limits on democracy in order to guarantee that rent-seeking politicians do not destroy society through their opportunism and myopia – the position of Buchanan. Let us first examine reduced form evidence and then employ structural model evidence.

A number of rankings of Central Bank independence have been carried out in the past ten years (Cukierman, 1992; Bernhard, 1998). They correlate highly, meaning that it is likely that they measure the same phenomenon (Table 10.7). A Central Bank has a high level of independence when it decides the monetary policy of a country without consultation from the Ministry of Finance. The European Central Bank in Frankfurt is such an independent Central Bank, which supplies the Euro to the member states in an autonomous manner, serving only the objective of keeping the value of the Euro stable.

Central Bank autonomy is measured by looking at whether the Central Bank can conduct monetary policy without seeking coordination with the Minister of Finance. The two classical models of Central Bank independence used are the American Federal Reserve Bank and the German Central Bank. However, the Swiss National Bank is also well known for its high degree of autonomy. On the other hand, there were countries which had linked Central Bank monetary actions with the Ministry of Finance in an overall economic policy determined by the government, as in the UK, France and the Nordic countries. The first model is often referred to as 'monetarist' whereas the second model used to be labelled as 'Keynesian'.

However, in the 1980s and 1990s, several countries moved in the direction of the Central Bank autonomy model, accepting more monetarism. In Western Europe the countries that have entered the European Monetary Union have delegated their monetary policy to the ECB, which has only one strict mission, namely to maintain the value of the Euro. Looking at data for a relatively long period of time, is it possible to find evidence for the claim that democracies would do better to rely on independent authorities than make policy themselves?

Table 10.7 Central Bank independence (correlations)

		CBANK1	CBANK2	CBANK3	CBANK4
CBANK1	r	1.00	–	–	–
	sig.	–	–	–	–
	N	–	–	–	–
CBANK2	r	0.86	1.00	–	–
	sig.	0.000	–	–	–
	N	18	–	–	–
CBANK3	r	0.71	0.82	1.00	–
	sig.	0.001	0.000	–	–
	N	18	18	–	–
CBANK4	r	0.67	0.80	0.89	1.00
	sig.	0.003	0.000	0.000	–
	N	18	18	18	–

Sources: see Appendix A1.

Testing the hypothesis that Central Bank independence improves economic outcomes can be done by either examining correlations or by resorting to regressions. One may debate which kind of evidence is superior. Here, we look first at reduced form evidence about any link between Central Bank independence on the one hand and inflation and economic growth on the other. We limit the test to the 1960s, 1970s, 1980s and 1990s, i.e. before the advent of the ECB, because it has replaced the many Central Banks in Western Europe to a considerable extent.

Table 10.8 suggests that Central Bank independence has the impact on inflation that monetarism predicts, namely reducing it. However, Central Bank independence has no impact on output, or economic growth. This result indicates that the relationship between a key institution like an independent Central Bank and outcomes is more complex than the argument scrutinized here entails. We suggest that deficit spending may be a key intervening factor. Table 10.9 tests a regression model which predicts inflation and economic growth from Central Bank independence and deficit spending by the national (federal) government.

The findings from the regression analysis support the previous analysis. Central bank independence was conducive to lower inflation rates, at least during the period 1973 to 1990, whereas the impact on economic growth is

Table 10.8 Central Bank independence and economic outcomes (correlations)

		CBANK1	CBANK2	CBANK3	CBANK4
GROWTH 1960–73	r	−0.20	−0.36	−0.19	−0.04
	sig.	0.375	0.148	0.444	0.878
	N	22	18	18	18
GROWTH 1973–85	r	0.02	−0.15	0.03	0.18
	sig.	0.938	0.558	0.906	0.476
	N	22	18	18	18
GROWTH 1985–94	r	−0.05	−0.15	−0.17	−0.00
	sig.	0.831	0.560	0.504	0.996
	N	22	18	18	18
GROWTH 1990–8	r	−0.02	−0.18	−0.17	−0.17
	sig.	0.940	0.469	0.500	0.491
	N	22	18	18	18
INFL 1961–73	r	−0.21	−0.41	−0.61	−0.40
	sig.	0.349	0.094	0.007	0.102
	N	22	18	18	18
INFL 1973–90	r	−0.03	−0.61	−0.76	−0.76
	sig.	0.895	0.008	0.000	0.000
	N	22	18	18	18
INFL 1990–8	r	0.19	−0.19	−0.25	−0.25
	sig.	0.396	0.442	0.317	0.325
	N	22	18	18	18

Sources: see Appendix A1.

Table 10.9 Central Bank independence and outcomes (regression)

Dependent variables:	Inflation 1973–90		Growth 1973–85	
Independent variables:	Coeffs	t-stat	Coeffs	t-stat
CBANK4	−10.626	−4.18	0.632	0.59
DEFICITS 1980	−0.149	−1.04	0.020	0.34
Constant	13.832	7.81	1.205	1.63
adj rsq	0.55	–	0.00	–
N	18	–	18	–

Sources: see Appendix A1.

non-existent. It is also obvious that deficit spending negatively matters not only for inflation but also for economic growth among the set of OECD countries. Independent bodies, to which policy-making and implementation has been delegated, may have an impact on economic outcomes like inflation. Thus, democracies may find it advantageous to decide themselves to limit their decision-making by creating independent authorities at arm's length from government. One key economic outcome, low inflation, is promoted by institutional devolution of economic policy-making to an independent monetary authority, as the existence of such a mechanism reduces inflation no matter what deficit spending takes.

It is not only the European Central Bank that could be interpreted as such a mechanism for independent monetary policy in the democracies in Western Europe. Actually, the entire EU Commission may be seen as such a mechanism, which democracies may profitably use for policy-making and implementation in certain well defined areas, such as economic regulation. The devolution of policy-making and implementation to an independent authority at arm's length from a democratically elected government may thus improve on outcomes, but the mission of the independent body must be clearly and transparently defined.

Conclusion

Democracy is not only a political regime which enforces human rights. It also contributes to other outcomes. One may look on people as being equipped with universal and unalienable rights or as adhering to different civilizations with their specific concepts of justice. According to the first approach, democracy is a universally valid regime which should be introduced in all countries of the world. However, using the second approach, democracy cannot claim such a universal status. There are other values at stake when one endorses a political regime, such as, for instance, religious or specific civilization values.

Democracy is not only to be looked on as a guarantee of human rights, whether considered as universal or local values of justice. It can also be seen as an instrument that enhances other outcomes. Thus, democracy is conducive to a large public sector, covering education, healthcare and social insurance programmes. It also counteracts corruption, as it tends to go together with the rule of law in the form of constitutional democracy.

Whereas democracy is conducive to 'cleanness' in government, we find no impact of democracy on environmental protection. Environmental outcomes depend on other factors than the political regime. First there is environmental vulnerability due to the physical structure of the country. Second there is pollution, which depends on the nature of the economy. Environmental pressure and environmental precariousness add up to environmental sustainability, which is not closely connected with the democracy–non-democracy separation.

It has been argued that democracies may improve on their outcomes by relying on policy delegation to independent authorities. If democratic politics may be invaded by political opportunism and myopia, then independent bodies like an autonomous Central Bank may improve policy outcomes by staying at arm's length from government. We found some evidence for the theory of monetarism, linking the fight against inflation with Central Bank autonomy. Democracies may use the delegation of policy and implementation to independent authorities, set up with a special mission, in order to improve on outcomes.

Appendix

Table 10.10 Country rankings on environment indices

Country	ECTOTAL: total ecological footprint	BIOCAPA: biological capacity	ECODEFI: ecological deficit	ENVSYS: environment system index
Afghanistan	0.58	0.38	−0.19	–
Albania	1.86	1.38	−0.48	62.2
Algeria	1.79	0.58	−1.21	50.3
Angola	0.82	2.74	1.92	62.6
Argentina	3.79	5.1	1.31	72.4
Armenia	1.16	0.69	−0.47	50.4
Australia	8.49	9.42	0.93	66.1
Austria	5.45	4.15	−1.3	64.6
Azerbaijan	2.18	0.64	−1.54	44.2
Bangladesh	0.6	0.08	−0.52	40.9
Belarus	5.27	3.47	−1.8	53
Belgium	5.88	2.3	−3.58	25.9
Benin	0.97	1.55	0.58	43
Bhutan	0.79	2.6	1.82	49.4
Bolivia	1.29	13.25	11.96	71.1
Bosnia and Herzegovina	1.29	1.39	0.1	45.8
Botswana	1.68	1.92	0.24	77.2
Brazil	2.6	11.56	8.96	66.3
Bulgaria	3.81	2.01	−1.8	35.9
Burkina Faso	0.9	0.79	−0.11	44.7
Burma-Myanmar	1.07	2.71	1.65	44.7
Burundi	0.75	0.5	−0.25	45.1
Cambodia	0.83	3.12	2.29	47
Cameroon	0.89	4.23	3.35	47.1
Canada	7.66	11.16	3.5	90.4
Central African Republic	1.12	14.51	13.38	68.6

Country	ECTOTAL: total ecological footprint	BIOCAPA: biological capacity	ECODEFI: ecological deficit	ENVSYS: environment system index
Chad	0.75	1.54	0.79	59.2
Chile	3.39	2.01	−1.38	50.3
China	1.84	0.89	−0.96	31.5
Colombia	1.9	5.66	3.76	69.8
Congo, Brazzaville	1.15	20.04	18.89	75.8
Congo, Kinshasa	0.69	6.94	6.25	53.1
Costa Rica	2.77	2.16	−0.6	51.5
Cote d'Ivoire	0.95	2	1.05	45.4
Croatia	2.35	2.19	−0.17	53.4
Cuba	2.1	1.11	−0.98	31.2
Czech Republic	6.3	2.93	−3.37	52.7
Denmark	9.88	5.68	−4.19	43.9
Dominican Republic	1.37	1.03	−0.34	36.9
Ecuador	2.26	4	1.74	65.3
Egypt. Arab Republic	1.7	0.64	−1.06	53.8
El Salvador	1.55	0.68	−0.87	50.1
Estonia	7.12	4.03	−3.1	57.7
Ethiopia	0.85	0.68	−0.18	43.6
Finland	8.45	9.77	1.32	78.7
France	7.27	4.27	−3.01	50.7
Gabon	2.06	33.77	31.72	81.2
Georgia	1.14	1.22	0.08	−
Germany	6.31	2.48	−3.83	45.3
Ghana	1.12	1.2	0.08	52.3
Greece	5.58	2.31	−3.27	43.7
Guatemala	1.4	1.76	0.36	54
Guinea	0.85	1.6	0.75	49.7
Haiti	0.78	0.3	−0.48	18.1
Honduras	1.43	2.26	0.83	57.2
Hong Kong, China	6.35	0.06	−6.28	−
Hungary	5.01	3.07	−1.94	53.7
Iceland	−	−	−	73.1
India	1.06	0.74	−0.32	27.4
Indonesia	1.48	3.18	1.7	32.6
Iran, Islamic Republic	2.47	0.76	−1.71	41
Iraq	1.73	0.35	−1.38	34.9
Ireland	9.43	6.71	−2.72	57.2
Israel	5.4	0.76	−4.64	39.2
Italy	5.51	1.92	−3.59	33
Jamaica	2.68	0.73	−1.95	21.4
Japan	5.94	0.86	−5.08	32.7
Jordan	1.71	0.21	−1.5	42.7
Kazakhstan	4.45	2.05	−2.4	50.6
Kenya	1.15	0.57	−0.59	51.9
Korea, North	1.92	0.73	−1.19	19.4
Korea, South	5.6	0.74	−4.86	21.7
Kuwait	10.31	0.65	−9.67	19.1
Kyrgyz Republic	1.87	1.5	−0.37	43.5
Lao PDR	0.91	7.29	6.39	57.6
Latvia	3.74	4.08	0.33	62.9
Lebanon	3.19	0.69	−2.5	35.5

Country	ECTOTAL: total ecological footprint	BIOCAPA: biological capacity	ECODEFI: ecological deficit	ENVSYS: environment system index
Lesotho	0.7	0.45	−0.24	−
Liberia	1.16	5.1	3.95	52.4
Libya	4.36	0.58	−3.78	53.7
Lithuania	4.76	3.72	−1.04	59.7
Luxembourg	−	−	−	−
Macedonia, FYR	3.24	1.19	−2.05	43
Madagascar	0.93	2.93	2	21.5
Malawi	0.87	0.77	−0.1	50.4
Malaysia	3.68	3.97	0.29	58.9
Mali	0.86	1.27	0.41	60.5
Mauritania	1.22	0.62	−0.6	55.4
Mauritius	2.45	2.23	−0.23	−
Mexico	2.69	1.65	−1.04	31.1
Moldova	2.47	1.7	−0.77	55
Mongolia	4.3	5.67	1.37	70.5
Morocco	1.56	0.99	−0.57	33.2
Mozambique	0.76	1.11	0.35	54.9
Namibia	0.66	1.83	1.17	75
Nepal	1.01	0.94	−0.07	37.8
The Netherlands	5.75	2.41	−3.35	44.7
New Zealand	9.54	15.8	6.26	49
Nicaragua	1.26	4.22	2.96	60.5
Niger	0.97	0.42	−0.56	53.3
Nigeria	1.31	0.88	−0.43	39.7
Norway	6.13	6.14	0.01	77.6
Oman	3.39	0.7	−2.69	46
Pakistan	1.09	0.68	−0.4	37.6
Panama	2.35	4.18	1.82	57.1
Papua New Guinea	1.4	31.6	30.2	66.9
Paraguay	2.84	5.53	2.68	63.8
Peru	1.33	9.23	7.9	69.3
Philippines	1.42	0.89	−0.54	19.6
Poland	5.4	2.35	−3.05	38.6
Portugal	4.99	2.23	−2.76	53.3
Romania	3.49	2.39	−1.1	48.1
Russian Federation	5.36	4.09	−1.26	72.2
Rwanda	0.9	0.42	−0.48	43.6
Saudi Arabia	6.15	0.41	−5.74	35
Senegal	1.06	0.95	−0.11	51.9
Sierra Leone	0.73	1.4	0.67	42.1
Singapore	12.35	0.13	−12.21	−
Slovak Republic	3.94	2.02	−1.92	59.3
Slovenia	5.4	2.63	−2.77	54.5
Somalia	0.97	0.74	−0.23	47
South Africa	4.04	1.39	−2.65	44.8
Spain	5.5	2.52	−2.98	41
Sri Lanka	0.95	0.52	−0.43	37.8
Sudan	1.14	1.76	0.62	53.1
Sweden	7.53	8.02	0.48	72.1
Switzerland	6.63	2.31	−4.33	52.4
Syrian Arab Republic	2.56	1.1	−1.46	48.3

Country	ECTOTAL: total ecological footprint	BIOCAPA: biological capacity	ECODEFI: ecological deficit	ENVSYS: environment system index
Taiwan	4.34	0.2	−4.14	–
Tajikistan	0.9	0.47	−0.44	42.5
Tanzania	1.02	1.34	0.33	54.9
Thailand	2.7	1.35	−1.35	50
Togo	0.82	0.83	0	47.1
Trinidad and Tobago	2.43	0.77	−1.66	49.7
Tunisia	2.27	1.22	−1.05	48.4
Turkey	2.73	1.49	−1.24	54.8
Turkmenistan	3.62	1.02	−2.6	38
Uganda	0.88	1.01	0.13	49
Ukraine	4.76	2.26	−2.49	42.7
United Arab Emirates	15.99	0.68	−15.31	27.3
United Kingdom	6.29	1.83	−4.46	38.5
United States	12.22	5.57	−6.66	60.1
Uruguay	4.91	5.13	0.22	65.4
Uzbekistan	2.65	0.96	−1.7	49.2
Venezuela	2.88	5.89	3.01	77.2
Vietnam	0.95	0.65	−0.3	42.7
Yemen	0.69	0.27	−0.42	–
Yugoslavia, FR	3.85	1.84	−2.01	–
Zambia	1.21	4.24	3.03	49.8
Zimbabwe	1.45	0.68	−0.77	56.5

Sources: see Appendix A1.

Part V
Conclusions

11 Participation, e-voting and principal–agent interaction

Introduction

Two new and interesting ideas about democracy have been introduced recently; one practical, the other conceptual. On the one hand we have the use of e-voting for increasing participation in elections. On the other, there is the emergence of the principal–agent framework for analysing the interaction between the voters and their representatives. In this chapter we combine these two developments, in relation to the problem of participation in democratic elections.

Let us start with the famous and immortal words of Abraham Lincoln in his Gettysburg address declaring that democracy is government of the people, for the people, and by the people. Lincoln was not aware of the tension between government *of* the people and government *by* the people. One may argue that the recent attention given to the principal–agent framework highlights this tension. Thus, we will discuss this approach to democracy, looking at the population as the principal and politicians and political parties as the agents of the population, receiving signals from the principal about what to do. However, when discussing the utility of the principal–agent framework for understanding the problem of participation in a democracy, we will choose a very special angle, namely the possibility of a participatory revolution accomplished by means of e-voting.

In this chapter we first analyse why participation rates differ so much between democracies. Then we look at the possibility of e-voting to promote more participation. Finally, we bring up the principal–agent framework and discuss its pros and cons when analysing the problem of democratic participation.

The problem of participation

The rate of participation in national elections varies in liberal democracies. It is a most important macro property of these political systems, as every democratic polity is characterized by popular participation in one form or another. First, the rate of participation is not constant within any one country: it may change substantially over time or hover closely around a mean. Second, there are national differences with regard to participation rates, with some countries scoring in the 90 per cent range and others having substantially lower rates of participation, such as 50 per cent of the electorate. Since the rate of participation may be measured as a macro property in a rather straightforward manner, taking voter turnout as a percentage of those eligible to vote, such aggregate scores invite macro modelling in a search for one or other macro properties as explanatory factors. At the same time, political participation may be approached by means of micro models focussing on individual level properties that are conducive to political interest and electoral participation. Thus, we arrive at the difficulty of how macro and micro level hypotheses are to be combined (Weber, 1949).

A number of macro hypotheses have been suggested in order to account for differential voter participation rates by means of statistically significant relationships with, among other things, (Crewe, 1981; Grofman and Lijphart, 1986; Lewis-Beck and Lockerbie, 1989; Flickinger and Studlar, 1992; Franklin, 1996, 2002; Gray and Caul, 2000; Wattenberg, 2000; Radcliff and Davis, 2002):

1 *legal factors:* a publicly sanctioned obligation to participate, registration laws, the use of various proportional electoral formulae.
2 *party system factors:* the extent of competition, the degree of polarization, the number of effective parties, the deviation from proportionality, volatility.
3 *political party factors:* support for protest parties, support for green parties, strong ties between social cleavage groups and parties, segmentation.
4 *political system factors:* unicameralism, Westminster model characteristics, political instability.
5 *economic factors:* affluence.

Whether these factors really have an impact on national voter turnout scores remains a contested issue. There are contradictory assumptions about the direction of the impact of some of these factors. It has been argued by Crepaz that political factors such as polarization and postmaterialist politics matter more than institutional factors such as compulsory voting, as emphasized by Jackman (1987). Blais and Carty (Crepaz, 1990) state that proportional electoral laws matter, contrary to the Powell argument (1980, 1986) which emphasized linkages between social groups and political parties as well as party competition in addition to compulsory voting.

The state of the debate is bewildering as it is argued that political competition drives up electoral participation whereas electoral disproportionality drives it down. At the same time, we know that proportional frameworks lessen party competition. Moreover, it is claimed that multi-partism lowers electoral participation at the same time as it is claimed that strict proportionality favours it. Yet we know that multi-partism feeds on proportionality.

Explaining the low degree of political participation in the USA, Switzerland, Japan and Ireland requires special knowledge about these political systems. Several plausible contributory conditions may be suggested – registration laws, discrimination against women, small public sector, confounded party cleavages – but none of them could count as necessary or sufficient conditions. It is not clear what is to be gained in moving from an interpretation of these deviant cases at the system level to a general aggregate level theory of electoral participation which is not capable of being understood in terms of micro level theory of human motivation in electoral contexts. Whereas micro hypotheses about electoral participation make sense, the macro hypotheses are difficult to interpret because they cannot be derived from any plausible theory of human motivation. The problem of finding general determinants of electoral participation at the system level is, in reality, only a question of why a few countries are deviant: the USA, Switzerland, Japan and Ireland.

The basic micro model of electoral participation is derived from a rational choice perspective. It explains participation with the expected utility of voting, which is a function of the probability of being effective in influencing outcomes that the participant favours less the expected utility of abstaining. The rational choice model has always been criticized for the falsification of one of its crucial implications, namely the irrationality of political participation in large groups. The model would imply, it is claimed, that self-interest-maximizing individuals will not participate in national elections because there is an infinitesimal probability that they could end up in a position to cast the decisive vote. This follows from the model only if one assumes that the positive utility in relation to the act of participation is smaller than the disutility of participation. However, this crucial assumption needs to be argued. Why could not the positive utility be larger than the negative utility in relation to the act of political participation? Thus it has been stated that the basic public choice model about the logic of political participation is erroneous, because it implies that it is always more rational to abstain than to vote (Crepaz, 1990 – *the paradox of participation*). The crux of the matter is that the costs of voting are small and there may be benefits involved in not abstaining.

The empirical analysis of micro factors that influence political participation has resulted in survey research findings that underline greater socio-economic resources and higher general levels of political awareness as conditions enhance the probability of participation (Milbrath and Goel, 1977; Verba *et al.*, 1978; Wolfinger and Rosenstone, 1980; Nelson, 1987; Jackman and Miller, 1995; Blais and Dobrzynska, 1998; Blais *et al.*, 2001). Participation expresses an *activist* attitude which is often correlated with socio-economic characteristics such as income, age and education. Given these findings about individuals from several voting studies, how are they related to the hypotheses that attempt to explain the variation in aggregate national turnouts?

It is claimed that the degree of party-polarization and the absence or presence of postmaterialism have a statistically significant impact on voter turnout (Crepaz, 1990). But others state that PR (proportional representation) fosters higher turnout (Blais and Carty, 1990). If, on the one hand, the Crepaz hypothesis was true, then the national participation rates would differ over time as a function of the change in polarization and the increase in the support for the Greens. If, on the other hand, the Blais and Carty hypothesis was true, then the participation rates would tend to be stable over time, because electoral systems do not normally change from one election to another. And countries with PR frameworks would display consistently higher participation rates than countries with majority frameworks. Let us look at the data for the post-World War Two period, covering elections from 1945 up until 1999 in democratic systems in the OECD group of nations (Table 11.1).

The *between-country differences* in average participation rates involve a few countries where only about half of the eligible population participates in national elections (the USA and Switzerland) as well as some countries where almost the entire eligible population votes (Italy, Austria, Australia and New Zealand). In most countries, however, the participation rate tends to hover

Table 11.1 Voter turnout 1945–99

Country	Voting in % of registered voters			Voting in % of voting age population (VAP)			Compulsory voting	Election system
	Mean	Std Dev	N	Mean	Std Dev	N		
Australia	94.5	1.936	22	84.3	2.948	21	Yes	Not PR
Austria	91.3	4.75	17	84.5	6.737	17	No	PR
Belgium	92.7	1.825	18	84.8	10.991	18	Yes	PR
Canada	73.8	5.157	18	68.4	4.739	17	No	Not PR
Denmark	85.6	2.562	22	83.6	3.766	22	No	PR
Finland	77.9	4.86	16	78.3	5.415	16	No	PR
France	76.6	6.088	15	67.3	5.524	15	No	Not PR*
Germany	85.4	4.407	14	80.4	5.193	14	No	Mixed
Greece	78.5	7.078	18	80.3	8.758	17	(Yes)***	PR
Iceland	89.5	1.988	17	89.2	1.888	17	No	PR
Ireland	73.2	3.381	16	74.9	4.218	16	No	PR
Italy	89.8	3.955	15	92.5	2.453	14	(Yes)***	Mixed since 1994
Japan	71.2	4.447	21	70.5	4.153	20	No	Mixed since 1995
Luxembourg	89.8	1.901	13	69.3	5.376	13	Yes	PR
The Netherlands	87.0	7.509	17	83.9	5.916	16	Yes to 1967	PR
New Zealand	88.7	3.932	19	86.6	7.232	18	No	Mixed since 1993
Norway	80.4	3.226	15	79.6	3.93	14	No	PR
Portugal	77.1	9.911	10	81.3	5.891	10	No	PR
Spain	73.3	4.632	8	76.8	4.497	7	No	PR
Sweden	85.6	4.671	18	83.1	4.175	17	No	PR
Switzerland	56.6	10.86	14	52.1	16.652	14	No	PR
Turkey	80.6	10.848	9	73.5	10.953	9	No	PR
United Kingdom	75.2	5.496	16	74.9	3.666	15	No	Not PR
USA**	47.0	8.062	28	48.3	8.335	26	No	Not PR
Total	79.6	13.452	396	76.7	12.971	383		

Sources: voting in % of registered voters is based on data reported in Mackie and Rose (1991, 1997) as well as IDEA (2001); voting in % of voting age population (VAP) is based on data reported in IDEA (2001).

Notes
* PR in France between 1945–56 and in 1986; ** registered voters for USA refers to estimates of the voting age population; *** the rule is only weakly implemented.

around the OECD average score for close to 400 elections since 1945 of about 80 per cent. The *within-country differences* over time are hardly extensive, except for a few countries like Switzerland, Spain and France. In some countries, the participatory behaviour is very consistent: Iceland, Austria and Belgium. An analysis of variance strongly confirms that participation rates tend to be stable over time. The total variation in national electoral participation rates in democratic elections since the end of the Second World War is almost completely a matter of between-country differences.

The fact that participation does not change much over time implies that we have to focus on a stable country variation which does not reflect short-term changes in the party system. If, indeed, there are factors that may account for the differences between Austria, Australia and New Zealand on the one hand, and the USA, Switzerland and Japan on the other, then they would have to be long-term factors.

Theoretically, there could be two sets of conditions for political participation in national elections. One set of conditions would include the factors that have an impact on *individual choice*, increasing or decreasing the likelihood that a citizen enters the election booth – that is, micro conditions. Another set of conditions would comprise those factors that explain why some countries on an aggregate level consistently display high participation rates, whereas other countries are characterized by low participation rates as a time invariant *political system property* – that is, macro conditions.

We face two problems in relation to the micro and macro conditions: *existence* and *reduction*. First, we have to ask whether we have any certain knowledge about micro and macro conditions, if indeed there are any such conditions at all. Second, following the Weberian philosophy of the social sciences (Weber, 1949), we have to find the relationship between micro and macro conditions, according to which the latter is a mere aggregation of the former. How could there be a set of conditions that explain individual voting and a quite different set of conditions that account for national participation rates which, after all merely summarizes individual choice behaviour?

The macro conditions are problematic in regard to both the existence and the reduction criteria. A *sufficient condition* for a high national rate of participation would be such that if a country had a low degree of participation, then that condition could not apply. And a *necessary condition* for a high rate of participation would be such that if a country has a high rate, then that condition must apply. How about the conditions that have been mentioned as candidates for macro conditions: do the various hypotheses about national turnout rates offer necessary or sufficient conditions?

It has been argued that *legal factors* make a difference in relation to voter turnout. However, compulsory voting is not a necessary condition for a high average turnout, as the cases of Austria, Iceland, Denmark and New Zealand indicate. Nor is compulsory voting a sufficient condition, as the case of Greece testifies. It is true that the countries that persistently display low participation rates lack a legally defined institution of obligatory participation, but there are several countries that also lack such a mechanism but score high on political participation. It has been claimed that the *electoral framework* makes a difference, in particular the employment of some system of proportional representation. However, proportional representation is not a necessary condition for high rates of political participation, as Australia and New Zealand show. Proportional electoral systems do not constitute a sufficient condition for a high rate of participation, as Switzerland, Spain and Ireland suggest. It seems indeed to be the case that the rate of political participation varies considerably within both subsets of countries, those with a proportional election framework and those without such systems.

When *party system factors* are referred to as explanations of participation rates, two contrary hypotheses are adduced. Either it is argued that the close competition between two major parties for a single majority government drives up the interest in participating, or it is stated that a broad system of representation involving several parties with a high level of polarization between some of these is conducive to citizen participation. More specifically, a low number of effective parties or fractionalization would go together with a high rate of participation; or it would be the other way around, where high fractionalization scores would covary with high participation rates.

High rates of participation are found in fractionalized Belgium and Holland, as well as in Australia and New Zealand, with a low number of effective parties – meaning that fractionalization cannot possibly constitute a necessary condition for citizen participation. At the same time, low levels of participation are to be found in the USA, which has a typical two-party system, as well as in Switzerland, which is a typical multi-party system, meaning that fractionalization cannot be a sufficient condition for citizen participation.

Similarly, if polarization is a candidate for constituting a sufficient or necessary condition, then we would expect polarized party systems to be combined with high participation rates and the opposite is true in non-polarized party systems. Polarization, or the conflict between extremist parties, used to be high in Finland, France and the United Kingdom, but the rate of participation is low in these countries. At the same time, the rate of participation has been high in Belgium, The Netherlands and the Federal Republic of Germany where the level of polarization has been low. How about volatility? Volatility characterizes both Belgium and Denmark, with high participation scores, and France, Greece, Spain and Portugal, with low participation scores. It is argued that the emergence of green parties in the late 1970s was significant, but the aggregate rate of participation does not vary as a function of the rise and decline of non-traditional parties.

Political system factors have been mentioned as necessary or sufficient conditions for citizen participation. However, we find low rates of participation in both Switzerland, adhering to a consensus model democracy, and the United Kingdom with its Westminster model of democracy. The opposite also holds, that is, high rates of participation are to be found in New Zealand, belonging to the Westminster type, and Austria, which is placed in the consensus type of democracy (Lijphart, 1999). What about political stability? Government instability is to be found in France, Italy, Finland and Portugal, yet these countries vary in terms of citizen participation. Government stability is high in the

United Kingdom, Switzerland, Sweden and Austria, but these countries also vary in citizen participation.

Affluence has been suggested as an *economic factor of* explanatory relevance: the higher the average income per capita, the higher the participation rate. Alas, we can find neither a sufficient nor a necessary condition here. Some affluent countries such as Denmark, Sweden and Norway are above the OECD average participation rate, while other rich countries such as the USA, Switzerland, Japan and Finland fall below it. And countries with a participation rate above the OECD average may have a modest GDP per capita as, for example, Italy and New Zealand.

The idea that a set of macro conditions for political participation exists stems from Tingsten's *Political Behaviour* (1937), where it was argued that the institutional set-up of obligatory participation affects voting behaviour. Once a *system property* like legal rules was accepted as a candidate for the causal mechanism involved in determining an *individual level property* like voting or abstaining, other relevant system properties were added. However, even if some minimum level of statistical evidence could be found for the existence of macro conditions for electoral participation, the severe problem of reduction and interpretation remains.

Understanding why people participate in elections (*micro*) as well as why countries differ in participation rates (*macro*) may offer some clues as to how participation can be increased. The new mechanism of e-voting should be discussed from a principal–agent framework on democracy for the purpose of strengthening the principal of a body politic, namely the electorate.

E-voting: ends and means

E-voting is a new mechanism of conducting democratic elections which is in need of a political theory. Thus, we need to clarify what are the ends and means of e-voting. Is it only a new technical device for lowering the costs of administering elections, or is it a future powerful instrument for increasing citizen participation? The problem of democratic participation is simply this: in one country after another the rate of participation tends to go down, meaning that, in some countries, less than 50 per cent cast a vote. One may suggest that this merely shows that citizens make rational choices, the so-called paradox of participation entailing that the costs of participation outweigh the probability of any one citizen becoming decisive. However, if e-voting lowers the costs of participation, then perhaps the seminal trend towards lower citizen participation can be reversed? After all, if the principal does not send signals to the agents, then how can the principal hold the agents responsible in elections?

The political theory of e-voting must address key questions concerning how it is to be administered, as well as what its potential is for democracy. One may look at alternative election techniques from two angles, namely:

- preference revelation: how well does one election mechanism reveal the preferences of the electorate compared with another election technique?

- impacts on politics: does one election mechanism such as PR affect the party system and the durability of governments differently from another mechanism such as majoritarian techniques?

E-voting has been examined from the first point of view but too little attention has been paid to its potential for improving democracy by reducing the costs of participation and making participation more interesting to ordinary citizens. Perhaps e-voting can solve the paradox of participation?

Before one can state the case for e-voting from the point of view of Rousseau's perspective of democracy – government by the people – the adherents of e-voting must make absolutely sure that e-voting achieves free and fair elections. The concept of *free and fair elections* is critical in election monitoring and it is as relevant in Zimbabwe as in the United States. However, the exact content of this conception is not easily spelled out. Based on a survey of the literature on free and fair elections, we suggest that they must accomplish the following:

- transparency of procedures;
- secrecy and authenticity;
- controllability.

First, e-voting must satisfy the criteria that account for transparency in elections: one person, one vote; no intimidation against candidates directly or indirectly, an independent, non-partisan electoral organization to administer the process. Second, e-voting must be based on a secret exercise of the franchise, resulting in casting a vote that corresponds to the voter's preferences. Third, e-voting must result in a documented outcome that can be controlled for accuracy by independent monitors. If the technical problems relating to authenticity can be solved, then e-voting could be the mechanism for stimulating political participation. There is a problem here, not only in relation to the European Union, but also in several countries where participation has gone down considerably in recent elections.

E-voting is not only to be seen from the perspective of the requirements on free and fair election, which is a problem of the design of election mechanisms. E-voting may also be related to democracy theory, especially as a tool for reinforcing the principal in relation to the agents in politics. As Rousseau emphasized, democracy without much citizen participation creates a basic difficulty for the idea of popular rule. At the same time, agents are not supposed to merely take care of the administration of democratic politics, as the representatives have an open mandate, as Burke emphasized. Thus, we arrive at the principal–agent interaction in democracies.

The principal–agent framework

The principal–agent framework has rapidly become a major approach to the analysis of contractual relationships within the private sector. We argue that it could be a promising approach to the analysis of democracy as well. As a matter of fact, it allows the statement of a number of governance problems in terms of an integrated framework. The making and implementation of policy in a democracy involve fundamental contractual problems referred to as asymmetric information, moral hazard, bounded rationality and adverse selection. Thus, the principal–agent framework could offer a new, promising approach to the analysis of democracy. The making and implementation of policies in the public sector involve the typical problems of principal–agent relationships within the private sector (Ricketts, 1987). As a matter of fact, the principal–agent problems within the public sector are even more severe, because they cannot be avoided. A minimum level of public policy is necessary in any society, and some agents have to be employed by the electorate.

However, principal–agent interaction in the public sector is not the same as principal–agent interaction within the private sector. One must make clear whether the agents are to allocate public goods (non-excludable, jointness) or whether they also supply private goods (excludability, rivalry). It is also important to realize that the public sector has a double principal–agent interaction, first between the electorate and the politicians (political parties), and then between politicians and bureaucrats. Thus, principal–agent interaction in the public sector is more complicated than in the private sector.

At the heart of the policy process is the attempt by the principal to monitor the efforts of the agent to live up to the terms of the policy contract. Whenever the interaction involves considerable transaction costs due to the intertemporal nature of the interaction, as well as the complexity of agreement involved, the principal–agent problem arises (Stiglitz, 1987; Laffont and Martimort, 2002). However, the principal–agent problems of designing a compensation system or contract that motivates the agent to act in the interests of the principal, as well as of monitoring the observation of the agreement, are not the same as those encountered in the private sector, for instance in credit and insurance institutions. The principal–agent relationship is constitutive of public sector institutions, in particular democracy. And the public contract between the principal and the agent concerns the exercise of power and the remuneration is not only financial but also political prestige.

To employ a principal–agent framework for the analysis of public policy involves a rejection of the notion of the public interest as the motivation within public sector institutions. The only interests that exist within a principal–agent modelling of policy-making are the interests that can be pinned down to either the principal or the agent. There is no separate room for the notion of the public interest as the driving force of policy-making and implementation within the public sector. In the principal–agent model, the outcome of the activities of the agent, Q, depends on the action taken by the agent, A, and a state variable, S.

The principal of the political body of a democracy is the electorate. Its individuals maximize a utility function involving the output of public policies. First and foremost they rely on public policy for the provision of a special set of goods and services: public goods. Assume that the various individuals within the electorate have a utility function over two goods, a public good, Qg, and a private good, Qp. Each individual faces a budget restriction, R, and is free to choose between various combinations of quantities of the two goods, provided that the budget restriction, R, is satisfied. Note that all individuals consume the same quantity of the public good, Qg. An optimal allocation of the public good, Qg, requires a decision procedure whereby the marginal willingness to pay of each individual is somehow aggregated. This expression involves a vertical aggregation of each individual's marginal rate of substitution in order to obtain optimality. Since the outlays on public and private goods must sum to R, each individual will be free riding with regard to the public goods, Qg, given the motivation to maximize. A variety of decision mechanisms have been suggested in order to find an aggregation rule that satisfies optimality. An efficient allocation of the public good, Qg, will only be forthcoming if the summation of each individual's marginal willingness to pay equals the marginal cost of producing the public good. If the group of individuals, n, is large, then the problem of collective action arises with regard to Qg (Olson, 1965). For each individual, it holds that the public good, Qg, is 'lumpy', meaning that Qg cannot be provided by a single individual within the group. According to Samuelson (1954), optimality requires the identification of a price mechanism that will equate the individual willingness to pay with the marginal cost of the good. The basic problem is to devise an institutional mechanism that will bring forward these optimal prices, p, or the so-called Lindahl prices. These prices cannot be market prices, since a voluntary exchange approach cannot bypass this fundamental difficulty.

The total quantity of Qp consists of the separate quantities, q, demanded by the individuals. An individual could maximize utility him or herself in relation to a strictly private good, Qp. Since it is not a question of a public good where each individual consumes the same quantity, a market allocation of a private good is efficient. Whereas a public policy involving only private goods could conceivably use market prices to allocate the goods, there has to be a different institutional mechanism for the allocation of public goods. Which one? If it is decided to allocate the private good, Qp, by means of public policy, the conditions for optimality are such that the marginal willingness to pay of each individual that benefits from the divisible good equals the marginal cost of providing the good. However, it is better to employ Walras markets in relation to pure private goods.

The Wicksell solution to the identification of the institutional device that will bring forward an optimal supply of public goods was the so-called unanimity rule (Wicksell, 1896). However, it fails because of the staggering decision costs involved in the individual veto (Buchanan and Tullock, 1962). Also, Wicksell's attempt at modifying the unanimity rule by various qualified majority rules – 3/4, 5/6 and 9/10 – in relation to the sensitivity of the public good involved, will not do, as nobody knows the exact shape of the cost curves involved: the external costs involved for the minority caused by a majority decision as well as the bargaining costs incurred by the need to negotiate with an increasingly smaller minority. The Lindahl suggestion that the mechanism would involve explicit negotiation between two major groups, each stating their preferences for a certain size of the public sector given a certain tax distribution between them, will not work. There is no reason to expect that the majority would not simply impose its will on the minority (Musgrave and Peacock, 1967). As Mueller has emphasized, unanimity targets efficiency in public resource allocation, whereas majority voting invites redistributional policies either in the form of redistribution of in kind (services) or redistribution of money (Mueller, 1989).

The Wicksell–Lindahl solution suffers from the preference revelation problem. Each individual maximizes utility according to their preferences. Yet, since an individual can consume the public good by free riding, there is an incentive to understate the preferences for public goods. The optimal prices, p, in relation to a public good, Qg, differ from one individual to another depending on the variation in the marginal willingness to pay, mv. The individually optimal prices, p, are not forthcoming on the basis of a voluntary exchange mechanism, because each individual has an incentive to understate his or her mv.

Any quantity of a public good provided in a large group must be decided on in a political setting in terms of a public policy programme decided on by means of some decision rule. More generally, as long as the marginal willingness to pay, if stated openly or *revealed* publicly, implies an actual willingness to pay, then each individual has strong incentives not to state their true preferences for public goods and services. Thus, we have that the optimal condition will fail. There is no other way to organize the supply of a public good, Qg, than to introduce a public authority based on the threat (or actual employment) of violence (Buchanan, 1968). There can be no other solution than the introduction of a state as the viable institutional mechanism for the provision of a set of public policies, because it can use tax prices, Pt, to cover the costs of Qg. The anarchist alternative (Taylor, 1987) fails for the same reason. The introduction of the state for the identification of tax prices, Pt, that will bring about a provision of public goods means that an institutional mechanism has been devised for defining the prices that will pay for public goods. Could these tax prices satisfy the conditions of optimality?

Bringing the state in means that politics enter the scene, which implies there is a strong likelihood that a number of difficulties, which we refer to as the public principal–agent problems, will manifest themselves. How is the electorate as the principal to interact with the agents of the state in order to bring about an optimal supply of public policies? The following difficulties arise in relation to public resource allocation and redistribution.

Assume that the public policies provided by the state and the tax prices used to pay for these are handled by means of a simple *referendum* mechanism. Strictly speaking, the referendum model involves the smallest possible margin for the agent to act on behalf of the principal. The electorate would decide each issue by means of a majority vote to be implemented by those occupying state authority positions. This assumes that the activities of the agent are observable to the electorate as well as that each issue can be decided and implemented on its own terms. However, even such a simple policy procedure would not bring forward efficient tax prices, Pt, that satisfy the optimality conditions because of fiscal illusions.

Public Goods. The introduction of taxes, that is, an obligation to pay, as the mechanism for financing the set of public goods also means that each individual faces what may be called the *reversed* logic of collective action. The tax mechanism as the institution for bringing forward revenues that match costs implies that costs may be diluted onto everyone. Consider that the electorate consists of an n large enough to exclude a voluntary exchange approach. According to the optimal Lindahl-prices, each individual should pay for the public good, Qg, in relation to each individual's marginal valuation of the good. Assume that aggregating their marginal willingness to pay adds up to the marginal cost of producing Qg.

However, tax prices have to be employed because of the group size n. Not knowing each individual's valuation of the good Qg, we assume that the state uses tax prices, dividing the cost of producing Qg equally between the individuals. There will then be an excess demand for Qg, because all individuals that have a marginal valuation for Qg less than the tax price, Pt, are forced to accept a larger quantity, whereas those individuals with a marginal valuation for Qg higher than the tax price will demand a larger quantity of Qg.

The use of tax prices, Pt, means that an individual will reveal a marginal willingness to pay in relation to a public good, Qg, in excess of the real marginal willingness to pay, because the cost of the public good, Qg, will be forced on all individuals within a group of size n larger than it is possible to handle by a voluntary exchange approach. Thus, we have a fiscal illusion: if referendum decisions about pure public goods are taken separately, there is a risk of systematic excess supply. However, there is an even larger risk of non-optimal resource allocation in the referendum model, because there is nothing to prevent the allocation of private goods by means of public decision-making.

Private Goods. If a simple majority rule is employed in referenda, then the tax mechanism may be used for allocating divisible private goods and services besides the indivisible public goods. A majority may provide itself with a set of private goods that benefits its individuals differently while, at the same time, using the tax mechanism to spread the cost over the minority. A majority may even introduce public policies that concentrate all the advantages with its individuals while placing all the costs with the minority. Thus, if the majority is denoted by ma and the minority by m, then the tax mechanism may be employed to exploit the minority.

If the majority and the minority groups are permanent within the political body, then tax prices invite severe forms of oppression. However, if the minority and majority can shift in relation to a number of private goods, Qp, there will be an oversupply of public policies in excess of the public goods set. Each group of individuals making up a majority, ma, has an incentive to introduce public policies beneficial to them as long as the cost is covered by some minority, m. Even if a majority of individuals only succeed in introducing public policies that concentrate programme advantages onto them while forcing the minority to share in picking up the costs, there will be an excess demand for public policies.

The referendum model invites fiscal illusions in the demand for and supply of public policies. To counteract these tendencies the electorate would have to create stable and enduring majorities that would control the setting of the policy agenda. In a large group, this would involve considerable transaction costs. Moreover, simply the employment of the referendum mechanism to decide on each and every social issue would lead to staggering transaction costs. To handle these difficulties, the electorate may organize political parties that constrain the making and unmaking of majorities and minorities, but introducing *party government* implies that we face the principal–agent relationship within the public sector. How can the electorate as the principal control its public agents in a liberal democracy – politicians and civil servants – to act in accordance with the contract agreed on in various settings: in the constitution, on the election day or in employment relations?

Typical of democracies in the world today is the fact that the distance between the electorate and the elected gives rise to all the kinds of principal–agent problems as encountered in the analysis of the private sector (Ross, 1973; Williamson, 1986). How would the electorate as the principal interact with the set of political parties and politicians as their agents, given that there is uncertainty about what action the principal wishes the agent to take, given, also, an original agreement and the impossibility of predicting the future state of the environment, and given that the actions of the agent cannot be monitored perfectly or costlessly? We argue that the principal–agent problems in the public sector are even more severe than those of the private sector, because the political contract is bound to be underspecified due to the ambiguities of political life and uncertainty about the state of the environment (March and Olsen, 1989).

Suppose that the politician is an agent that faces the following maximization problem:

$$\max E\ (U(Y, Q, A, S)) \tag{1}$$

where Y is the compensation paid by the principal to the agent, which is a function of the outcome, Q, observable to both the principal and the agent *ex post*, A is the action taken by the agent known only by the agent *ex ante* and S is the state of the economy not known with certainty by any part. The outcome, Q, depends on actions taken by the agent and the state of the economy, as given by equation (1) above.

The electorate as the principal would have a corresponding maximization problem:

$$\max E\ (U(Y, Q, A, S)) \tag{2}$$

Whereas the agent maximizes a utility function consisting of the tax income, Y, with regard to his or her actions, A, the principal maximizes a utility function consisting of the outcomes desired Q^* with regard to tax income paid to the agent.

Different states of the economy, $S_1, S_2, \ldots S_n$, may require various actions, $A_1, A_2, \ldots Am$, taken by the agent in order to increase the probability that the outcomes desired by the principal materializes. The contract between the principal and the agent may involve the agent taking different actions in alternative states of the economy. As a matter of fact, this is what election campaigns are typically concerned with. This means that if the principal considers A^* to be the best action, given a state S, then the compensation scheme must involve an expected utility function of the agent that satisfies:

$$E\ (U(Y,\ Q,\ A^*,\ S)) = E\ [U(f(Q\ (A^*,\ S)),\ A^*,\ S)] > E\ (U(f(Q(A,\ S)),A,\ S,)) \qquad (3)$$

for all actions A, provided that only the output Q is observable to the principal. The basic problem in politics is for the principal to monitor which actions the agent takes in various states of the economy as well as to establish whether what actually takes place is in agreement with the original contract. The agent may claim that the state of the economy was not the one expected and that it called for different actions.

A principal–agent approach modelling the interaction between the voters and the politicians would predict that the agent is in a strategically advantageous position in relation to the principal. Since the contractual relationships within the public sector are characterized by fuzziness arising from partial unobservability of the agent's effort, bounded rationality, asymmetrical information and strategic moves, there are bound to be transaction costs in the operation of party government.

Asymmetrical information, moral hazard and adverse selection enter the basic political contract between the electorate and the politicians. First, there is ambiguity about whether the actions, A, taken by the agent under the circumstances, S, were the correct or desired ones, as well as whether the outcomes, Q, are acceptable to the principal to call forth the rewards, Y, demanded by the agent. The politicians may argue their case by pledging that the actions desired by the principal, A^*, were not feasible under the circumstances, S^1, or that the outcomes, Q^1, were the only feasible ones in S^1 on the basis of their information advantage. Or the politicians may argue that the divergence of the actual outcomes, Q, from the desired ones, Q^*, does not involve a breaking of the election contract, because there is bound to be a moral hazard about what actions, A, are to be taken given the election promise of bringing about a desired outcome, Q^*. Moreover, opportunities exist for the manipulation of the ambiguous terms of the political contract by politicians who wish to engage in irresponsible behaviour or political symbolism, meaning that there is a danger of adverse selection of some politicians.

The Brennan and Buchanan model of the revenue maximization Leviathan deals with the principal–agent relation between the electorate and the politicians in power (Brennan and Buchanan, 1980). The Leviathan model entails that there is a conflict between the rewards provided the agent government, Y, and the amount of resources allocated to produce the outcomes, Q^*, desired by the electorate. This gives rise to a set of reaction functions where the principal tries to maximize the resources allocated to the provision of policies while minimizing the income to the agent who acts in the opposite manner.

Yet, one does not have to derive such extreme predictions from the principal–agent model, which is also true of the Niskanen model. According to the public choice model of Niskanen, these principal–agent difficulties are so severe that the budget results in a bureau budget that is twice as large as the optimal one (Niskanen, 1971). If one assumes that the principal is aware of asymmetric information and is able to arrange for competition between agents, then less extreme predictions would follow. One may wish to apply the insights from the new economics of information to the democratic games which arise when principals choose agents to make public policy, who in their turn select agents to implement them (Rasmusen, 1994). Incentives and institutions are critically important in politics, but they need to be modelled differently from the private sector.

Conclusion

Democracy secures human rights better than other kinds of regime. It is also conducive to equality. Thus, it is concluded that it is the best political regime mankind has invented. However, democracy has an internal problem referred to either as the paradox of participation or as a principal–agent difficulty. It is not quite clear that the population is really in the driving seat, as participation tends to be low and politicians/political parties play a dominating role in deciding policies.

Democracy may be approached by means of a principal–agent framework. Allocating public policies creates principal–agent relationships between the electorate and government. Monitoring politicians and civil servants involves the difficulties encountered in principal–agent relationships in the private sector. Principal–agent problems of asymmetrical information, bounded rationality, ambiguous contracting, moral hazard and adverse selection occur to a high extent in the public sector.

One could argue, however, that the principal can counteract the difficulties of instructing, paying and monitoring the agent by employing many agents as well as agents of different kinds. Thus, it has been suggested that politicians should be seen as supervisors or regulators (Laffont, 2000), but how can the principal make sure the supervisors do not collude with each other? Yet, one could interpret public principal–agent interaction in terms of the Montesquieu framework (*trias politica*) as an institutional mechanism for controlling all kinds of political agents by playing them out against each other. Any theory of incentives and institutions in a democracy must take into account the insights in political theory concerning the separation of powers, as well as the erection of the Rule of Law by means of human rights and immunities. Such institutions make democracy more probable at the same time as they reduce the so-called 'shirking proclivities' of agents working for the principal of democratic governments, the people. Political institutions may also restrict the allocation of private goods, such as redistribution and rent-seeking behaviour by special interest agents.

12 Conclusion

How can we enhance democracy?

Il faut en outre connaitre la vrai nature des choses par rapport a l'ordre de faits sur lesquels on veut etre instruit; il faut les classer methodiquement, pouvoir en montrer la liason, c'est-a-dire les rapports qui font de l'un une cause et de l'autre un resultat.

(Say, 1996: 84–5)

Introduction

'Democracy' is first and foremost a word. It has today an immense positive evaluation, but what we are searching for is what it refers to in reality. We will take the normative meaning of 'democracy' as given, and then look for what it stands for in the real world which we observe with our senses. Alas, it is all too well known that 'democracy' is an ambiguous word with many meanings. How can one enhance conceptual clarity in relation to the various concepts of 'democracy'?

The uses of 'democracy' have been examined in several major semantic investigations. A number of scholars have distinguished between various meanings of the word, and have come up with a different set of concepts. We will not multiply these enquiries into the meaning of 'democracy', but we do accept that the word is ambiguous. We will distinguish between three key concepts of 'democracy':

- democracy as constitutional government today;
- democracy as citizen participation in politics;
- democracy as an egalitarian society.

It is quite obvious that 'democracy' is used in all three of these meanings. What is perhaps not equally clear is that these three concepts overlap only to a certain extent. In reality, these conceptions are quite distinct as a country may practise constitutional government but give little scope for citizen participation in politics and embrace an economy which contains lots of inequalities. Perhaps this is a description of the United States or Switzerland today, where less than 50 per cent of the population participates in ordinary elections? However, both of these countries employ the referendum institution to express citizen preferences which is a positive. Most so-called democracies concentrate on representation by providing Parliaments with a major role in channelling citizen preferences into government policies. Finally, some democracies underline equality more than others; for example, the Nordic countries, where both income equality and gender equality are higher than in many other democratic countries.

Constitutional democracy may be practised in different ways. The political system of democratic countries offers a large set of different institutions in terms of which the Rule of Law may be guaranteed. Usually two questions are raised in relation to institutions that guarantee the 'Rule of Law' or 'Rechtsstaat', namely:

- why is constitutional democracy stable in some countries but not in others?
- are different institutions for constitutional democracy conducive to different policy outputs or outcomes?

Constitutional democracy is a system of government where procedures are respected and citizens can seek redress against wrong decisions as well as express grievances against the administration. Constitutional democracy is government through checks and balances, where centres of power constitute counter-veiling forces. Why is it the case that constitutional democracy works in some democracies but remains fragile in others? A number of hypotheses have been suggested to account for the probability that one country succeeds in establishing the Rule of Law. We will examine these hypotheses here using the most recent data possible about almost all the countries of the world. Interestingly, one finds that all the major factors employed in social science theories have been suggested, such as economic factors, social structure, culture, history and the very institutions of constitutional democracy themselves.

Another major problem in relation to constitutional democracy is whether certain institutions matter more than others, or if some institutions have a different impact than others. Constitutional democracy may be based on a plethora of institutions safeguarding decentralization of power as well as human rights. A country may opt for a thin or a thick institutional set up to protect and enhance its Rule of Law. Does it matter for outcomes? There are a number of theories that argue that democracy can be carried out under various institutions and it matters which institutions a country chooses and implements. Thus, Robert Dahl opposed Madisonian democracy to Rousseau democracy and Arend Lijphart suggested that Westminster democracy operated very differently from Consensus democracy. What evidence is there that actually confirms these ideas that alternative models of democracy result in different styles of decision-making or outcomes?

We have here three sets of problems concerning the interpretation of democracy today. The first set includes all kinds of questions about the stability of the democratic regime. What are the sources of political stability in a democracy and why do some democratic countries hover between the Rule of Law and authoritarianism? The second set deals more with democratic politics than with democratic procedures. It asks a number of questions about who participates in politics and how citizen preferences are translated into government decisions. Third, there is the problem of inequality in democratic countries, which calls for an analysis of whether democratic policy-making can reduce social and gender inequalities.

Three perspectives of democracy

While it is true that these three sets of problems of democratic government do not constitute an exhaustive listing of questions social scientists tend to raise in relation to democracy, they cover a fair amount of territory. Thus, they include the constitutional perspective of democracy, the behavioural perspective as well and the policy view. Let us comment further on each of these perspectives.

The constitutional perspective

To a constitutionalist, the rules of democracy are at the centre of interest. They must satisfy a number of requirements, including transparency, stability, procedural accountability, human rights and division of power. In a constitutional approach to democracy, these requirements are not only means to the accomplishment of citizen rule but they are regarded as goals in themselves. When they collide with the expression of the will of the people, then institutionalism would favour that the rules prevail.

The constitutional perspective focuses on the Rule of Law in the context of a democratic regime. The idea of a Rechtsstaat was launched before the advent of democracy, however. Universal male and female suffrage was introduced after the erection of Rule of Law. Thus, the constitutional monarchies in Western Europe practised the Rechtsstaat before they accepted universal suffrage. And the theory of the constitutional state underlined the requirements of Rule of Law without emphasizing universal suffrage or even demanding it.

The great theoreticians of the constitutional state in the nineteenth century emphasized other things than one person, one vote. They focussed on the exercise of power within the limits of the law – the requirement of legality. As a consequence they demanded that the state should be based on a fundamental law – *lex suprema* – which outlined the structure of government and identified both its possibilities and limits. Such a basic law could be codified, as with Continental Europe, or it could consist of conventions, as in the United Kingdom.

Constitutionalism in the early nineteenth century dealt more with the procedures of government than with universal human rights. A constitutional state would respect certain human rights, such as the classical negative freedoms, but it was not considered essential that all people could vote. Freedom of thought, of expression and of religion together with property rights constituted vital elements of a constitutional state, but it was not until the late nineteenth century that universal suffrage was made part of the constitutional state. Several constitutional scholars pressed more for parliamentarism than for democracy, as they often looked on people as belonging to different categories of citizens.

Yet, in the twentieth century, the constitutional state has been married to the democratic regime. Constitutional democracy is based on broadly defined human rights, of which one is universal suffrage for men and women. One may discuss the voting age limit, as some have claimed that eighteen years of age is not the lowest level possible. A few countries have actually accepted sixteen years of age. In the new constitutions of many states, the list of human rights is long, comprising both negative freedoms and positive freedoms, but the emphasis is on procedures within the institutionalist approach. The key question is how thick should the institutional fabric be in order to guarantee Rule of Law?

Politics may be considered as a game in which various players interact. The rules of the game matter very much to decide which strategies various players engage in, especially whether the rules are stable or not. Institutional stability is a major concern for democratic regimes. Although the question of the nature of democratic institutions is a major issue in democratic theory, it is still the case that the stability of the institutions is of equal importance. When a country fails to stabilize its political rules, then it is likely that it will hover between democracy and dictatorship.

One may calculate the longevity of the democratic institutions of a country in order to separate between countries that are democratically stable and countries that are stable dictatorships, as well as countries that are unstable democracies. An unstable democracy could be a country that has introduced a new democratic constitution but fails to consolidate a democratic regime. The institutions introduced are not respected, at least not fully. They may either be implemented in a manner that leaves considerable doubt about which rules more exactly apply, or some of the rules may be entirely pushed aside for a shorter or longer time period.

An unstable democracy could also be an authoritarian country that initiates a process of institutional change but it does not achieve institutional stability. There is a grey zone between stable democracy and stable dictatorship where many countries are to be placed, but for different reasons. Transition countries moving from authoritarianism to democracy may get stuck in the process of change, as some players do not respect the new democratic institutions or they interpret them in an ambiguous manner. It may be easier to initiate a process of democratization than to fulfil such a process.

Finally, we have the case of an unstable democracy, when government itself does not function. It seems as if more and more countries in the world face the risk of anarchy. The collapse of government may be witnessed in not only countries where there is civil war between various ethnic or religious factions, but also in countries where warlords and the crime economy more or less replace the state and bureaucratic political authority. Sometimes it is difficult to distinguish political conflict resulting from deep-seated cleavages from mere political disobedience due to the breakdown of law and order.

Constitutional stability may be characterized as a conservative approach to democracy. One may wish to talk about the need for democratic reform, choosing between alternative institutions which all result in the Rule of Law. Some theoreticians of democracy have preferred thick institutionalism to thin institutionalism, partly because it is believed that thick institutionalism enhances political stability more than thin institutionalism. When we speak about democratic stability we will, however, refer to the grey zone between democracy, dictatorship and anarchy. The increase in anarchy in several parts of the world also makes the classical focus on political stability relevant today. Why does the Ivory Coast, for example, fail to stabilize a democratic regime?

The late 1980s and early 1990s was an exceptional time for institutional change. One may enquire into how countries differ on democratic longevity in the 1990s, after the starting-point of the wave of democratization in the late 1980s when several communist and fascist regimes crumbled. Or one may cast a broader net, investigating how countries have differed in terms of democratic longevity during the entire post-war period since 1945.

Constitutional democracy underlines liberties and plays down the relevance of equality and brotherhood or community – see the interpretation of John Rawls in *Political Liberalism* (1993). It has been criticized from several angles, but it remains true that a country which adheres to constitutional democracy, and only this type of democracy, is a more attractive country to live in (a well-ordered society) than a country where constitutional democracy is lacking.

The behavioural perspective

Democracy could not only be the Rule of Law. Somehow democracy entails that the people govern. Thus, participation is a key element in democracy. And the major problem is how participation may be achieved. Let us separate between two models, the majoritarian and the minoritarian.

The majoritarian model of democracy underlines the capacity of the polity to take decisions quickly on the basis of the preferences of a majority among the voters. What is emphasized is the expression of majority will in the electorate. The majority should be articulated as clearly as possible and there should be as few hindrances to its manifestation as possible, given a respect for the Rule of Law. Majoritarian democracy endorses the referendum, majoritarian election techniques and a unitary state. Perhaps civic republicanism is today the leading interpretation of what majoritarian democracy requires?

Minoritarian democracy, according to Lijphart, stresses the importance of minority participation in political decision-making. Society is fragmented into a fabric of minority groups which have a right to participate in decision-making even when there is a clear majority in the population. Minorities must have a say in politics – this the basic position that distinguishes the minoritarian model from the majoritarian one. A number of participation channels are open for minority participation or representation:

a   proportional election systems;
b   two-chamber Parliaments;
c   federalism;

d   special territorial autonomy;
e   legal review.

Minoritarian democracy aims at bringing all players on board. It is prepared to allow for a veto, meaning that minorities can block any decision, even majoritarian ones. According to the minoritarian model of democracy, political decision-making is a process of negotiation during which not only are all points of view heard but, also, that all decisions must reflect the taking into consideration of the standpoints of all choice participants. To some, the minoritarian model of democracy implies deliberative democracy, whereas others connect it with the power of veto players.

The behavioural perspective on democracy involves a number of questions about democratic politics. It looks on decision-making as controlled by organized groups such as political parties, interest organizations and citizen groups, social movements or by state bureaucracies including the judiciary. In the countries with a stable democratic regime, politics tends to be dominated by the organizations that are positioned between the citizens and the key political bodies such as the Parliament and the Presidency. One may then ask whether the people are sovereign or not in today's democracy. In American political science this question has been debated in the famous power debate initiated by Robert Dahl in the 1950s, including the influential analysis by Schattschneider in *The Semi-Sovereign People* (1960).

From the perspective of minoritarian democracy the problem of whether the people are sovereign or semi-sovereign or not sovereign at all is not a very relevant one, because politics is always a game involving minorities, which tend to organize themselves in order to have a say. However, from the majoritarian perspective, the many organizations between the key bodies and the people can involve a threat against the majority, which is more or less crushed when faced with lots of special interests. The majority may still be out there but it remains a silent one, overshadowed by all the special interest groups.

One may separate between participatory democracy and representative democracy, which is a distinction that cross-cuts the distinction between majoritarian and minoritarian democracy. In participatory democracy, the emphasis is on various forms of democratic participation including the referendum, the activity of action groups as well as the use of political strikes and demonstrations. Representative democracy is well anchored in the Houses of Parliament and focuses on the political parties, favouring the institutionalization of their work.

Party government has become the standard conception of modern democracy and it is a firmly representative notion. Party government tends to be interpreted in terms of a minoritarian approach, meaning that a multi-party system is considered more legitimate than a two-party system. A one-party system may occur in a democracy, but it is looked on as a destabilizing phenomenon, as a party with such a powerful position would be tempted to misuse it for various purposes, including corruption. A major classical question in democratic theory is: which party system operates best? This problem involves a whole set of questions concerning the performance of party government and the evaluation of the outputs and outcomes of different party systems.

The position of organized interests in democratic politics has been much debated. Although organized interest groups belong to the world of minoritarian democracy, it is true that they may figure prominently in both the participatory view and the representative view. In the latter, organized interests target the political parties in Parliament or the bureaucracy directly. In the former, organized interests employ the participatory channel, making use of demonstrations and action groups. It is an open question as to which form is the most effective in bringing about policy outputs that are in the interest of these groups. Differences in policy-making styles between countries structure the way interest organizations relate to the political process.

The policy perspective

In the constitutionalist view, democracy is basically a broad set of rights and duties which have to be more or less fully implemented in a transparent manner. In the behavioural view, democracy is an activity or a set of behaviour through which people become active in politics in various ways, and somehow affect how the key political bodies operate. The constitutionalist question is: what are my rights and how can I protect them? The behaviouralist asks: how are democratic decisions forthcoming? And the policy view complements these two perspectives by looking at the impact of democratic decision-making on society. It asks: can democratic governance enhance social equality in a society with massive inequalities? It focuses on the outcomes of democratic politics.

One may somewhat schematically say that the constitutionalist perspective deals with the presuppositions of the game of democracy; the behavioural perspective examines the process of democratic politics and the policy view deals with the results of democratic policy-making. Whereas constitutional democracy safeguards liberty and a set of individual freedoms, democratic policy-making may be employed to enhance social equality, that is, either income equality between the various social groups in society or gender equality.

The policy perspective asks whether democracy matters for the transformation of society. It entails an extrinsic perspective of democracy, which makes it different from the constitutionalist perspective and the behaviouralist perspective approaching democracy as a value in itself. A democratic government may have an impact on society in various ways, but it is equality that must be given priority from a democratic point of view. With some of the classical theoreticians of democracy, equality was the first and foremost preoccupation. Under what circumstances can a democratic government succeed in enhancing equality?

A libertarian view of democracy may rest content if there is constitutional democracy, meaning basically a set of liberties protected by the state. A pluralist perspective of democracy would require that interest groups have channels open to the politicians and the bureaucracy so that groups can organize and have an influence on politics. Yet, in an egalitarian approach to democracy, this is not enough. Only if constitutional democracy or pluralist democracy enhances equality is there 'real' democracy, to use an often misused phrase.

The demand for social and economic equality has been raised in relation to capitalist democracies, where government possesses sufficient resources for intervening in society by means of egalitarian programmes. It is argued that the capitalist organization of society poses considerable threats for democracy – this is the thesis of Charles Lindblom in *Politics and Markets* (1977). Lindblom was partly inspired by the dream of a new type of economic system – market socialism or the Yugoslav model – which is hardly as relevant as it was in the 1970s. However, capitalism in the twenty-first century does challenge democratic governance, especially in the context of a global economy.

What democratic theory must discuss today is whether markets are strong enough to dictate policy-making or undo policy-making by democratically elected politicians. Since markets are orientated first and foremost towards economic efficiency, it has been required that governments correct market outcomes by redistribution. What needs to be researched is whether government really can increase equality or whether inequalities are beyond the control of the state.

Two hypotheses confront each other in relation to equality. The optimistic hypothesis claims that government by means of its public sector is a major determinant of equality in society, whereas the negative hypothesis suggests that the private sector is itself the source of as much equality as is possible.

The preceding chapters have examined the key theoretical approaches to democracy as a political regime in existing societies. The enquiry has come up with a number of new findings when key hypotheses have been tested against a database comprising information about a large set of countries. Sometimes one speaks about empirical democratic theory in order to separate the enterprise above from the enquiry into democracy as an ideal – associative or deliberative democracy (Hirst, 1994; Elster, 1998). Thus, we have not said much about various possibilities for reforming existing democratic countries so that their level of democracy increases. Our focus is on democracy as an existing macro regime, its causes and its effects.

What do the findings in this book all add up to? The answer is that they reinforce our scepticism against democratic exogeneity. Democracy may be modelled as the outcome of factors that are either within the political system or outside of it. The findings reported on in this book suggest that democratic stability or the longevity of a democratic political system should be modelled in terms of endogenous democracy and not, as is the main approach in the literature, as exogenous democracy. Let us explain why, and develop a new model of endogenous democracy.

Towards a theory of endogenous democracy

The first key framework for the analysis of democracy, the modernization approach initiated *inter alia* by Lipset and further developed by Diamond, entails that the democratic regime is a function of macro forces determined outside of the political system. These socio-economic forces are analysed at great length in this modernization framework. Thus, democracy is modelled as a function of socio-economic modernization covering a host of variables which are strongly related to each other: GDP, industrial employment, urbanization, etc. The country scores on these variables are taken as given and the extent of democracy is predicted from the country scores on these exogenous factors.

The second main framework for analysing democratic stability is the Rokkan approach to democracy, focussing on the impact on democracy from external cleavages. Thus, the emphasis with Lijphart is on the impossibility of majoritarian democracy in a deeply divided society, characterized by profound ethnic and religious fragmentation. Again, cleavages are taken as given and their negative impact on democracy can only be mitigated through consociational practices, such as the making of pacts and the use of the grand coalition. Although institutions can be framed by political elites in order to improve on democratic stability or democratic consolidation (veto points), the emphasis is again on exogeneity, as social fragmentation and cultural diversity are basically determined outside of the political system.

These two approaches – the modernization and cleavages frameworks – offer cross-sectional hypotheses about the variation in democracy between countries. Both underline exogenous democracy, although they also include institutional factors to some extent. A third chief type of exogenous approach to democracy focuses on time and the impact of history. Thus, democracy is modelled by Huntington as being determined by the historical evolution of the state within the country in question. The basic hypothesis is that the longer the time span of uninterrupted growth of state institutions, the more stable is the democratic regime in a country. As a country cannot control its past, this factor is basically an exogenous one. What one is referring to in models focussing on the impact of variables such as institutional sclerosis, modernized leadership and year of birth of a modern state, is basically state age. The key hypothesis is that the older the state, the more probable it is that it is democratic.

To what extent is democracy determined outside of the political system? Table 12.1 combines the key variables mentioned in the models of exogenous democracy we have discussed. The test of this regression model shows clearly that democracy may be modelled as determined by factors outside of the political system.

A model combining a number of often mentioned exogenous factors accounts for less than half of the variation among democracies. The partial effects are in accordance with the models of exogenous democracy, although only affluence and state age throw up significant effects. Perhaps one can explain more if one resorts to endogenous democracy?

It is not our intention to deny the usefulness of exogenous democracy. Enquiring into which external factors impact on democracy and in what direction and with which strength is a worthwhile effort. That both affluence and state age have an impact on democracy entails that poor new countries face a significant challenge when opting for a democratic regime. But these inter-

Table 12.1 Exogenous democracy I (regression)

| *Dependent variable: DEM 1995–2001* | | |
Independent variables:	*Coeffs*	*Model 1*
LNGDP/CAP 1998	Coeff	1.071
	t-stat	4.81
STATEAGE	Coeff	0.011
	t-stat	2.62
ELF1	Coeff	−0.604
	t-stat	−0.83
RELFR1	Coeff	0.011
	t-stat	1.14
Constant	Coeff	−3.823
	t-stat	−2.16
adj rsq		0.42
N		135

Sources: see Appendix A1.

actions are all probabilities meaning that a young, new nation in a poor environment like East Timor is not doomed to democratic failure. A key question for mankind is whether Islam can accommodate democracy more successfully. Emphasizing the negative influence of a large Muslim population on the probability of a democratic regime or the success of democratic consolidation is again to offer a model of exogenous democracy. Table 12.2 tests such an exogenous model, predicting democracy from affluence, state age and strength of Islam.

Table 12.2 Exogenous democracy II (regression)

| *Dependent variable: DEM 1995–2001* | | |
Independent variables:	*Coeffs*	*Model 2*
LNGDP/CAP 1998	Coeff	0.929
	t-stat	4.81
STATEAGE	Coeff	0.008
	t-stat	2.26
MUSLIM	Coeff	−0.028
	t-stat	−5.95
Constant	Coeff	−1.663
	t-stat	−1.16
adj rsq		0.54
N		135

Sources: see Appendix A1.

Entering a variable to capture the strength of Islam increases the amount of explained variation. It is also evident that this variable has the strongest impact on the variation in the level of democracy at the end of the twentieth century. Exogenous factors matter for democracy.

An alternative perspective on democracy only includes endogenous factors. Table 12.3 tests a regression model of thin constitutionalism. As stated in the Introduction, the new idea that we launch in this book is a model which endogenizes democracy. Thus, we suggest the following democracy model (DM1):

DEMO = *d* (Election system, Corruption, Size of the largest party),

and we estimate the corresponding regression model in Table 12.3 in order to specify the democracy function, *d*, above. Democracy depends here on factors which are determined within the political system.

The finding from testing a model of endogenous democracy explains most of the country variation very well. Corruption and a dominant political party strongly diminishes the probability of democracy whereas the employment of PR election techniques enhances democratic stability. When one party achieves a dominant position, scoring electoral support between 55 per cent and 100 per cent of the electorate and, in addition, the bureaucracy is characterized by large-scale corruption, then democracy cannot stabilize. If, in addition to widespread corruption, majoritarian election methods are employed to overemphasize the role of one party, then authoritarian rule will be the result.

We regard the finding in Table 12.3, concerning the positive contribution of PR election techniques to democratic stability, as a confirmation of the consociationalist approach. As a matter of fact, PR is essentially what remains of consociationalism when one bypasses the grand coalition which is an impractical institution.

The endogenous model tested in Table 12.3, receiving such a high good-

Table 12.3 Endogenous democracy (regression)

Dependent variable: DEM 1995–2001		
Independent variables:	Coeffs	Model 1
NEWCORR	Coeff	−0.447
	t-stat	−7.03
ELSYS	Coeff	0.749
	t-stat	2.39
LGSTPTY	Coeff	−0.05
	t-stat	−6.58
Constant	Coeff	11.933
	t-stat	20.97
adj rsq		0.69
N		102

Sources: see Appendix A1.

ness of fit, may develop into a deductive framework for democracy analysis. The basic endogenous model would be the following (DM2):

$$\text{DEMO} = \frac{\text{Election system}}{\text{Corruption} \times \text{Largest party size}}$$

In Appendix 12.1 this endogenous model is developed deductively together with a model which combines endogeneity with exogeneity, namely (DM3):

$$\text{DEMO} = \frac{\text{State age}}{\text{Corruption} \times \text{Largest party size}}$$

Now, following the core of our argument that democracy should be endogenized, we then ask: which institutions enhance endogenous democracy in accordance with the model tested in Table 12.3? Should government in constitutional choice opt for *thin* institutionalization or *thick* institutionalization of democracy?

Thin constitutionalism matters more

The findings in this book have convinced us that thin constitutionalism is a sufficient condition for democracy. Institutions constitute a major condition for democratic longevity and consolidation, but thick constitutionalism is not a necessary condition for democracy. Democracy can be introduced in societies with adverse economic, cultural and social conditions as long as three sets of rules are enforced:

1 parliamentarism;
2 the Ombudsman; and
3 economic freedom.

We claim that thin constitutionalism adhering to these three rules is sufficient to make democracy workable.

We have shown that parliamentarism supports democracy better than presidentialism. Yet, parliamentarism needs a legal structure to tame the Caesarist dangers involved in unrestrained majoritarian democracy under parliamentarism. Rights in combination with the Ombudsman temper these Caesarist tendencies in parliamentarism. In addition there is the market economy whose institutions (property, contact) also restrain parliamentarism.

Rights and immunities

Democracy promises the hope of the rule of the people. But it also contains the seeds of the tyranny of the majority. Tocqueville saw both the opportunity that populist democracy provides and the danger that it harbours. When a majority can decide over a minority with merely 51 per cent of the votes, then

oppression may result. This is the wisdom developed in the theory of the seg-
mented society where deep ethnic or religious cleavages hinder the alterna-
tion in power which majoritarian democracy prospers from.

Populist democracy is a necessary condition for a stable democratic regime,
but it is not a sufficient condition. Unrestrained populist democracy suffers
from two weaknesses which do not tend to occur simultaneously. Thus, populist democracy may be conducive to two kinds of instability which may lead
to the replacement of the regime by non-democratic forms of government.
They are:

- *Lijphart instability*: a majority suppresses a minority along ethnic or religious cleavages: for example, Northern Ireland, Sri Lanka, Lebanon,
  Egypt, Spain, etc.
- *Arrow instability*: the majority and the minority changes side so quickly that
  decisions become volatile: cycling, log-rolling, etc.

The remedy against both types of instability, although altogether different in
nature, is the enforcement of a list of fundamental rights, especially immunities, as well as the enforcement of economic freedom. The key mechanism for
enforcing rights is, in our view, the Ombudsman – the peculiar Scandinavian
contribution to making democracy concrete and meaningful. When democracy is restrained by such a mechanism, then we arrive at constitutional
democracy.

Constitutional democracy may be practised through parliamentarism. Presidentialism may express populist democracy, but it then requires thick constitutionalism to restrain the dangers of a powerful executive. Thick
constitutionalism is advocated as the best form of democracy. We disagree,
and the findings reported in this book support our doubts about consociationalism, federalism, consensus democracy and veto players. Thick constitutionalism makes democracy too complicated, reducing decisiveness, if indeed thick
institutionalization is feasible at all given its risks for blockage and constitutional crisis.

Parliamentarism offers a set of efficient executive institutions for a democratic regime. The will of the people is more easily expressed under these
institutions than under presidentialism. The 51 per cent principle decision
rule makes it possible for a polity to come to a decision, whereas requirements
of larger majorities or unanimity block the operation of democracy. Parliamentarism focuses on the legislative assembly and the Premier who emerges as
the natural leader of the work of Parliament. The institutions of parliamentarism – investiture, no-confidence and dissolution – make the executive
reflect the popular will in the legislative assembly, avoiding conflicts and stalemate between the executive and legislative branch of government, as Bagehot
emphasized more than one hundred years ago.

Parliamentarism may employ a range of election techniques, including the
various PR methods. What should be avoided are grand coalitions or institutions which reduce decisiveness. Yet, parliamentarism needs a legal structure
to tame the Caesarist dangers involved in unrestrained majoritarian demo-

cracy. Rights in combination with the Ombudsman temper these Caesarist tendencies. In addition the institutions of the market economy also restrain majoritarian democracy.

Tocqueville suggested that political decentralization in various forms was the key remedy against this tendency towards the tyranny of the majority. Political decentralization may, however, be pursued so far that it hurts majoritarian democracy. If each minority could claim a veto, then democracy as the rule of the people loses its rationale. Negotiated democracy would be based on unanimity rule where each group would be able to block decisions. It could be implemented through both territorial and functional decentralization. In federalist theory, veto powers would comprise of nullification and secession whereas functional decentralization would focus on corporatist institutions.

Yet federalism or corporatism could come into conflict with democracy, hindering the popular will to express itself. This is likely to occur under thick constitutionalism which reinforces the role of veto players in the political system. Thin constitutionalism avoids the problem by maintaining a balance between majoritarian democracy and the capacity of minorities to block decisions. There need to be some blocking powers but not to such an extent that the expression of popular will becomes impossible. We suggest the remedy is parliamentarism, fundamental rights and the Ombudsman. These institutions constitute a necessary and sufficient condition for constitutional democracy.

A list of fundamental rights and duties appear in all constitutions. Such a list typically contains a mixture of negative and positive rights. In some constitutions, the list is short and concise, whereas in others it is very long and comprehensive. What matters is the enforcement of whatever list of rights a country may have written down in its formal constitution. And the enforcement task rests with the legal system, including an Ombudsman.

Constitutional democracy is the marriage of populist democracy with the Rule of Law. Popular governance is transformed into constitutional democracy when a list of rights is added to parliamentarism. We may follow the Hohfeld scheme for analysing rights. All of his four categories are relevant in a constitutional democracy: claim-rights, liberties, competences and immunities (Hohfeld, 2001). Rights which are not discussable constitute immunities. As states hesitate to make rights without any restriction on their exercise, true immunities hardly exist in any constitutional democracy. Yet, the following immunities are often mentioned as being key in a constitutional democracy, constituting the *set of fundamental rights and liberties*:

a   habeas corpus rights;
b   religious tolerance;
c   freedom of thought and expression;
d   freedom of association;
e   the right to vote.

None of these rights, however, are perfect immunities, as governments in democratic countries restrict them somewhat for security reasons. At the end of the day, the contents of these rights are decided by the courts – in case law or precedents. Yet, these classical rights help to stabilize democracy by both protecting minorities and reducing the negative effects of cycling. Legislation that attacks these rights will not get through Parliament, at least not without much difficulty and resistance. How can the rights and liberties a–e be enforced?

Legal institutions

It is argued that only legal review can secure the basic immunities in a constitutional democracy. We disagree. Legal review is neither a necessary nor a sufficient condition for constitutional democracy. It creates a strong veto player that may change the will of the people in ways that are hardly in agreement with the requirements of justice, such as, for instance, the infamous Dred Scott decision by the US Supreme Court in 1857. On the contrary, several countries in Latin America have introduced legal review but it has not secured constitutional democracy.

The Ombudsman – the peculiar Scandinavian contribution to constitutional democracy – is the little man's protection against the abuse of government authority. It is extremely effective through its anticipation effect. The people in the Ombudsman Office do not engage in the kinds of spectacular political intervention typical of courts where legal review is practised. However, they check the bureaucracy and they offer a safe channel for complaints and remedies in relation to the rule of law. In very few countries where the Ombudsman has been introduced has it been a failure. There are two basic versions of the Ombudsman, the Swedish model (1809) and the Danish model (1954). Both bite when it comes to enforcing the Rule of Law.

The risk of Arrow instability is high in relation to economic legislation. To reduce the probability of cycling, the institutions of the market economy offer a complex system of rights which, when enforced, stabilize democratic policy-making. Economic rights including:

- private property;
- limited liability companies;
- contractual freedom;
- labour rights; and
- financial markets

restrain policy-making, although none of these rights are immunities in the strict sense.

Thus, the set of institutions create the same kind of barrier against majoritarian Caesarism, making up the rules of the market economy. When the market economy is put in place, then economic rights are enforced concerning land, property, capital and ownership: the institutions of the market economy may not protect minorities (Lijphart instability) as much as they limit cycling (Arrow instability). Yet, they restrain government decision-making considerably and they enhance stability by reducing the range and scope for policy-making.

Economic rights tend to go hand-in-hand with civil and political rights. The rationale of this strong association is that states cannot guarantee the one and not the other. When government invades rights, then they tend to attack both political and economic rights. Conversely, when governments respect economic rights, then they also tend to respect civil and political rights.

Structural model evidence

To substantiate our claim that thin constitutionalism is enough for democratic stability, we will test a regression model that explains the variation in democracy with the following institutions which are singled out as key:

- parliamentarism;
- the Ombudsman;
- the market economy.

Democracy would be a function of these three sets of institutions, which governments can promote to a considerable extent. Table 12.4 shows the findings of the test of this regression model.

This model estimation suggests that full and transparent institutionalization of a market economy matters most for democracy. The Ombudsman institution also has a strong positive impact, while, for the case of parliamentarism, it holds that it only has a weak positive impact in this model.

One may contrast the test of this model of thin constitutionalism with the test of a model of thick constitutionalism. In order to maximize the number of veto points, one would construct a constitutional democracy out of the following institutions: federalism, presidentialism, symmetrical bicameralism and legal review. Ideally, a country with such an institutional set up would be democratically stable. But how about the reality: do the rules of thick constitutionalism enhance democracy? Table 12.5 suggests an answer.

Table 12.4 Thin constitutionalism (regression evidence)

Dependent variable: DEM 1995–2001 Independent variables:	Coeffs	Model 1
PARLIAM	Coeff	0.309
	t-stat	1.72
OMBUDS	Coeff	0.811
	t-stat	3.87
ECFREE	Coeff	2.279
	t-stat	9.99
Constant	Coeff	1.994
	t-stat	2.73
adj rsq		0.67
N		128

Sources: see Appendix A1.

Table 12.5 Thick constitutionalism (regression)

Dependent variable: DEM 1995–2001		
Independent variables:	Coeffs	Model 1
FEDER	Coeff	−0.420
	t-stat	−0.56
PRES(A)	Coeff	−0.663
	t-stat	−1.44
BICAMER	Coeff	2.107
	t-stat	4.11
LEGREV	Coeff	1.267
	t-stat	2.82
Constant	Coeff	2.909
	t-stat	4.04
adj rsq		0.16
N		145

Sources: see Appendix A1.

The amount of explained variation is distinctively lower for this model. Legal review and bi-cameralism is positively related to democracy, but neither federalism nor presidentialism enhances it. Thick constitutionalism, as specified in this model, has only a modest positive impact on democracy. In constitutional choice, countries would do better opting for thin institutionalization of democracy than thick institutionalization. To state our basic point in a succinct manner: a compact unitary state with parliamentarism and the Ombudsman in a setting with a market economy has a higher probability of succeeding from a democratic point of view than a federal state with lots of veto points or veto players.

Conclusion

Democratic stability, our evidence suggests, is more endogenous than exogenous. Although economic and cultural factors impact on democracy, institutions play a crucial role; and institutions can be promoted from within the political system through constitutional policy-making (Sartori, 1994).

Affluence promotes democratic stability. There can be no doubt that poverty is a major hindrance to democracy in Third World countries. However, economics does not determine politics. Poor countries can overcome the negative consequences of mass poverty through institutional design. Ethnic and religious cleavages reduce democratic longevity and democratic consolidation. However, countries may overcome these negative effects through firm institutions. In relation to ethnic and religious cleavages it is crucial that governments can guarantee a body of basic rights which counteract racism and religious intolerance. Whether democracy is possible in Islamic countries remains doubtful, but one may point out that Buddhism has proved that it can accommodate a democratic system.

When endogenous democracy is emphasized, then one always underlines thick constitutionalism. Somehow, democracy must be protected against its own tendencies towards instability. And the only remedy against democratic instability is to create such strong checks and balances that the will of the people is virtually dissipated. Thick constitutionalism creates too many veto players, who employ their blocking power to further their interests, which sometimes occurs at the expense of the will of majorities.

Our basic argument is that thin constitutionalism is enough for safeguarding constitutional democracy. The key institutions are parliamentarism, the Ombudsman and the market economy. If a country implements these three sets of institutions, then it has a very good chance of remaining democratic or becoming a consolidated democracy. These three institutions favourably influence the basic conditions for endogenous democracy, reducing corruption and the size of the largest party.

Appendix: on the mathematics of democracy

By Florent Dieterlen (Lausanne) and Jan-Erik Lane

We want to find out how democracy (which we will call a function D) varies with factors that are determined within the polity – endogenous democracy. Thus, we will *not* examine how democracy is a function of major social and economic or cultural forces – exogenous democracy. In the comparative research on the conditions for democratic stability and the consolidation of democracy in transition countries, the impact of external forces has been well researched. It remains to map the influence of internal factors.

The factors that would constitute endogenous democracy could be, in our approach, the following: the election system $= E$, the level of corruption $= C$, the size of the biggest party $= B$ and the state age $= S$.

The first three are clearly determined within the polity. State age measures the length of time of uninterrupted government institutionalization. And it is only partially an internal factor, as it is endogenous only from a dynamic perspective.

We could search for linear relationships, but the data is arranged on curves, except for the election system which takes only two values, which excludes another curve than a line. The other data look like polynomial curves, for example, $y = x^2$, or $y = \text{sqrt}(x)$. Our goal is therefore to find the exponents of these polynomials. In the two preceding examples, the exponents are 2 and ½. The general form of our functions will look like this:

$$y = x^a \tag{1}$$

where y is the function democracy, x is one of the three variables we consider and a is the exponent. In order to find these exponents, we take the logarithm of both sides of equation 1:

$$\text{Log} y = a \log x \tag{2}$$

At this point, we just have to find the linear regression line that best fits equation 2. Democracy is measured by a standard index which ranges from 0 to 10.

The estimation of the linear regression applied to the election system, *E*, gives the following equation:

$$D = 4.83 + 3.11\ E \tag{3}$$

We know that presidential regimes tend to use majoritarian election systems whereas parliamentary regimes tend to employ PR election methods. To go deeper into the impact of the election system, we will construct a new variable using two other variables, which are:

1   presidential/parliamentary/mixed;
2   proportional/non-proportional.

We give the maximum for parliamentary and proportional. There are two ways of computing this:

1   Elsys1: presidential/parliamentary is more important than proportional/non-proportional. Thus, we put 0 for presidential, 4 for mixed, 8 for parliamentary, and add 2 if it is proportional. We finally add 1 in the non-linear case, to avoid $\log(0)$, which is not possible mathematically.
2   Elsys 2: proportional/non-proportional is more important than presidential/parliamentary. Thus, we put 0 for non-proportional, 6 for proportional, and add 2 if mixed, and 4 if parliamentary. We finally add 1 in the non-linear case, to avoid $\log(0)$, which is not possible mathematically.

Let us first estimate the equation for Elsys1: presidential/parliamentary before proportional/non-proportional. Thus, we get:

$$D = 6.26\ \text{Elsys}\,1^{0.17}$$

We show here the linear and non-linear fits. We have put here $D = 6.26^{*}E\char`^0.2$, because $E\char`^0.17$ is not possible.

Democracy is strongly associated with a combined institutional set up of parliamentarism and PR.

Second, we look at Elsys2: proportional before presidential/parliamentary. Thus, we get:

$$D = 4.96\ \text{Elsys}\,2^{0.12}$$

We may certainly conclude that the combination parliamentary regime and PR election method is more conducive to democracy than the institutional combination of presidentialism and a majoritarian election system.

The next endogenous factor to look at is corruption. Estimating a regression equation from the data gives us the following:

$$D = 3.74 \ (10 - C)^{0.40} \tag{4}$$

Equation 4 shows the form of this equation where democracy is negatively affected by the level of corruption in a country.

Thus, we may establish that D is naturally related to $10-C$, which is the lack of corruption, which we could also call 'probity'.

Let us look at the impact of big party size (i.e. whether there is a dominant party scoring more than 50 per cent of the vote). We have:

$$D = 636.77 \ \frac{1}{B^{1.20}} \tag{5}$$

Finally, we have state age. Here we get:

$$D = 1.29 \ S^{0.31} \tag{6}$$

Finding a slope of the preceeding curves at certain points means to calculate the derivative of the equations of these curves at defined points. We first calculate the general equation for the slopes, and then see what values they take for certain defined points.

For the derivative function of election system, we have:

$$\frac{dD}{dE} = 3.11$$

This derivative is constant, therefore we do not need to calculate its value for different points, as it is always equal to 3.11: when E goes from 0 to 1, D is, on average, approximately doubled.

For the derivative function of corruption, we have:

$$\frac{dD}{dC} = -1.496 \frac{1}{C^{0.6}}$$

It means that when corruption increases, democracy generally decreases.

For the derivative function of big party size, we have:

$$\frac{dD}{dB} = -757.7563 \frac{1}{B^{2.2}}$$

It means that when the largest party size increases, democracy generally decreases.

For the derivative function of state age, we have:

$$\frac{dD}{dS} = 0.39835 \ \frac{1}{S^{0.69}}$$

It means that when the age of the state increases, democracy generally increases. Here we can see the derivative function of corruption at two points:

$$C = 0.1: \qquad\qquad \frac{dD}{dC} = -5.955683270$$

$$C = 0.9: \qquad\qquad \frac{dD}{dC} = -1.593624830$$

This means that when corruption is at a very low value, or when the state is very 'clean', an increase in corruption will give a large decrease in democracy. But if instead, the corruption is very big, an increase in corruption will still give a decrease in democracy, but about four times less than before.

The derivative function of big party size at two points:

$$B = 30\%: \qquad\qquad \frac{dD}{dB} = -0.4264447729$$

$$B = 90\%: \qquad\qquad \frac{dD}{dB} = -0.03803610476$$

This means that when the biggest party is relatively small, an increase in the size of that party will generally give a relatively large decrease in democracy. But if, instead, the leading party dominates almost completely, an increase in size will still generally give a decrease in democracy, but ten times lower.

The derivative function of state age at two points:

$$S = 1: \qquad\qquad \frac{dD}{dS} = 0.39835$$

$$S = 200: \qquad\qquad \frac{dD}{dS} = 0.01029328801$$

From when a state was just created, its increase in democracy over time will be generally quite big. But when a state has already 200 years of age, its increase in democracy over time will be, on average, forty times lower.

To compute $D = D(S, E, C, B)$, one generally uses a linear multiple regression. This gives us D as a linear function of the four variables. Splus computes this very easily, and for both election systems we get:

$$D = 12.3426 + 0.0028\ S - 0.4354\ C - 0.0577\ B + 0.0274\ \text{Elsys1}$$

$$D = 10.7581 + 0.0031\ S - 0.364\ C - 0.0474\ B + 0.1304\ \text{Elsys2}$$

When one knows for sure that the main variable is a product of the other variables, one can do a linear multiple regression on the logs. For both election systems we have:

$$D = 1.7771 \; \frac{S^{0.058} \; \text{Elsys1}^{0.0692}}{C^{0.1049} \; B^{0.565}}$$

$$D = 1.5135 \; \frac{S^{0.0539} \; \text{Elsys2}^{0.1258}}{C^{0.0987} \; B^{0.4763}}$$

Thus, we may conclude that democracy is directly related to state age and the electoral system as well as inversely related to the level of corruption and the size of the largest party.

We thus suggest an endogenous model of democracy to explain these national differences. We find that democracy is positively related to parliamentarism and the PR methods of election and inversely related to corruption multiplied by the size of the largest party. State age affects democracy positively. The endogenous model should be useful in predicting democracy scores.

Appendix A1

Variable list for the sample of the countries of the world (at most $N = 150$)

Abbreviation	Description	Sources
ABSOLUT	Tradition of absolute rule	Derbyshire and Derbyshire 1996, 1999
AGREMPL	Share of labour force in agriculture c. 1990	UNDP, 1995
BICAMER	Chamber system as a dummy variable where 1 = Bi-cameral systems and 0 = one-cameral systems	Encyclopaedia Britannica
BIOCAPA	Biological capacity index which measures the biological production capacity within a country	WWF, 2000
BRITLEG	Legacy of British colonial rule as a dummy variable where 1 = British legacy and 0 = no such legacy	Based on de Blij, 1996
BUDD	Percentage of the population estimated to adhere to the Buddhist creed	Barrett, 1982
CBANK1	Index of Central Bank independence based on Cukierman; the higher the score, the more independence	Cukierman, 1992
CBANK2	Index of Central Bank independence based on a revision of Cukierman; the higher the score, the more independence	Bernhard, 1998
CBANK3	Index of Central Bank independence based on Grill *et al.*; the higher the score, the more independence	Bernhard, 1998
CBANK4	Index of Central Bank independence based on Alesina *et al.*; the higher the score, the more independence	Bernhard, 1998
CENTPERI	Center-periphery index where higher scores refer to the core and lower scores to the periphery	Terlouw, 1989
CGCON	Central government consumption as a percentage of GDP	World Bank, 2000c
CGDEBT	Central government debt as percentage of GDP	World Bank, 2000c

Abbreviation	Description	Sources
CGEXP	Central government expenditure as a percentage of GDP	World Bank, 2000c
CONYR	Number of years of current constitution at a certain time-point	Banks, 1978; Encyclopaedia Britannica, 1986, 1996
CORR	Perceived corruption, where higher scores indicate less corruption, and lower scores more corruption	Transparency International
COUPS	Number of coups d'etat in a country in the period 1970 to 1996	Banks, 1996
DEFICITS	Central government deficits	World Bank, 1992, 1997
DEM	The democracy scores are based on the Freedom House scores where a low degree of democracy scores 1 and a high degree of democracy scores 10	Freedom House, 2002
ECODEFI	Ecological deficit index which measures how much the 'ecological footprint' (ECTOTAL) exceeds the 'biological capacity' (BIOCAPA)	WWF, 2000
ECTOTAL	Index on ecological footprint which estimates the ecological impact of humanity on the environment	WWF, 2000
ELF1	Ethno-linguistic fragmentation index based on the division of the population into different ethno-linguistic groups	Based on Encyclopaedia Britannica, 1998
ELF2	Ethno-linguistic fragmentation index based on the division of the population into different ethno-linguistic groups	Based on Barrett, 1982
ELF3	Ethno-linguistic fragmentation index based on the division of the population into different ethno-linguistic groups	Taylor and Hudson, 1972
ELSYS	Election system as a dummy variable where 1 = proportional systems and 0 = non-proportional systems	Reynolds and Reilly, 1997; Rose, 2000
ENVSYS	Environment system index which captures the environmental system of a country	WEF, 2002
ESI	Environmental sustainability index	WEF, 2002
FAMFARM	Percentage of family farms of total holding area *c.* 1990	Vanhanen, 1997
FAMSYST	Classification of countries as belonging to family systems according to degree of individualism, where the absolute nuclear family scores high and the African family system scores low	Todd, 1985
FEDER	Federalism as a dummy variable where 1 = federalism and 0 = non-federalism	Encyclopaedia Britannica

Abbreviation	Description	Sources
FRASER	Index of economic freedom as estimated by the Fraser Institute, and where high scores indicate a high degree of economic freedom and low scores indicate a low degree of economic freedom	Gwartney and Lawson, 2001
FREEDOM HOUSE	The Freedom House scores have been added and normalized so that a low degree of democracy scores 1 and a high degree of democracy scores 10	Freedom House, 2002
GCON	General government consumption as a percentage of total consumption	Gwartney and Lawson, 2001
GDI	Gender-related development index	UNDP, 2001
GDP in PPP	Gross Domestic Product per capita expressed as purchase power parities in US$	World Bank, 2000c
GDPC	Gross Domestic Product per capita expressed as purchase power parities in US$	World Bank, 2000c
GEM	Gender empowerment measure	UNDP, 2001
GGEXP	General government consumption as a percentage of total consumption (GCON) plus transfers/subsidies as a share of GDP (TRANS)	Gwartney and Lawson, 2001
GINI 1970	Gini coefficient measuring inequality of income distribution within countries estimated by the World Bank	Deininger and Squire, 1997
GINI 1980	Gini coefficient measuring inequality of income distribution within countries estimated by the World Bank	Deininger and Squire, 1997
GINI 1990	Gini coefficient measuring inequality of income distribution within countries estimated by the World Bank	Deininger and Squire, 1997
GINILIS	Gini coefficient measuring inequality of income distribution within countries estimated by the Luxembourg Income Study	LIS, 2002
GINIMIL	Gini coefficient measuring inequality of income distribution within countries estimated by the World Bank	Milanovic and Yizhaki, 2000
GINIWB	Gini coefficient measuring inequality of income distribution within countries estimated by the World Bank	World Bank, 2000c
GINIWDI	Gini coefficient measuring inequality of income distribution within countries estimated by the World Bank	World Bank, 2000c
GNP Atlas	Gross National Product per capita estimated in US$ following the World Bank Atlas method	World Bank, 2000c

Abbreviation	Description	Sources
GNP Constant	Gross National Product per capita estimated in US$ at constant prices	World Bank, 2000c
GNP in PPP	Gross National Product per capita expressed as purchase power parities in US$	World Bank, 2000c
GOVSP	Government spending as a percentage of GDP as estimated by the Global Competitiveness Report	Schwab *et al.*, 1999; Porter *et al.*, 2000
GROWTH	Annual per capita economic growth	World Bank, 2000c
HDI	Human Development Index	UNDP, 2001
HERITAGE	Rescaled index of economic freedom as estimated by the Heritage Foundation, and this means that here high scores indicate a high degree of economic freedom and low scores indicate a low degree of economic freedom	O'Driscoll *et al.*, 2002
HPI	Human Poverty Index	UNDP, 1999
IBERLEG	Legacy of Iberian colonial rule as a dummy variable where 1 = Iberian legacy and 0 = no such legacy	Based on de Blij, 1996
IMPEX	Imports and exports in percentage of GDP	World Bank, 2000c
INDFRIND	Democracy scores for India as estimated by the Freedom House	Freedom House
INFL	Average inflation rates for various periods of time	World Bank, 2000c
LANDAREA	Land area in sq. km.	World Bank, 2000c
LATITU	Distance from the Equator in absolute degrees – latitudes	CIA, 1999
LEGREV	Presence of legal review as a dummy variable where 1 = legal review and 0 = no legal review	Based on Rhyne, 1978; CIA, 1994; Maddex, 1996
LGSTPTY	Estimated size of the largest party at an election as a percentage of the total vote	Vanhanen, 2000
LNGDP/CAP	Natural logarithm of GDP per capita in US$ expressed as purchasing power parities	World Bank, 2000c
MADD	Gross domestic product per capita in international US$ as estimated by Maddison	Maddison, 1995
MUSL	Percentage of the population estimated to adhere to the Muslim creed	Barrett, 1982
MUSLARAB	Dummy variable where Arab countries within the Muslim world (= 1) and non-Arab countries are coded as (= 0)	Authors' own coding
NEWCORR	Rescaled perceived corruption index (CORR) which means that high scores stand for high levels of perceived corruption and low scores for low levels of perceived corruption	Transparency International

Abbreviation	Description	Sources
OMBUDS	Occurrence of the Ombudsman institution as a trichotomous variable where 2 = early institutionalization, 1 = later institutionalization, and 0 = no institutionalization	International Ombudsman Institute, 1999
ORTH	Percentage of the population estimated to adhere to the Orthodox creed	Barrett, 1982
PARL	Parliamentarism scored as 2 = parliamentarism 1 = semi-presidentialism 0 = presidentialism	Derbyshire and Derbyshire, 1996, 1999
PARLIAM	Parliamentarism as a dummy variable where 1 = parliamentarism and 0 = non-parliamentarism	Derbyshire and Derbyshire, 1996, 1999
POLITY	The polity score has been arrived at from subtracting the original autocracy score from the democracy score and then the index is normalized to go from 0 (no democracy) to 10 (democracy)	Gurr and Jaggers, 2000
POPGRO	Annual growth in population	World Bank, 2000c
POPUGRO	Annual growth in world population	US Bureau of Census, 2000
PPPCGRO	Annual growth in gross world product/capita expressed in PPP	IMF, 2000
PPPCGROW	Annual growth in gross domestic product/capita expressed in PPP	World Bank, 2000c
PPPGRO	Annual growth in gross world product expressed in PPP	IMF, 2000
PPPGROW	Annual growth in gross domestic product expressed in PPP	World Bank, 2000c
PQLI	Physical quality of life index	Morris, 1996
PRES(A)	Presidentialism as a dummy variable where 1 = presidentialism and 0 = non-presidentialism	Encylopaedia Britannica
PRES(B)	Presidentialism as trichotomous variable where 2 = presidentialism, 1 = semi-presidentialism and 0 = non-presidentialism	Derbyshire and Derbyshire, 1996, 1999
PRES(C)	Presidentialism as a dummy variable where 1 = presidentialism and 0 = non-presidentialism	Derbyshire and Derbyshire, 1996, 1999
PROT	Percentage of the population estimated to adhere to the Protestant creed	Barrett, 1982

Abbreviation	Description	Sources
PRZEWORSKI	The score has been multiplied by 10, ranging from 0 (no democracy) to 10 (democracy)	Przeworski *et al.*, 2000
PWT	Gross domestic product per capita in international US$ as estimated by the Penn World Tables	Summers and Heston, 1994
RC	Percentage of the population estimated to adhere to the Roman Catholic creed	Barrett, 1982
RELFR1	Religious fragmentation index based on the division of the population in the major world religions	Barrett, 1982
RELFR2	Religious fragmentation index based on the division of the population in the major world religions, as well as the major subgroups within Christianity	Barrett, 1982
RSAFRIND	Democracy scores for South Africa as estimated by the Freedom House	Freedom House, 2002
SINGFRIN	Democracy scores for Singapore as estimated by the Freedom House	Freedom House, 2002
STATEAGE	Number of years since the introduction of modernized leadership	Based on Black, 1966
TAXREV	Tax revenues as a percentage of GDP	World Bank, 2000c
TOTDEB	Total debt service as a percentage of GDP	World Bank, 2000c
TOTOUT	Total government outlays as a percentage of GDP	Gwartney and Lawson, 2001
TRANS	Transfers/subsidies as a percentage of GDP	Gwartney and Lawson, 2001
TRUST	Percentage of a sample in a country expressing interpersonal trust	Inglehart *et al.*, 2000
TUD	Trade union density	ILO, 1997
U5MR	Under-five mortality rate per 1000	UNICEF, 2001a
VANHANEN	The Vanhanen score is arrived at by multiplying participation with competition, and the higher the score, the more democracy	Vanhanen, 2000
WATER	Percentage of population having access to an improved water source	World Bank, 2001
WOM	Percentage of female parliamentarians	IPU, 2000

Appendix A2

Variable list for the sample of Central and East European countries, and the CIS countries

Abbreviation	Description	Sources
BRUSSELS	Distance between Brussels and the capital of the country in km.	Based on Byers, 2002
CIS	Dummy variable where 1 = country is part of the CIS (Commonwealth of Independent States) and 0 = not part of CIS	Authors' own coding
CIVILSOC	Civil society index; here rescaled to go from lowest (= 0) to highest (= 10)	Karatnycky *et al.*, 2001b
DEM	The democracy scores are based on the Freedom House scores where a low degree of democracy scores 1 and a high degree of democracy scores 10	Freedom House, 2002
DEMOINTER	Democracy index for the interwar years going from no democracy (= 0) to democracy (= 10)	Authors' own coding
ECFREE	Rescaled index of economic freedom as estimated by the Heritage Foundation, and this means that here high scores indicate a high degree of economic freedom and low scores indicate a low degree of economic freedom	O'Driscoll *et al.*, 2002
ELF	Ethno-linguistic fragmentation index based on the division of the population into different ethno-linguistic groups	Based on Encyclopaedia Britannica, 1998
ELSYS	Election system as a dummy variable where 1 = proportional systems and 0 = non-proportional systems	Reynolds and Reilly, 1997; Rose, 2000
FDI	Foreign direct inflows in percentage of GDP	EBRD
GDP/CAP 1973	GDP per capita in 1990 international US$	Maddison, 2001
GDP/CAP 1985	GDP per capita in US$	Kitschelt, 1999
GDP/CAP 1998	Gross Domestic Product per capita expressed as purchase power parities in US$	World Bank, 2000c

Abbreviation	Description	Sources
GDP/CAP 2000	Gross Domestic Product per capita in US$	EBRD, 2001
GDPINDEX	Index for level of GDP where 1989 = 100	EBRD
GGBAL	General government balance in percentage of GDP	EBRD
GGEXP	General government expenditure in percentage of GDP	EBRD
GINIA	Gini coefficient measuring inequality of income distribution within countries estimated by the World Bank	World Bank, 2000a
GINIB	Gini coefficient measuring inequality of income distribution within countries estimated by UNICEF	UNICEF, 2001b
GROW9098	Annual per capita economic growth averaged for the period 1990–8	World Bank, 2000c
GROW9000	Annual per capita economic growth averaged for the period 1990–2000	World Bank, 2000c
INTERNET	Internet hosts per capita	ISC
INVEST	Investment rate in percentage of GDP	EBRD
LABPROD	Change in labour productivity in industry, 1991–7: averages	EBRD
LATITU	Distance from the Equator in absolute degrees – latitudes	CIA, 1999
LNINFLA	Natural logarithm for the inflation rate for the period 1990–6	World Bank, 1998
LONGITU	Distance from the zero meridian in absolute degrees – longitudes	CIA, 1999
MUSLIM	Percentage of the population estimated to adhere to the Muslim creed	Barrett, 1982
NOGOV	Number of governments during the period 1990–2001	Authors' own coding
OMBUDS	Occurrence of the Ombudsman institution as a trichotomous variable where 2 = early institutionalization, 1 = later institutionalization, and 0 = no institutionalization	International Ombudsman Institute, 1999
ORTH	Percentage of the population estimated to adhere to the Orthodox creed	Barrett, 1982
PRESIDIND	Presidential power index	Frye, 1997
PRIVIND	Privatization index	EBRD
PRIVSHARE	Estimates of the private sector share of the economy	EBRD
RC	Percentage of the population estimated to adhere to the Roman Catholic creed	Barrett, 1982

Abbreviation	Description	Sources
REFYEAR	Year and month of introduction of stabilization programme	EBRD
RELFR	Religious fragmentation index based on the division of the population in the major world religions	Barrett, 1982
TERTIARY	Tertiary education enrolments as a percentage of the 18–22 age population	UNICEF, 1999
TURN	Number of main political executive turnovers 1989–99	World Bank, 2002
TYPEGOV	Type of government, where 2 = one-party governments, 1 = mixed governments, 0 = mostly coalition governments	Authors' own coding
U5MR	Under-five mortality rate per 1000	UNICEF, 2001a
VETO	Veto points index 1989–99	World Bank, 2002

Bibliography

Abbinnett, Ross (1998) *Truth and Social Science: From Hegel to Deconstruction.* London: Sage.

Abootalebi, Ali Reza (2000) *Islam and Democracy: State–Society Relations in Developing Countries, 1980–1994.* New York, NY: Garland.

Abrams, Burton A. and Kenneth A. Lewis (1995) 'Cultural and institutional determinants of economic growth: a cross-section analysis.' *Public Choice,* 83: 273–89.

Adelman, Irma (2000) 'Fifty years of economic development: what have we learned?' Paper prepared for the ABCDE/Europe, Paris 26–28 June (available at: http://www.worldbank.org/research/abcde/eu_2000/papers_eu2.html).

Adelman, Irma and Cynthia Taft Morris (1967) *Society, Politics and Economic Development: a Quantitative Approach.* Baltimore, MD: the Johns Hopkins University Press.

Adminstrations fédérale des finances (2001) *Finances Publiques en Suisse: Dépenses, Recettes, Dettes: Confédération, Cantons, Communes, Assurances Socials 1990–2000.* Bern: Adminstrations fédérale des finances.

Ahluwalia, Montek S. (2000) 'Economic performance of states in post-reform period.' *Economic and Political Weekly,* 35, 6 May: 1637–48.

Ake, Claude (1996) *Democracy and Development in Africa.* Washington, DC: Brookings.

Alesina, Alberto and Roberto Perotti (1994) 'The political economy of growth: a critical survey of the recent literature.' *The World Bank Economic Review,* 8: 351–71.

Almond, Gabriel A. (1956) 'Comparative political systems.' *Journal of Politics,* 18, 391–409.

Anand, Sudhir and Amartya Sen (1994) 'Human development index: methodology and measurement.' *Human Development Report Office Occasional Papers,* 12 (available at: http://www.undp.org/hdro).

Anand, Sudhir and Amartya Sen (1995) 'Gender inequality in human development: theories and measurement.' *Human Development Report Office Occasional Papers,* 19 (available at: http://www.undp.org/hdro).

Anand, Sudhir and Amartya Sen (2000) 'The income component of the human development index.' *Journal of Human Development,* 1: 83–106.

Anglade, Christian (1994) 'Democracy and the rule of law in Latin America.' In: Budge, Ian and David McKay (eds) *Developing Democracy: Comparative Research in Honour of J.F.P. Blondel.* London: Sage, pp. 233–52.

Aristotle (1981) *The Politics.* Harmondsworth: Penguin.

Arndt, Heinz Wolfgang (1989) *Economic Development: the History of an Idea.* Chicago, IL: the University of Chicago Press.

Aron, Janine (2000) 'Growth and institutions: a review of the literature.' *The World Bank Research Observer,* 15: 99–135.

Åslund, Anders (1992) *Post-Communist Economic Revolutions: How Big a Bang?* Washington, DC: The Center for Strategic and International Studies.

Baechler, Jean (1995) *Democracy: An Analytical Survey*. Paris: UNESCO.

Bagehot, Walter (1993) [1867] *The English Constitution*. London: Fontana.

Banks, Arthur S. (ed.) (1978) *Political Handbook of the World, 1978*. New York: McGraw-Hill.

Banks, Arthur S. (1996) *Cross-national Time–Series Data Archive*. Binghampton, NY: Center for social analysis, State University of New York at Binghampton.

Barber, Benjamin R. (1984) *Strong Democracy: Participatory Politics for a New Age*. Berkeley, CA: University of Carlifornia Press.

Bardhan, Kalpana and Stephan Klasen (1999) 'UNDP's gender-related indices: a critical review.' *World Development*, 27: 985–1010.

Barker, Ernest (1942) *Reflections on Government*. Oxford: Clarendon Press.

Barraclough, Solon L. (2001) 'Toward integrated and sustainable development?' *UNRISD Overarching Concerns Paper, 1*. Geneva: UNRISD.

Barrett, David B. (ed.) (1982) *World Christian Encyclopedia: A Comparative Study of Churches and Religions in the Modern World, AD 1900–2000*. Nairobi: Oxford University Press.

Barro, Robert J. (1996) 'Democracy and growth.' *Journal of Economic Growth*, 1: 1–27.

Barro, Robert J. (1999) 'Determinants of democracy.' *Journal of Political Economy*, 107: S158–83.

Barry, Brian (1989) *Democracy, Power and Justice: Essays in Political Theory*. Oxford: Clarendon Press.

Barry, Norman (1982) 'The tradition of spontaneous order.' *Literature of Liberty*, V, 2: 7–58.

Baylis, Thomas A. (1996) 'Presidents versus prime ministers: shaping executive authority in Eastern Europe.' *World Politics*, 48: 297–323.

Beetham, David (ed.) (1994) *Defining and Measuring Democracy*. London: Sage.

Bell, Daniel A. and Kanishka Jayasuriya (1995) 'Understanding illiberal democracy: a framework.' In: Bell, Daniel A., David Brown, Kanishka Jayasuria and David Martin Jones (eds) *Towards Illiberal Democracy in Pacific Asia*. Basingstoke: Macmillan, pp. 1–16.

Bernhard, William T. (1998) 'A political explanation of variation in central banks independence.' *American Political Science Review*, 92: 311–27.

Beteille, Andre (1999) 'Empowerment.' *Economic and Political Weekly*, 34, 19 March: 589–97.

Bhagwati, Jagdish (1998) *A Stream of Windows: Unsettling Reflections on Trade, Immigration, and Democracy*. Cambridge, MA: the MIT Press.

Bhalla, Surjit S. (1997) 'Freedom and economic growth: a virtuous cycle?' In: Axel Hadenius (ed.) *Democracy's Victory and Crisis*. Cambridge: Cambridge University Press, pp. 195–241.

Bhardwaj, R.C. and K. Vijayakrishnan (1998) *Democracy and Development: Allies or Adversaries?* Aldershot: Ashgate.

Black, Cyril E. (1966) *The Dynamics of Modernization: A Study in Comparative History*. New York, NY: Harper and Row.

Black, Max (ed.) (1961) *The Social Theories of Talcott Parsons: A Critical Examination*. Englewood Cliffs, NJ: Prentice-Hall.

Blais, André and R.K. Carty (1990) 'Does proportional representation foster voter turnout?' *European Journal for Political Research*, 18: 167–81.

Blais, André and Agnieszka Dobrzynska (1998) 'Turnout in electoral democracies.' *European Journal of Political Research*, 33: 239–61.

Blais, André, Louis Massicotte and Antoine Yoshinaka (2001) 'Deciding who has the right to vote: a comparative analysis of election laws.' *Electoral Studies*, 20: 41–62.

Blaug, Mark (1992) *The Methodology of Economics: Or How Economists Explain*. Cambridge: Cambridge University Press.

Boix, Carles (2000) 'Democracy and inequality.' MIT working papers on political economy (available at: http://web.mit.edu/polsci/polecon/www/).

Bollen, Kenneth A. (1980) 'Issues in the comparative measurement of political democracy.' *American Sociological Review*, 45: 370–90.

Bollen, Kenneth A. (1986) 'Political rights and political liberties in nations: an evaluation of human rights measures, 1950 to 1984.' *Human Rights Quarterly*, 8: 567–91.

Bollen, Kenneth A. (1990) 'Political democracy: conceptual and measurement traps.' *Studies in Comparative International Development*, 25: 7–24.

Bollen, Kenneth A. (1993) 'Liberal democracy: validity and method factors in cross-national measures.' *American Journal of Political Science*, 37: 1207–30.

Bollen, Kenneth A. (1995) 'Measures of democracy.' In: Lipset, Seymour Martin (ed.) *The Encyclopedia of Democracy. Volume III*. London: Routledge, pp. 817–21.

Bollen, Kenneth A. and Robert W. Jackman (1985) 'Political democracy and the size distribution of income.' *American Sociological Review*, 50: 438–57.

Bollen, Kenneth A. and Pamela Paxton (2000) 'Subjective measures of liberal democracy.' *Comparative Political Studies*, 33: 58–86.

Boserup, Ester (1970) *Woman's Role in Economic Development*. London: Allen and Unwin.

Botchway, Karl (2001) 'Paradox of empowerment: reflections on a case study from northern Ghana.' *World Development*, 29: 133–53.

Brennan, Geoffrey and James M. Buchanan (1980) *The Power to Tax: Analytical Foundations of a Fiscal Constitution*. Cambridge: Cambridge University Press.

Brennan, Geoffrey and James M. Buchanan (1985) *Reason of Rules: Constitutional Political Economy*. Cambridge: Cambridge University Press.

Brooker, Paul (2000) *Non-Democratic Regimes: Theory, Government and Politics*. New York, NY: St. Martin's Press.

Brunetti, Aymo (1997) 'Political variables in cross-country growth analysis.' *Journal of Economic Surveys*, 11: 163–90.

Brunetti, Aymo and Beatrice Weder (1995) 'Political sources of growth: a critical note on measurement.' *Public Choice*, 82: 125–34.

Bryce, James (1921) *Modern Democracies*. London: Macmillan.

Buchanan, James M. (1968) *The Demand and Supply of Public Goods*. Chicago, IL: Rand McNally.

Buchanan, James M. (1989) *Explorations into Constitutional Economics*. College Station, TX: Texas A&M University Press.

Buchanan, James M. and Gordon Tullock (1962) *The Calculus of Consent: Logical Foundations of Constitutional Democracy*. Ann Arbor: MI: University of Michigan Press.

Bunce, Valerie (1998) 'Regional differences in democratisation: the east versus the south.' *Post-Soviet Affairs*, 14: 187–211.

Bunce, Valerie (2001) 'Democratization and economic reform.' *Annual Review of Political Science*, 4: 43–65.

Bundesamt für Statistik (annually) *Statistisches Jahrbuch der Schweiz*. Zürich: Verlag NZZ.

Bunge, Mario (1980) 'Development indicators.' *Social Indicators Research*, 9: 369–85.

Burkhart, Ross E. (1997) 'Comparative democracy and income distribution: shape and direction of the causal arrow.' *Journal of Politics*, 59: 148–64.

Burkhart, Ross E. and Michael S. Lewis-Beck (1994) 'Comparative democracy: the economic development thesis.' *American Political Science Review*, 88: 903–10.

Burnham, James (1987)[1943] *The Machiavellians: Defenders of Freedom*. Washington, DC: Gateway.

Byers, John A. (2002) *Great Circle Distances Between Cities* (available at: http://www.wcrl.ars.usda.gov/cec/java/lat-long.htm).

Calhoun, John C. (1992) *Union and Liberty: The Political Philosophy of John C. Calhoun.* Indianapolis, IN: Liberty Fund.

Carothers, Thomas (1997) 'Democracy assistance: the question of strategy.' *Democratization*, 4, 3: 109–32.

Carothers, Thomas (2000) 'The Clinton record on democracy promotion.' *Working papers*, 16. Carnegie Endowment for International Peace, (available at: http://www.ceip.org/files/publications/Pub_by_type.asp#anchor).

Castles, Ian (1998) 'The mismeasure of nations: a review essay on the Human Development Report 1998.' *Population and Development Review*, 24: 831–45.

Census of India (2001) (available at: http://www.censusindia.net/).

Chardonnens, Pierre and Peter Saurer (2002) 'Quote-part d'impot, quote-part fiscale, quote-part de l'état: une exégese.' *La Vie Économique: Revue de Politique Economique*, no 2.

Chebabi, H.E. and Juan J. Linz (eds) (1998) *Sultanistic Regimes.* Baltimore, MD: the Johns Hopkins University Press.

Cheibub, José Antonio (2002) 'Presidentialism and democratic performance.' In: Reynolds, Andrew (ed.) *The Architecture of Democracy: Constitutional Design, Conflict Management, and Democracy.* Oxford: Oxford University Press, 104–40.

Chiriyankandath, James (1996) 'Hindu nationalism and regional political culture in India: a study of Kerala.' *Nationalism & Ethnic Politics*, 2, 1: 44–66.

Chiriyankandath, James (1997) '"Unity in diversity"?: coalition politics in India (with special reference to Kerala).' *Democratization*, 4, 4: 16–39.

Christophersen, Jens A. (1968) *The Meaning of 'Democracy' as Used in European Ideologies from the French to the Russian Revolution: an Historical Study in Political Language.* Oslo: Universitetsforlaget.

CIA (1994) *The World Factbook 1994–95.* Washington, DC: Brassey's.

CIA (1999) The world factbook 1999 (available at: http://www.odci.gov/cia/publications/factbook/).

Clague, Christopher, Suzanne Gleason and Stephen Knack (2001) 'Determinants of lasting democracy in poor countries: culture, development and institutions.' *Annals of the American Academy of Political and Social Science*, 573: 16–35.

Clark, Barry (1998) *Political Economy: A Comparative Approach.* 2nd edn. Westport, CT: Praeger.

Collier, David and Robert Adcock (1999) 'Democracy and dichotomies: a pragmatic approach to choices about concepts.' *Annual Review of Political Science*, 2: 537–65.

Collier, Paul (2000) 'Ethnicity, politics and economic performance.' *Economics and Politics*, 12: 225–45.

Collins, Randall (1998) 'Democratization in world-historical perspective.' In: Schroeder, Ralph (ed.) *Max Weber, Democracy and Modernization.* Basingstoke: Macmillan, pp. 14–31.

Connors, Michael Kelly (1996) 'The eclipse of consociationalism in South Africa's democratic transition.' *Democratization*, 3, 4: 420–34.

Costanza, Robert (2000) 'The dynamics of the ecological footprint concept.' *Ecological Economics*, 32: 341–5.

Couvalis, George (1997) *The Philosophy of Science: Science and Objectivity.* London: Sage.

Crawford, Beverly and Arend Lijphart (1995) 'Explaining political and economic change in post-communist Eastern Europe: old legacies, new institutions, hegemonic norms, and international pressures.' *Comparative Political Studies*, 28: 171–99.

Crawford, Gordon (1997) 'Foreign aid and political conditionality: issues of effectiveness and consistency.' *Democratization*, 4, 3: 69–108.

Crepaz, Markus M.L. (1990) 'The impact of party polarization and postmaterialism on voter turnout: a comparative study of 16 industrial democracies.' *European Journal of Political Research*, 18: 183–205.

Crepaz, Markus M.L., Thomas A. Koelble and David Wilsford (eds) (2000) *Democracy and Institutions: The Life Work of Arend Lijphart*. Ann Arbor, MI: University of Michigan Press.

Crewe, Ivor (1981) 'Electoral participation.' In: Butler, David, Howard R. Penniman and Austin Ranney (eds) *Democracy at the Polls: A Comparative Study of Competitive National Elections*. Washington, DC: American Enterprise Institute, pp. 216–63.

Cukierman, Alex (1992) *Central Bank Strategy, Credibility, and Independence: Theory and Evidence*. Cambridge, MA: the MIT Press.

Cunningham, Frank (1987) *Democratic Theory and Socialism*. Cambridge: Cambridge University Press.

Cunningham, Frank (2002) *Theories of Democracy: A Critical Introduction*. London: Routledge.

Cutright, Philippe (1963) 'National political development: measurement and analysis.' *American Sociological Review*, 28: 291–308.

Dahl, Robert A. (1963) *A Preface to Democratic Theory*. Chicago, IL: the University of Chicago Press.

Dahl, Robert A. (1971) *Polyarchy: Participation and Opposition*. New Haven, CT: Yale University Press.

Dahl, Robert A. (1985) *A Preface to Economic Democracy*. Cambridge: Polity.

Dahl, Robert A. (1986) *Democracy, Liberty and Equality*. Oslo: Universitetsforlaget.

Dahl, Robert A. (1989) *Democracy and its Critics*. New Haven, CT: Yale University Press.

Danner, Mona, Lucia Fort and Guy Young (1999) 'International data on women and gender: resources, issues, critical use.' *Women's Studies International Forum*, 22: 249–59.

Darnell, Adrian C. (1994) *A Dictionary of Econometrics*. Aldershot: Edward Elgar.

Dawisha, Karen and Bruce Parrott (eds) (1997) *Democratization and Authoritarianism in Postcommunist Societies: 4 Volumes*. Cambridge: Cambridge University Press.

De Blij, Harm Jan (1996) *Human Geography: Culture, Society and Space*. 5th edn. New York, NY: Wiley.

Deininger, Klaus and Lyn Squire (1997) *The Deininger–Squire Data Set* (available at: http://www.worldbank.org/research/growth/dddeisqu.htm).

Derbyshire, J. Denis and Ian Derbyshire (1989) *Political Systems of the World*. Edinburgh: Chambers.

Derbyshire, J. Denis and Ian Derbyshire (1996) *Political Systems of the World*. 2nd edn. Oxford: Helicon.

Derbyshire, J. Denis and Ian Derbyshire (1999) *Political Systems of the World*. 3rd edn. Oxford: Helicon.

Desai, Meghnad (1991) 'Human development: concepts and measurement.' *European Economic Review*, 35: 350–7.

Dethier, Jean-Jacques, Hafez Ghanem and Edda Zoli (1999) 'Does democracy facilitate the economic transition?: an empirical study of Central and Eastern Europe and the former Soviet Union.' *Policy Research working paper* #2194. Washington, DC: World Bank.

Dewey, John (1966) *Democracy and Education: An Introduction to the Philosophy of Education*. New York, NY: Free Press.

Diamond, Larry (1992) 'Economic development and democracy revisited.' *American Behavioral Scientist*, 35: 450–99.

Diamond, Larry (1997a) 'Is the third wave of democratisation over?: an empirical assessment.' *Working Paper*, 236. University of Notre Dame, IN: Kellogg Institute for International Studies.

Diamond, Larry (1997b) 'Is the third wave of democratisation over?: the imperative of consolidation.' *Working Paper*, 237. University of Notre Dame, IN: Kellogg Institute for International Studies.

Diamond, Larry, Juan J. Linz and Seymour Martin Lipset (eds) (1988) *Democracy in Developing Countries: Volume Two: Africa.* Boulder, CO: Lynne Rienner.

Didia, Dal O. (1997) 'Democracy, political instability and tropical deforestation.' *Global Environmental Change*, 7: 63–76.

Diener, Ed and Eunkook Suh (1997) 'Measuring quality of life: economic, social, and subjective indicators.' *Social Indicators Research*, 40: 189–216.

Dobb, Maurice (1963) *Economic Growth and Underdeveloped Countries.* New York, NY: International Publishers.

Dollar, David and Roberta Gatti (1999) 'Gender equality, income, and growth: are good times good for women?' *Policy Research Report on Gender and Development: Working Paper Series*, 1 (available at: http://www.worldbank.org/gender/prr/wp.htm).

Doveton, Daniel (1994) 'Marx and Engels on democracy.' *History of Political Thought*, 15: 555–91.

Downs, Anthony (1957) *An Economic Theory of Democracy.* New York: Harper & Row.

Downs, Anthony (1960) 'Why the government is too small in a democracy.' *World Politics*, 12: 541–63.

Downs, Anthony (1998) *Political Theory and Public Choice: The Selected Essays of Anthony Downs: Volume One.* Cheltenham: Edward Elgar.

Drèze, Jean and Amartya Sen (1989) *Hunger and Public Action.* Oxford: Clarendon Press.

Durham, J. Benson (1999) 'Economic growth and political regimes.' *Journal of Economic Growth*, 4: 81–111.

Duverger, Maurice (1980) 'A new political system model: semi-presidential government.' *European Journal of Political Research*, 8: 165–87.

Dyson, Tim and Mick Moore (1983) 'On kinship structure, female autonomy, and demographic behavior in India.' *Population and Development Review*, 9: 35–60.

Eckstein, Harry (1966) *Division and Cohesion in Democracy: a Study of Norway.* Princeton, NJ: Princeton University Press.

Elazar, Daniel J. (1987) *Exploring Federalism.* Tuscaloosa, AL: University of Alabama Press.

Election Commission of India (2001) (available at ⟨http://www.eci.gov.in/⟩).

Elgie, Robert (ed.) (1999) *Semi-Presidentialism in Europe.* Oxford: Oxford University Press.

Elgström, Ole and Goran Hyden (eds) (2002) *Development and Democracy: What Have We Learned and How?* London: Routledge.

Elkins, Zachary (2000) 'Gradation of democracy?: empirical tests of alternative conceptualizations.' *American Journal of Political Science*, 44: 287–94.

Elster, Jon (ed.) (1998) *Deliberative Democracy.* Cambridge: Cambridge University Press.

Elster, Jon, Claus Offe and Ulrich K. Preuss (1998) *Institutional Design in Post-Communist Societies: Rebuilding the Ship at Sea.* Cambridge: Cambridge University Press.

Emizet, Kisangani N.F. (2000) 'The relationship between the liberal ethos and qualiy of life: a comparative analysis of pooled time-series data from 1970 to 1994.' *Comparative Political Studies*, 33: 1049–78.

Encyclopaedia Britannica (annually) *Britannica World Data.* Chicago, IL: Encyclopaedia Britannica.

Esman, Milton J. (ed.) (1977) *Ethnic Conflict in the Western World.* Ithaca, NY: Cornell University Press.

Esping-Andersen, Gøsta (1990) *The Three Worlds of Welfare Capitalism.* Cambridge: Polity Press.

Esposito, John L. and John O. Voll (1996) *Islam and Democracy*. New York: Oxford University Press.

Estes, Richard J. (1984) *The Social Progress of Nations*. New York, NY: Praeger.

Estes, Richard J. (1996) 'The world social situation, 1970–1995: professional challenges for a new century.' Philadelphia, PA: University of Pennsylvania (available at: http://caster.ssw.upenn.edu/~restes/jak2.html).

European Bank for Reconstruction and Development (EBRD) (annually since 1994) *Transition report*. London: EBRD.

Evnine, Simon (1991) *Donald Davidson*. Cambridge: Polity Press.

Feng, Yi (1996) 'Democracy and growth: the sub-Saharan African case, 1960–1992.' *Review of Black Political Economy*, 25: 93–124.

Feng, Yi (1997) 'Democracy, political stability and economic growth.' *British Journal of Political Science*, 27: 391–418.

Feng, Yi (2001) 'Politics and development.' *Journal of Democracy*, 12, 1: 170–4.

Fields, Gary S. (1999) 'Distribution and development: a summary of the evidence for the developing world.' *Background Paper for the 2000/2001 World Development Report on Poverty*. Washington, DC: the World Bank (available at: http://www.worldbank.org/poverty/wdrpoverty/background/index.htm).

Firebaugh, Glenn (1999) 'Empirics of world income inequality.' *American Journal of Sociology*, 104: 1597–630.

Fish, M. Steven (1998a) 'Democratization's requisites: the postcommunist experience.' *Post-Soviet Affairs*, 14: 212–47.

Fish, M. Steven (1998b) 'The determinants of economic reform in the post-communist world.' *East European Politics and Societies*, 12: 31–78.

Fisher, Stanley and Ratna Sahay (2000) 'The transition economies after ten years.' *IMF Working Paper* 00/30. Washington, DC: IMF.

Fisher, Stanley, Ratna Sahay and Carlos A. Végh (1998) 'How far is Eastern Europe from Brussels?' *IMF Working Paper* 98/53. Washington, DC: IMF.

Flickinger, Richard, S. and Donley T. Studlar (1992) 'The disappearing voters?: exploring declining turnout in Western European elections.' *West European Politics*, 15, 2: 1–16.

Flora, Peter, Stein Kuhnle and Derek Urwin (eds) (1999) *State Formation, Nation-Building, and Mass Politics in Europe: The Theory of Stein Rokkan Based on his Collected Work*. Oxford: Oxford University Press.

Foweraker, Joe and Roman Krznaric (2000) 'Measuring liberal democratic performance: an empirical and conceptual critique.' *Political Studies*, 48: 759–87.

Franklin, Mark N. (1996) 'Electoral participation.' In: LeDuc, Lawrence, Richard G. Niemi and Pippa Norris (eds) *Comparing Democracies: Elections and Voting in Comparative Perspective*. Thousand Oaks, CA: Sage, pp. 216–35.

Franklin, Mark N. (2002) 'The dynamics of electoral participation.' In: LeDuc, Lawrence, Richard G. Niemi and Pippa Norris (eds) *Comparing Democracies: Elections and Voting in Comparative Perspective*. 2nd edn. Thousand Oaks, CA: Sage.

Freedom House (1978 annually) *Freedom in the World*. New York, NY: Freedom House.

Freedom House (2002) 'Annual survey of freedom country scores 1972–73 to 2000–01' (available at: http://www.freedomhouse.org/ratings).

Frey, R. Scott and Ali Al-Roumi (1999) 'Political democracy and the physical quality of life: the cross-national evidence.' *Social Indicators Research*, 47: 73–97.

Frieden, Jeffry A. (1991) *Debt, Development, and Democracy: Modern Political Economy and Latin America, 1965–1985*. Princeton, NJ: Princeton University Press.

Friedman, Milton (1953) *Essays in Positive Economics*. Chicago, IL: University of Chicago Press.

Friedman, Milton (1962) *Capitalism and Freedom.* Chicago, IL: University of Chicago Press.

Frye, Timothy (1997) 'A politics of institutional choice: post-communist presidencies.' *Comparative Political Studies*, 30: 523–52.

Frye, Timothy (2002) 'Presidents, parliaments, and democracy: insights from the post-communist world.' In: Reynolds, Andrew (ed.) *The Architecture of Democracy: Constitutional Design, Conflict Management, and Democracy.* Oxford: Oxford University Press, 81–103.

Fukuyama, Francis (1992) *The End of History and the Last Man.* New York, NY: Free Press.

Fukuyama, Francis (1995) 'Confucianism and democracy.' *Journal of Democracy*, 6, 2: 20–33.

Gais, Thomas L. (1996) *Improper Influence: Campaign Finance Law, Political Interests Groups, and the Problem of Equality.* Ann Arbor, MI: University of Michigan Press.

Gallagher, Michael, Michael Laver and Peter Muir (2000) *Representative Government in Modern Europe.* Boston, MA: McGraw-Hill.

Gasiorowski, Mark J. (2000) 'Democracy and macroeconomic performance in under-developed countries: an empirical analysis.' *Comparative Political Studies*, 33: 319–49.

Geddes, Barbara (1999) 'What do we know about democratisation after twenty years?' *Annual Review of Political Science*, 2: 115–44.

Geweke, John (1987) 'Endogeneity and exogeneity.' In: Eatwell, John *et al.* (eds) *The New Palgrave. A Dictionary of Economics.* Volume 2. London: Macmillan, 134–5.

Giliomee, Hermann (1995) 'Democratization in South Africa.' *Political Science Quarterly*, 100: 83–104.

Gill, Anthony (2001) 'Religion and comparative politics.' *Annual Review of Political Science*, 4: 43–65.

Glasure, Yong U., Aie-Rie Lee and James Norris (1999) 'Level of economic develop-ment and political democracy revisited.' *International Advances in Economic Research*, 5: 466–75.

Goldsmith, Arthur A. (1995) 'Democracy, property rights and economic growth.' *The Journal of Development Studies*, 32: 157–74.

Goldsmith, M.M. (1985) *Private Vices, Public Benefits: Bernard Mandeville's Social and Polit-ical Thought.* Cambridge: Cambridge University Press.

Goodin, Robert E., Bruce Headley, Ruud Muffels and Henk-Jan Dirven (1999) *The Real Worlds of Welfare Capitalism.* Cambridge: Cambridge University Press.

Goodman, Nelson (1972) *Problems and Projects.* Indianapolis, IN: Hackett.

Gough, Ian and T. Thomas (1994) 'Why do levels of human welfare vary among nations?' *International Journal of Health Services*, 24: 715–48.

Goulet, Denis (1989) 'Participation in development: new avenues.' *World Development*, 17: 165–78.

Goulet, Denis (1995) *Development Ethics: A Guide to Theory and Practice.* New York, NY: the Apex Press.

Gradstein, Mark, Branko Milanovic and Yvonne Ying (2000) 'Democracy and income distribution: an empirical analysis.' *Policy Research Working Papers*, 2561. Washington, DC: World Bank (available at: http://wbln0018.worldbank.org/research/workpapers.nsf/policyresearch?openform).

Gray, Mark and Miki Caul (2000) 'Declining voter turnout in advanced industrial democracies, 1950 to 1997: the effects of declining group mobilization.' *Comparative Political Studies*, 33: 1091–122.

Grofman, Bernhard and Arend Lijphart (eds) (1986) *Electoral Laws and their Political Consequences.* New York, NY: Agathon.

Gunther, Richard, P. Nikiforos Diamandouros and Hans-Jürgen Puhle (eds) (1995) *The Politics of Democratic Consolidation: Southern Europe in Comparative Perspective.* Baltimore, MD: the Johns Hopkins University Press.

Gurr, Ted Robert and Keith Jaggers (2000) 'Polity98 project: regime characteristics, 1800–1998' (available at: http://www.bsos.umd.edu/cidcm/polity/).

Gwartney, James and Robert Lawson (2001) *Economic Freedom of the World 2001 Annual Report.* Vancouver, BC: the Fraser Institute (available at: http://www.freetheworld.com/release.html).

Haan, Jacob de and Clemens L.J. Siermann (1995) 'New evidence on the relationship between democracy and economic growth.' *Public Choice,* 86: 175–98.

Haber, Stephen (ed.) (2000) *Political Institutions and Economic Growth in Latin America: Essays in Policy, History and Political Economy.* Stanford, CA: Hoover University Press.

Habermas, Jürgen (1984) *The Theory of Communicative Action.* London: Heinemann.

Hadenius, Axel (1992) *Democracy and Development.* Cambridge: Cambridge University Press.

Harriss, John (1999) 'Comparing political regimes across Indian states: a preliminary essay.' *Economic and Political Weekly,* 34, 27 November: 3367–77.

Hayek, Friedrich August von (1944) *The Road to Serfdom.* London: Routledge.

Haynes, Jess S. (2001) *Democracy in the Developing World: Africa, Asia, Latin America and the Middle East.* Cambridge: Polity Press.

Heller, Patrick (1995) 'From class struggle to class compromise: redistribution and growth in a south Indian state.' *Journal of Development Studies,* 31: 645–72.

Heller, Patrick (1996) 'Social capital as a product of class mobilization and state intervention: industrial workers in Kerala, India.' *World Development,* 24: 1055–71.

Heller, Patrick (2000) 'Degrees of democracy: some comparative lessons from India.' *World Politics,* 52: 484–519.

Helliwell, John F. (1994) 'Empirical linkages between democracy and economic growth.' *British Journal of Political Science,* 24: 225–48.

Henderson, David (2000) 'False perspective: the UNDP view of the world.' *World Economics,* 1, 1: 1–19.

Henderson, Hazel (1996) 'What's next in the great debate about measuring wealth and progress?' *Challenge,* 39, 6: 50–6.

Hesse, Mary (1974) *The Structure of Scientific Inference.* London: Macmillan.

Hicks, Douglas A. (1997) 'The inequality-adjusted human development index: a constructive proposal.' *World Development,* 25: 1283–98.

Hirst, Paul (1994) *Associative Democracy: New Forms of Economic and Social Governance.* Cambridge: Polity Press.

Hohfeld, Wesley Newcomb (1964) *Fundamental Legal Conceptions as Applied in Judicial Reasoning.* New Haven, CT: Yale University Press.

Hohfeld, Wesley Newcomb (2001) *Fundamental Legal Conceptions as Applied in Judicial Reasoning.* Eds David Campbell and Philip Thomas. Aldershot: Ashgate.

Holmes, Leslie (1997) *Post-Communism: An Introduction.* Cambridge: Polity Press.

Hook, Steven W. (1998) '"Building democracy" through foreign aid: the limitations of United States political conditionalities, 1992–96.' *Democratization,* 5, 3: 156–80.

Hookway, Christopher (1988) *Quine: Language, Experience and Reality.* Cambridge: Polity Press.

Horowitz, Donald L. (1985) *Ethnic Groups in Conflict.* Berkeley, CA: University of California Press.

Horowitz, Donald L. (1993) 'Democracy in divided societies.' *Journal of Democracy,* 4, 4: 18–38.

Huff, Toby E. and Wolfgang Schluchter (eds) (1999) *Max Weber and Islam*. New Brunswick, NJ: Transaction.

Huntington, Samuel P. (1984) 'Will more countries become democratic?' *Political Science Quarterly*, 99: 193–218.

Huntington, Samuel P. (1987) 'The goals of development.' In: Weiner, Myron and Samuel P. Huntington (eds) *Understanding Political Development*. Boston: Little, Brown and Company, pp. 3–32.

Huntington, Samuel P. (1991) *The Third Wave: Democratization in the Late Twentieth Century*. Norman, OK: University of Oklahoma Press.

IDEA (2001) *Voter Turnout: A Global Survey* (available at: http://www.idea.int/ Voter_turnout/voter_turnout.html).

IMF (2000) The World Economic Outlook (WEO) database September 2000. Washington, DC: IMF (available at: http://www.imf.org/external/pubs/ft/weo/2000/02/ data/index.htm).

Inglehart, Ronald *et al.* (2000) *World Values Surveys and European Values Surveys, 1981–1984, 1990–1993, and 1995–1997*, ICPSR version, Ann Arbor, MI: Institute for Social Research.

Inkeles, Alex (ed.) (1990) 'On measuring democracy.' *Studies in Comparative International Development*, 25, 1.

International Labour Office (1997) *World Labour Report 1997–98: Industrial Relations, Democracy and Social Stability*. Geneva: ILO.

International Ombudsman Institute (1999) *International Ombudsman Institute directory of World-Wide Ombudsman Offices*. Edmonton: International Ombudsman Institute.

Internet Software Consortium (ISC) (2002) *Internet Domain Survey* (available at: http://www.isc.org/ds/).

IPU (2000) 'Women in national parliaments' (available at: http://www.ipu.org/ wmn-e/world.htm).

Iqbal, Farrukh and Jong-Il You (eds) (2001) *Democracy, Market Economics, and Development: An Asian Perspective*. Washington, DC: World Bank.

Isaac, T.M. Thomas and S. Mohana Kumar (1991) 'Kerala elections, 1991: lessons and non-lessons.' *Economic and Political Weekly*, 26, 23 November: 2691–704.

Ishiyama, John T. (1997) 'The sickle or the rose?: previous regime types and the evolution of the ex-communist parties in post-communist politics.' *Comparative Political Studies*, 30: 299–330.

Ishiyama, John T. and Matthew Velten (1998) 'Presidential power and democratic development in post-communist politics.' *Communist and Post-communist Studies*, 31: 217–33.

Jackman, Robert W. (1987) 'Political institutions and voter turnout in the industrial democracies.' *American Political Science Review*, 81: 405–23.

Jackman, Robert W. and Ross A. Miller (1995) 'Voter turnout in industrial democracies during the 1980s.' *Comparative Political Studies*, 27: 467–92.

Jänicke, Martin (1996) 'Democracy as a condition for environment policy success: the importance of non-institutional factors.' In: Lafferty, William M. and James Meadowcroft (eds) *Democracy and the Environment: Problems and Prospects*. Cheltenham: Edward Elgar, pp. 71–85.

Jayal, Niraja Gopal (ed.) (2001) *Democracy in India*. New Dehli: Oxford University Press.

Jeffrey, Robin (1992) *Politics, Women and Well-being: How Kerala Became a Model*. Basingstoke: Macmillan.

Johnson, R.W. and Lawrence Schlemmer (1996) *Launching Democracy in South Africa: The First Open Election, April 1994*. New Haven, CT: Yale University Press.

Jolly, Richard (2000) 'False attack: misrepresenting the Human Development Report and misunderstanding the need for rethinking global governance.' *World Economics*, 1, 3: 1–15.

Jordan, Thomas E. (1993) 'Estimating the quality of life for children around the world: NICQL '92.' *Social Indicators Research*, 30: 17–38.

Joseph, Richard A. (1987) *Democracy and Prebendal Politics in Nigeria: The Rise and Fall of the Second Republic.* Cambridge: Cambridge University Press.

Joseph, Richard A. (ed.) (1999) *State, Conflict, and Democracy in Africa.* Boulder, CO: Lynne Rienner.

Jung, Courtney and Ian Shapiro (1995) 'South Africa's negotiated transition: democracy, opposition, and the new constitutional order.' *Politics and Society*, 23: 269–308.

Kabeer, Naila (1999) 'Resources, agency, achievements: reflections on the measurement of women's empowerment.' *Development and Change*, 30: 435–64.

Kabeer, Naila (2001) 'Conflicts over credit: re-evaluating the empowerment potential of loans to women in rural Bangladesh.' *World Development*, 29: 63–84.

Kanath, Shyam J. (1999) 'Indian development and poverty: making sense of Sen *et al.*' *Critical Review*, 13: 315–36.

Kang, David C. (2002) *Crony Capitalism: Corruption and Development in South Korea and the Philippines.* Cambridge: Cambridge University Press.

Kaplan, Abraham (1964) *The Conduct of Inquiry: Methodology for Behavioural Science.* San Francisco, CA: Chandler.

Karatnycky, Adrian, Alexander Motyl and Aili Piano (eds) (2001a) *Nations in Transit 1999–2000: Civil Society, Democracy, and Markets in East Central Europe and the Newly Independent states.* Piscataway, NJ: Transaction Publishers.

Karatnycky, Adrian, Alexander Motyl and Amanda Schnetzer (eds) (2001b) *Nations in Transit 2001: Civil Society, Democracy, and Markets in East Central Europe and the Newly Independent states.* Piscataway, NJ: Transaction Publishers.

Kaviraj, Sudipta (1996) 'Dilemmas of democratic development in India.' In: Leftwich, Adrian (ed.) *Democracy and Development: Theory and Practice.* Cambridge: Polity Press, pp. 114–38.

Kenworthy, Lane and Melissa Malami (1998) 'Gender inequality in political representation: a worldwide comparative analysis.' *Social Forces*, 78: 235–69.

Khng, Heng Hiang (1997) 'Economic development and political change: the democratization process in Singapore.' In: Laothamatas, Anek (ed.) *Democratization in Southeast and East Asia.* Singapore: Institute of Southeast Asian Studies, pp. 113–40.

Kitschelt, Herbert (1999) 'Accounting for outcomes of post-communist regime change: causal depth or shallowness in rival explanations.' Paper presented at the 1999 annual meeting of the American Political Science Association.

Knack, Stephen (1999) 'Social capital, growth and poverty: a survey of cross-country evidence.' *Social Capital Initiative: Working Paper*, 7 Washington, DC: the World Bank (available at: http://www.worldbank.org/poverty/scapital/wkrppr/index.htm).

Knack, Stephen (2000) 'Does foreign aid promote democracy?' *IRIS Working paper*, 218 (available at: http://www.iris.umd.edu/publications/browse.asp?pn=1&how=wp).

Koelble, Thomas and Andrew Reynolds (1996) 'Power-sharing democracy in the new South Africa.' *Politics and Society*, 24: 221–36.

Kohli, Atul (ed.) (2001) *The Success of India's Democracy.* Cambridge: Cambridge University Press.

Kopstein, Jeffrey S. and David A. Reilly (2000) 'Geographic diffusion and the transformation of the postcommunist world.' *World Politics*, 53: 1–37.

Korzeniewicz, Roberto Patricio and Timothy Patrick Moran (1997) 'World-economic trends in the distribution of income, 1965–1992.' *American Journal of Sociology*, 102: 1000–39.

Kumar, G. Gopa (2001) 'Kerala: defensive left and divided congress.' *Economic and Political Weekly*, 36, 12 May: 1581–4.

Kymlicka, Will (1995) *The Rights of Minority Cultures*. Oxford: Oxford University Press.

Laffont, Jean-Jacques (2000) *Incentives and Political Economy*. Oxford: Oxford University Press.

Laffont, Jean-Jacques and David Martimort (2002) *The Theory of Incentives*. Princeton, NJ: Princeton University Press.

Landman, Todd (1999) 'Economic development and democracy: the view from Latin America.' *Political Studies*, 47, 607–26.

Lane, Jan-Erik (ed.) (2001) *The Swiss Labyrinth: Institutions, Outcomes, and Redesign*. London: Frank Cass.

Lange, Oscar (1963) *Economic Development, Planning and International Cooperation*. New York, NY: Monthly Review Press.

Laski, Harold J. (1931) 'Democracy'. In: *Encyclopaedia of the Social Sciences*. Vol. 5. London: Macmillan: 76–85.

Lauth, Hans-Joachim, Gert Pickel and Christian Welzel (eds) (2000) *Demokratiemessung: Konzepte und Befunde im internationalen Vergleich*. Wiesbaden: Westdeutscher Verlag.

Laver, Michael and Kenneth A. Shepsle (1996) *Making and Breaking Governments. Cabinets and Legislatures in Parliamentary Democracies*. Cambridge: Cambridge University Press.

Laver, Michael and Kenneth A. Shepsle (eds) (1994) *Cabinet Ministers and Parliamentary government*. Cambridge: Cambridge University Press.

Leblang, David A. (1996) 'Property rights, democracy and economic growth.' *Political Research Quarterly*, 49: 5–26.

Leblang, David A. (1997) 'Political democracy and economic growth: pooled cross-sectional and time-series evidence.' *British Journal of Political Science*, 27: 453–72.

Lee Kuan Yew (2000) *From Third World to First: The Singapore Story 1965–2000*. Singapore: Singapore Press Holdings.

Lerner, Daniel (1964) *The Passing of Traditional Society: Modernizing the Middle East*. New York, NY: the Free Press.

Lewis, Bernard (1996) 'Islam and liberal democracy: a historical overview.' *Journal of Democracy*, 7, 2: 52–63.

Lewis-Beck, Michael S. and Brad Lockerbie (1989) 'Economics, votes, protests.' *Comparative Political Studies*, 22: 155–77.

Li, Jinshan and Jørgen Elklit (1999) 'The Singapore general election 1997: campaigning strategy, results, and analysis.' *Electoral Studies*, 18: 199–216.

Lijphart, Arend (1977) *Democracy in Plural Societies: A Comparative Exploration*. New Haven, CT: Yale University Press.

Lijphart, Arend (1984) *Democracies: Patterns of Majoritarian and Consensus Government in Twenty-One Countries*. New Haven, CT: Yale University Press.

Lijphart, Arend (1985) *Power-Sharing in South Africa*. Berkeley, CA: Institute of International Studies.

Lijphart, Arend (1994a) *Electoral Systems and Party Systems: A Study of Twenty-Seven Democracies, 1945–1990*. Oxford: Oxford University Press.

Lijphart, Arend (1994b) 'Prospects for power-sharing in the new South Africa.' In: Reynolds, Andrew (ed.) *Election '94 South Africa: The Campaign, Results and Future Prospects*. London: James Currey, 221–31.

Lijphart, Arend (1996) 'The puzzle of Indian democracy: a consociational interpretation.' *American Political Science Review*, 90: 258–68.

Lijphart, Arend (1998) 'South African democracy: majoritarian or consensual?' *Democratization*, 5, 4: 144–50.

Lijphart, Arend (1999) *Patterns of Democracy: Government Forms and Performance in Thirty-Six Countries*. New Haven, CT: Yale Univerity Press.

Lijphart, Arend (2002a) 'The wave of power-sharing democracy.' In: Reynolds, Andrew (ed.) *The Architecture of Democracy: Constitutional Design, Conflict Management, and Democracy*. Oxford: Oxford University Press, 37–54.

Lijphart, Arend (2002b) 'The evolution of consociational theory and consociational practices, 1965–2000.' *Acta Politica*, 37: 11–22.

Lijphart, Arend and Bernhard Grofman (eds) (1984) *Choosing an Electoral System: Issues and Alternatives*. New York: Praeger.

Lijphart, Arend and Carlos H. Waisman (eds) (1996) *Institutional Design in New Democracies: Eastern Europe and Latin America*. Boulder, CO: Westview Press.

Lindblom, Charles (1977) *Politics and Markets: The World's Political–Economic Systems*. New York, NY: Basic Books.

Lindblom, C. (2002) *The Market System*. New Haven, CT: Yale University Press.

Linz, Juan J. (1994) 'Presidential or parliamentary democracy: does it make a difference?' In: Linz, Juan J. and Arturo Valenzuela (eds) *The Failure of Presidential Democracy: Comparative Perspectives: Volume 1*. Baltimore, MD: the Johns Hopkins University Press, 1–87.

Linz, Juan J. (1997) 'Democracy, multinationalism and federalism.' *Estudio/Working paper* #103, Centro de Estudios Avanzados en Ciencias Sociales, Madrid.

Linz, Juan J. (2000) *Totalitarian and Authoritarian Regimes*. Boulder, CO: Lynne Rienner Publishers.

Linz, Juan J. and Alfred Stepan (1996) *Problems of Democratic Transition and Consolidation: Southern Europe, South America, and Post-Communist Europe*. Baltimore, MD: the Johns Hopkins University Press.

Linz, Juan J. and Arturo Valenzuela (eds) (1994) *The Failure of Presidential Democracy*. 2 volumes. Baltimore, MD: the Johns Hopkins University Press.

Lipset, Seymour Martin (1959) 'Some social requisites of democracy: economic development and political legitimacy.' *American Political Science Review*, 53: 69–105.

Lipset, Seymour Martin (1963) *Political Man*. London: Mercury Books.

Lipset, Seymour Martin (1994) 'The social requisites of democracy revisited.' *American Sociological Review*, 59: 1–22.

Lipset, Seymour Martin (1995) 'Introduction.' In: Lipset, Seymour Martin (ed.) *The Encyclopedia of Democracy: Volume 1*. London: Routledge, pp. v–xxvi.

Lipset, Seymour Martin, Kyoung-Ryung Seong and John Charles Torres (1993) 'A comparative analysis of the social requisites of democracy.' *International Social Science Journal*, 45, 2: 155–75.

Lively, Jack (1962) *The Social and Political Thought of Alexis de Tocqueville*. Oxford: Clarendon Press.

Lively, Jack (1975) *Democracy*. Oxford: Blackwell.

Locke, John (1991) [1699] *A Letter Concerning Toleration*. London: Routledge.

Lodge, Tom (1996) 'South Africa: democracy and development in a post-apartheid society.' In: Leftwich, Adrian (ed.) *Democracy and Development: Theory and Practice*. Cambridge: Polity Press, pp. 188–208.

Lomborg, Bjørn (2001) *The Sceptical Environmentalist: Measuring the Real State of the World*. Cambridge: Cambridge University Press.

Luckham, Robin, Anne-Marie Goetz and Mary Kaldor (2000) 'Democratic institutions and politics in contexts of inequality, poverty, and conflict.' *IDS working paper*, 104 (available at: http://www.ids.ac.uk/ids/bookshop/wp.html).

Luxembourg Income Study (LIS) (2002) *LIS Key Figures: Income Inequality Measures* (available at: http://www.lisproject.org/).

Machlup, Fritz (1963) *Essays on Economic Semantics*. Englewood Cliffs, NJ: Prentice-Hall.

MacIver, R.M. (1965) *The Web of Government*. New York, NY: the Free Press.

Mackie, Thomas T. and Richard Rose (1991) *The International Almanac of Electoral History*. 3rd edn. Basingstoke: Macmillan.

Mackie, Thomas T. and Richard Rose (1997) *A Decade of Election Results: Updating the International Almanac*. Glasgow: Centre for the Study of Public Policy.

McFaul, Michael (2002) 'The fourth wave of democracy and dictatorship: non-cooperative transitions in the postcommunist world.' *World Politics*, 54: 212–44.

McGranahan, Donald (1971) 'Analysis of socio-economic development through a system of indicators.' *Annals of the American Academy of Political and Social Science*, 393: 65–81.

McGranahan, Donald (1995) 'Measurement of development: research at the United Nations Research Institute for Social Development.' *International Social Science Journal*, 47, 1: 39–59.

McGranahan, Donald, Eduardo Pizarro and Claude Richard (1985) *Measurement and Analysis of Socioeconomic Development: An Enquiry into International Indicators of Development and Quantitative Interrelations of Social and Economic Components of Development*. Geneva: UNRISD.

McHenry, Dean E. (2000) 'Quantitative measures of democracy in Africa: an assessment.' *Democratization*, 7: 168–85.

MacPherson, C.B. (1966) *The Real World of Democracy*. Oxford: Clarendon Press.

MacPherson, C.B. (1973) *Democratic Theory: Essays in Retrieval*. Oxford: Clarendon Press.

Maddala, G.S. (1977) *Econometrics*. New York: McGraw-Hill.

Maddala, G.S. (2001) *Introduction to Econometrics*. 3rd edn. Chichester: Wiley.

Maddex, Robert L. (1996) *Constitutions of the World*. London: Routledge.

Maddison, Agnus (1995) *Monitoring the World Economy 1820–1992*. Paris: OECD.

Maddison, Angus (2001) *The World Economy: A Millennial Perspective*. Paris: OECD.

Mainwaring, Scott (1993) 'Presidentialism, multipartism, and democracy: the difficult combination.' *Comparative Political Studies*, 26: 198–228.

Mainwaring, Scott and Matthew S. Shugart (1997a) 'Juan Linz, presidentialism, and democracy.' *Comparative Politics*, 29: 449–70.

Mainwaring, Scott and Matthew S. Shugart (eds) (1997b) *Presidentialsim and democracy in Latin America*. Cambridge: Cambridge University Press.

Mandeville, Bernhard (1970)[1714] *The Fable of the Bees: Or, Private Vices, Public Benefits*. Harmondsworth: Pelican.

Marc-Wogau, Konrad (1968) *Studier till Axel Hägerströms Filosofi*. Stockholm: Prisma.

March, James G. and Johan P. Olsen (1989) *Rediscovering Institutions: The Organizational Basis of Politics*. New York, NY: Free Press.

Markoff, John (1999) 'Where and when was democracy invented?' *Comparative Studies in Society and History*, 41: 660–90.

Mather, A.S. and C.L. Needle (1999) 'Development, democracy and forest trends.' *Global Environmental Change*, 9: 105–18.

Mauro, Paul (1995) 'Corruption and growth.' *Quarterly Journal of Economics*, 110: 681–712.

Mayer, Peter (2001) 'Human development and civic community in India: making democracy perform.' *Economic and Political Weekly*, 36, 24 February: 684–92.

Mbaku, John Mukum (1994) 'The political economy of development: an empirical analysis of the effects of the institutional framework on economic development.' *Studies in Comparative International Development*, 29, 2: 3–22.

Means, George P. (1996) 'Soft authoritarianism in Malaysia and Singapore.' *Journal of Democracy*, 7, 4: 103–17.

Midlarsky, Manus I. (1998) 'Democracy and Islam: implications for civilizational conflict and the democratic process.' *International Studies Quarterly*, 42: 485–511.

Midlarsky, Manus I. (1998) 'Democracy and the environment: an empirical assessment.' *Journal of Peace Research*, 35: 341–61.

Milanovic, Branko (1999) 'True world income distribution, 1988 and 1993: first calculations based on household surveys alone.' *Policy Research Working Papers*, 2244. Washington, DC: World Bank (available at: http://wbln0018.worldbank.org/research/workpapers.nsf/policyresearch?openform).

Milanovich, Branko and Shlomo Yitzhaki (2000) 'Decomposing world income distribution: does the world have a middle class?' *World Bank Policy Research Working Papers*, #2562. Washington, DC: World Bank.

Milbrath, Lester W. and M.L. Goel (1977) *Political Participation*. Chicago, IL: Rand McNally.

Miller, David (2000) *Citizenship and National Identity*. Cambridge: Polity Press.

Montinola, Gabriella R. and Robert W. Jackman (2002) 'Sources of corruption: a cross-country study.' *British Journal of Political Science*, 32: 147–70.

Moon, Bruce E. and W.J. Dixon (1985) 'Politics, the state, and basic human needs: a cross-national study.' *American Journal of Political Science*, 29: 661–94.

Moore, George Edward (1959) *Philosophical Papers*. London: Allen and Unwin.

Moore, George Edward (1960) *Philosophical Studies*. London: Routledge and Kegan Paul.

Moore, Mick (1995) 'Democracy and development in cross-national perspective: a new look at the statistics.' *Democratization*, 2, 2: 1–19.

Moore, Mick, Jennifer Leavy, Peter Houtzayer and Howard White (1999) 'Polity qualities: how governance affects poverty.' *IDS Working Paper*, 99 (available at: http://www.ids.ac.uk/ids/bookshop/wp.html).

Morris, Matthew (1998) 'Social capital and poverty in India.' *IDS Working Paper*, 61 (available at: http://www.ids.ac.uk/ids/bookshop/wp.html).

Morris, Morris David (1979) *Measuring the Condition of the World's Poor: The Physical Quality of Life Index*. New York, NY: Pergamon Press.

Morris, Morris David (1996) 'Measuring the changing condition of the world's poor: the physical quality of life index, 1960–1990.' *Working Paper* #23/24. Brown University: Thomas J. Watson Jr. Institute for International Studies (available at: http://www.brown/edu/departments/Watson_Institute/Publications/OP/CCSD_toc.shtml).

Mueller, Dennis (1989) *Public Choice II*. Cambridge: Cambridge University Press.

Muller, Edward N. (1988) 'Democracy, economic development, and income inequality.' *American Sociological Review*, 53: 50–68.

Muller, Edward N. (1995) 'Economic determinants of democracy.' *American Sociological Review*, 60: 966–82.

Munck, Gerardo L. and Jay Verkuilen (2002) 'Conceptualizing and measuring democracy: evaluating alternative indices.' *Comparative Political Studies*, 35: 5–34.

Musgrave, Richard A. and Alan T. Peacock (eds) (1967) *Classics in the Theory of Public Finance*. New York, NY: St. Martin's Press.

Mutalib, Hussin (2000) 'Illiberal democracy and the future of opposition in Singapore.' *Third World Quarterly*, 21: 313–42.

Myrdal, Gunnar (1969) *An Asia Drama*. Harmondsworth: Penguin.

Naess, Arne, Jens A. Christophersen and Kjell Kvalø (1956) *Democracy, Ideology and Objectivity: Studies in the Semantics and Cognitive Analysis of Ideological Controversy*. Oslo: Universitetsforlaget.

Nagel, Ernest (1957) 'Determinism and development.' In: Harris, Dale B. (ed.) *The Concept of Development: an Issue in the Study of Human Behavior.* Minneapolis, MN: University of Minnesota Press, pp. 15–24.

Nagel, Ernest (1961) *The Structure of Science.* London: Routledge and Kegan Paul.

Nelson, Joan M. (1987) 'Political participation.' In: Weiner, Myron and Samuel P. Huntington (eds) *Understanding Political Development.* Boston, MA: Little, Brown and Company, pp. 103–59.

Nelson, Michael A. and Ram D. Singh (1998) 'Democracy, economic freedom, fiscal policy, and growth in LDCs: a fresh look.' *Economic Development and Cultural Change,* 46: 677–96.

Niskanen, William A., Jr (1968) 'The peculiar economics of bureaucracy.' *American Economic Review,* 58: 293–305.

Niskanen, William A., Jr (1971) *Bureaucracy and Representative Government.* Chicago, IL: Aldine.

Noorbakhsh, Fahrad (1998) 'A modified human development index.' *World Development,* 26: 517–28.

North, Douglass C. (1990) *Institutes, Institutional Change and Economic Performance.* Cambridge: Cambridge University Press.

North, Douglass C. (1997) 'The contribution of the new institutional economics to an understanding of the transition problem.' *WIDER Annual Lectures,* 1. Helsinki: United Nations University.

North, Douglass C., William Summerhill and Barry R. Weingast (2000) 'Order, disorder, and economic change. Latin America versus North America.' In: Bueno de Mesquita, Bruno and Hilton L. Root (eds) *Governing for Prosperity.* New Haven, CT: Yale University Press, 17–58.

Nossiter, T.J. (1982) *Communism in Kerala: A Study in Political Adaptation.* Dehli: Oxford University Press.

Nurmi, Hannu (1987) *Comparing Voting Systems.* Dordrecht: Reidel.

Nussbaum, Martha C. (1995) 'Human capabilities, female human beings.' In: Nussbaum, Martha and Jonathan Glover (eds) *Women, Culture and Development: A Study of Human Capabilities.* Oxford: Clarendon Press, pp. 61–104.

Nussbaum, Martha C. and Jonathan Glover (eds) (1995) *Women, Culture and Development: A Study of Human Capabilities.* Oxford: Clarendon Press.

Nwabueze, Ben O. (1974) *Presidentialism in Commonwealth Africa.* London: Hurst.

O'Donnell, Guillermo A. (1979) *Modernization and Bureaucratic-Authoritarianism: Studies in South American Politics.* Berkeley, CA: Institute of International Studies.

O'Donnell, Guillermo and Philippe C. Schmitter (1986) *Transitions from Authoritarian Rule: Tentative Conclusions about Uncertain Democracies.* Baltimore, MD: the Johns Hopkins University Press.

O'Donnell, Guillermo, Philippe C. Schmitter and Laurence Whitehead (eds) (1986) *Transitions from Authoritarian Rule: Comparative Perspectives.* Baltimore, MD: the Johns Hopkins University Press.

O'Driscoll, Gerald P. Jr., Kim R. Holmes and Mary Anastasia O'Grady (2002) *2002 Index of Economic Freedom.* Washington, DC: Heritage Foundation.

Offner, Avner (2000) 'Economic welfare measurements and human well-being.' University of Oxford: discussion papers in economic and social history, 34.

Okun, Arthur M. (1975) *Equality and Efficiency: The Big Tradeoff.* Washington, DC: Brookings.

Olson, Mancur (1982) *The Rise and Decline of Nations: Economic Growth, Stagflation, and Social Rigidities.* New Haven, CT: Yale University Press.

Olson, Mancur (1965) *The Logic of Collective Action.* Cambridge, MA: Harvard University Press.

Oppenheim, Felix E. (1971) 'Democracy – characteristics included and excluded.' *The Monist*, 55: 29–50.

Ottaway, Martina and Theresa Chung (1999) 'Toward a new paradigm.' *Journal of Democracy*, 10, 4: 99–113.

Pap, Arthur (1949) *Elements of Analytic Philosophy*. New York, NY: Macmillan.

Parayil, Govindan (ed.) (2000) *Kerala: The Development Experiences: Reflections on Sustainability and Replicability*. London: Zed.

Pateman, Carole (1970) *Participation and Democratic Theory*. Cambridge: Cambridge University Press.

Pateman, Carole (1989) *The Disorder of Women: Democracy, Feminism and Political Theory*. Cambridge: Polity Press.

Paxton, Pamela (1997) 'Women in national legislatures: a cross-national analysis.' *Social Science Research*, 26: 442–64.

Payne, Rodger A. (1995) 'Freedom and the environment.' *Journal of Democracy*, 6, 3: 41–55.

Pennock, J. Roland (1979) *Democratic Political Theory*. Princeton, NJ: Princeton University Press.

Persson, Torsten and Guido Tabellini (2000) *Political Economics: Explaining Economic Policy*. Cambridge, MA: the MIT Press.

Porter, Michael E., Jeffrey D. Sachs, Andrew M. Warner, Peter K. Cornelius, Macha Levinson and Klaus Schwab (1999) *The Global Competitiveness Report 2000*. New York, NY: Oxford University Press.

Powell, G. Bingham (1980) 'Voting turnout in thirty democracies: partisan, legal and socio-economic influences.' In: Rose, Richard (ed.) *Electoral Participation: A Comparative Analysis*. Beverly Hills, CA: Sage, pp. 5–34.

Powell, G. Bingham (1982) *Contemporary Democracies: Participation, Stability and Violence*. Cambridge, MA: Harvard University Press.

Powell, G. Bingham (1986). 'American voter turnout in comparative perspective.' *American Political Science Review*, 80: 17–43.

Powell, G. Bingham (2000) *Elections as Instruments of Democracy: Majoritarian and Proportional Visions*. New Haven, CT: Yale University Press.

Prakash, B.A. (ed.) (1999) *Kerala's Economic Development: Issues and Problems*. Thousand Oaks, CA: Sage.

Przeworski, Adam (1991) *Democracy and the Market: Political and Economic Reforms in Eastern Europe and Latin America*. Cambridge: Cambridge University Press.

Przeworski, Adam (1999) 'Minimalist conception of democracy: a defense.' In: Shapiro, Ian and Casiano Hacker-Cordón (eds) *Democracy's Value*. Cambridge: Cambridge University Press, pp. 23–55.

Przeworski, Adam, Michael E. Alvarez, José Antonio Cheibub and Fernando Limongi (1996) 'What makes democracies endure?' *Journal of Democracy*, 7, 1: 39–55.

Przeworski, Adam, Michael E. Alvarez, José Antonio Cheibub and Fernando Limongi (2000) *Democracy and Development: Political Institutions and Well-Being in the World, 1950–1990*. Cambridge: Cambridge University Press.

Przeworski, Adam and Fernando Limongi (1993) 'Political regimes and economic growth.' *Journal of Economic Perspectives*, 7, 3: 51–69.

Przeworski, Adam and Fernando Limongi (1997a) 'Democracy and development.' In: Hadenius, Axel (ed) *Democracy's Victory and Crisis*. Cambridge: Cambridge University Press, pp. 163–94.

Przeworski, Adam and Fernando Limongi (1997b) 'Modernization: theories and facts.' *World Politics*, 49: 155–83.

Putnam, Hilary (1979) *Mind, Language and Reality*. Cambridge: Cambridge University Press.

Quine, Willard van Orman (1960) *Word and Object*. Cambridge, MA: the MIT Press.

Quine, Willard van Orman and Julien S. Ullian (1978) *The Web of Belief*. New York: McGraw-Hill.

Rabushka, Alvin and Kenneth A. Shepsle (1972) *Politics in Plural Societies: A Theory of Democratic Instability*. Columbus, OH: Charles E. Merrill.

Radcliff, Benjamin and Patricia Davis (2000) 'Labor organization and electoral participation in industrial democracies.' *American Journal of Political Science*, 44: 132–41.

Ramachandran, V.K. (1998) 'On Kerala's development achievements.' In: Drèze, Jean and Amartya Sen (eds) *Indian Development: Selected Regional Perspectives*. Oxford: Oxford University Press, pp. 205–356.

Rasmusen, Eric (1994) *Games and Information: An Introduction to Game Theory*. 2nd edn. Cambridge, MA: Blackwell Publishers.

Ravallion, Martin and Gaurav Datt (1999) 'When is growth pro-poor?: evidence from the diverse experience of India's states.' *Policy Research Working Papers*, 2263. Washington, DC: World Bank (available at: http://wbln0018.worldbank.org/research/ workpapers.nsf/policyresearch?openform).

Rawls, John (1993) *Political Liberalism*. New York, NY: Columbia University Press.

Razavi, Shahra (1997) 'Fitting gender into development institutions.' *World Development*, 25: 1111–25.

Razavi, Shahra (1999) 'Gendered poverty and well-being: introduction.' *Development and Change*, 30: 409–33.

Razavi, Shahra (2000) 'Women in contemporary democratisation.' *Occasional Paper*, 4. Geneva: UNRISD.

Reilly, Benjamin (2001) *Democracy in Divided Societies: Electoral Engineering for Conflict Regulation*. Cambridge: Cambridge University Press.

Reynolds, Andrew (ed.) (2002) *The Architecture of Democracy: Constitutional Design, Conflict Management, and Democracy*. Oxford: Oxford University Press.

Reynolds, Andrew and Benjamin Reilly (1997) *The International IDEA Handbook of Electoral System Design*. Stockholm: IDEA.

Rhyne, Charles S. (1978) *Law and Judicial Systems of Nations*. Washington, DC: World Peace Through Law Center.

Ricketts, Martin (1987) *The Economics of Business Enterprise: New Approaches to the Firm*. Brighton: Wheatsheaf.

Riggs, Fred W. (1984) 'Development.' In: Sartori, Giovanni (ed.) *Social Science Concepts: A Systematic Analysis*. Beverly Hills, CA: Sage, pp. 125–203.

Riker, William H. (1982) *Liberalism Against Populism: A Confrontation Between the Theory of Democracy and the Theory of Social Choice*. San Francisco, CA: Freeman.

Rodrik, Dani (1997) 'Democracy and economic performance.' Harvard University (available at: http://ksghome.harvard.edu/~.drodrik.academic.ksg/papers.html).

Rokkan, Stein (1970) *Citizens, Elections, Parties: Approaches to the Comparative Study of the Processes of Development*. Oslo: Universitetsforlaget.

Rose, Richard (ed.) (1980) *Electoral Participation: A Comparative Analysis*. London: Sage.

Rose, Richard (ed.) (2000) *International Encyclopedia of Elections*. London: Macmillan.

Ross, Stephen A. (1973) 'The economic theory of agency: the principal's problem.' *American Economic Review*, 63, 2: 134–9.

Rueschemeyer, Dietrich, Evelyne Huber Stephens and John D. Stephens (1992) *Capitalist Development and Democracy*. Cambridge: Polity Press.

Sachs, Jeffrey (1993) *Poland's Jump to the Market Economy*. Cambridge, MA: the MIT Press.

Saith, Ruhi and Barbara Harriss-White (1999) 'The gender sensitivity of well-being indicators.' *Development and Change*, 30: 465–97.

Samuelson, Paul A. (1954) 'The pure theory of public expenditure.' *Review of Economic Studies*, 36, 387—9.

Sartori, G. (1976) *Parties and Party Systems.* Cambridge: Cambridge University Press.

Sartori, Giovanni (1987) *The Theory of Democracy Revisited: Part One: The Contemporary Debate.* Chatham, NJ: Chatham House Publishers.

Sartori, G. (1994) *Comparative Constitutional Engineering.* New York: New York University Press.

Say, Joseph (1996) [1815] *Cours D'economie Politique et Autres Essais.* Paris: Flammarion.

Scarritt, James R. and Shaheen Mozaffar (1999) 'The specification of ethnic cleavages and ethnopolitical groups for the analysis of democratic competition in contemporary Africa.' *Nationalism and Ethnic Politics*, 5, 1: 82–117.

Schattschneider, Elmer Eric (1960) *The Semi-Sovereign People: A Realist's View of Democracy in America.* New York, NY: Holt, Rinehart and Winston.

Scheffler, Israel (1982) *Science and Subjectivity.* Indianapolis, IN: Bobbs-Merrill.

Schmidt, Manfred G. (1999) 'On the political productivity of democracies.' *Scandinavian Political Studies*, 22: 281–94.

Schmidt, Manfred G. (2000) *Demokratitheorien: Eine Einführung.* 3rd edn. Opladen: Leske and Budrich.

Schumpeter, Joseph A. (1976) *Capitalism, Socialism and Democracy.* London: Allen & Unwin.

Schwab, Klaus, Michael E. Porter, Jeffrey D. Sachs, Andrew M. Warner and Macha Levinson (1999) *The Global Competitiveness Report 1999.* New York, NY: Oxford University Press.

Seguino, Stephanie (2000) 'Gender inequality and economic growth: a cross-country analysis.' *World Development*, 28: 1211–30.

Sen, Amartya (1983) 'Development: which way now?' *Economic Journal*, 93: 745–62.

Sen, Amartya (1988) 'The concept of development.' In: Chenery, Hollis and T.N. Srinivasan (eds) *Handbook of Development Economics: Volume 1.* New York, NY: North-Holland, pp. 9–26.

Sen, Amartya (1997) 'Population policy: authoritarianism versus cooperation.' *Journal of Population Economics*, 10: 3–22.

Sen, Amartya (1999) *Development as Freedom.* Oxford: Oxford University Press.

Sen, Amartya (2000) 'East and West: the reach of reason.' *The New York Review of Books*, 47, 12: 33–8.

Serra, Renata (1999) '"Putnam in India": is social capital a meaningful and measurable concept at Indian state level?' *IDS Working Paper*, 92 (available at: http://www.ids.ac.uk/ids/bookshop/wp.html).

Serra, Renata (2001) 'Social capital: meaningful and measurable at the state level?' *Economic and Political Weekly*, 36, 24 February: 693–704.

Shin, Doh C. (1989) 'Political democracy and the quality of citizens' life: a cross-national study.' *Journal of Developing Societies*, 5: 30–41.

Shugart, Matthew S. and John M. Carey (1992) *Presidents and Assemblies: Constitutional design and Electoral Dynamics.* Cambridge: Cambridge University Press.

Shvetsova, Olga (2002) 'Institutions and coalition-building in post-communist transitions.' In: Reynolds, Andrew (ed.) *The Architecture of Democracy: Constitutional Design, Conflict Management and Democracy.* Oxford: Oxford University Press, pp. 55–78.

Simpson, Miles (1990) 'Political rights and income inequality: a cross-national test.' *American Sociological Review*, 55: 682–93.

Sirowy, Larry and Alex Inkeles (1990) 'The effects of democracy on economic growth and inequality: a review.' *Studies in Comparative International Development*, 25: 126–57.

Smith, Anthony D. (1998) *Nationalism and Modernism.* London: Routledge.

Solow, Robert M. (2000) *Growth Theory: An Exposition.* Oxford: Oxford University Press.

Sørensen, Georg (1991) *Democracy, Dictatorship and Development: Economic Development in Selected Regimes of the Third World.* Basingstoke: Macmillan.

Sørensen, Georg (1993) *Democracy and Democratization: Processes and Prospects in a Changing World.* Boulder, CO: Westview Press.

Southall, Roger (2000) 'The state of democracy in South Africa.' *Commonwealth & Comparative Politics,* 38, 3: 147–70.

Stark, David and László Bruszt (1998) *Postsocialist Pathways: Transforming Politics and Property in East Central Europe.* Cambridge: Cambridge University Press.

Steiner, Jürgen and Thomas Ertman (eds) (2002) 'Consociationalism and corporatism in Western Europe: still the politics of accommodation?' *Acta Politica,* 37: Spring/Summer.

Stepan, Alfred (2001a) 'The world's religious systems and democracy: crafting the "twin tolerations".' In: Stepan, Alfred *Arguing Comparative Politics.* Oxford: Oxford University Press, 213–53.

Stepan, Alfred (2001b) *Arguing Comparative Politics.* Oxford: Oxford University Press.

Stepan, Alfred and Cindy Skach (1993) 'Constitutional frameworks and democratic consolidation: parliamentarianism versus presidentialism.' *World Politics,* 46: 1–22.

Stigler, George J. (ed.) (1988) *Chicago Studies in Political Economy.* Chicago, IL: University of Chicago Press.

Stiglitz, Joseph E. (1987) 'Principal and agent.' In Eatwell, John, M. Milgate and P. Newman (eds) *The New Palgrave Dictionary of Economics.* London: Macmillan.

Streeten, Paul (1995) 'Human development: the debate about the index.' *International Social Science Journal,* 47, 1: 25–37.

Summers, Robert and Alan Heston (1994) 'Penn world tables, mark 5.6' (available at: http://pwt.econ.upenn.edu/).

Svensson, Jakob (1999) 'Aid, growth and democracy.' *Economics and Politics,* 11: 275–97.

Talmon, Jacob Leib (1960a) *The Origins of Totalitarian Democracy.* New York, NY: Praeger.

Talmon, Jacob Leib (1960b) *Political Messianism: The Romantic Phase.* London: Secker and Warburg.

Talmon, Jacob Leib (1981) *The Myth of the Nation and the Vision of Revolution: The Origins of Ideological Polarisation in the Twentieth Century.* London: Secker and Warburg.

Tanzi, Vito and Ludger Schuknecht (2000) *Public Spending in the 20th Century: A Global Perspective.* Cambridge: Cambridge University Press.

Taylor, Charles Lewis and Michael C. Hudson (1972) *World Handbook of Political and Social Indicators.* 2nd edn. New Haven, CT: Yale University Press.

Taylor, Michael (1987) *The Possibility of Cooperation.* Cambridge: Cambridge University Press.

Terlouw, Cornelis Peter (1989) 'World-system theory and regional geography: a preliminary exploration of the context of regional geography.' *Tijdschrift voor Economische en Sociale Geografie,* 80: 206–21.

Therborn, Goran (1977) 'The rule of capital and the rise of democracy.' *New Left Review,* 107: 3–41.

Thompson, Michael, Richard Ellis and Aaron Wildavsky (1990) *Cultural Theory.* Boulder, CO: Westview Press.

Tingsten, Herbert (1937) *Political Behaviour: Studies in Election Statistics.* London: P.S. King & Son.

Tingsten, Herbert (1965) *The Problem of Democracy.* Totowa, NT: Bedminster Press.

Tocqueville, Alexis de (1990) [1835, 1840] *Democracy in America,* I–II. New York: Vintage.

Todd, Emmanuel (1985) *The Explanation of Ideology: Family Structures and Social Systems.* Oxford: Blackwell.

Todd, Emmanuel (1987) *The Causes of Progress: Culture, Authority and Change.* Oxford: Blackwell.

Törnquist, Olle (1995) *The Next Left?: Democratisation and Attempts to Renew the Radical Political Development Project: The Case of Kerala.* Copenhagen: Nordic Institute for Asian Studies.

Transparency International (yearly from 1995) *Corruption Perceptions Index* (available at: http://www.transparency.org/surveys/index.html#cpi).

Treisman, Daniel (2000) 'The causes of corruption. A cross-national study.' *Journal of Public Economics,* 76: 399–457.

Tsebelis, George (2002) *Veto Players: How Political Institutions Work.* Princeton, NJ: Princeton University Press.

Tsebelis, George and Jeanette Money (1997) *Bicameralism.* Cambridge: Cambridge University Press.

US Bureau of Census (2000) 'World population information' (available at: http://www.census.gov.ipc/www/world.html).

UNCTAD (2000) *The Least Developed Countries: 2000 Report.* Geneva: UNCTAD.

UNICEF (1979–) *The State of the World's Children.* New York, NY: UNICEF.

UNICEF (1999) 'Women in transition.' *Regional Monitoring Report,* no. 6. Florence: UNICEF Innocenti Research Centre.

UNICEF (2001a) *The State of the World's Children 2001.* New York, NY: UNICEF.

UNICEF (2001b) 'A decade of transition.' *Regional Monitoring Report,* no. 8. Florence: UNICEF Innocenti Research Centre.

United Nations Development Programme (UNDP) (1990–) *Human Development Report.* New York, NY: Oxford University Press.

Vanhanen, Tatu (1997) *Prospects of Democracy: A Study of 172 Countries.* London: Routledge.

Vanhanen, Tatu (2000) 'A new dataset for measuring democracy, 1810–1998.' *Journal of Peace Research,* 37: 251–65.

Varshney, Ashtosh (1999) 'Democracy and poverty.' *Background Paper for the 2000/2001 World Development Report on Poverty.* Washington, DC: the World Bank (available at: http://www.worldbank.org/poverty/wdrpoverty/background/index.htm).

Verba, Sidney, Norman H. Nie and Jae-om Kim (1978) *Participation and Political Equality: A Seven-Nation Comparison.* New York, NY: Cambridge University Press.

Véron, René (2001) 'The "new" Kerala model: lessons for sustainable development.' *World Development,* 29: 601–17.

Waal, Alex de (2000) 'Democractic political process and the fight against famine.' *IDS Working Paper,* 107 (available at: http://www.ids.ac.uk/ids/bookshop/wp.html).

Wackernagel, Mathis and William E. Rees (1996) *Our Ecological Footprint: Reducing Human Impact on the Earth.* Gabriola Island, BC: New Society Publishers.

Walker, Peter A. (1999) 'Democracy and environment: congruencies and contradictions in southern Africa.' *Political Geography,* 18: 257–84.

Wattenberg, Martin P. (2000) 'The decline of party mobilization.' In: Dalton, Russell J. and Martin P. Wattenberg (eds) *Parties Without Partisans: Political Change in Advanced Industrial Democracies.* Oxford: Oxford University Press, pp. 64–76.

Weber, Max (1949) *The Methodology of the Social Sciences.* Glencoe, IL: Free Press.

Weber, Max (1978) *Economy and Society I–II,* Berkeley: University of California Press.

Weber, Max (1993) *The Sociology of Religion.* Boston, MA: Beacon Press.

Weber, Max (1994) *Political Writings.* Cambridge: Cambridge University Press.

Wedberg, Anders (1984) *A History of Philosophy: Volume 3: From Bolzano to Wittgenstein.* Oxford: Clarendon Press.

Weede, Erich (1993) 'The impact of democracy or repressiveness on the quality of life, income distribution and economic growth rates.' *International Sociology*, 8: 177–95.

Weintraub, E. Roy (1983) *Microfoundations: The Compatibility of Microeconomics and Macro-Economics*. Cambridge: Cambridge University Press.

White, Morton (1956) *Toward Reunion in Philosophy*. Cambridge, MA: Harvard University Press.

Wicksell, Knut (1896) *Finanztheoretische Untersuchungen*. Jena: Gustav Fischer.

Wildavsky, Aaron (1993) *Craftways*. New York: Transaction.

Wildavsky, Aaron (1995) *But Is It True?: A Citizen's Guide to Environmental Health and Safety Issues*. Cambridge, MA: Harvard University Press.

Wilensky, Harold L. (2002) *Rich Democracies: Political Economy, Public Economy, and Performance*. Berkeley, CA: University of California Press.

Williamson, Oliver E. (1986) *Economic Organization: Firms, Markets and Policy Control*. Brighton: Wheatsheaf.

Wilson, Edward O. (1998) *Consilience: The Unity of Knowledge*. New York, NY: Alfred A. Knopf.

Wolfinger, Raymond E. and Steven J. Rosenstone (1980) *Who Votes?* New Haven, CT: Yale University Press.

Woolcock, Michael and Deepa Narayan (2000) 'Social capital: implications for development theory, research, and policy.' *The World Bank Research Observer*, 15: 225–49.

World Bank (1992) *World Bank Report, 1992*. New York: Oxford University Press.

World Bank (1996) *From Plan to Market: World Development Report 1996*. New York, NY: Oxford University Press.

World Bank (1997) *World Development Indicators 1997*. Washington, DC: World Bank.

World Bank (2000a) *World Development Indicators 2000*. Washington, DC: World Bank (in print).

World Bank (2000b) *World Development Report 2000/2001: Attacking World Poverty*. New York, NY: Oxford University Press.

World Bank (2000c) *World Development Indicators 2000*. Washington, DC: World Bank (on CD-ROM).

World Bank (2000d) *Making Transition Work For Everyone: Poverty and Inequality in Europe and Central Asia*. Washington, DC: World Bank.

World Bank (2001) *World Development Indicators 2001*. Washington, DC: World Bank.

World Bank (2002) *Transition: The First Ten Years: Analysis and Lessons for Eastern Europe and the Former Soviet Union*. Washington, DC: World Bank.

World Commission on Environment and Development (WCED) (1987) *Our Common future*. Oxford: Oxford University Press.

World Economic Forum (WEF) (2001) *2001 Environmental Sustainability Index* (available at: http://www.ciesin.columbia.edu/indicators/ESI/).

World Economic Forum (WEF) (2002) *2002 Environmental Sustainability Index* (available at: http://www.ciesin.columbia.edu/indicators/ESI/).

World Wide Fund for Nature (WWF) (2000) *Living Planet 2000 Report* (available at: http://panda.org/livingplanet/lpr00/).

Zachariah, K.C. and S. Irudaya Rajan (eds) (1997) *Kerala's Demographic Transitions: Determinants and Consequences*. New Dehli: Sage.

Zweifel, Thomas D. and Patricio Navia (2000) 'Democracy, dictatorship and infant mortality.' *Journal of Democracy*, 11, 2: 99–114.

Index